BOTH FEET IN THE
Stirrups

BILL HUNTINGTON

ILLUSTRATED BY
J.K. RALSTON

Copyright 1999 by Huntington Trust, Inc.

All rights reserved.

This book may not be reproduced in whole or part by any means
(with the exception of short quotes for the purpose of review)
without the permission of the publisher.
Printed and published in the United States of America.
Huntington Trust, Inc.
Third printing, 2015.

Bill Huntington, the author, died October 15, 1969, at the age of 93.
Following his death, requests began coming in for copies of this, his second book.
This printing reflects the continued interest in his books.

ISBN-13: 978-1519179777
ISBN-10: 1519179774
Library of Congress Control Number: 2015918786
CreateSpace Independent Publishing Platform, North Charleston, SC

Written by William C. "Bill" Huntington
Illustrated by J.K. Ralston
Edited by Linda Grosskopf & Nancy Morrison
Typeset by Nancy Morrison

To purchase additional copies of Bill Huntington's books:
They Were Good Men and Salty Cusses
Both Feet in the Stirrups
Treasures from Bill's Warbag

Mail request to:
Word Wright Women
PO Box 85
Billings, MT 59103

Or email request to:
wordwright@nemont.net

For complete catalog, go to:
www.wordwrightwomen.com

Dedicated to the Pioneers
and Trail Blazers
of the West

Foreword - Second Printing

On February 1, 1959, *Both Feet In The Stirrups* was presented to the readers within the livestock industry of the West. We're proud to present the second edition of a book that is a second volume of memories by the late, great Bill Huntington.

Bill Huntington started his writing career after he was 70 years old. You'll notice the book is full of tales—some funny, some poignant, some fiercely competitive—but they're all presented in a free western style as only Bill Huntington could write.

The third and fourth generations of Bill Huntington's family have urged that this book be presented once again to the western world. The first three printings of *They Were Good Men and Salty Cusses* and the first printing of *Both Feet In The Stirrups* have been sold out for many years, and the demand keeps rising from the industry to own and have this book for their private libraries.

There is a great richness in the western past that will enlighten you. It will give the reader a chance to observe and digest first hand the accounts that happened in this rugged, independent part of western history and the development of the western United States.

You'll note that this book has not been created by any form or pattern that is necessarily prescribed by schools of writing. It is rather the writings and thoughts of Bill Huntington as only he could put them on paper.

WLR Publications is happy to present this book to the readers, both young and old, who want to get a real feel of the maturing West.

Patrick K. Goggins
Publisher
WLR Publications, April 20, 1998

Family Note

Not too long after his wife died, Gramps—also known as Bill Huntington—moved in with his younger daughter, our grandmother, Georgia Blake, on her ranch east of Billings where she raised Herefords, wheat, and grandkids ... in that order!

Gramps was a fixture of our youth. Hunched over a table in the corner of the kitchen with a sheaf of typing paper, a couple of dull pencils, and a smoldering pipe, he scribbled page after smudged page of colorful memories.

Gramps never tired of inspecting the passing parade of kids and cowponies that trotted through the yard over the years, and he took great interest in their every detail, usually with a few stories from his past woven in with his approval of the present.

During fair time, he was a godsend to small, broke, hungry grandkids. And he wasn't hard to find when one needed a stake either—under the big, cool grandstands placing a bet or standing spellbound along the racetrack fence, rooting on his favorite!

Gramps died when he was 93. His going left a great big hole in our family, but not in our family history because we had the best of his rich memories and the very essence of his sparkling personality captured on paper. The best part about the books, of course, is that they allow us—who either were too young to know him in his youth or who weren't lucky enough to have known him at all—to vicariously relive the Old West in its heyday through Grampa's twinkling eyes and humorous outlook.

Gramps was not politically correct. In fact, he would never have considered that the way he spoke of those long distant days needed any correction. He wrote the way he lived. And it was a different world in those days, for better or worse. Many would say better. That being said, Gramps spoke in ways that do not recognize the respect due all cultures, perhaps because, in those days, that respect wasn't part of the landscape. Whatever the reason, he spoke like the rest of his world, and we have not changed it to reflect changed sensibilities. It was the world he lived in, and this is his story in his words.

It is with great pleasure that we—Bill's family which now is in its seventh generation on the ranch east of Billings—watch these books come rolling off the presses. Our only regret is that Bill cannot be here to personally autograph them for you.

Linda Grosskopf, Editor
Nancy Morrison, Editor and Typesetter
November 1, 2015

Table of Contents

1: Boyhood Days 1
2: Cattle 31
3: Utah 79
4: Cowboys 99
5: Mrs. Huntington 145
6: Freighting 161
7: Indians 179
8: Sheep Business 209
9: Rustlers and Killers 235
10: Horse Breaking and Filly Chasing 263
11: Bucking Horses 303
12: Wild West Shows 319
13: Iowa 347
14: With the Carnival 355
15: Rodeos 387
16: Moonshine 399
17: The Last of the Show Stock 415

1: Boyhood Days

AFTER my parents separated, I spent most of my time at my grandparents' home. There was always something doing there as they had a large family. Grandma had six children when she married Grandpa and he had three children, together they had three more.

Grandma had come from England when she was eleven years old. She talked like the English as long as she lived. She was a little bit of a woman under five feet and never weighed over a hundred pounds. She was like a little wren always on the go. She was good hearted and quick tempered.

I can remember so well when she used to bake bread. She would take a loaf right from the oven, break it up, cover the chunks with butter and give it to us kids. When we came back for more she would open her eyes wide and stare at us and say, "Your little guts hold more than a man's." We generally got the second helping.

Her medicine cabinet didn't look like the ones nowadays. She made us wear asafetida bags around our necks to keep away diseases. She kept skunk oil and goose grease to rub on us when we had croup, for all other ailments she kept laudanum and whiskey.

Now my grandpa was altogether different. His folks came to America before the Revolution. He was a tall man well proportioned. He was a cabinet maker and an undertaker. He made his own coffins. He was a deeply religious man but not a fanatic. He believed in the Golden Rule and lived it. He fought in the Civil War and was a prisoner for a short time in Andersonville Prison. Where Grandma was peppery, he was calm. He never used tobacco and had a deep dislike of liquor.

I remember one time when Grandpa wasn't feeling well. He was not a man to complain about his ailments and usually let nature take its course. He really must have been sick for he asked Grandma if she couldn't fix him some medicine. She bustled to her medicine chest and got out the laudanum and fixed a dose but deciding that wasn't good enough she put in a good slug of whiskey with some hot water and ginger to hide the taste. She told him to drink every swallow and lay down, which he did.

He went right to sleep but must have had a nightmare for pretty soon he rared up in bed, blinked his eyes a time or two and began to yell "Whoopee-whoopee" as loud as he could.

Grandma rushed in the bedroom, followed by a pack of us kids. Grandpa was setting up in bed, his hair standing on end, his eyes bugging out, waving his arms, still yelling.

Grandma was sure scared. She shooed us kids out of his room. She was wringing her hands, saying, "Grandpa's gone crazy. Quick! Go get Doctor Langley."

Doctor Langley only lived about a block from our house. He grabbed his satchel and made some pretty fast tracks. When he got there, he asked Grandma all about Grandpa's sickness and what medicine he'd been taking.

Grandpa let out another loud yippy and Doctor Langley looked him over. One look was enough or maybe he smelled his breath for he said, "He's not crazy, he's just good and drunk."

It wasn't a good idea for a long time for us kids to mention the time Grandpa had a crazy spell.

MONEY wasn't so plentiful when I was a boy and everyone had a lot of respect for a dollar. I remember one time when I was staying with my grandparents in North Platte that a silver dollar caused me a lot of grief. I can't remember exactly how old I was but I don't think I could have been over eight years old.

BOYHOOD DAYS

It was in the evening. My grandmother needed something from the store. She gave me a note with her list to give the store keeper and handed me a silver dollar and said, "Now Willie, hold the money in your hand and don't lose it. Give it to Mr. Gilman and hurry back."

It was only about three blocks to Gilman's store. I know I ran all the way over there. In those days the sidewalks was wide steps made of planks with big cracks between the planks.

I stumbled on the steps as I went to go in the door and lost the dollar through a crack. I could see the dollar but I couldn't get it. I went in and gave Mr. Gilman the note and told him the money was under his steps.

He was an awful cranky old fellow and jawed around about how I ought to be careful with my money. I wanted to pry up a plank and get the money but he wouldn't let me. He finally gave me the groceries and said he would charge them to my grandfather.

When I got home, grandmother scolded me too and I cried. I thought the whole world was against me. I was still pretty unhappy when I went to bed.

I was telling my troubles to my uncle Lew who was only two years older than me. He said we'd wait until the folks went to bed and go get that dollar.

We was sleeping upstairs. We waited until everyone had gone to bed and we figured they was asleep. We got our clothes on and with our shoes in our hands, sneaked downstairs and outside. We got our shoes on and went to the barn and got a spade and was off to Gilman's store.

The Gilmans lived in the back of the store. Their lights was out, too. You'd have thought we was bank robbers the way we was sneaking around but we thought old man Gilman would put us in jail if he caught us.

There was stringers under the planks. We dug under the first stringer until we made a little hole. I was the smallest and knew where the dollar was so I crawled in the hole. I was scared for it was darker than the devil.

Of course, the dollar was under the next stringer. We tried to dig under it but couldn't. I clawed and scratched with my hands until I could get my arm under the stringer. I could almost reach it but not quite. I dug and scratched some more like a dog after a bone and managed to feel around until I got the dollar.

I tried to get back but I was stuck and just couldn't make it. Lew got hold of my legs and tried to pull me out but he couldn't get it done. I was latched on to that dollar but it wasn't doing me much good. When Lew couldn't pull me out of the hole, I sure got scared and began to bawl.

Lew was scared too and told me to be still or Gilman would hear me and have us both put in jail. He whispered, "I'll go home and get a crow bar to dig you out. Don't make any noise while I'm gone."

He probably wasn't gone very long but it seemed like hours to me. I kept trying to make the hole bigger with my one hand, the other one I kept clinched around the dollar.

When Lew got back, he used the bar to pry one plank off. It didn't make much noise. They was six inch planks so it wasn't a big enough space so he pried on the next plank. When he started to pull the next plank up it made a loud screeching noise. He had to use the spade to loosen the dirt so I could get out from under the stringer.

Just as I was crawling out of the hole, we saw a light go on in Gilman's store. Lew grabbed the crowbar and I got the spade. We tore out of there and ran all the way home. We put the spade and crowbar back where they belonged and sneaked back up to bed.

I don't know if Gilman saw us or just suspected us but early next morning, before us kids was out of bed, he came over to Grandpa's and raised a ruckus with the old man. He was sure talking with his mouth and his hands about his steps being dug up and the planks sticking up in the air.

We was two scared kids when Grandpa came up the stairs to find out if we was the guilty parties. Grandpa gave us a good talking to, but there was a twinkle in his eyes. He went over to Gilman's and fixed the steps but after that Grandpa and Grandma traded at Foley's store.

MY GRANDPARENTS had moved to Brady Island, Nebraska, on the Union Pacific railroad. Grandpa had just built a hotel there, it was called the Brady House.

I can remember when the Union Pacific had just got a contract from the government to deliver the mail from Omaha, Nebraska, to the coast and was making a test run. The train was supposed to make sixty miles an hour and everybody was talking about such fast dangerous time.

People came for miles to see the mail train go by. It just stopped at division points. It picked up the mail on the fly as it went by the little towns. The mail hung in a canvas bag and then there was sort of an artificial arm that grabbed it and pulled it into the baggage car.

It was an exciting day for Brady Island as everybody gathered to see the "Flyer" as it was called go through. There was all kinds of stories about how dangerous it was and nobody got any closer than a couple hundred yards to the track. It was a short train as I remember it, an engine and four or five coaches. One old nester said that he never thought that he would ever see any manmade machine that would outrun a horse and he'd bet that it never made the coast. That it was just a damn man killer.

GRANDPA HAD two boys Bert and Lew. Lew was two years older than me and Bert was two years younger. We was just the right age to be adventuresome. Brady Island didn't offer much entertainment for kids but we used to swim a lot in the North Platte River until a man drowned in it and the folks forbid us to swim there after that. About the only thing left to do was go over to the railroad and ride the freight trains that stopped to get water.

One time one of our neighbors was going to North Platte in a wagon a distance of about twenty-three miles. He was going one day, stay overnight, and come home the next day. We got permission to go with him as we had an aunt to visit in North Platte.

We made the trip and stayed overnight with our aunt but thought it would be a lot more fun to beat our way back on the freight train than ride in the wagon. Most all of the freight trains stopped at Brady for water.

We got on the freight train at North Platte without telling anyone of our plans. We got in an empty box car and was having a lot of fun thinking of beating our neighbor home. When the train got to Brady instead of stopping it went on through and never stopped 'til it got to Gothenburg. As the train passed through Brady we began to get scared. We got off just as soon as the train stopped but we was farther from home than we had been at North Platte.

It was somewhere near noon when we got off at Gothenburg. We hung around the water tank all afternoon waiting to catch a train to take us back. One came along about four in the afternoon but the brakeman saw us getting in a car and ran us out. We found out there wasn't any more trains until the next day.

We was pretty unhappy kids—broke, hungry and a long ways from home. We went down by the stockyards that night and made a fire. It was in the fall of the year and got pretty chilly at night. We shivered around all night—cold, hungry and sleepy.

In the morning we went up the track to where there was a flour and grist mill. We found some corn in a car and ate some, then we went in the mill. There was some bran, we sure took to that bran and was poking it in our mouths with both hands when the miller discovered us.

He asked us if we was hungry and where we lived. We was three dirty faced, scared little boys. We had not washed since we left North Platte. We told him our story.

He told us there was a train due in a few minutes and he would square us with the conductor if we would promise never to try to bum another ride. We was more than happy to promise for we hadn't found our adventure of riding the freight much fun.

The miller had a little talk with the conductor and he told us to go back to the caboose and sit down or we might get run over and he would see we got off at Brady.

When we got to Brady we made tracks to the back of the hotel, as we didn't want to meet Grandpa. We met Grandma. She threw up her hands at the sight of us. She cleaned us up, fed us and sent us to bed. We never got a licking but we got some strict orders about freight trains.

Grandpa and Grandma hadn't been worried, they thought the neighbor was just spending an extra day in town.

MY MOTHER went to visit her sister who lived in the Sand Hills of Nebraska. That was before she took a claim there. My uncle was an old cowpuncher who had made several trips with trail herds from Texas. He had taken up a claim and had a little bunch of cattle.

My uncle Hop gave me an old Texas horse to ride that was perfectly gentle. I used to have a lot of fun riding old Tex around. I don't think I was a mean kid but I didn't have any playmates and had an adventurous spirit. I used to get in some awful messes.

My aunt had a few chickens. She had quite a struggle to keep them from the coyotes and skunks. One time she had set a couple of hens. When the little chickens hatched she wanted to keep them separated from the big chickens.

Uncle Hop turned a wagon box upside down and put a door in one end. She put the two hens and little chickens in it.

One night a skunk came. It dug a hole under the wagon box and killed most of the little chickens. My aunt was awful mad at the skunk for killing the little chickens.

A few days after that I was out riding around on Tex. I run onto a skunk. It ran under a pile of posts. I thought I'd do my Aunt Clara a favor and kill the skunk so it wouldn't get any more chickens.

I got off Tex and tied him to a bush. I went over to the post pile and pulled them over 'til I could see the skunk. It wasn't alone, there was five little skunks there too. I got a club and killed them but that old skunk sure perfumed me up plenty.

After I had them all killed, I smelled so bad that Tex wouldn't let me close enough to him to get on so I had to walk and lead him. I thought I had done something really worthwhile and was right pleased with myself. However, when I got almost to the house they smelled me a coming.

My mother and Aunt Clara went on something horrible. They told me I was always getting into trouble. Mother took some clothes for me to the barn and told me not to come near her until I had changed into them. Uncle Hop had a water tank in the corral. I got in the tank thinking I'd wash off the smell.

I left my clothes with the skunk smell in the barn. Uncle Hop made me take a spade and bury them. The horses wouldn't drink out of the tank so Uncle Hop was mad at me too. After that I never bothered any more skunks.

Uncle Hop was working for the C Bar **C—** cow outfit which was a pretty big spread. The **C—** was only about six miles from where my Aunt Clara and Uncle Hop lived. Uncle Hop used to take me with him on short trips.

As a special favor sometimes he would let me go with him to the **C—**. I sure liked to go there because there was several cowboys working there. I was the only small boy in that part of

BOYHOOD DAYS

the country. The cowboys liked to tease me and tell me some whopping big stories. At that time, I believed them all.

THE OLD ROUNDUP cook that was cooking at the ranch was a homely, long geared individual with red hair. He was minus one ear. It was chopped off close to his head. I was mighty curious how the cook lost his ear and asked one of the cowboys.

The cowboy told me that after the Civil War there was lots of unbranded cattle in Texas that was called mavericks. It was all right for any cowman to brand them. The cowboy said that the cook was such a big thief that he was working over brands as well as getting mavericks so they cut his ear off to mark him as a cattle thief.

"I used to have a lot of fun riding old Tex."

When I went home I told the folks about how the cook lost his ear. They laughed so much that I knew something was wrong. The next time I went to the C—, I asked another one of the hands what had happened to the cook's ear.

He told me that the first trip that the cook made to Nebraska with a bunch of cattle, it was pretty late in the season. They got caught in a blizzard. The cook froze his ear so hard that when his horse stumbled, the cook's ear fell off.

It seemed that it was a pretty touchy subject to the cook to mention his minus ear. I was curious, hearing two different stories. I wasn't satisfied which was the right one so I decided to ask the cook.

He was standing by a table cutting beef steak with a large steak knife in his hand when I asked him if he got his ear cut off for stealing cattle or did it freeze and drop off.

He gave me an awful mean look. His big butcher knife was poised in the air as he said, "None of your damn business. Get out of here!" I left pretty fast and I never did find out how the cook lost his ear.

There was one outfit in the Sand Hills that used what was called a dewlap. They would cut the skin on the neck and it would hang down. It was used instead of an earmark.

Whenever I asked them cowboys a question they always answered me. I asked, "What do they cut that skin in the neck for?"

An old waddy blinked his eyes and said that when they fetched the cattle from Texas they was so wild the cowboys would cut a hole in the dew lap and stick a front leg through it so the cattle couldn't run so fast.

If I could remember all the windy stories them cowboys told me, it would make a big book.

One day after I had got in a mix up, Uncle Hop took me out for a ride with him. He told me I pulled some foolish stunts. He said, "Bill, I don't think you do it to be mean, just use your head a little more. When you get a little older I will learn you to be a good cowboy. I'll learn you to be a good roper and a good bronc rider but you are a little too young yet."

I sure liked Uncle Hop that day and I told him I'd sure use my head from now on and wouldn't worry my mother and Aunt Clara anymore. I told him I didn't think women understood men like he did.

About a week after Uncle Hop gave me the nice talk, another uncle of mine that was riding for the C— had a horse buck him off. The horse either jumped on him or kicked him I have forgotten which. He was layed up for a while and came over to Uncle Hop's to get well.

I had always rode Tex bareback as I didn't have a saddle. I saw Uncle Earn's nice saddle hanging in the barn and as I was going to ride aways with Uncle Hop, I asked him if I could ride Uncle Earn's saddle.

He said yes but that it was too big for me to put on a horse so he would put it on for me as I had got to be a pretty good boy. He said he was sure going to make a good cowboy out of me.

I was really proud riding along beside Uncle Hop on a real cowboy saddle with a rope fastened on the swell of the saddle with a leather strap.

We rode perhaps a mile or two when he told me that he was going up country several miles and I had better go back home.

I started back. I saw some red willows that Burton had told me was kinnikinnick that the Indians smoked for tobacco. I peeled off a pocket full and started on.

I ran into a bunch of cows and calves. I looked at them and thought I had better do a little cowboying if Uncle Hop was going to make me a top hand.

I thought I would rope me a small calf. I took down the rope and threw at a small calf. I missed it but caught a big husky calf. I'd had a pretty big loop and he had one front foot over the rope and was caught right around the shoulders.

Tex knew what to do even if I didn't. When the calf hit the end of the rope it turned him over. The calf got up scared and how he did bawl. He ran against the rope again and had another fall. He was a good big bull calf and he sure was a bellow box. The old cows all came a running and bawling.

I was getting scared. I didn't know what to do. I was too scared of the cows to get off and take the rope off the calf. I thought I would just untie the rope from the saddle and turn the calf loose. I hadn't had any experience in tying ropes and couldn't get the rope untied.

I was in another mess and didn't know how I was going to get out of it. I thought I would take the calf with me so I could get the rope off him in the corral.

After he had busted himself several times the calf quit running against the rope but he never quit bawling. I started to take him home. I was dragging him. He was a bawling and a bunch of cows was running around with their tongues out bawling and making a lot of noise. I would drag him aways until Tex would get tired, then I'd rest and start dragging again and the music would start.

Uncle Hop was on his way back when he heard the noise and came to my rescue. He took the rope off the calf. He didn't scold me. About all he said was that I had over matched myself.

I told him that I had throwed at a little calf but caught a big one. I couldn't untie the rope so I was just taking the calf to the corral. I told him if I was going to make a cowboy I ought to practice. Uncle Hop laughed at me but I didn't get to ride a saddle again for quite a while.

I WENT TO SCHOOL for a while in Gordon, Nebraska. It was a small town on the Elkhorn, Fremont and Missouri Railroad in the northern part of Nebraska close to the South Dakota line where the Sioux Indian Reservation was located.

That was about 1887 or 1888 and at that time it was all "blanket Indians." There was just a few of them that could speak other than their own language and sign language. I never seen or heard of an old Indian that didn't know sign language. While each tribe had a different lingo they could all talk to one another by means of the sign language.

The Indians used to get rations from the government. They included sugar, coffee, flour, beef and blankets, clothing and shoes or boots. They hardly ever wore the clothes but would fetch them in to sell or trade. You could buy a good Indian blanket for a dollar or a pair of shoes for fifty cents. They would buy "fire water" with the money. They would trade you most anything for whiskey. There was a lot of bootleggers that lived off them Indians.

The Indians used to have a camp about a half mile north of Gordon on a creek. Saturdays and Sundays us kids used to hang around the Indian camp. We'd sell a dog or two, maybe buy a pair of moccasins or some beadwork as the squaws did a lot of beadwork to sell, and play with the Indian kids.

The Sioux Indians sure liked a fat dog to eat. We was sure to get a dollar to a dollar and a half for a dog. There wasn't too many dogs around Gordon as us kids used to keep all the stray dogs cleaned up and some that wasn't strays.

I used to chum around with a couple of boys by the name of Swaggert. The oldest boy's name was Lash and the youngest boy's name was Rudy. All the spare time we had we was over to the Indian camp. It is astonishing how fast a kid can pick up a language. Lash got to be an Indian interpreter and then in later years I heard he became the agent at Standing Rock Agency in South Dakota.

I remember one time when Rudy and me was going to the Indian camp. We saw a big fat squaw coming down the road with a big load of wood on her back. It looked like a wagon box full. It didn't look like it was possible for anyone to tie that much wood in a rope and carry it on their back.

She stopped at the bridge that crossed the creek, put her load of wood down beside the road and went under the bridge. We stayed at the camp perhaps half an hour. As we came back to the bridge, the squaw was coming out from under it. She had a brand new baby. She went on to camp carrying the baby but she left the wood. We looked under the bridge. It looked like some cow had just had a calf. The grass and weeds was all tore up.

I have been to a good many Indian dances, Sun dances and war dances by the Crow Indians. I have also attended several dances of the Flathead, Shoshoni, Arapahoe and Ute Indians but the Sioux Indians' war dance skins anything I ever saw.

Their regalia and war bonnets was outstanding, buffalo heads fastened on their heads with a lot of eagle feathers. They was great for different colors on their faces and bodies, with just a G-string around their body, scalps hanging on their scalp pole.

While I was going to school at Gordon the Sioux Indians put on some kind of a special war dance. There must have been four or five hundred of them camped at the campgrounds. They had just got their rations and had lots of blankets, clothing and other stuff to sell or trade for whiskey. I will try to describe it just as I remember it.

The Indians formed a large circle and took hold of hands. There was a large tom tom in the center with about six singers. Their songs are a lot of hollering, but they keep time and it sounded nice to hear about a half a mile away.

There was quite a lot of special dancers in the center of the ring and they was going through a lot of fancy stepping. Some would be bent over nearly touching their heads on the ground. Then they would raise up slowly until they was standing on their toes. All the time the outside was all going around in a circle the inside warriors would dance until they would fall down exhausted. They would lay right where they fell until they rested. Some of the others took their place. They kept that up for hours that night.

They had lots of liquor and they all got to hollering. They had started to dance just when it got dark. They had two big bonfires going and I could see them all the time.

BOYHOOD DAYS

ABOUT TWELVE O'CLOCK it was really getting wild. They all seemed to be hollering. Then they opened the circle up and turned in a wild white horse all dabbed with blood, or anyway it looked like blood, it may have been paint. Then they closed the gap so the horse couldn't get out. The horse was crazy scared running around trying to get out and the Indians trying to keep him in. It sure was a spooky sight.

There was about a hundred and fifty white people from town and the surrounding country watching the Indians dance. Finally, an old half breed that used to hang around town told the white people they had better leave as the Indians was all getting drunk and was talking bad about the white people.

Of course we all got going. The last I seen was the white horse going round and round scared crazy. As I remember, the white horse represented the white people and the Indians had them corralled. If they could hold the horse in, it was good but if he got out that was bad.

"The Sioux put on a war dance."

I REMEMBER when the cavalry had the last skirmishes with the Sioux Indians at the Pine Ridge Agency in South Dakota. About that time Bartlett Richards had the contract to deliver so many beef each month to the agency at Pine Ridge.

Bartlett Richards ran lots of cattle in the Sand Hills of Nebraska and his spread was known as the Spade outfit. At the time I am telling you about, Sidney Erwin was foreman. Bartlett Richards must have had it fixed with the Indian Agent for they turned in the sorriest looking cattle you can imagine. There was big jaws, old bulls and poor shelly cows. It didn't look like a beef herd but the culls of their entire spread. They got by with it for quite a while.

AT ABOUT THAT time it seemed like the government didn't have anything to do except make and break treaties with the Indians. In some of their pow wows over the beef issue there was such a squawk made about the kind of beef issued that the government stopped the beef issue and granted them so much cash in place of beef along with blankets, clothes and provisions. The money never done the Indians much good as there was too many white men selling them liquor.

The Indian reservation wasn't too far from the Fremont and Missouri railroad. The Indians used to come over to Shadron, Rushville and Gordon, Nebraska to buy or trade anything they had for liquor. Outside of a few young Indians, the half breeds and squaw men, they couldn't talk our language. They was all blanket Indians and the bucks wore their hair in braids. They was sporting people with lots of time. They lived each day and let the white men worry about tomorrow. They would bet their last bead on a horse race.

There was always some of them camped on a little creek about a half a mile north of Gordon. The young bucks was always playing games. They threw arrows, they ran, they jumped, they wrestled and ran their ponies in races. In fact their life seemed good to them and they enjoyed it. They held lots of dances and I don't think many of them was war dances, just friendly get togethers like we have. I don't believe I ever heard of Sioux Indians having quarrels among themselves. They showed a lot of respect toward their chief and the medicine men.

GORDON WAS JUST a new little town but it had a half mile race track. Any kind of amusement took place at the race track, because everyone owned horses and always thought theirs was the best and tried to prove it. They started a little fair in the fall and it seemed like all the ranchers was there as was the whole Indian tribe.

The Spade outfit raised a lot of good horses for saddle stock. They had one thoroughbred stallion they had shipped all of the way from England. It seemed like some of the Spade outfit was on hand at any doings to run a race with the Indians and generally always beat them.

I remember one race that the Indians cleaned up on the Spade outfit. It was at one of those first fairs at Gordon. The Indians had just got their government issue. They had lots of new blankets, clothes and money outside of about fifty head of betting horses.

There was an old Indian that could talk a little called Bird On Top. He had a horse he wanted to race. The Spade cowboys was raring for some easy money. They hit Bird On Top for a race. The Spade outfit wanted to bet fifty dollars on a half mile race. Bird On Top wanted to run a mile. There was a big pow wow and much sign language before they got the betting and the race compromised at three quarters of a mile.

Bird On Top and a young breed squatted on a blanket and covered all bets. Bird On Top didn't savvy paper money but the breed did and when someone gave a bill he would hold up his fingers to show the amount and Bird On Top would put silver dollars alongside it. When they ran out of money they would point to a horse for ten dollars.

Bird On Top's squaw had fetched in a nail keg and the money was put into it. He said, "You horse win, you ketchum keg. My horse win, me ketchum keg. All a same. Heap a good." They turned the keg to the judges to keep.

Bird On Top's horse was a raw boned sorrel horse not exactly pretty but built for speed and endurance. It looked like it had quite a lot of age. It was branded U S on the left shoulder, and must have been a cavalry horse at one time. Whether he had been stolen from the government or obtained otherwise I don't know but anyway, he was a running old fool.

The Spade horse was a very pretty grey that showed a lot of breeding. He was young and looked in tip top shape. I think Shorty Truacks was riding him that day.

Bird On Top had an old cavalry saddle without any stirrups on his horse. He picked up a little Indian boy that didn't look to be over ten years old and small for his age. He set him in the saddle, then tied the boy's ankles to the cinch rings. The horse had only a rope in his mouth with just one rein. The kid had that rein in one hand and an Indian whip in the other. He wore paint instead of clothes except for a G string.

They loped up to the starting line and the judge hollered, "Go!" It was a good even start. The grey horse was about a neck ahead of the sorrel for about a quarter of a mile. Then the kid hit the sorrel horse a couple of licks down the hind leg and he went up about a half a length ahead and that's the way they finished. Both of them was licking their horses at the finish but the little buck had the strongest arm. There was about three hundred Indians yelling and whooping as they crossed the finish line.

That night the Indians had a big dance to celebrate the winning of the race. They had a big circle of Indian dancers dressed in all their finery and in the center of the ring they led the sorrel horse. He was also decorated for the dance. They had put an Indian war bonnet on his head and had eagle feathers and ribbons tied in his mane and tail.

I REMEMBER one Sioux Indian dance in particular that took place before the massacre at the Wounded Knee Agency in South Dakota. It was held north of Gordon, Nebraska on a small creek. I don't know whether it was a shadow dance, a ghost dance or a regular war dance but it was plenty scary.

My folks was living in the Sand Hills about forty miles from Gordon. My mother, sister and I was going to Gordon with my Aunt Clara and Uncle Hop. He was at one time a scout for the government and had a lot of experience in Indian affairs.

When we got about twenty miles from Gordon we began to see smoke. Uncle Hop said it was Indian smoke signs and described how they was made. He said the Indians would have a fire going, then would throw some weeds and grass on the fire. They would throw a hide or wet blanket over the fire until it kind of smothered the fire. When they pulled the hide off the fire, the black smoke would just boil up into the air.

When we got to Gordon we heard that the Indians had had their smoke signals going for several days. The dance was to be that night and like everybody around close to Gordon we went to it.

The little creek where the dance was held was an old stomping ground of the Indians for there was always Indians camping there. They had been coming for three days before the dance. I don't know how many Indians was there but there must have been several hundred as the whole flat was covered with tepees. They seemed to be peaceable.

As I remember it, there was quite a big circle made with a rawhide rope stretched about three feet above the ground. The only gap in the enclosure was just next to the creek where there was a brush patch. The dancers came in or went out of the circle through that gap.

It was just dark when we got there but we was in time to see the dance start. The Indians had two big fires going, one on each side of the circle. I can't remember all the stunts they pulled but these stand out in my memory.

One big bellied buck was pounding on the tom tom in the center of the circle. It was some kind of a hide stretched over a hoop. There was about ten singers that yelled and kept time with the beat of the tom tom.

The dancers came in the circle single file. The bucks was all decked out with war bonnets that had eagle feathers hanging down their backs, just a breach clout on in place of clothes, beaded moccasins on their feet. Their faces and bodies was all painted. The squaws all wore bright colored blankets belted down with a wide beaded belt with a knife fastened to it. Their faces was painted too.

A big tall Indian buck led the bunch. He had some kind of a bird fastened on top of his war bonnet. He must have been a chief or a medicine man.

They all went around the circle singing in rhythm with the tom tom for a couple of rounds. Then the tall buck hollered something. The bucks all went in the middle of the circle yelling and going through all kinds of antics. Some of them bending so far over that they looked like they would fall on their faces, then straighten up gradually, all in perfect time with the singers and the tom tom.

Some of them must have been doing kind of a scare dance. They would look at the ground as though there was something spooking them. They'd leap to the side and then they would sneak a few steps, jump into the air and yell and repeat the maneuver.

One dancer had a skull on a short pole and several was dancing around him. All the time, the squaws was going around the circle slowly chanting a low humming song of some kind. As the dance progressed it seemed to get faster, wilder and crazier.

Some of the dancers would dance and yell until they would fall down exhausted but the dance never slowed up as another Indian would take the tired one's place. Some of them just layed where they fell but most of them went out of the circle into the brush to rest.

There was an Indian came running into the circle with a white sheet covering him all over. He was holding the sheet with his hands, all you could see of him was his eyes. Several Indians was chasing him flashing tomahawks. One had a spear and made like he speared him. As he fell down, a squaw came from the circle with a long knife and made a wild slash at a scalp that was fastened on his hair with her knife. As she pulled the scalp off, the Indians really went wild hollering and doing a crazy dance around the squaw. They made so much racket that you couldn't hear the tom tom.

There was a cottonwood log standing in the circle too. It was about the size of a man. It was white with a face painted on it. As the Indians with the tomahawks passed the log they let fly with their hatchets. They never missed a throw and there was hatchets sticking all over the log.

One buck came running in from the entrance. He had something in his hands. Several other bucks was in close pursuit grabbing at him. One caught him by the G string or breech clout, whatever you might call it. He jerked away minus his clout but joined right in the dance. Whether it was an accident or on the program no one seemed to know.

After that, Uncle Hop said we had better go as things was getting pretty rough. He said he thought the Indians had whiskey in the brush patch.

We had all just started away when something special must have happened as the Indians was putting out some awful blood curdling yells. The dance lasted three nights. They would rest in the days and dance all night.

I have seen several Indian dances since then but nothing compared with that one. Not even the one that had a wild white horse dabbed with blood that they kept in the circle was as spooky.

AFTER WE visited my Aunt Clara and Uncle Hop my mother took up a claim in the Arkansas valley in Cherry County, Nebraska close to the Enlow Land and Cattle Company C— headquarters. John Enlow was the principle owner of the company. During haying season my mother cooked for the hay crews of the C—.

John Enlow was a noted character in Nebraska, a leader among men. Enlow trailed several herds of cattle from Texas to the northern states before he settled down to ranching. I once heard him say that Texas cowboys was the best hands he ever worked with and the meanest.

I can still remember what a kick I got listening to the cowboys tell stories in the evenings around the stove in the bunkhouse. I remember one story I heard John Enlow tell. He wasn't a man to tell windy stories so I have always believed every word of it. I will tell his story as near as I remember it.

Enlow was trailing cattle from Texas. They had to trail through Indian Territory. I believe he called it the Indian Nation, anyway, it was somewhere in what is now Oklahoma.

I think he said it was Kiowa reservation. He said at that time they was a very mean treacherous tribe. Anyone going through that country had to be mighty careful or the Kiowas would steal their whole herd of cattle.

The men taking herds through that territory had to get a permit to cross it. If the herd crossed any Indian land and it was grazed on or the cattle was watered, the herd owner had to pay a fee to the Indian owning the land. There was creeks and places to water along the trail belonging to Indians that just had to be used. The Indians took advantage of anyone with a herd and bled the trail herds for all they could get.

Enlow said that one place that they came to was a pretty barren country. Several trail herds had gone through ahead of him. They had eaten most of the grass close to the trail.

They was just pulling into a small creek when three Indians met them. The Indians pow wowed a while and with much use of sign language said that for three head of cattle they would let the herd graze on some bottom land where there was better grass.

Enlow had one of the punchers cut them out three head. While the Indians drove the cattle off, Enlow's crew camped the wagon on the creek. All the cowboys took a swim except one that guarded the herd. That part of the country was hilly and the herd was never left alone at no time.

Enlow said there never was a time on that drive, through the Indian country, that if you looked you couldn't see an Indian up on some hill watching the trail herd. The Indians was keeping cases on them, always ready to slip in and cut off a little bunch of cattle.

The next morning they had the cattle all rounded up ready to start the day's drive when about fifteen Indians came riding up. There was one breed with them that could talk. He said that the Indian who owned the bottom land wanted twenty head of cattle for the feed and water the trail herd had used. According to the breed, the Indian that owned the land hadn't given his consent for them to use it.

Enlow told the breed he'd given three head for the privilege but as he didn't want any trouble he told one of the cowboys to cut out five more head.

The Indians wasn't satisfied with five head. One started in the herd to cut out some more cattle. Enlow rode right in behind the Indian with his six-shooter aimed at the Indian's back. Another Indian rode in behind Enlow with a gun pointed at his back.

That's the way they went through the herd. The cowboys all lined up with their guns out. Enlow pointed to the five head of cattle.

The Indians never showed fight but took the five head and drove them off. Enlow said there wasn't a shot fired but it had been close. After that, he kept a double guard until they got out of the Indian territory.

PEOPLE DIDN'T USED to make all the fuss and commotion about Christmas they do now. I want to tell you about Christmas when I was about eleven years old. That was in 1887. My mother was cooking for John Enlow. Gordon was the closest town and was about forty miles from the ranch.

Enlow's C— ranch on Clifford Creek was a pretty big spread. He used to put up a lot of hay in the valleys for winter feed. He didn't stack the hay, just run it up in big bunches. He'd have the cowboys hold the cattle in a valley until they'd eaten all the hay, then move them into another valley.

It had been a nice fall, just a few light storms. Enlow had all the work done and was ready for winter. The fire guards had been plowed and burned around the hay meadows. A big stack of hay was hauled into the ranch for the stock there. There was no timber in that country, everyone burned cow chips for fuel. There had been two men picking up cow chips for three weeks and piling them in a great big shed to keep them dry.

The winter supply of groceries was layed in. There was a barrel of green coffee beans. I remember my mother roasting those beans in the oven in a big pan and then grinding them in a small coffee grinder nailed on the wall. I turned that coffee grinder for her many a time.

The men had been paid off except two, my Uncle Hop, who had a place about seven miles from the home place and Burton, who had a homestead about five miles in what was called north valley. Burton could live on his claim and hold the cattle in the hay meadows at the same time.

A week or ten days before Christmas my mother and little sister went to Gordon in a buggy to get some things. I suppose the things was for Christmas but I don't remember. I stayed at the ranch with Mr. Enlow.

The day after my mother left, a man brought a message to Enlow to come to North Platte which was about a hundred and fifty miles away. Mr. Enlow was in a spot, he didn't want to leave me and I don't think he wanted to take me with him although he asked me to go with him. I thought I was about a man and said I would see to things until my mother got back.

Mr. Enlow left a note for me to give Burton when he came to the ranch. In the note he asked Burton to stay at the ranch with me until he got back from North Platte. I remember Enlow telling me, "Stay at the house and don't be riding around the hills on old Peggy until your mother gets back."

When my mother got to Gordon she heard that Mrs. Murray, a very good friend, was awfully sick. My mother went to see Mrs. Murray and found her in very bad shape. There was a doctor but no nurses or hospitals at that time. In case of sickness neighbors or friends had to stand by. Mother stayed with Mrs. Murray a few days to nurse her and take care of the small children.

While mother was taking care of Mrs. Murray, thinking I was with John Enlow and he was in North Platte thinking my mother was back at the ranch, I was alone at the ranch a couple of weeks. Burton was busy taking care of the cattle in the north valley and didn't come to the ranch so didn't get Enlow's orders to stay with me.

There was a milk cow, a few chickens, a work team and twelve or fifteen poor cows to take care of so I was busy most of the time. I was doing alright until a big storm came.

It snowed a little and was cold for two days, then a big wind hit and it really got cold. I don't believe you could see fifteen feet. It looked like you was trying to look through a wall of snow. I tried to feed the poor cows but as soon as I'd lift a fork of hay, the wind would blow it all away.

That night, I forgot I was a man and really wanted my mother. There was the howl of the wind and a knocking and bumping around the house. I shivered in my bed and wondered if there was such things as ghosts and goblins.

Finally, I couldn't stand it any longer. I got up and lit the lamp. I tried to look out the windows but they was all covered with frost, then I opened the door a crack to see out. I could see a lot of cattle had drifted around the buildings and the noise that had scared me so bad I couldn't go to sleep was made by the cattle knocking and rubbing their horns against the house.

I had thought the storm was bad but next morning I knew what a ring tailed blizzard was. I couldn't feed those hungry cows because of the wind. I couldn't stand to hear them bawl and see them shiver from the cold so I opened the gate and let them go into the hay stack. That was Christmas Eve.

In the afternoon sometime, Burton rode in about half frozen. He came to tell Enlow that the storm had drifted the cattle out of north valley. Boy, was I glad to see him!

Christmas morning the storm was still raging. There was no gifts, no Christmas tree and no turkey in the oven but Burton tried to make us something special for dinner. There was a quarter of beef hanging in a shed. Burton carried it in. It was frozen hard as glass. He took the axe and chopped us off some steak.

He made a custard pudding in a tin pan and put some raisins or currants in it. He opened a can of corn and made some coffee. It don't sound like much of a feast now but I think it was the best Christmas dinner I ever ate.

I WAS ABOUT fifteen years old. I was exploring the west by way of fast freight trains. When I got to Rawlins, Wyoming I decided I'd have to pick up some kind of a job helping a freighter if I was to get over in the Lander country which didn't have a railroad. I don't know why I wanted to get to Lander unless it was because I'd heard about the gold mines near there and the large cattle and sheep ranches.

There was a stage route that had stations about twenty miles apart that went from Rawlins to Lander but I didn't have enough money to pay my way on the stage. The freighters, at that time, drove jerk line outfits using eight to twenty horses hauling two to three wagons. I hit several of them for a swamping job to Lander but I was small for my age and I guess they didn't think I could do anything. Anyway, I didn't get a job with a freight outfit.

I was determined to get to Lander. Like any kid, I thought I'd get a job as a cowboy and get some money together and find me a gold mine, if I could just get there. Like all air castles mine tumbled down as time went on.

I was down to ten dollars and thirty five cents when a Mexican propositioned me to drive a small bunch of horses, perhaps twenty head, while he drove his wagon to Lander. I didn't like his looks but I thought I could get along with him for a hundred and fifty miles.

He was short and heavy set. He was anyways from thirty eight to forty five years old. He had a scar from his ear to his chin and smallpox pits all over his ugly, black, wrinkled face. He had little pig eyes that just looked mean. He carried a big knife in his boot and a .45 buckled around his waist all the time. I found out on the trip that he was even meaner than he looked. In fact, he was the cruelest meanest man to his stock I ever run into.

I didn't know when I took the job of driving the horses that they was stolen horses. I learned that after we had parted company. He was the only man in all my life that I was mad enough to kill and come close to doing it, but I told that story in *Good Men and Salty Cusses* and won't repeat it.

It was in the spring of the year and we had got the wagon stuck in snow drifts several times. By the time we got to South Pass there was no snow there.

We camped a short ways east of the gold camp to let the horses rest up as they was thin and weak and tired. The Mexican went in to South Pass and left me to hold the horses.

While I was killing time waiting for the Mexican to come back, I ran into an old prospector by the name of Jimmie. He was working the creek where we was camped. The horses was tired and never tried to get away so I helped Jimmie cradle for gold.

He was a real old man all crippled up. He had a burro that he used to pack his stuff on. He told me he was a Confederate soldier in the Civil War. He was quite a talker and told me a lot of Civil War stories.

Jimmie told me that the little creek where we was camped went dry in the summer and that the only time he could work it was in the spring when the snow melted and made a runoff. He had to have water to use his cradle.

The cradle was kind of a trough about four feet long, two and a half to three feet wide. It had slats nailed along the bottom and sides to catch the gold, and a hole in the end to let the water out. It worked like an old washing machine, one of the kind that you worked back and forth with a lever.

To get the gold, first you have to dig down to gravel which was about two feet deep there. You carried the gravel to the cradle and put it in, then throwed water in and rocked the cradle. When the water had all worked through the gravel, you had to throw off the coarse rocks on top and put in more water and keep rocking the cradle.

The gold, if any, would settle to the bottom and get caught along the slats. It was awful hard discouraging work even though we was getting a little fine gold. Jimmie wanted me to stay and help him but I thought it was too slow as we had worked for three days and only had about six dollars' worth of gold. My back was about broke and my hands all blistered. Jimmie gave me a small nugget for helping him but he had dug

BOYHOOD DAYS

it out somewhere else as the gold we had been cradling was fine gold.

When the Mexican came back after his three day stay in South Pass he was all skinned up. He said he had been in a poker game, lost his money and been in a big fight.

We was all out of groceries. In fact all we had on the trip was a little flour, sow belly, some black Mexican beans and coffee. The Mexican was in a ugly temper, cussing everything. He wanted to borrow my ten dollars and go back to South Pass.

I wouldn't let him have it until we got to the grocery store. We got enough grub to last us to Lander. I never got my ten dollars back as we dissolved partners before we got to Lander but I was close enough to walk in, jingling my thirty five cents.

I did odd jobs around Lander all summer and winter. I tried to get jobs around the cow outfits but they thought I was too young.

I saved my money. Early the next spring I went over to Rawlins on the stage, caught a freight and beat my way to Cheyenne.

2: Cattle

I USED TO hear a lot of stories from the cowboys that had brought trail herds up from Texas. Those stories was full of the grief and hardships the cowboys endured on those long drives. It took a tough breed of men to take that punishment and be ready to repeat the trip.

Them long drives from Texas was plenty tough. The outfit consisted of what was called the chuck wagon, bed wagon, the cavvy and the cowboys.

The chuck wagon was generally moved by a four horse team. The chuck wagon had a chuck box or cupboard built in the back of the wagon box. It had shelves built in for the tin dishes, knives and forks, pots and pans. There was a door in the front of the grub box on hinges. When let down the door made a kind of a table for the cook to work on. The cowboys just filled their plates and sat cross legged on the ground to eat their meals.

The chuck wagon was made for traveling. The wagon box held the groceries. There was places made on each side of the wagon for two water barrels, in case they had to make a dry camp. The bed wagon held the tents, bed rolls and other equipment used on the trail.

Those drives was made in the summer when it was hot as Hades. Millions of flies, gnats, chiggers, wood ticks and flying ants made life miserable. There was no comfort at night with tarantulas, scorpions, sand fleas, even rattle snakes ready to crawl into their beds.

Fifteen hundred to twenty five hundred head of cattle can kick up an awful lot of fine dust that settles all over a man, in his ears, hair and all over his hat and clothes. It poisons his eyes until they are sore and he can hardly see.

They had all kinds of weather to contend with. Heat, wind, hail storms, cyclones. Rains that would last a week or more which meant mud and sleeping in a wet bed. Then mile after mile where there wasn't a drop of water, where they had to drive the cattle at night when it was cooler in order to get the cattle through to water before they perished. They generally made eight to ten miles a day unless they was in the dry country, then they had to make longer drives.

The dust, hair and filth would settle on their clothes so that when they got off their horses to walk around and shake themselves they made a regular fog. The cattle made so much dust that they couldn't see ten feet ahead of them especially if they was in the drag end of the herd.

On bad windy days the cattle didn't like to travel and the cowboys had to work hard to keep them moving. They said it seemed like every head of them was bawling at the same time.

"Horse grazing, rider sitting."

CATTLE

CATTLE DRIVE [handwritten]

They had to night herd the cattle all the time to keep the Indians and thieves from stealing them, and to keep them from drifting away. Night herding in a bad thunder and lightning storm was a spooky proposition when the forked lightning jumped from horn to horn on the cattle lighting the grim darkness as light as day. Cattle stampeding in the dark when they had to run their horses in all kinds of rough country where they was likely to fall in a hole any old time.

The cowboys had to ride their horses with a hackamore so they could grab a mouthful of grass any time they could find one. After they had traveled from eight hundred to a thousand miles, the horses was wore down and sore footed. Most of them had sores on their back that the cowboys called a pie or a set fast, as big as a hat. When they saddled a sore backed horse up in the morning and stepped up on him, he generally went down to his knees, it hurt so bad.

The grub wasn't anything to brag about, sow belly, beans, baking powder biscuits and strong coffee. Sometimes they had canned corn or tomatoes. Any fresh meat was game, for the cattle of the herd wasn't in any condition to butcher.

They all said they suffered for good water more than anything else. The water in some of that southern country was just not fit to drink. Sometimes they said it was warm with thousands of wiggle tails in it and they had to strain it through a cloth to catch the wiggle tails and bugs.

The flies made life miserable for the cattle too. The worst of all was the small black flies. They would get on an animal just back of the front legs on the back where it was too far for the tail to switch them off and hard for the critter to knock them off with its horns. The cattle would fight with no results. The flies just sat there and sucked blood until they got full of blood and fell off. They bothered the light colored cattle the most.

After a while the animals would finally give up fighting the flies. The flies never left the cattle's backs. The hair soon all disappeared and there was a blanket of flies all over their backs which was all raw and bloody. The cowboys would have to rope and tie them down and rub axel grease mixed with creosote to keep the flies off or they would just stay there until they killed the animal.

The cooks on them long drives had plenty of grief too, through rain and wind storms, dry camps and what not for the cowboys had to eat. Sometimes he had wood to burn, other times just buffalo or cow chips. He had to cook on a little old sheet iron camp stove or on a camp fire in Dutch ovens.

No wonder those cowhands was a little trigger fingered and spoiling for a fight when they reached a town. Those cowboys worked from sun up until sun down outside of standing two to three hours night guard. Sometimes they was on guard half the night or all night in case of a scare or a storm.

I REMEMBER the first big cattle roundup that I took a small part in. I was just a boy. The roundup took place in the Sand Hills of Nebraska near the old Spade ranch. The foreman's name was Sidney Erwin.

The Spade was a big outfit and ran a lot of cattle from the Running River in the Hat Creek country, east as far as Brush Lake and Snake Creek. The roundup was starting from the Spade ranch about thirty five miles south of Gordon.

At that time, I was living at the Enlow Land and Cattle Company C— ranch that was located on Clifford Creek. Enlow was sending a rep to the roundup by the name of Dave Tate. He was a very good Texas cowhand that had several notches on his gun. Dave had come up the trail from Texas with the early day herds.

I helped Tate take a bunch of saddle horses to the roundup. We took twenty four head of horses as Enlow was getting a couple of men from the Spade outfit and was furnishing them horses. At that time, each man that worked on the roundup was furnished eight head of horses to ride in what was called "his string."

CATTLE

I was too young to make a hand but I had permission from my folks to stay with the roundup a few days.

The Spade outfit's cowboys was mostly Texas men that had trailed in the country with southern herds. They was the real McCoy, all trail hardened men that had never done any kind of work except work cattle. They all carried a gun belted around their middle. There was several different wagons from different spreads but we stayed at the Spade wagon.

It was the spring roundup. Most of the saddle horses hadn't been rode since the fall roundup. The first time or two they was rode, they generally tried to buck their rider off. I remember the first morning when the cowboys started out there was fifteen to twenty horses bucking at one time. The cowboys was hollering, "Stay with him, Cowboy. He's just a pet."

They wasn't real hard horses to ride as they was all broke saddle horses. As soon as they got through their first spasm they was good gentle horses that you could do anything on.

The roundup cook that was working on the Spade wagon was a big red headed Irishman. He was a good cook but he was cranky and tough. If anything went wrong, he was the swearingest man I ever heard. He could make a bull whacker's profanity sound like a Methodist minister's sermon. He never lacked for a cuss word. They just rolled out naturally in a blue smoke with all the frills attached.

It is a very interesting sight to see a roundup branding a bunch of calves. The cowboys holding a bunch of cattle together while the ropers are catching the calves out of the herd at the rate of from forty to sixty calves per hour, dragging them to the fire for branding. The calf wrestler grabs the calf, releases the rope and the roper is after another calf.

There is a lot of today's cowboys that will say that I'm crazy. It can't be done. Of course it will seem unreasonable to some of the boys that have to run his calf down to catch it. I don't say there was many that could catch sixty calves an hour, forty was about the average.

The Spade outfit had a lot of good saddle horses. Of course, like all big outfits, they had a few old benches. In their cavvy they had a horse they called Badger as he was kind of a grey color. He was a real outlaw horse. He had bucked all the good riders off on the Spade ranch and got so no one would ride him. When a new man started to work, he generally got jobbed and bucked off Badger. The foreman said they would make a bell horse out of him so he always wore a bell.

The second day of the roundup there was a tall, slim, nice looking waddy rode into camp and asked the foreman for a job. He said he would take the rough string.

Sidney told him that their horses was all pretty gentle except for three head. He asked the cowboy where he had been working. The cowboy said he had broke out some horses at Deadwood. He got a name right then.

Sidney said, "All right, Deadwood, you got a job. I'll give you a string of horses in the morning."

Of course all the cowboys knew that Deadwood would draw Badger in the morning.

The horse wrangler had the horses in the rope corral about daylight. He caught Badger and took the bell off. Cowboys always caught their horses before breakfast. Sydney told Deadwood to saddle up Badger as he hadn't been rode for quite a while and he might buck a little and to take a little of the rough out of him before breakfast.

Badger wasn't a hard horse to saddle. Several of the boys got on their horses in order to catch Badger if he threw Deadwood off. Deadwood stepped on. Badger unwound fast and furious, bucking right toward the mess wagon and the campfire. The cook began to swear. The cowboys was hollering for Deadwood to stay on top.

Old Badger was coming straight for the campfire with his mouth wide open bawling like a Texas steer. Deadwood had both hands full of leather. He was in the saddle, out of the saddle, in all kinds of shapes.

The cook grabbed a pole that held up a canvas in the back of the wagon placed for shade and ran over to protect his fire and breakfast, cussing something awful.

Deadwood was just swinging around in the air when the cook swung at Badger's head with the pole. Badger dodged away but the pole caught Deadwood right across the back and broke.

When Deadwood managed to pick himself up and the cook got through swearing, breakfast was eaten and the roundup went on its way.

I REMEMBER a drive with a bunch of beef steers that I helped take from the old C— ranch to a small station called Cody on the Fremont, Elkhorn and Missouri Railroad. It was about forty miles north of the ranch.

It had been an early spring with lots of rain. The grass was knee high. This was sometime about the last of August. The grass was still green and the beef steers was loaded with tallow.

There was a man fetched a message to John Enlow. It was an order from Clay Robinson and Company of Omaha for two hundred head of fat steers at a fancy price. Most of the big outfits didn't ship their cattle until the last of September or sometime in October. They liked to get the benefit of the late grass as the cattle weighed more and shipped better on the cured dry grass.

It was about three o'clock in the afternoon when the message got to Enlow. He sent two men to the east and told them to throw as many cattle as it was handy to gather in the Burton valley and we would round up more cattle in the morning and cut out two hundred of the fattest steers and move them over on Snake Creek for the night.

Enlow sent an order for cars in by the messenger. He told the cook to have a four o'clock breakfast and be over in the Burton valley with the roundup wagon to have dinner for us at noon.

We was sure busy getting ready, helping the cook grease and load his wagon for the trip, getting some extra saddle horses to take along and a lot of other little things done so we could get started early in the morning.

We had our horses all saddled next morning ready to start as soon as we had breakfast. Burton valley was about five miles north of the ranch toward Cody.

We had good luck as it was a small valley about two miles long and it didn't take long to bunch the cattle and cut out two hundred head of the oldest and fattest steers. We had dinner about eleven and started the beef herd for Cody.

We hit Snake Creek about three in the afternoon. We stayed there about an hour. We had our supper early and changed saddle horses while the cattle was taking on water and grass. Enlow thought it would be a good thing to drive on as there wasn't water for fifteen miles after we left the Snake.

We left Snake Creek and drove on several miles and made a dry camp. We had a natural bed ground. It was a very pretty star light night. The cattle was tired and hardly moved all night. As soon as it was daylight we started to move the herd.

There was five of us driving the cattle. The cook and horse wrangler started on to a water hole about five miles from Cody where we would eat and change horses.

Everything was working fine. There was an old trail that went right through Cody. The steers was traveling it like a bunch of soldiers. One of the men said, "This is a snap, moving these cattle. All we have got to do is ride along behind them."

Burton, an old cowhand, told him, "We are having plenty of good luck but I never feel satisfied with a bunch of cattle until they are in the stock yards with the gate shut."

There was three nester shacks in about fifteen miles as the country had begun to settle up. They was little sod houses. One in particular, I remember had some kids watching us go by with the cattle. There was a few chickens and a milk cow in the

CATTLE

yard, a small garden and a patch of corn. It was out on a lonesome flat full of cactus.

We had gone by it about a half a mile. The cattle was strung out for a quarter mile. All at once I thought I heard dogs barking. I looked and saw a bunch of hounds running a coyote, hell for leather, right at about the center of the beef herd. Business picked up right now!

The coyote went right through that line of cattle. A blue hound grabbed him just after they got through the cattle. The rest of the dogs got in the struggle and they tore that coyote in strips.

The cattle was sure scared. They exploded like powder. They cut in two, one bunch running straight ahead, the others back the way they had come. Being so fat, they couldn't keep it up for long.

When we got them together and milling around, they had their tongues out and was puffing like steam engines. We had lost our luck.

There was two boys about thirteen and fifteen years old with the dogs. While we was getting the cattle together the boys skinned the coyote's head out for the bounty. I guess they thought they had scared the cattle and would come over and help us hold them. They was coming on a long lope toward us with the hounds following.

Burton was an old salty Texas cowboy. He knew that if the boys came close to the cattle with those hounds that the cattle would scare again.

He jerked out his six-shooter and shot just ahead of the horse that the oldest boy was riding, who was ahead. When the bullet kicked up sand in front of the horse, it put on the brakes but the boy traveled straight on.

I think the other boy thought Burton had shot his brother for he whirled his horse and started for home. As soon as the boy on the ground got his gas, he got on his horse and went for home on the run, too.

"Those cattle exploded like gun powder."

The cattle was so busy milling and bawling that they didn't pay no attention to the shot. Burton was sure painting the air blue cussing the damn grangers.

We finally got to the water hole. The cattle was too excited to drink and just wanted to mill and bawl and hook each other. It took a lot of yelling, cussing and rope snapping to get them on to Cody.

The cars was strung along the stock yards waiting for us. Cody was just a depot, section house and stock yard. The cattle had cooled off and we was handling them just as careful as we could.

It was getting along about sundown and clouding up like it might rain. We had the steers just at the stock yard's gate and it looked like a cinch to corral them. Then a freight train came by.

It scared them and how they did run. We managed to hold them together but we couldn't get them near the stock yards in the dark. There was nothing to do only hold them until morning.

It started to rain in the night. The cattle milled and bawled. Our horses was about all in but we was all so busy we couldn't leave the herd to get fresh ones.

CATTLE

At daylight the cattle quieted down so we could relay and get a fresh horse and some coffee.

We worked until ten o'clock before we got those steers in the stock yards. They didn't look so good and neither did we.

AROUND 1890 there was several big cattle outfits running cattle on the Sioux Reservation in South Dakota near the Nebraska line. Most of the cattlemen was running Texas steers. They would buy yearlings and two year olds cheap, trail them north, run them a couple of years and make good money.

It was in the fall of the year. The beef roundup had finished gathering and was preparing to break up and the various outfits return to their own range. They was camped at Walk A Palmoney Lake. (Note: Perhaps this is his spelling of Wakpala.) There had been a dispute over the ownership of a X I T steer. A squaw man and another outfit had both bought X I T cattle and the re-brand didn't show up too plain.

This squaw man was a former Texas man. He was pretty hard to get along with. He thought he had more privileges coming to him on account of having an Indian woman.

That evening a bootlegger that was selling liquor to the Indians came to the roundup camp. Naturally, they all got liquored up. Now that squaw man was hard to get along with when he was sober, mean as hell when he was drunk. The argument over the X I T steer flared up and led to a big fight. Several got skinned up, one cowboy got shot in the arm.

The squaw man had about eight hundred head of steers gathered that he was going to ship. He was figuring on getting some of the boys from the roundup crew to help him get the steers to the railroad. After the fight they was all sore and wouldn't help him.

He had to close herd the steers until he could get some more help. Gordon, Nebraska was the closest town, about thirty miles away. There was more or less always a few cowboys hanging around Gordon. He wanted six men but only managed for three.

As Bill Burton and I had come to Gordon together, when he hired Burton I hit him for a job too. He told me that I was a little young but he would take me to jingle the horses.

The squaw man had his roundup wagon five or six miles northeast of Walk A Palmoney Lake at a water hole. Two cowboys and the cook was holding the cattle. As we rode into camp we saw his saddle horses. There was about twenty five head and they was a sorry looking bunch, poor with sore backs. He had a crummy looking outfit all around.

It was just about sun down. We saw the two cowboys fetching a bunch of steers over to the bed ground where they was night herding the cattle. It was a real bed ground against a rimrock which made a circle back in the rim. The cowboys just had to ride the front end and there was no way for the cattle to get out.

The steers was all colors of the rainbow with longhorns and was fat, wild and rollicky. One cowpoke was a half breed Indian. He was sure good looking. He had a dark velvety round face. His hair was long and he had the prettiest set of even white teeth that I ever saw. He was a nice breed just as pleasant as he looked. The other fellow was short and stubby. He had pox marks all over his homely face. He was wearing a pair of bull hide chaps.

They looked awfully tired and their horses was all sweaty and just about played out. You could tell they had had plenty hard work holding that eight hundred steers together. We rode over and helped them on the bed ground. The cook had supper, then two of the men took their bed over to the bed ground. One stood guard until midnight, then the other took over.

The boss told me, "You saw the saddle horses when we come in. Have them in the rope corral at four o'clock in the morning. Don't fail. They won't be far, you will hear the bell. After breakfast, help the cook get started, then fetch the saddle

CATTLE

horses. Trail along, not too far from the herd so we can get fresh horses if we need them. Now I am paying good wages to those men and I'll pay you the same if you earn it, if you don't earn it I'll just pay you what I think you earned. I hadn't ought to have hired a damn kid anyhow."

The way he said it made me mad and I told him I'd do my work alright but I didn't like to be swore at by a damn squaw man. I was a pretty cocky kid.

He reached up and pulled three or four red hairs out of his head and pulled a knife and whacked them off and said, "Better keep your damn mouth shut or I'll trim your ears for you."

I told Burton about it that night. He said, "You'll be okay, kid. He was just trying to scare you."

I was plenty scared even if I didn't let on to the squaw man. I had the horses in at three-thirty in the morning. I borrowed Burton's watch. I think that I looked at it fifty times and at three o'clock I went after them. They was about a quarter of a mile from camp.

It was cloudy and the wind was in the north. They made a dry camp at noon and camped on a little creek that night, about a fifteen mile drive. About four o'clock it began to rain, not too hard but a slow drizzle and cold. We was about a mile from the Nebraska line.

Just over the line there was about twelve or fifteen farmers that had taken up some homesteads. The reservation cattle had got in their crops the year before and they had had some trouble. The cowmen told the farmers they would pay for about nine miles of material if the farmers would put in a fence. The fence was put in. It was a good deal, for the cowmen used it as a drift fence in the winter.

Just before dark we rounded the cattle on a flat about a half a mile south of the creek. It was still raining. The cattle was cold and nervous. They wouldn't stand at all, just milled and bawled. It looked like a tough night and we was going to be lucky if we didn't lose some cattle. The squaw man told me to put the horses in the rope corral and leave them until morning as he might have to double up the guard.

There was eight men all together including the cook and me. Four men went on first guard. It was still raining and dark as pitch. You could hardly see your hand in front of your eyes. About ten o'clock one of the hands came in and said that the boss sent him in for all hands and the cook to come to the herd as the cattle was giving them hell.

There wasn't no thunder or lightning. It would have been better if there was, for then you could see by the lightning. We had been out about two hours when the cattle got an awful scare. It seemed right in the middle of the herd and they went in all directions.

Burton was at the south end of the herd and so was I. It was too dark to see him but I could hear him singing. Oh Lord, how those cattle did run. You could hear their horns knocking together and it was an awful noise. My horse was plenty scared and so was I. Every once in a while I would hear Burton holler. I didn't know just what to do, in fact there was nothing to do only stay with the cattle until they run down, then try to mill them.

I knew that damn wire fence was ahead but couldn't tell how far for I couldn't see a thing. I heard Burton on the east side of me and a little ahead as though he was trying to swing the herd west so I run my horse to the west. I just got out of the way when the cattle hit the fence.

It was a good thing that I had turned west for I couldn't have been over forty feet from the fence and I would have hit the fence on the run. No doubt that it would have knocked my horse down and that bunch of cattle would of run over me. It gives me chills yet to think of it.

I heard Burton holler and I answered back. I rode toward him. When we met Burton said when the leaders hit the fence they couldn't of been over fifteen feet ahead of him. We could hear the cattle still running, the fence didn't seem to bother them cattle. We got off our horses and walked across the fence leading our horses for they was afraid of the loose wire. The cattle had left a clear trail.

Burton had rode that country before and said, "If they kept going as they was headed, there was a range of hills ahead and a canyon that goes right through them but if they swing, they will hit the rough country."

We rode hell for leather and soon began to pass cattle.

It had just about quit raining and the clouds was moving. We could see a little better. All at once it was pretty light and I saw the moon. We had a good look. The leaders had hit the canyon and had slowed down.

Burton told me to go back and get behind the cattle we'd passed, he thought he could get to the lead and stop them as they couldn't get out of the canyon. He did just that and we got them bunched up, me behind them, him in front.

The clouds got over the moon and it was black as ink. It began to rain but lots harder, big drops and the wind began to blow. I thought I'd freeze to death. I was shaking and my teeth was rattling. I thought I saw a little flash. I looked again and sure enough Burton had a fire going. There was a little patch of pines alongside of the canyon. He had managed to roll over an old tree and get some dry twigs and start a fire. My God, that fire looked good. The more I looked the colder I got.

The cattle was bawling, making an awful noise. Where I was there was nothing to burn. I just had to shake and wait. It finally stopped raining and the clouds was moving so it lightened up.

Just after daylight the squaw man and the good looking breed came up. He said that they had lost a bunch in the rough country and as there was a lot of cattle in there, they was all mixed up. He wanted to know how many we had. I told him quite a bunch. He decided that he would take what cattle we had and by making a long drive that day we could corral at Cody that night.

He told us to keep them going and he would go back for the outfit. We was about six miles from the wagon. It must have been nine o'clock before the wagon caught up with us. We had some coffee and a lunch, then changed horses.

I drove the saddle horses on to Cody. Them steers sure did travel. We made about twenty five miles to Cody by five o'clock and got them corralled. We had about five hundred head. It didn't seem to me that I had been in bed fifteen minutes when the cook hollered, "Come and get it."

After breakfast the squaw man was sending his two breeds back with the saddle horses and the cook with the chuck wagon. He was giving the cowboys their checks. I asked Burton how much he gave him and he showed me his check.

When he'd paid the men he said, "Where is that damn kid?"

I said, "I don't like to be swore at by a Texan. You better get your knife out."

He kind of grinned and the fellows laughed. When he handed me my check I saw it was two dollars more than Burton's. I asked him if he had made a mistake. He said, "No, the two dollars is for you to buy candy with."

I BLOWED INTO CHEYENNE on a freight train when I was just a kid (around sixteen). I had nineteen dollars in my pocket and I was looking for a job. I had been raised in the cow country and didn't have any experience in other kinds of work.

After a couple of days I landed a job in a restaurant washing dishes for four dollars a week. I didn't like it but knew I had to do something until I could land a better job.

Around Cheyenne, at that time, was all big cattle country. The cowboys used to come into Cheyenne to drink, gamble and have a good time. They generally done their drinking and gambling at Harry Hines' Saloon and Gambling Hall.

After I got through washing dishes I'd go over to Hines' to watch them do their stuff. I understood cowboys better than other people and wanted to land a job on some cow outfit. Being young and small for my age and not having a saddle or bed I wasn't having any luck. One cow foreman that I hit for a job told me they didn't have anyone at the wagon to change my didies.

That sure riled me up and I told him to go to hell. That I'd bet I could read brands as good as he could.

The cowboys laughed and went over to the crap table and began to shoot craps. They didn't seem to be lucky and one cowboy asked me if I ever shot any craps.

I told him I did and I was lucky and could generally make three passes and then shoot craps.

He said, "Maybe this kid is lucky."

He threw two dollars on the line and said, "Here kid, let's see you make three passes. One of them dollars is yours."

I took the dice and threw seven. They had all bet but the foreman who had a lock of red hair that hung down over one eye. He had a little too much liquor under his belt and was a little sore at me for telling him I could read brands as good as he could.

I made another throw and made eleven and won again. The cowboys was taking my word for making three passes and letting their money ride. The third throw I hit ten, a hard point to make. Threw several times and made ten. The fellow that staked me had sixteen dollars on the line.

I took up eight dollars and passed the dice to Red. I had a hunch that it was time for "craps" and asked the dealer what were the odds for craps. He said, "Five to one, but you have to put something on the line. You can bet as much on craps as you put on the line."

Red threw two aces which was craps. He paid me ten dollars for the craps but won the two dollars on the line. Red didn't like it when I bet against him on craps and gave me an ugly look.

I never bet anymore until the dice went around the table and come to me. I was eighteen dollars winner and thought I'll quit if I win or lose.

I bet six dollars on the line and made two passes. I throwed the dice to Red and left the saloon forty dollars winner and never lost a bet. That was some luck! I felt like a millionaire as I'd only spent three dollars and had a week's wages coming to me.

I worked the next day as that made out my week. I had counted my money several times. I had $56.00. I told the restaurant man I didn't like dish washing and was quitting.

I thought if I got out of town I could get a riding job. At one of the feed stores, they bought and sold horses. I went to the feed yards and told the man what I wanted.

He said, "Kid, I got just what you want. I bought a small horse and a saddle from a Mexican yesterday. It is a good little horse but the saddle ain't much. I can sell you both for forty five dollars."

I looked at the horse. He looked good to me but the saddle, bridle and blanket wasn't much. The saddle was a Mexican rig with a low cantle, two cinches and a saddle horn that was as big around as a tin plate. The saddle skirts was all wrinkled up.

I bought the works, then went up town, bought two soogan quilts, and a cotton blanket for $3.50. A coffee pot, some coffee, a piece of bacon, salt and some flour completed my outfit. I tied it all behind my saddle and started out for Chugwater where I heard they wanted some men.

I RODE into a ranch which was about four miles from the present town of Chugwater. Two men was building a pole corral, I rode up to them and asked for the boss. They told me he had gone to Buffalo and wanted to know what I wanted.

I said that I'd heard in Cheyenne that he needed some men and thought maybe I could get a job. They looked me over, then looked at each other. I guess they thought I couldn't do much as they sized up my old saddle with the pack tied on behind.

One of them asked me if I'd had dinner and when I said, "No," he said to go over to the house and the cook would fix me something as they had just finished eating.

CATTLE

That night the boss came. He said he didn't have a job for me but he said he had some **C Y** horses that he'd promised to deliver to Buffalo. He would pay me $5.00 to deliver them. I took the horses to Buffalo.

When I got to Buffalo, Pike a **C Y** hand was waiting for the horses. I went with him to the **C Y** wagon which was camped on Crazy Woman.

It started to rain as we left Buffalo. It rained for three days and nights. It was sometime in May and it was a cold rain. I liked to froze to death as all the clothes I had was two light shirts and two pair of overalls and a light summer coat.

When we got to the wagon, Pike pointed out Bob Devine, the wagon boss, and I hit him up for a job. I was cold and shivering so hard I could hardly talk.

He didn't give me much satisfaction. He said they was full handed but told me to turn my horse in the cavvy and stay until the storm was over. He said, "You might help the cook a little."

I went over to the roundup wagon where there was a small tent stretched. I told the cook the boss had told me to help him.

The cook was a sour old cuss. He asked me if I could wash dishes. When I said I could, he pointed at the dishpan and said, "Get busy."

I washed the tin dishes, saw he was about out of wood and went out to where one of the cowboys had drug up some. I cut it up and put it behind the stove to dry. I peeled about a bushel of potatoes and got some water. Then I went over to a tent where the waddies slept. It had a sheet iron stove in it.

I asked one of the cowboys if there was room to put my bed in there. He said, "We are pretty crowded."

I blowed up and said, "This is a hell of an outfit. I was raised in a cow country and never saw the time there wasn't room for one more bed in a tent when it was raining."

I took my soogans and blanket, wrung the water out of them and put them under the wagon box. I like to froze that night.

Next morning it was still raining, a slow cold drizzle. I got up about four o'clock and built a fire in the cook tent. It was nice and warm when the cook got up. As soon as the horse jingler corralled the horses, I caught my horse, saddled up and tied my pack behind my saddle ready to travel.

Bob, the boss, who had his own tepee came out and talked to me when he saw I had my pack tied on. He asked me where I came from. I told him I'd come from Cheyenne but I was from the Sand Hills of Nebraska.

He said, "That's cow country. Do you know any cowmen there? How about the Spade outfit, ever heard of it?"

I told him, "Yes, I've been to the Spade outfit lots of times. Johnny Riggs, a Texas man with a broken nose used to be the foreman but I've heard he's gone back to Texas and Bennet Erwin is running the spread now."

He asked me my name and when I told him he said, "Bill, I'm going to give you a job helping the horse wrangler night hawk as he is losing horses. Last night he lost five head. We are short of horses, you can ride your own horse and I'll give you three more for your string when we find the horses we lost. Help the cook whenever you can. We pay $30.00 and $35.00 a month. I will give you $30.00, if you earn it."

That evening when we was taking the horses out, I noticed that Shorty the wrangler had a bed tied on behind his saddle. Just after dark he rolled out his bed that had a tarp on it and said, "I never had any sleep today, was hunting horses. You watch the cavvy. Call me if you can't hold them."

They was hard to hold. They never scared, they was just cold and wanted to travel. I called the wrangler about two o'clock. When it got light enough to see he made a count and we was seven short. The wrangler told me to see if I could find them as they couldn't be very far away.

I struck their trail as it was muddy. I followed them about twelve miles before I found them. They was the horses I had fetched from the Chugwater. I run onto the horses too that Shorty had lost the night before.

My horse was tired as I had set on him all night so I didn't get into the wagon until about noon. As I went into camp Bob said, "I'm glad you fetched the horses in but seems to me that you both had ought to hold them."

I said, "Maybe so, but this is the first time I ever saw a night hawk take his bed out to wrangle horses."

THE **C Y** ROUNDUP WAGON worked the Crazy Woman, the Clearwater, around the Big Horn Mountains as far as the steep canyon that goes down to Ten Sleep, the Powder River up to where it turns north through the badlands, the Pumpkin Butte country and the head of the Belle Fourche. There was lots of cattle in that country. We made one roundup a day and sometimes two. Rob Devine, the wagon boss, was a good cowman. I remember some of the names of the **C Y** crew.

"Portrait of Slats."

There was George Pike that was full of fun and always jobbing someone. Shorty Krisler, the night hawk horse wrangler, was a Texas man about forty years old. He wore a longhorn moustache and had a crooked leg. He was always talking about the way they handled cattle in Texas.

One cowboy was called Happy Jack and one they called Slats. I never spoke to Slats all the time I was working for the **C Y**. He was the one that told me the tent was too crowded for my bed. In those days they used lots of nick names and you hardly ever asked a man his real name.

Most all them old waddies had a six-shooter buckled around their middle. They was good to get along with except when they was drinking, then they was mean as the devil.

When the roundup got to going the saddle horses was getting lots of work and they wasn't trying to get away. There was four reps at the wagon and it kept the cook pretty busy. Bob told me to help the cook until noon, then to come to the roundup and carry brands from the fire to the calf as they didn't drag the calf very close to the fire.

Every hand left his saddle at the rope corral so it would be handy when they saddled up. My saddle was old with square skirts. The corners curled up and looked queer sticking straight up in the air. One windy day someone (I layed it to Slats) drove two big stakes in the ground and tied my saddle to the stakes. There it was, perched up on a sage brush with the stirrups anchored to the stakes. It looked like it was going to fly away.

I was mad but couldn't say much as they was all joshing me. Pike asked me if I always staked my saddle. The next day I took my knife and cut the corners off. It looked like a muley cow and the fellows all laughed at it.

In my string of horses, I had a very nice sorrel horse. When Bob gave him to me he said, "That sorrel hasn't been broke too long but I don't think he will pitch with you as he has quit that. Watch him in the mornings. You can get along with him if you

CATTLE 53

hold his head 'til he gets started. Don't let him buck for if you do, he will slip you."

I had rode the sorrel horse several times and liked him. He was the best horse in my string. One morning I was going to ride him. Someone had put some cockle burrs in the inside of my saddle blanket where I couldn't see them.

When I stepped on, the cockle burrs hurt his back. I tried to hold him up but he went to pitching with me. I rode him about four jumps when my front cinch busted. The saddle slipped over on his side. I lit on my head and rolled over. It knocked the wind out of me and I had a stiff neck for a while.

"Saddle on a sagebrush."

It sure tore that old saddle up a plenty. Both stirrup fenders was tore off. I found one stirrup hanging in a sage brush. The leather in the cantle was tore and the saddle was scattered over an acre of ground. It took me half a day to fix it but I rode it until the roundup was over.

THERE IS ALWAYS something happening around a roundup wagon to cause a little excitement. The **C Y** roundup had worked the upper country around the mountains and was on the Powder River.

Someone had put some salt out on the flat for the cattle. They had left a five gallon can setting there. A two year old steer was hunting salt. He stuck his head in the can and gave it a root. The bail dropped over his horns.

It scared the steer, plenty. He made a blubbering bellow and started whirling around trying to kick the can off his head. When he couldn't kick it off he began to run. The five gallon can was over his eyes so he couldn't see where he was going.

The steer headed right into camp where we was all sitting down eating our dinner. Cowboys dropped their plates and was scrambling to get out of the way as the steer ran right through the fire knocking the coffee pot over, then ran into the roundup wagon. That stopped him but he started to running in a circle.

The cook had a fly stretched at the back of the roundup wagon for shade as he hardly ever stretched a tent or set up the stove when the weather was good, just cooked in the Dutch ovens. The steer knocked down the fly and was tearing up the whole camp.

The old cook was sure on the fight. He grabbed a cleaver and was swinging it around trying to hit the steer. He sure looked scary with his apron flying in the breeze and his hair standing straight up.

One of the hands got on a horse and roped the steer and threw it down. When one of the boys took the can off, the steer

CATTLE

was sure on the fight. He had his long tongue out bawling and was frothing at the mouth. The cowboys knew that business was going to pick up when the steer got up.

The cook was cussing as he was picking up the wreck at the campfire. I think Pike headed the steer toward the cook whose back was turned to see a little more excitement.

Everyone else was in the clear. All the steer could see was Sandy, the cook, and his apron. The steer made a run at Sandy. The cowhands began to holler, "Look out, Sandy, he's after you."

The cook stood his ground for a minute, then made a run for the wagon. It was a pretty close finish. The steer was blowing bubbles on Sandy's rear end as Sandy made a dive to get under the wagon. He hit his head on the edge of the wagon box as he dived.

When they got the steer out of camp and the boys was laughing at the cook's little race, the cook crawled up on the wagon and opened a case of tomatoes and began to throw cans at the cow punchers saying, "Now laugh, you damn fools, that's all the dinner you get."

While we was sitting down eating cold tomatoes, Pike discovered a lock of the cook's hair hanging on the wagon. He pointed to it and everybody began to laugh again.

It was more than the cook could take. He grabbed his cleaver and ran everybody out of camp.

"Steer with a bucket on his head."

AFTER THE C Y ROUNDUP I went back to Lander. Lander was a red hot burg. There was lots of cattlemen, sheepmen, miners and freighters made the town. For a small place there was lots of money changed hands.

There was two banks, three hotels, two livery stables, a brewery, a court house, a jail that was always pretty well filled up and ten saloons which done a land office business. The town had electric lights which was a luxury in those early days. Like every early day frontier town there was lots of gambling, drinking and painted ladies.

The biggest saloon and gambling house was owned and run by a man by the name of Bill Coulter. Every saloon had gambling in them but Coulter's was where the big money changed hands. You could see a thousand to five thousand dollars on the table at one time.

I remember one time a cowpuncher went broke and raffled off his horse at Coulter's Saloon. It was a dollar a chance with three shakes of the dice for each person that had a chance. The high score got the saddle horse.

Everybody that had a dollar took a chance including several painted ladies and me. Three dice was throwed out of a leather box. As each person throwed three times the score was counted and marked on a black board. They had a rule on the game that if anyone threw three sixes at one throw, the house stood drinks for the ticket holders, but whoever won the house was stuck for the house.

There was a long bar. All the dice throwers was lined along the bar waiting their chance to throw the dice. I was standing, waiting my turn pretty well toward the end of the line next to Calamity Jane and her soldier man. Nobody had made a very big score. It was still anybody's horse. When it come to me, I pushed the dice box over to Calamity Jane and told her to spit in the box to make it lucky.

She shook her head and said, "No, Kid, I ain't lucky. If I spit in the box you would get nothing but aces and deuces."

Standing on the other side of me was a big, long, tall freighter as long as a piece of rope and about as limber with a big cud of tobacco in his jaw. He let fly and it filled the leather box half full of tobacco juice outside of what slobbered over onto the bar.

The bartender grabbed up a towel, wiped off the bar and reached for the box, which I had picked up, to give it a wipe too.

I said, "Never mind, I don't want you to wipe off the luck."

I raised it above my head and rattled the dice through the tobacco juice and made my throw. Was I ever surprised! I had thrown three sixes. Everybody began to holler and laugh and pound me on the back for I had won a drink for the dice throwers.

We didn't throw any more dice until the bartender served us. It seemed like everybody was pulling for me to win. I made my other two throws and they was pretty fair. I was away ahead on the blackboard.

Everyone had throwed but Razor Dick, a gambler. I was afraid of him for some reason. I guess it was a hunch.

Razor Dick propositioned me. He said, "Kid, if you give me ten dollars you can have the horse. I won't shake."

I told him that I only had eight dollars but I would give him that.

He said, "Okay, Kid, show money."

As I was high man on the board, if I bought his throw, naturally the horse was mine. It seemed to me that it would be cheap at that as he was a good looking horse, probably worth about forty dollars.

As Razor Dick put the money in his pocket he said, "I will just throw to see what I get."

He throwed and tied my score but I had bought him off. The horse was mine and the drinks was on me for winning the horse. That was one thing I hadn't figured on when everybody was patting me on the back. The eight dollars that I gave Razor Dick was all the money I had.

Everyone was feeling pretty high ordering special drinks. I had mine with the rest. The bartender said, "Kid, you got off cheap. The drinks are only $11.60."

Coulter was having a shot with everybody else when I told him that I would have to stand him off until I could raise the money to pay for the drinks.

He said, "Oh, that's all right, Kid, I will just keep the horse until you pay your bill."

It was funny to the crowd. They was all laughing and joshing me. It was getting serious with me as I knew Coulter would put the horse in the livery barn at a dollar a day.

I was sure hustling around trying to borrow that $11.60. Finally I went down to the Saint John saloon and he lent me the money. I hurried back to pay for the drinks at Coulter's. As I started to hand Coulter the money he said, "Everything is okay. The crowd took up a collection and paid me. The horse is yours."

By that time the crowd was pretty well juiced up. When they spotted me trying to pay Coulter, someone said, "There's the kid. He's got money."

A couple of the painted ladies grabbed me and said, "Buy us a drink, Kid." The crowd all bellied up to the bar. I threw my money on the bar and said, "That's all I have and that has to do as I want to keep my horse."

Coulter made money on the deal as there was others willing to set them up.

I HAD BEEN on the spring roundup for the Flying W outfit over in the Wind River country in Wyoming. After the last calves was branded a cowboy by name of Johnny Lynch and myself drawed our time and went in to Lander to celebrate the Fourth of July. From there we went over in Gooseberry Basin to break out a bunch of horses for the Dickey outfit.

CATTLE

We got through with the horses at the Dickey outfit and headed for Johnny's folks. They lived on a creek called the Fontenelle, not far from Douglas. Johnny had made arrangements with a horseman named Wheelock to break some horses for him after the roundup. He wanted me to help him get them broke before the beef roundup in the Powder River country that fall.

It was about the tenth of August when we left the Dickey ranch and started for the Fontanelle. It was about a hundred and fifty mile trip. We had a packhorse to carry our bed and grub.

When we got to the **K C** ranch between Buffalo and Douglas we camped for the night. A cowhand from Glen Rock, that Johnny knew, told us that the **C Y** outfit had got a special order from Clay, Robinson and Co. of Omaha for five hundred head of heavy steers three and four years old. He told us that he had talked to the foreman just before he left Glen Rock. It was too early for regular beef roundup and they just had a small outfit. A foreman with a chuck wagon, a horse wrangler, cook and six riders was to go over on the Powder River and ship from Orin Junction.

It looked like a two or three week job and we would still have plenty of time to break the horses before the regular beef roundup in the fall.

It was about twenty miles from where we was, on the middle fork to where the Powder River turned north into the bad land country where we figured to find the outfit working.

We had gone down the Powder about twelve or fifteen miles when we saw a horse coming down the trail on a long trot. At first we thought it was a cow poke but after he got closer, we saw it was a horse with a saddle on and no rider.

Of course, we had to catch the horse. We thought he had perhaps fell down and hurt his rider or jerked away. We tied the packhorse to a sage brush, took our ropes down and spread out so the horse would come between us. By that time the horse stopped and threw up his head and snorted. We spread out farther so he would come through as he seemed determined to come on up the river.

We discovered that the horse had only one rein dragging as he had tromped on the other one and broke it off. When he saw the gap between us he started on a dead run to pass us. We closed in so one of us would get a throw at him.

Johnny was the closest to him and he made the throw. He missed the horse's head but caught the saddle horn. Both horses was doing their damnedest and Johnny's rope was tied to his saddle horn.

The loose horse was going down grade when he hit the rope. It threw both horses down. I saw Johnny go up in the air about ten feet and come down like a ton of rock. He lit in a bunch of sage brush on his head and shoulders. He never moved and I thought for sure he was killed.

About that time, the loose horse got up and as Johnny's horse was getting up, the other one took another run on the rope and knocked both of them down again. Things was happening so fast that I couldn't do anything but I made a run to catch the horse. I threw my rope on him, got up to him and took Johnny's rope off the saddle horn and went to see if Johnny was killed.

He had come out of it and was on his hands and knees, all bent over trying to get some air. One side of his face was all tore up. He was bleeding like a stuck hog and gasping for breath. I sure thought he was a goner.

He finally got some air and I looked him over. He didn't have any bones broken but his neck was stiff, his arm sprained, his back hurt and his face was tore all to hell.

After a little while he was able to get on his horse. We hadn't gone very far until we met a waddy from the outfit hunting the horse Johnny had roped.

He said that the horse wrangler had seen the horse come out of the badlands and start up the river. The wrangler was fetching in the saddle horses to camp and was too far away to catch it, anyway he wanted to tell the other boys to get to looking for the rider.

By the time we got to the wagon they had found the cowboy. He hadn't been too far away. He had started some cattle in. They was awfully wild and when he went to turn them his horse had stumbled. He had probably hit the horse with his spur as he recovered from the stumble and the old pony just slipped his pack and run off as he was only partly broke. In his fall, the cowboy had broke his leg just above the ankle.

When we rode in to camp, he was laying on a bed and the cook was cutting up a canned goods box with a big butcher knife to make a splint for his leg, while two of the other boys was holding the leg in place.

Johnny was in bad shape too. He was just hurt all over. We all looked him over but decided he was just bruised up. He was a hard looker, with his face and shirt all bloody.

The foreman said that they ought to both go to a doctor. So early the next morning we unloaded the chuck wagon and sent them to Douglas, as it was the closest place where there was a doctor. I stayed on with the outfit to help gather the beef steers.

I HAD NEVER RODE in the Powder River country before that year of 1895. There wasn't much grass growing in the valley but lots of sage brush and alkali flats. There was some cotton wood trees along the river. The river was not very wide and when I was there in August, there wasn't very much water in it. The river bed was sand. You could scoop the sand out with your hands most anywhere and find water. A bunch of cattle could walk in the river bed and the water would come up in their tracks so they could get a drink. It was a treacherous, dangerous stream, had lots of quicksand. In case of a cloud burst or the runoff of spring snows the Powder River got plenty high. Many a cow lost her life in the Powder River.

For what I thought of the Powder River country, we stole it from the Indians, we ought to have given it back. Although there was lots of grass when you got out in the rolling country there was lots of coulees and water washes that you couldn't cross and you would have to ride way around them. There is lots of badlands where it is hard to ride for cattle although cattle gets fat as the grass is of a very good quality.

At the time I was there working for the **C Y** outfit there was more steers than cows and calves in that country. Most of the outfits used to stock it with southern steers, keep them a couple of years and ship them to Omaha for beef. They was all longhorn cattle of all colors of the rainbow and wild as deer. They was hard to handle. Some of those Texas steers could run about as fast as a good horse.

There was thousands of cattle in that country. It was a hard job shorthanded to gather those wild cattle and hold them. There was lots of big outfits and different brands running in that country.

We had only eight men, a cook, horse wrangler and six riders. It took two men to hold the beef herd and those steers tried to get away all the time. We had to let them scatter to graze. If we let them scatter too much, a bunch would throw up their heads and start off on a long trot. By the time we headed them, some on the other side of the herd was going the other way. As they was on their own range they didn't care which way they went just so they got away.

We rode herd all day and rode night guard three hours. It took two men on each guard and sometimes it took us all if the cattle got scarey or it was an extra dark night. We didn't dare take any chances of a stampede and losing them for they would mix with the other cattle and we would have all the work to do over again.

The weather was hot as hell. The water wasn't fit to drink as it was warm and had lots of alkali in it.

CATTLE

After gathering the middle fork and the south fork of the Powder River we crossed over the old Bozeman trail toward Pumpkin Buttes and the head of the Belle Fourche. We had about two hundred seventy five head. As there was several little creeks south toward Orin Junction the foreman said that with good luck we could get enough cattle in the next two days. The third day we would corral at Orin.

It was awful hot with a hot wind coming from the southeast. It seemed to burn your face and eyes so you could hardly stand it. When we got our tally it took us all to hold the cattle that night. It was a windy, hot night. It seemed that there was dust in the air or something as it was so dark and hazy.

We got started early in the morning. You couldn't see very far. The sun looked like a twenty dollar gold piece way off in space. The wind quit blowing about noon and my God, it was so hot and close you could hardly get your breath.

We camped early as it was too hot to drive cattle. Just before sundown a big white cloud with a reddish cast to it came sailing from the southeast.

The foreman cocked his weather eye on it and said, "We'll probably get a water spout out of that and when it hits, I want every man on herd. I sure don't want to lose them steers now."

Just a little after sundown the storm hit. There was a big gust of wind and big drops of rain, then a loud clap of thunder and hailstones about the size of hickory nuts with some as big as baseballs hit. You couldn't see nothing it was so dark. The noise and roar from the hail storm was terrific.

Before the storm hit, that bunch of steers all had their heads up smelling at the air. I remember it very well. Their longhorns and tails up, their eyes bugging out. They was scared stiff.

The jagged, forked lightning and the clap of thunder touched them off and the hail kept them going. There was nothing we could do, only try to protect ourselves. We was on a flat where there wasn't any protection whatever. We never tried to stop the cattle, just jerked our saddles off our horses and put them over our heads.

The hail didn't last over thirty minutes but it was followed up with a heavy rain and turned so dark that you couldn't see your hand in front of your eyes.

We had had a tent stretched with our beds in it but the wind blew the tent down, stampeded the saddle horses, wet our beds, tipped the camp stove over and filled it full of hail, blowed the stove pipe away and raised particular hell.

The horse wrangler managed better than the rest of us. He had a slicker. He got his horse in a plum thicket that gave a little protection. The horse herd headed toward a little canyon. He figured that they would hump up and stay there. As soon as it quit hailing he started after them. He'd look ahead and get his bearings when the lightning flashed. When he found the horses he stayed with them until morning and was in camp before breakfast.

The cattle had went down a ridge. There was a coulee on both sides of the ridge. The coulees got full of water and the cattle didn't try to cross. When they struck South Fork it was bank-full so we found most of them okay and not scattered too bad. They had picked up a few odd head in their run but it didn't take long to cut them out.

When we got back to camp, the whole crew went on night guard as it was the last night out and we wasn't taking any chances of losing them. We was a tired and sleepy bunch when we got them corralled at Orin Junction.

I WAS WORKING for the Flying W outfit. It was in the fall of the year. The year before had been a hard, dry summer and consequently there had been a lot of late calves that the spring roundup didn't get branded. We was making a general roundup to brand up the late calves and gather beef.

CATTLE   65

The wagon was camped on Bull Lake. We was making a four or five day camp there as we could gather upper and lower Wind River and the north side from there. It was a good place to hold the beef cattle while we was branding the late calves.

It was in the middle of September. There was mountains all around us and the nights was cold and frosty. Just as we had camped at Bull Lake, it started to rain. It rained all the next day, then turned into a wet snow.

We had about three hundred head of steers to night herd and they was cold and hard to hold. I don't think I was ever so cold in my life as I was the second night. We had been out on the range for about three months and all we had was our summer clothes. We managed to hold the steer herd by doubling the guard but the horse wrangler lost most of the saddle horses and he never found them for several days.

"It didn't take long to cut them out."

The third day it cleared up but was cold. There was about two inches of snow on the ground with a north wind blowing. Don't ever think we wasn't earning our money. We all had plenty money coming and wanted to get into Lander to get some winter clothes. There wasn't any chance of that until we had cleaned up that country.

It was getting late and the foreman wanted to get the beef herd started as it was about two hundred miles to the railroad to ship the cattle to Omaha. That evening, a cowboy came from Lander with a letter for the wagon boss. It said that if he had three hundred fifty head gathered to start the beef herd and the outfit would send another wagon to finish gathering the late calves.

We only needed about fifty head more to get our number. All the horses we had to gather them on was the night horses we was riding when the night hawk had lost the cavvy. The foreman said, "I think we can gather enough steers today on these horses. The men had ought to be in with the horses pretty soon." He had sent two extra men to find them.

I told the foreman that the horse that I had was all in and I didn't think he could go anywhere.

They always hobbled the four horses they used on the roundup wagon so they hadn't got away. One of the four was a brown horse with a white face named Headlight. He had been a saddle horse but was getting old and stiff and they broke him to work.

The foreman, whose name was Howard, said, "We need all the help we can get today. You can ride old Headlight. There is a bunch of cattle just across the river not too far. I saw them the day we made camp. The cattle may be hard to cross on account of it being so cold. You go with us as far as the river crossing and stay there until Kirkendall and I make a ride. You can help cross the cattle."

There was an old camp ground near the crossing. As we hit the crossing there was a big bull that had stepped in a tin bucket and was in bad shape for the bucket had got stuck on the bull's hind foot. It must have been on him several days as his foot was plenty sore and he couldn't travel. He sure was one mad bull on the fight.

When we rode up to inspect him he just began to roll his eyes, shake his head and bellow. He was a horrible scary animal. Howard said we would have to take the bucket off his foot and that he would be plenty hard to handle as he judged the bull would weigh close to eighteen hundred pounds.

He said, "I don't think that any one horse can hold that bull by the head. I will try to catch him by the head and one front foot. If I don't get a front foot, Kirkendall, you catch his head too. We can hold him while Bill can catch a hind leg and we can handle him."

Howard didn't get a front foot so Kirkendall caught him by the head too. They both had their ropes pretty tight on each side of him. The bull just froze there. I rode up to catch a hind leg but had to move him in order to rope his leg.

I hit him on the back with my rope. He gave a jump and I caught the leg with the bucket on it and gave the rope a jerk. It must have hurt pretty bad for he give a big jump and broke the rope that Kirk had on his neck, whirled around and broke Howard's rope. About that time the rope that was caught on the bucket pulled the tin bucket off and the bull was loose.

He saw me and took a dive at my horse. Old Headlight stumbled when I hit him with the spurs and the bull hit him in the rear and turned him plumb over. I tried to get out of the way so he wouldn't fall on me and that was the last I remember for a while as the fall knocked the wind out of me.

Headlight floundered around to get up. The bull made another ram at him. That settled Headlight. The bull hadn't noticed me laying where I had lit, about ten feet from the horse.

Kirkendall ran his horse between me and the bull. The bull took after his horse and that's what saved me. When I got some gas I made a run toward Howard. He pulled me up on his horse.

The bull was bawling and pawing up the ground when he couldn't catch Kirkendall.

We went over to try and help Headlight up but couldn't get him up. Howard said he thought his back was broke so he shot him. When we got back to the wagon the wrangler had found the horses.

The fall from Headlight had dislocated my shoulder. It was giving me a lot of grief. The boys layed me on a bed and two held me down while another pulled my shoulder in place.

The wagon with a three-horse team and the beef cattle started for the railroad. The cowboy that had brought the letter and I started for Lander. I wanted to get my shoulder doctored.

IN THE EARLY DAYS they ranged cattle on grass the year around in this western country. It was a pretty hard job for the cowboy in the late fall and winter months.

If he was in a mountain country the cowboy had to get all the cattle out of the mountains into the foot hills where there wasn't so much snow. In the lower country the cowboys had to keep the water holes open, see that the cattle didn't drift away and keep them on the best range.

The cattlemen had what they called line camps. There was generally a small one room log shack and a barn and corral to keep saddle horses in and two men at a line camp. These camps was sometimes fifty to seventy-five miles from a town or settlement.

When the weather was good the men at the line camps didn't have too much to do. It was a lonesome, disagreeable life at the best. Cook your grub, wash your clothes and count the days until spring time and grass. I put in one winter in a line camp in Wyoming and I promised myself never to do it again.

I was working for the Flying W outfit. It was after I hurt my shoulder. The cattle was mostly Texas steers that was coming three year olds. They had been wintered one year in the

Wyoming country, which helped as they was climated to the cold weather.

My pardner at the line camp was a Texas man about forty years old. His name was Jim Sawyer and he was a good cowboy. He told me that he had never done any other kind of work. His one weakness was liquor. Whenever Jim went to town he got drunk and stayed that way as long as he had a cent. When he couldn't get anything more to drink he would get on his horse and ride grub line until he got another job.

The Flying W had bought forty head of green broke saddle horses that fall over in Idaho. They wanted to go back to their home range and we had a hard time holding them.

About Thanksgiving there wasn't too much snow. We had all the cattle out of the mountains. Then there came a storm and the horses started for Idaho. We started to hunt them. We found them about fifteen miles from camp.

It was really storming, the wind and snow was sure howling in the mountains. We had to drive the horses back right against a northwest wind. It was awful cold, the horses hated to go against the wind. Jim and I about froze to death. We never got in to camp until about ten o'clock that night. Our saddle horses was just about played out.

Jim cussed those Idaho horses with words that had hair on them. We had to ride every day to keep them from leaving and it was mean cold work.

About two weeks before Christmas there was a trapper came by and stayed all night with us. He said he was going to Lander for supplies and to spend Christmas. He was a-foot leading a burro. It was about sixty miles to Lander. The trapper said it would take him three days to get there.

Jim wrote a letter to the Flying W boss at Lander. In the letter he told the boss that we would never be able to hold those horses until spring and he had better see if he could get them in a pasture down around Lander. Jim told the trapper not to forget to deliver the letter for if he did it wouldn't be healthy for him at our camp.

Every day one of us would ride to throw the horses back so they wouldn't get away, while the other one would look after the cattle.

About four days before Christmas a waddy rode into camp. It was a cold, snowy day but he was lit up like a church. He had come to take the horses down to a pasture close to Lander. He had fetched us a gallon jug of liquor to celebrate Christmas.

The log shack where we was staying just had a dirt floor but it had a nice fireplace built out of flat rocks. Whoever had built it had laid some big flat rocks in front of the fireplace.

We was just getting supper when he rode up. He wobbled in to the shack with the jug in a gunny sack. He went over to the fireplace as he was cold, carrying the jug with him. He bumbled around trying to untie the knot at the top of the sack, dropped the jug on the rocks and broke the bottom out of it. There went our Christmas glee after it had been carried sixty miles tied behind the saddle.

The liquor run all over the dirt floor except a little that stayed on the rocks. Jim grabbed a dish towel and soaked up a couple of tin cupfuls. It didn't look very tempting to me after he squashed it out of the dish rag with all the dirt in it.

Jim was a liquor fiend and got away with those two tin cups in about ten minutes. Jim and the waddy was feeling their liquor. They told some wild stories, finally got in a fight, tipped the table over and messed things up. Anyhow, it broke the monotony for a little while.

The next morning they started the horses for Lander. Jim told me that he would help get the horses started, then ride the lower country. He said he probably wouldn't be back until late. He said, "Bill, you better take my saddle gun and go up a quaking asp grove and see if you can get a deer for Christmas dinner. I'm sure tired of eating sow belly."

That was the last I saw of Jim for over two weeks. When he came back he had quite a story to tell.

It seems he just couldn't turn back when he got headed for Lander. The liquor he'd sopped up the night before just kept begging for more.

He had gone on into town and was putting on a celebration worthy of the occasion. Somehow or another he matched himself a fight with Stub Farlow in Lanagon's Saloon. Stub worked him over pretty good until they was throwed in jail for disturbing the peace.

The next morning when he went before the judge he got a nice talk about it being Christmas time and all and that he would be let off light for a ten dollar fine.

Jim wasn't feeling so good and he said, "Can the talk, Judge, I have the fine in my hip pocket."

The judge said, "I wasn't through—ten days in jail. Have you got that in your hip pocket too?"

For the kind of a Christmas day I had, I might as well have been in jail with Jim.

WHEN I SEE a big truck loaded with cattle going to market it reminds me of the one hundred and fifty to two hundred and fifty mile drives we used to have to make to get cattle to the railroad. In Wyoming the Union Pacific had a branch line from Cheyenne to Casper, Douglas and Orin Junction. Most of the southern cattle was unloaded at Orin Junction.

I had been working over on Bear River in Utah. I was in Montpelier, Idaho, scouting around for a job. I happened to run into Jean Emmeretta, a Lander man. He had bought some doggie cattle from the Mormons and was looking for cowboys to trail them over into the Wind River country.

We trailed from Montpelier over the head of Green River through Fremont Pass and left them on Horse Creek, a small stream that comes into Wind River from the north.

On my way to Lander I struck the fall beef roundup at the Sinks. They was shorthanded so I stayed at the Stagner wagon and worked a week or ten days.

They started the beef herd south to the U. P. railroad about a hundred and fifty miles away. The boss sent Jim Kirkendall and me over the Wind River Mountains north to hit another roundup wagon of Stagner's on Gooseberry Creek.

We had to hurry because we was afraid the crew had worked that country and would be gone. The roundup was going to work the Gooseberry country, the Ten Sleep country and on over the south side of the Big Horn Mountains in the Crazy Woman country, then wind up on Powder River.

It was a fifty or sixty mile ride to where we thought we would strike the roundup wagon. The ride across the mountains was the toughest trail I ever went over.

We had to ride around the side of a mountain that looked impossible but Jim knew the country and said it would save fifteen miles. There was one place we had to get off and lead our horses for about a mile. Then we got down on the north side of the mountain we hit a creek that flowed north and east through a deep narrow canyon. The mountains was straight up of solid black rock and so high that you had to lay on your back to see the tops. We rode down the canyon about ten miles, then went east, maybe a little south, until we hit Gooseberry Creek. I remember Jim saying that Meeteetse wasn't too far north of us.

When we was about eight miles from Gooseberry Creek we saw a small bunch of steers. There was seven head, traveling the same direction as we was. We loped up to see what they was. When we got in about two hundred yards of them they broke into a run. Jim said, "Well, I'll be damned."

Then he told me about that bunch of steers. The year before they was running over in the badlands close to Ten Sleep. The roundup had run on to them but it was late and the steers had got away. He said that they belonged to Stagner and was outlaw steers six or seven years old. He said he knew them as there was a marker in the bunch, a big brindle one.

We fell in behind them and had gone about two miles when we met a couple of riders from the roundup that was looking for the steers. When we got to the wagon and threw the steers with the herd, Tex, the roundup boss, was well pleased as he had orders to try and get them.

Those steers had been gathered several times but had always managed to get away. That night Tex doubled the night guard on the beef herd. Next morning all the cowboys was sure on the prod. They said those old outlaw steers kept the bunch of cattle milling all night for they kept going through the herd hooking any of the cattle that tried to bed down, all of the time trying to sneak away.

It seemed that the big brindle steer was the worst as he was kind of a leader. He was a big steer, probably weighed fourteen or fifteen hundred pounds. He was wild as an elk and mean as sin. He had a big pair of ugly horns and knew how to use them.

Tex, the roundup boss, was a small man about fifty years old. He wore a long, droopy moustache and had a loud voice. He had come into Wyoming with a bunch of cattle from Texas. When anyone asked him his name he told them he'd been called Tex so long he'd forgot his other name. Anyhow, he sure savvied cattle.

In the morning after the cowboys had saddled up and was waiting for orders, Tex said that there was a little job to do before we made a ride.

He said, "Boys, we're going to take those outlaw steers to the railroad or kill 'em all. I want you to catch old Sullivan (a big, old, fighting bull that had whipped every bull on the range) and tie him down. I want that big brindle steer tied to him head and tail. Then I want the other six steers tied in pairs head and tail. It's going to take some hard work for we will have to drag them together in order to tie them. I think we can hold them."

Everybody shook out their ropes for they didn't want any of them to get away. A cowboy dabbed a rope on old Sullivan but that old bull snapped it like it was a twine string. Those cowboys had plenty grudge against him so in less time than it takes to tell about it that old bull had three ropes on him and was tied down hard and fast.

Then they went after old Brindle who was taking for the hills. That old wild steer sure done his share of bawling and fighting before they got him down. There was plenty of cowboys to do the job and in just a little bit all the outlaw steers was hanging on the end of a rope.

After they was all tied down the hard job started. We had to hitch four or five saddle horses on them to drag them together. We put ropes around their necks and tied their tails together with some rawhide strings.

When they was all tied together Tex said, "Now throw dirt in their eyes so they can't see and let them up."

They was all on the fight, bawling and running in circles, hooking one another, trying to get away. That old Sullivan bull had one horn on the outside but the other one had been broke off sometime and growed down and made sort of a loop. In the mix-up, the brindle steer got his longhorn caught in the loop and broke it. Blood was spurting on Sullivan's head and that bull smelled the blood and was crazy mad. They was going around in a circle like a whirligig. The rest of the steers was bawling and fighting and running around in circles trying to get away from each other. It was plenty rough on them but nobody cared if they killed themselves.

The next morning those steers was pretty docile. Outside of the brindle steer who was awfully lame, they was okay. Tex said to turn the brindle steer and old Sullivan loose as they would never get to the railroad. That old Texan knew his stuff for he delivered six of the outlaw steers.

IN MY EXPERIENCE as a cowhand, the wildest cattle I ever saw and the hardest to handle was in Wyoming. They was out of Texas cows that had been trailed up from the south and turned loose. After a calf was branded it hardly ever saw a man until it was three or four years old. They sure was wild. If for some

CATTLE

reason you had to rope one, things picked up. They would bawl and fight like wildcats.

The cattle that was trailed up from Texas got used to being drove and handled. After they got rested up and turned on the range, they got pretty wild but they never forgot the handling. When they got over their first scare and cooled off you could handle them okay. Those that never had been trailed or handled much was sure hard to get along with.

Christman had made the spring roundup and gathered about six hundred head. He was waiting until the calves got old enough to travel over to the Union Pacific railroad, a distance of about two hundred twenty-five miles.

These cattle was running on the Arapahoe Indian Reservation in the Wind River country. They was really wild cattle. There was about fifty head of cows and calves. The rest was yearlings, twos and threes and a few old renegade steers that had been missed from time to time on the beef roundup.

Our crew was Jim Kirkendall, a real good hand about forty years old, a Mexican, two breed Indians, Christman and myself. We didn't have a wagon but a pack outfit as it was too hard to get a wagon through the mountains between Wind River and the head of Green River. There wasn't no road, just a cow trail through the timber over the mountains.

We gathered them in one day as the Mexican had been riding on them since they had been gathered in the roundup. We got them altogether and drove about three miles. We was going to night herd them that night. It had been a hot day as it was some time about the middle of July. About six or seven o'clock there was a greenish black cloud coming from the west. There was a flash of lightning and a big crash of thunder. It began to hail and rain.

We was all on herd but fifty men couldn't have held those cattle. We just had to pull our saddles off and put them over our heads and get out of the way. Those hail stones was as big as eggs.

We was all wet and scared almost to death. The hail stones would hit on the ground and bounce fifteen feet. It was sure spooky with the hail bouncing around us, forked lightning flashing and the thunder crashing. The roar of the storm and the noise of the cattle running was deafening.

The lightning was striking all around us. It was just like a streak of fire jumping from horn to horn. There was nothing we could do to stop those crazy cattle when they started to run.

It hailed for about thirty minutes, then it started to rain. It was just as if the plug had been pulled out of the sky.

The Wind River was on the north of us and we knowed the cattle wouldn't try to cross it. When the storm let up a little, Christman sent the other boys up the river to where the camp was. He said, "Me and the kid (meaning me) will ride down on the south side and try to get ahead of the cattle before they scatter. We never can get them in a close herd tonight. Everybody be on their horses at daylight."

It was still raining hard when Christman and I started out. Water was running everywhere and we couldn't ride too fast. The lightning would flash and we could get our bearing and look for cattle or tracks. Then it would be pitch black; we couldn't see our hands in front of our face.

We must have rode twelve or fifteen miles to get ahead of the cattle. We found the lead cattle had got in a bend of the river in the brush out of the fury of the storm.

It was just before daylight when we located them by a flash of lightning. We couldn't see any tracks farther on so we knew the cattle was behind us. When we started them, they came rushing out of the brush and tried to run down the river. Christman went one way and I went the other. I made a hell of a fuss and turned them.

I didn't know where Christman was but thought he was ahead of me but I was too busy to worry. I met the other boys and we got the cattle in a bunch and realized Christman was missing. Two of the boys was just starting out to hunt him when we saw him limping in. He was bunged up, all covered with mud and plenty hostile.

CATTLE

His horse had fallen down. It had knocked Christman out for a while. When he come out of it he figured his horse had gone on with the herd and followed a foot.

We was in a bad fix as the hail had stampeded the cavvy. The grub was all wet as the tent had blowed down. We was all riding tired horses. Christman and I hadn't eaten since dinner the day before and nobody had got any sleep.

We finally found the cavvy and got some fresh horses and moved the cattle about four miles to Thompson's Fork. We had to night herd the cattle as they was still spooky.

There was no songs sung or tall stories told around the camp fire that night. We was just a bunch of dead-tired cow hands all dragging a bush.

It was a little too early to ship so they left the cattle north of Wind River close to Indian's Peak. I stayed with the cattle while the other hands was riding the Owl Creek country for cattle the roundup had missed.

"Hail storm."

3: Utah

I WAS IN Lander, Wyoming, during the big panic of Cleveland's administration when Jacob Coxey's Army went to Washington, D.C., to protest against the hard times. I had got acquainted with a man whose name was Tom Johnson and his wife. They was taking a trip to Salt Lake City, Utah, and wanted me to go with them.

Times was real tough, and it was hard to get a job. Johnson was going to pay all the expenses of the trip. I thought I would get to see some new country so I agreed to go with them. There was no railroad to or out of Lander at that time so we was going in a prairie schooner.

We got as far as Bear Lake, Utah, and stopped at a horse ranch owned by Newt Austin, a friend of Johnson's. Austin had several racehorses. He said he was up against a tough race at Montpelier. His racehorse was hard to control. Five of the boys that was home was too heavy to ride the horse and the other one wasn't stout enough to hold the horse as it was nervous and hard to control.

Tom told Newt to let me try the horse. He did, and we got along pretty well. I stayed at Austin's ranch and helped train the horse. I rode him in the race and won it, but not easy, for it was a close, hard race.

Tom and his wife went on to Salt Lake while I was training the racehorse and that was the last time I ever saw them. After the race, Newt and his family was going up to the head of the lake to visit some of his relations named Cheaney and invited me to go with them. The Cheaneys was putting up hay and was shorthanded so they hired me to help. That was strictly a

Mormon settlement. There wasn't a Gentile in that whole settlement but me.

I had worked for the Cheaneys about a couple of weeks when there was a Mormon celebration. I have forgotten whether it was Brigham Young's birthday or some other occasion.

The Mormons all turned out for miles around. They had foot races, a horse race, a three legged race, a ladies' race and a greased pig. They rode some bucking horses. The purse wasn't much as the whole thing was for amusement. The first prize for the bucking horse riding was a pair of high heeled boots, the second prize was a dress shirt, and the third a red handkerchief that wasn't silk.

I sure got jobbed by the boys that was riding the bucking horses. There was lots of range horses in Utah at that time and wild ones too. All the young men was horsey as that was all the transportation there was and you thought as much of your horse as you did of your brother.

Of course the Mormons had all heard about the race in Montpelier that I had won for Newt Austin. It gave me a little pull. At that time the Mormons didn't care much about a Gentile coming in their country and mingling in their company. There was about ten girls to every boy. The girls was more sociable than the boys.

The morning before the entertainment all the hay crew including myself went to the general store. There you could buy lemonade for five cents a quart. They gave you two glasses if you had your girl with you.

I saw the new boots that the storekeeper was giving to the best rider. There was quite a lot of young people there and when I was looking at the boots I made the mistake of asking him if he had any smaller sizes.

He said, "Yes, if you win the boots, I'll fit you out." I told him that I had no intention of riding. Not being a Mormon, I wasn't nosing in.

When we went to the picnic grounds the boys acted awfully nice and asked me to ride with them. I took the bait, hook, line, and sinker.

If I had kept my big mouth shut I might of had a chance for a new pair of boots. Those Mormons was pretty forked. Like all westerners they had growed up among bucking horses and they was all after a new pair of boots too. I didn't have a chance, they took care of that. They wanted some amusement and they got it off me and very embarrassing it was too.

They tied four horses in a row and gave us four numbers. We was to ride as they called the numbers. They gave me number four so I would get a big grey.

I didn't pay any attention to the horses as I had got in a croquet game with three girls which was framed to hold my attention. When the horses would do their stuff we would stop and watch them, then continue the game.

The horses was all halter broke stuff and they wasn't having any trouble saddling them. We was riding out in the open. There was two men saddling and when they called a man's number all he had to do was step on. The girls was entertaining me so royally that I had never looked at the mare I was going to ride.

When they called me I ran over. At first glance I saw some harness marks but I have seen some good bucking horses that had been worked. She was a gray mare, perhaps weighed 1,200 pounds, and looked to me like she was pretty fat to buck much.

She just stood there froze like. I hit her with the end of my bridle reins. She exploded, with her tongue hanging out, gave a loud cough and a big snort. She wasn't bucking much but she was making a lot of noise, coughing and snorting— the loudest I ever heard. She could make a brass band sound like a toy rattle box.

They really had her loaded for me. They had tied her up all the day before. That night they had given her a lot of alfalfa hay and a drink of water. She was just in the right condition to make a lot of noise at both ends. She soon got out of wind and turned off the gas.

The Mormons was sure getting a big kick out of me riding that old heavy work mare. I saw I was jobbed and I hit her with the spurs a few times. She made so much noise coughing and the loud snorts that I quit and got off, horribly embarrassed.

I never heard so much hollering and laughing in my life. I got on my horse and tore out of there. I didn't attend the dance that night. The ride, however, made a hit. They all treated me fine after that. I guess it was because they all got such a kick out of it. I worked there for the Cheaneys nine months and was never treated any better in my life or had so much fun.

AFTER THE HAYING, Mr. Cheaney said he'd like to keep me longer but couldn't pay me until he sold some cattle in October or I could take my wages in horse flesh.

Ready cash was mighty scarce. Wages wasn't very high. At that time, a dollar a day was top wages. I agreed to work forty days for two head of horses.

Mr. Cheaney had some horses to deliver to Montpelier. When he got them in the corral he gave me the pick of the bunch and I picked a very pretty sorrel and a bay. We vented the brands and turned them back on the range.

Mr. Cheaney ran a bunch of cattle. He summered them in the mountains and wintered them on Stump Creek, a little valley about ten miles from the home ranch. Stump Creek was a small creek that came off the mountains into a little valley where there was a small settlement of twelve or fifteen ranches, a post office and a school.

It had been a nice warm fall. I had gathered all the cattle and put them in a pasture at the foot of the mountains so they wouldn't get snowed in when the snow got too deep for them to rustle. It was a handy place to feed them hay. He had a log shack, a barn, corrals and a wild hay meadow just about half a mile from the settlement where I batched for the winter.

In November it snowed and had cold nights but warm, sunny days until just before Christmas. Then we got a regular old mountain blizzard. The wind blowed the snow so bad you couldn't see. Oh Mister, it was cold, a regular ring-tailed son of a gun!

It all started one still December day. It was not too cold but there must have been a heavy wind high overhead for the clouds was traveling rapidly from the southeast. Those clouds was a regular circus if you had a good imagination. You could see a big camel and then it would break up and change into an elephant, a house, or maybe an alligator.

It was Sunday. I had been over to Bear Lake to a dance, stayed all night and was riding back on my way to Stump Creek. By four o'clock it had clouded over and begun to snow. The wind changed to the northwest and all at once it looked like a wall of snow coming off the mountain. I think the wind had gathered all the cold this side of the North Pole and was blowing it ahead of that storm.

It was getting dark and I had about six miles to go right against that snow bank and I was about half froze at that. I remembered there was a man named Ferguson who lived about two miles from where I was. I knew I couldn't ride my horse six miles against that whirling mass of snow so I thought I'd better turn east and hit for Mr. Ferguson's ranch.

I had just started on the trail that led to his place when I saw someone coming right in my direction. It was the school teacher who taught at Stump Creek. She had gone over to visit her folks Friday night and was coming back to the settlement when the storm caught her. She had got off the trail. She was lost, scared and near froze.

It was a good thing that I happened to meet her or no doubt she would have frozen to death. The wind was so bad that we had to holler to hear one another. I told her that I was going over to Ferguson's to stay all night.

Ferguson's ranch was in an easterly direction so the storm didn't hit us right in the face. I took her reins and lead her horse so we wouldn't get separated. By that time, it was dark as ink and I was getting scared, for when we crossed a ridge I couldn't see their light. We finally got to his wire fence and followed it down to the house. You couldn't see at all and if it hadn't been for that wire fence we would surely have got lost.

Ferguson was a widower but had two grown daughters living with him. They was visiting and nobody was home. I put the horses in the barn, then went to the house, struck a light and built a fire as quick as I could.

The teacher's ears, face and the end of her nose was froze and she was shaking all over. Luckily she had overshoes on her feet; they wasn't froze but awfully cold.

She was about twenty years old, a small attractive girl, built rather frail, with blue eyes and a pretty head of auburn hair. Her first name was Mary.

I was okay, not froze anywhere but just cold all over. We made some coffee and built some supper to eat. I told Mary she had better go to bed and get some sleep as she had told me that she also had gone to a dance on Saturday night.

She went in the girls' room and went to bed but she was in so much pain I don't think she slept much. She looked a fright in the morning. Her face had turned black and her ears was swollen and still pained her.

By morning, the wind had gone down some but it was still blowing snow and about fifteen below zero. The shape Mary was in, I told her it was too cold for her to ride, so we decided that we would stay over that day. We was expecting the Fergusons to come home that day but due to the drifts and cold they didn't show up.

By the next morning the wind had gone down and the sun came out. It was still cold and the snow had drifted bad which made hard traveling.

We had some excitement when Mary's horse fell down. Mary made a dive in the loose snow. Nothing could be seen of her except her feet sticking out of the drift.

We finally got to the settlement but Mary was all in. We was both lucky to get out of that storm alive.

Well, it shortened that cold winter for me, for after I fed the cattle and was at loose ends, I would go over and visit with Mary during the long evenings.

I worked for Cheaney all that winter and until about the middle of May. They was nice folks to work for. He had a couple of cousins come from Salt Lake so he didn't need me anymore.

I had only been to the railroad once while I was working for the Cheaneys so I had saved my money. When I was about ready to leave, young Joe Cheaney went with me to help get my horses which was ranging about fifteen miles from the ranch up on the mountain.

We was both riding horses that hadn't been rode much that spring. They was fat and soft. We didn't find my horses until about two o'clock in the afternoon. When we did find them, Joe's horse was about played out and the horse I was riding was awful tired. We knew that if we started in with the range horses our saddle horses would never make it and we would spill them.

The horses was watering in a deep canyon where there was a spring in a quaking asp grove. Just where the grove was, it was a wide place in the canyon but above it and below, it was just a narrow trail with steep rock on both sides. There was big rocks to go around and a few quaking asps along the edge of the trail.

Our horses was too tired out to get close enough to the bunch of horses to rope one of them, though there was three saddle horses in the bunch. We thought maybe, with a lot of luck, we could snare two of them at a narrow place where the trail passed around a big rock and some trees hung over the trail.

We tied our two ropes together, hung the rope over a limb and tied it to the top of another behind it. We wet the loop of the rope so it would stand open. We had it fixed so Joe could pull it up or let it down.

As the horses went by the first time Joe let the rope down a little too quick and caught a snuffy old mare. Being in so narrow a place she finally choked down. Joe got the rope off just in time or she would have choked to death. I couldn't help him or the rest of the horses would get away and we would never get them in the canyon again.

We tried again and got a gentle saddle horse. As soon as he saw he was caught he gave up. We tried several times and finally after two hours of snaring got another saddle horse.

We got saddled up on the two fresh horses, turned the tired ones loose and started for the ranch on high. We had a lot of trouble getting them in but made it okay.

I stayed at the ranch four days handling my horses, then started for Wyoming, riding one and leading the other with my pack on its back.

ONE OF THE most horrible things that can happen to a cowboy is to get lost in the mountains or even in a prairie country. You know that you have got turned around and try to figure just which direction to go. If it is foggy or cloudy or dark, you can't see any land marks or stars to straighten yourself out. If a person has never been in that particular situation he can't realize what an awful feeling comes over you. If you are riding a horse that knows the country you can give him his head and he will take you to camp.

Just such a circumstance happened to me in Utah. It was late in the fall and there hadn't been any snow to speak of. Generally, the snow comes in the mountains and the stock will come down to the foothills. The snow will get deep in the upper country, naturally the stock will drift down where the snow ain't so deep.

I was working for Austin. He had a bunch of cattle that ranged south and east of Bear Lake. He was also running a bunch of steers for a man that lived in Montpelier by the name of Johnson. They was Texas steers and they run the winter before in southern Colorado. We had gathered them and threw them down in the valley but some of them had gone back in the mountains, and they was high, rugged mountains broken up by a thousand canyons.

Johnson had come over from Montpelier to gather his steers to put them on feed for the winter. They was two and three years old and wild, as they hardly ever saw a man all summer in those mountains. As we was expecting him we had throwed them all down in the valley. When they counted them they was short forty head.

It was about noon. Austin told me to get a fresh horse and go up on the mountain. If I didn't find them, to stay up there in a log cabin that had a bed and some groceries in it and I could pick them up in the morning.

There was quite a fog on the mountain and the farther I rode the thicker the fog got. There was a lot of quaking asp patches, some of them ten or fifteen acre patches. I could hardly see at all so it took me a long time to ride them out so I wouldn't miss any cattle, if they was in them. I had got up about twelve miles and it began to snow awful hard and the wind began to blow. I just couldn't see at all. I wasn't lost then but thought I would go to the line camp, which wasn't over four miles.

I could have rode around a ridge and probably made it but cutting across would be shorter and I'd have the wind to my back. It began to get dark and it seemed that the wind had changed. It hadn't, I had got in a canyon that swung to the east and I wanted to go south.

I was all mixed up. The farther I rode up that canyon the farther I got away from the cabin. It was almost dark with a genuine rip-roaring blizzard muddling me up. I knew that I was lost. I was getting cold and my horse was tired. I could stand a cup of coffee and a hunk of beef without bothering me. I wasn't getting anywhere. I knew if I kept riding my horse would play out. Finally, I came to a shelf that stuck out over the canyon enough so the snow couldn't hit me and it offered some protection from the wind. I got off and led my horse under the shelf and made a fire as there was lots of timber on each side of the canyon.

After I got a fire so I could see, I gathered a lot of dry wood for I knew that I was stuck there for the night. I thought that it would clear up in the morning and I could figure out where I was.

That was a tough old night. I had a fire but it smoked awful. I'd get pretty close to the fire and the fire would smoke me out. I'd back away and get some fresh air and try it again, so on all night.

Instead of clearing up in the morning, it was worse and the snow was drifting. It was a cold, regular stem winder of a blizzard. I knew if I kept in the canyon it would have to come out in the valley somewhere. I was hungry, cold and sleepy as I couldn't sleep that night. My eyes felt like two holes in a burned blanket from the smoke and my horse was shivering.

We made a start down the canyon. That canyon was just like a funnel. The wind seemed to twist the snow into a big rope. The rope was as big as the canyon. I knew that I could never ride far against that rope of snow and wind. Just imagine how I felt. I was sure spooky. I didn't know what to do, go back to the shelter of that ledge, or go ahead a little farther and maybe I could find a north wind break. I came to where the canyon split, one to the right, the other to the left.

I didn't know which one to take. The horse wanted to go to the left, I felt like I should go to the right. I decided to let the horse have his way. I hadn't gone more than a hundred yards down that left fork when I run right into a shack built back in the mountain, logged up in front.

I jumped off my horse and went in. There was a little sheet iron stove, a home-made table and a bunk made of poles in a corner, a few sticks of wood by the stove. I got a fire started, warmed up a little and tried to get my horse in.

He was a small horse and had lots of room to get in but he wouldn't come in. I was getting cold so I warmed up and tried him again. No good. He was shaking and nearly froze but was afraid to go in that hole. Someone had been staying in that shack not too long ago for there was some hay in the bunk and it didn't look too old. I took some in my hand and held it out to him. He was hungry and finally I coaxed him in with the hay.

There was a quaking asp grove just across the canyon. I went out to hustle more wood. I thought I saw something in the brush. Finally I saw it was cattle. I knew that it must be the ones I was after. I wasn't worrying too much about them steers. I was worrying about the storm and I was getting plenty hungry. I knew that it was impossible to ride against that storm as the snow was drifting something awful. I was worrying how I was going to get out of there. Of course I was glad to find the cattle as they would break trail for me. I knew they would never leave that quaking asp shelter in that storm.

When I got enough wood I started to inspect the shack to see if perhaps there wasn't something to eat in a box cupboard that was nailed on the wall. All I could find in the cupboard was an old frying pan with the handle broke off, a coffee pot with a hole in the side, a big old tablespoon and two big, healthy looking pack rats. I killed the rats and wondered if I had guts enough to eat one of them but I hesitated. Then I saw a sack hanging from the roof. I looked in it and there was about a pint of pinto beans in the sack. I throwed the rats out, tied a rag in the hole in the coffee pot and put the beans on to boil.

If you have ever tried to boil beans in the mountains you know how hard they are to cook. Every little while I would put the spoon in and see if they was done enough to eat. They never did get done but I ate them. They tasted pretty good but if they had had a little salt in them they would have tasted better. But at that, I think they tasted better than those rats would have. If I hadn't found those beans I could tell you how boiled pack rats taste.

I put a lot of wood in the stove and layed down by it and went to sleep while the horse ate the hay on the bunk. When I woke up the fire had gone out. I was cold and built up the fire, then I thought I would take a look and see how the weather was and see if the steers had moved. When I opened the door there must have been a wagon full of snow fell in the house on me, giving me a morning bath. It must have been ten o'clock and I was kind of sorry that I had throwed the rats out. Every time I moved I could hear those beans rolling in my stomach. It sounded like a lot of pebbles rolling around in a tin pan.

The steers was edging around for something to eat. After tramping a trail so I could get the horse out, I made a brave start. The wind had quit blowing but it was still snowing and plenty cold. There was some bad drifts and it was slow going with those steers. One would get down in a drift and I would have to snake him out with my rope. I made it into the ranch about four that evening, cold, hungry and tired. I have never liked beans since then.

I HAD WINTERED in Utah with Austin. They lived on Indian Creek right at Bear Lake about a mile from a large, hot spring that boils out at the foot of Hot Springs Mountain.

Newt Austin had settled at Bear Lake when the first Mormons came west. He had a very nice motherly wife, six boys and one girl. At that time the Mormons believed in polygamy and some of them had several wives but Newt had only one. Newt trained racehorses and pacers, while the boys broke the common stuff.

The winter I stayed with them was the second winter I was in Utah. Us boys used to have some great times going to parties and dances. We all slept upstairs and used to play seven-up at night to see which one of us would ride out a bronc in the morning before breakfast. We would put a bronc in the chute and the loser of the seven-up games would have to ride it out bareback with nothing but the mane hold. The broncs kept us pretty well skinned up but we was young and tough and liked it.

One of the boys named Buck was breaking horses for a cow outfit owned by a man named Strong that lived on Bear River right near the Idaho, Utah and Wyoming boundary. I went over to the Strong ranch with Buck to help him finish up the bunch of horses he was breaking to ride and was there two or three weeks.

The Strong outfit ran several hundred head of range stuff. They was all southern long-horned cattle. Strong had been feeding a large bunch of three and four-year-old steers for the early market. It wasn't very often in those days that they fed cattle in that part of the country. If I remember right, it was sort of an experiment.

These Texas steers had been kept in a corral for three or four months stuffed with good wild hay and grain and was fat and rollicky! They had been bought in Texas and trailed up when they was yearlings and two year olds. On reaching that country they had been turned loose in the mountains for a couple years. They was wild and buggery. It didn't take much to get them riled up and on the rampage.

It was only about six miles from the Strong ranch to a station on the Union Pacific Railroad. There was a stock yard, water tank and section house there. I have forgotten its name but it wasn't too far from Montpelier, Idaho. The cars was all ordered and waiting at the station. The cattle was to be loaded at four o'clock. If everything went smoothly it would take perhaps a little over two hours to drive the cattle that six miles.

There was six of us all riding good horses and we didn't think we would have much trouble getting them to the station.

The foreman was called Peggy Smith as he had his leg cut off below the knee and wore a peg leg. He was a good cow hand. He was originally from Texas. He had come north with a trail herd, got lost in a blizzard and nearly froze to death. One foot was froze so bad he got gangrene in it and had to have it cut off. It didn't seem to bother him any to ride. Peggy was a good, hard, salty cuss.

When we was ready to start the cattle to the station Peggy called us together and said, "You waddies be careful when we turn them billies out for they feel so good that they will all want to run and play." He said, "Me and Bill will ride in front to hold them up. Buck and Jim ride the middle, Sleepy and Idaho the drag end. I don't want any visiting. Everybody ride his own horse."

We turned them out of the feed lot about ten o'clock, giving us about six hours to get them to the stockyards to load up. Them billies was a pretty sight coming out of the corral. They was fat and slick with their heads and tails up. They all had great big long horns. Their eyes was bugging out and they was all colors of the rainbow.

They was all raring to go. It was sure something to see them steers play. They was just bucking and kicking up. We could handle them easy as they wasn't scared, just feeling good.

We had to go right down Bear River. It was a valley with the railroad on the north end and the river on the south. A range of mountains was on either side of the valley. The river wasn't very wide but being early spring it was high and bank full.

We was about half way to the station, the steers had got their play out and we was getting along just fine. At that particular place, we was close to the river and there was a lot of bushes along the edge. The steers threw up their heads and looked at the brush as a big, black dog came out of it. He saw the cattle and gave a loud bark.

Those cattle just stopped and stood and looked. That damn dog looked just like a bear. Then a man came out of the brush after the dog, hollering, "Here Tige. Here Tige." He had an old sour dough coat that was a-flopping in the wind and looked more like a scarecrow than a man.

That was too much for them cattle. They was off like dynamite. They split right in two in the middle, some going up the river and some going down the river. What I mean "going," almost flying. It takes a good horse to outrun a Texas Billy when he gets scared into a stampede.

Peggy and I was in the lead. When they started to run Peggy hollered, "Ride like hell, don't let any of them get by, we can't turn them until we have more room."

We must have run a half mile, there the river made a turn to the south. The valley widened out there and we had more room. Peggy began shooting in front of the steers. I would have too only I didn't have a gun, so I yelled and swung my rope. Finally they turned and we got them to milling.

The other cowboys had got their bunch turned and they was coming hell bent to get away. Just then an engine pulling three coaches came along. There was about forty head in the lead and when the train came around a curve the train looked to those cattle like it was coming right at them. They whirled to the south and jumped in the river.

The river was bank full and when they got in they couldn't get out as there was six or seven feet of water where they jumped in. They had to go down stream about three hundred yards before they came to a kind of crossing where the banks widened out.

Peggy and I was having trouble keeping our bunch milling so they wouldn't take another run. Then Buck came with the other bunch. When we got them all milling, Peggy told me to go over to the river and head off the ones that was coming down the river.

I just got to the crossing when the last of them was going out on the other side. There was nothing to do but take to the river. My God, that water was cold. I got around them, they was crazy scared cattle. I couldn't do much with them, only keep them from going to the mountains. I got them back to the crossing but couldn't get them to take the river. When I crowded them they would break out and run.

The rest of the boys got the main bunch quieted and was holding them. As soon as he wasn't needed Sleepy came over to help me. Even the two of us couldn't make them take the water.

Peggy saw what we was up against so he and the other boys worked the bunch near the crossing so our steers could see them. Finally our steers crossed. We had them all together again and got them started for the stock yards. We got them in about five thirty.

They didn't look so pretty as when we started from the ranch. When you run a bunch of fat cattle that have been on a lot of good feed it loosens up their bowels. By the time we got them all corralled they was pretty near all the same color—green.

The old coot and his dog that had caused all the trouble was a trapper that had been trapping beaver in the river. We looked for him as we went back to the ranch. We found his tent but I guess he didn't want to meet us after all the trouble he caused and so had business elsewhere.

Cattle will scare and stampede in the daylight but they generally see what scares them and you can handle them. The worst stampedes are at night when it is real dark. The leaders run and the cattle back of them run to follow. That scares the leaders more and they run to get away.

When a large bunch of cattle get to running you would be surprised at how much noise they make. About all you can do is try to turn them until they finally get to milling. It takes a lot of time to quiet them down and it is very dangerous. If a cowboy's horse happens to fall with him, there is another good cowboy gone to "The Big Roundup."

I WORKED for Strong a while. Jim Strong had more horses than money. Whenever he settled with a man, he always tried to settle in horse flesh instead of cash.

I had sold my packhorse to a sheep outfit so I could use a horse. We made a deal, I settled for a very nice unbroke gelding for twenty dollars. At that time it was a pretty good price but I knew that after I broke him I could sell him to most any cow outfit for thirty-five or forty dollars.

When I bought the horse we caught it and vented the brand. Jim Strong handled lots of horses and never let one go unless vented. He said that made everyone honest. As I wanted to get another job and buy some clothes I just turned the horse back on the range with his horses while I went to Montpelier, Idaho, which was just across the state line.

At Montpelier I got a job helping take a bunch of cattle over in Wyoming. I wintered in Lander. During the winter I got acquainted with a young man about my own age whose home was in Utah. After the calf roundup in the spring he was going home. As I had a horse over in that country and nothing to do, we made the trip together.

When I got to the Strong ranch after an absence of about eight months, Mr. Strong told me where my horse was running. I brought him in and made a deal with Strong to stay with him about a week to break my horse. I was to help Strong's bronc stomper with a bunch of green horses he was breaking and handle my horse at the same time.

I had a packsaddle at Strong's as I had packed in there and sold my packhorse. I want to explain the reason for a packhorse. In those days if you traveled around with a roundup or other jobs, you needed a bed, some grub and what few clothes or other belongings that you owned with you. Wherever you went all you needed was grass and water for your horses, a few groceries for yourself and you was at home.

If you was going across country you was lucky to hit a town within two or three hundred miles. From the Union Pacific Railroad to the Northern Pacific Railroad was a distance of about four hundred miles, all open space.

When I started from the Strong horse ranch I didn't know just where I was headed but thought I probably would end up in the Lander country where I was acquainted, or wherever I heard of a suitable job.

It was a good day's ride to the Sweet Water. I made it by about five o'clock. About an hour before I got in, I shot a couple of nice young sage hens and thought I would have a big feed that night. As I was riding up to the camp grounds I saw a covered wagon, and thought it would be nice to have company that night.

After I had unsaddled and staked out my horses, the man from the covered wagon came over to my camp fire where I was cooking supper. We got acquainted.

I could tell by his talk that he had been drinking. I gave him one of the sage hens and he gave me a drink of Duff's malt whiskey out of a quart bottle. He said his name was Pat. He said he was going to Butte to work in the mines. I could tell by his brogue that he was a full-blooded Irishman. We had visited a while when his wife hollered to him that supper was ready. I could tell by her speech that she was Irish, too.

The sun was just going down when I heard them quarreling. It was loud fighting talk. Then they came rolling out of the wagon like a couple of tom cats. They finally got on their feet, stood toe to toe fighting like a couple of pugilists.

She knocked him down. When he got up he clinched her and down they went. Pat had a hold of her red hair and he sure was working on her, holding her down by the hair and punching her in the ribs with his other hand. She was hollering for him to let her up.

I had got over close to them by that time. When she saw me she gasped, "You are a hell of a fine man to let a man get a woman down and beat her. Pull him off, he's killing me."

I thought it was time to interfere so I got hold of Pat's leg and managed to get them untangled.

When he got on his feet he said, "You damn spalpeen, we've had many a fight and this is the first time I ever had the best of it and you pulled us apart. You ought to have more sense than to interfere in family trouble. Square yourself, I'm just getting started."

I was trying to talk him out of it but his Irish temper and the whiskey he had drunk made no argument worthwhile. He came at me and about all I could do was fight.

He sure was a scrapper. I saw right away that I didn't have much chance with him. He hit me on the bridge of the nose and I couldn't see out of one eye but when he went to finish me up I made one lucky punch and knocked him down. I had a little of the best of it then. As he came up I layed another on him but that was the last I remember for a while.

She had rested up and didn't want to see her better half get the worst of it. She layed one on my jaw. When I come to, her and Pat was having it out again toe to toe. She put a hay maker on him and he went out. She looked at him, turned around, and got in the wagon. That was the last I heard of them until the next morning.

I had just made some coffee and eaten a couple of flapjacks when I saw them coming. I thought, My God, they have come over to finish me up. I couldn't see out of one eye and the other was swelled almost shut. My jaw felt like it was broke. Though I couldn't see myself I don't think I looked any worse than he did. She was scratched up a little, but nothing like we was.

I reached over and got hold of the frying pan and thought I would use it for a weapon if they started anything. I was really scared stiff.

Pat said, "Good mornin'. I guess we had quite a time last night." He handed me a bottle with just about a drink in it and said, "I thought you'd like to have a little nip this mornin'." I took the drink.

She said, "You have a bad eye, come over to the wagon, and I will give you something for it."

I went over and she fixed a poultice for my eye. She said they was sorry but they generally had a little fuss when they got to drinking. She said that Pat was a good man with a heart of gold. We shook hands and parted good friends.

I had learned a lesson the hard way, from rough experience. I made up my mind that I would never mix up with no family affairs again.

4: Cowboys

DOUGLAS, WYOMING, was a wide open little town when my Uncle Bert and I rode into it in 1897. There was lots of cattle on Powder River and the surrounding country and sheep east and north. Douglas was just a small place but had several saloons. There was several gambling tables in all the saloons. They used to get pretty wild some times and the games played for pretty high stakes.

Abe Daniels' Saloon seemed to get the big play. There was a sign hung on the wall by the poker tables that said, "If you play poker, deposit your gun with the bartender."

Abe Daniels was a red-faced, good-natured man with a pleasant laugh that everyone liked. He was a big man with lots of frontage. He always wore a bright, loud shirt, pink, red or blue.

Bert and I was heading for Yellowstone Park as the government was wanting men to work there. We was leaving our saddles and horses with Cackling Tate. He used to laugh a great deal. He had a very funny cackle with his laughter that you could hear all over town. We'd made all arrangements to leave the next morning.

We was in Abe Daniels' Saloon. I was visiting with a man by the name of Bennie Wheelock that I knew from Lander. Bennie was a gambler and a good one. He was a fine looking man and always wore good clothes. He seemed to always beat the big games.

George Pike, a cow hand and gambler, was also in Abe's place, probably waiting for a game to start as the poker games hardly ever opened until afternoon.

While I was setting visiting with Bennie two hands came in. They bellied up to the bar, took off their six-shooters, handed them to the bartender and ordered drinks for the house. There wasn't many in the saloon at that time. After they got their drinks they went down to Reid's restaurant to get a feed.

When they'd left I asked Bennie who they was. He said the light complexioned fellow that bought the drinks was called Whiskey Bill and that he worked for a cow outfit over on Chugwater. That he sure was a hard drinker and a plunger in a poker game, generally won all the money in town until he got drunk, then lost it all. The other fellow Bennie didn't know.

Abe Daniels got out his poker chips and said, "Let's start a poker game. Whiskey Bill will be raring to play as soon as he gets his dinner."

Bennie, Pike, a sheepman that had just blowed in, a tin horn gambler that was hired for the house to start a game and fall out as soon as the game got under way, and myself took out ten dollars' worth of chips.

Bert didn't play poker and he cautioned me, "Bill, remember we are starting for the park in the morning. Don't get stuck and lose all your money as I haven't got enough to take us both."

I told him that I would only play the ten and if I lost it I wouldn't buy any more chips.

The game had been going on for about an hour and I was lucky, didn't seem like I could lose a pot. The sheepman seemed like he couldn't win one. He had got in about fifty dollars and I had about sixty dollars when Whiskey Bill and his friend came in.

Bill bought a drink for all of us and said, "Let's turn this into a poker game."

They set in and bought a hundred and fifty dollars' worth of chips. The sheepman, Bennie and Pike done likewise. I told them I was trying to make a scratch and would just play mine as they was.

Bert motioned at me from the bar. He wanted me to quit while I was ahead fifty dollars. I told him I was going to try and run it up to a hundred but if I lost it would only be ten dollars.

Whiskey Bill liked lots of liquor while he was gambling. Every little while he would buy a drink for us all. He'd say, "Hell, fellows, I don't like to drink alone." Whenever someone would win a good pot he would buy a drink for the bunch.

We was all getting pretty well organized except Whiskey Bill. You couldn't tell he'd had a drink. It was just like pouring water down a rat hole. He said it took a week of drinking to make him drunk and two weeks to sober up.

The sheepman was about four hundred dollars the loser. Bill had the most of it. The sheepman was bleating like a ewe that had lost her lamb. Bill told him to cheer up, that the worst was yet to come, that when the game was over that he (Bill) would be driving a bunch of sheep to Chugwater. The sheepman about throwed a fit and bought some more chips. Everybody laughed but the sheepman.

The way they was all plunging I thought I would quit. I counted my chips and had about eighty dollars. My uncle was looking over my shoulder and Abe kicked me on the leg. I knew I ought to quit but the liquor was working.

While I was counting my chips Abe Daniels was dealing.

I looked at my hole card and I had the joker. The sheepman anteed. You could ante whatever you wanted. He was loser and trying to get even. He anteed $2.50. We all called.

When the cards was dealt, I got the ace of clubs. I was high and bet ten dollars. They all called. The sheepman was the last to call and raised the bet fifty dollars. They all called. I put all my chips in on a pair of aces, the best hand, but you never can tell in a poker game.

The next card the sheepman drew was a queen. It was a cinch he had three queens. He had drawed out on my aces but there was two cards yet to fall. He bet fifty dollars. They all quit but Whiskey Bill, he called the fifty.

When the cards was dealt, the sheepman bet a hundred. Bill didn't help so turned his cards down. I had three clubs up with the joker in the hole. As I was all in I was entitled to a show down. I got the club that I needed, making a double ace flush, beating the sheepman's three queens.

It was a nice pot for me, over three hundred dollars, and all I was in was ten dollars. Abe Daniels paid me in gold and silver. There was a small side pot that the sheepman got.

Bert and I was both feeling mighty good about my poker game. It was raining hard. Our camp was about a half a mile from town. While we was killing time waiting for the rain to slack up every once in a while we would take just one more, until we had a glorious jag on.

We started for camp finally. There was a sidewalk for a ways but it wasn't wide enough. We took the middle of the muddy street with locked elbows singing on our way to camp, "The night is dark and the road is muddy. We got a jag and we can't walk steady."

We met Cash Lewis and Bill Rayome. We left our horses in a pasture and went on to the Yellowstone Park and worked there. That winter Bert and Cash went back to Nebraska and Bill and I spent the winter in Billings.

EVER SINCE its beginning Billings has been a lively town, a distributing center for a large territory. In the early days there wasn't any railroad on the north until Great Falls and south to Casper, that made Billings the trading center for a large scope of country.

There was a lot of big sheep, cattle and horse outfits that had to be supplied, so there was a lot of freight haulers. In June and July I've seen all kinds of freight teams from four horses up to a twelve horse team lined up for a quarter of a mile waiting to be unloaded at the wool house. Most of them stopped at Donovan & McCormick's or Yegen Brothers' store to pick up a load of salt and supplies to haul back. Donovan & McCormick's and Yegen's handled all kinds of merchandise including harness, wagons and machinery. In fact, you could get anything you wanted at either place.

Most of the boom towns of the west had their saloons, dance halls, painted ladies and Chinese restaurants. Billings had hers and in the 1890s it was a wide open town. There was gambling of all kinds in every saloon, a large Red Light district on the south side. On Minnesota Avenue there was three big sporting houses, Dutch Mary's, Etta Feely's, and Quittor's. They had fifteen to twenty women working in each place, they had a dance hall and served beer for a dollar a bottle. There was a lot of cribs and three Saloon Show Houses, as I remember, they was Diego Frank's, The Globe and the Topic and they was plenty tough. They was big beer halls with a stage in the back where they had all forms of entertainment. There was singing, dancing, ladies, prize fights, wrestling matches, any kind of amusement to draw and hold a crowd. There was tables all around the hall and a gallery with booths and rooms upstairs.

The beer slingers that fetched drinks to the tables was pretty hard customers. One in particular was Broken Nose Slim. It seemed like he could get into more fights than the rest of them. He seemed to have a kind of special talent for getting into trouble. It got so that when a fight started, so many had it in for Slim, that a fight was never over until old Slim got crowned. He was plenty tough and could take a lot of punishment. Many a beer bottle was cracked over his head but he seemed to thrive on it.

Wherever there are cowboys, sheep herders, freighters, floaters and decent married men mixed together with a lot of hard liquor there's always lots of fights take place. There never was a night but what there was two or three fights.

One night there was a prize fight between a black man and a white man. The black man whipped the white man but he was a dirty fighter. The audience didn't like the results and they threw about three cases of beer bottles at the black man. It wasn't uncommon for a fight to start in the balcony and somebody to get heaved over the edge on the crowd below.

A fight at the Topic for entertainment was what they called a "battle royal." There was eight men, some white and some black, that got in the ring and any man that was knocked down was out of the fight. At the last there was a black man and a white man fighting. It was really rough and tough, the stage was covered with blood. The black man finally got the decision.

Another fight I'll never forget happened in the Globe. Four of us went in for a drink. There was Joe Poor, his son Rube, Whitey Boggus and me. Joe Poor was an Irishman. He weighed about two hundred pounds and he was knowed as a fighting man. He was a good, honest, hardworking man but liked to fight when he'd had a few drinks.

Joe bought us all a drink and paid the bartender. The bartender was a tough man, an ex-prize fighter by the name of Barry. He took the money but didn't ring it up. When Joe asked for his change Barry started an argument. He had a habit of putting his hand on the bar and jumping over the bar and knocking out the other guy.

This time it worked the other way for Joe was ready for him and knocked him down. The other beer slingers and housemen rushed into the fracas to help Barry. Right then it turned into a free for all.

The four of us was battling the saloon crowd and doing a lot of business. Joe Poor was knocking bartenders right and left. He hollered to me, "Sure, and they are falling before me, Billy," just before somebody hit him on the head with a beer bottle and knocked him into the big window where there was a lot of flowers.

Whitey was standing by the swinging door that went into the beer hall and when they hollered, "Fight!" the beer slingers and housemen began coming through the door. Whitey stood by the door and knocked them down as they came through. We was doing all right and making a good showing when somebody hollered, "Police!" We gathered up Joe and drug it.

At that time nobody was ever arrested for fighting in a saloon unless the saloon keeper made a complaint, which they hardly ever done for they didn't want to lose a customer.

BEFORE THE DAY of gas and electric stoves, there was an old timer by the name of Arch Clark used to haul and sell firewood. He was a tall, limber jointed individual usually in bad need of a haircut. He was a harum scarum bugger, always ready for anything.

He had a couple of little thin Indian diggers on his wagon. One day as he was coming down Minnesota Avenue the fire whistle blowed. Arch naturally was looking for the fire which was down in the Red Light district behind Dutch Mary's parlor house.

The horse drawn fire wagon came across the tracks on Twenty-seventh Street and made the turn east. They was making a pretty good run when they came up to Arch's wood wagon.

It was just a challenge to Arch as he was headed for the fire too. He stood up in his wagon and started his team on a dead run. They was neck and neck. Arch was hollering but his team seemed to lose ground. He reached down and began to throw stove wood at his horses. It was rough along the street and there was stove wood bouncing off the wagon and off the horses.

Folks that was hurrying to the fire stopped to see the race between the fire wagon and Arch's scrawny team. The fire gong a-ringing, Arch throwing stove wood and people cheering the race, it made quite a commotion.

They was neck and neck 'til they got to the corner, then the fire team slowed a little to make the turn.

Arch just kept heaving firewood at his team and took it on two wheels and beat them to the fire, waving his old floppy hat to come on. When the fire wagon got to the fire, which was an old shack, and backed up to get their hose in place, Arch drove alongside and saluted them.

The pride of the fire department was wounded. Their honor was at stake and the speed of their team questioned. They had to take legal action.

So next morning Arch, with a long face, was seen at police court trying to argue the judge out of a twenty-five dollar fine. He said he was just having a little fun.

ONE OF THE outstanding cowboys of Montana's early days was George Williams. The first I heard of him, he was in the western part of the state working for horse outfits around the Madison, Jefferson and Ruby country.

He came to Billings with a bunch of horses about 1900 and went to work for John Conway, one of the horse buyers for the English during the Boer War. It was at Conway's that George made a marvelous record. He rode from fifteen to twenty-five horses a day for two years and a half, through the entire inspection period and was never bucked off.

The horses we rode was mostly range horses that had never been handled and was plenty salty. When you screwed down in your saddle you knew you was going to have a rough ride. You had to ride them until they was tired enough to let the inspector look in their mouth to tell their age.

There is an old saying among the bucking horse riders, that "All horses get rode and all riders get throwed." It's a true saying, I never saw it fail but once. In that inspection there was a horse that slipped every rider that tried to ride him. He was a very pretty horse, kind of a blue cast. The owner would run him through the inspection as often as he could for the English wouldn't take a horse that wasn't rode.

The riders never knew what they was getting to ride as the horses was put through a chute and each rider rode in rotation. Whoever got Blue got spilled. Whenever a rider got throwed he would want to bet some of the other riders that he couldn't ride the blue horse but no one would take him up. George never drew the blue horse to ride. The other riders wanted him to take him on but George said, "I would just as soon hug a bear as try to ride him but if ever I draw him I'll do my damnedest."

Loud windy talk and bad liquor got lots of the boys' backs dusted. At the beginning of the Boer War inspections, there was seventeen of us riding. They have all died except Mark Newman and myself. We both live around Billings. I got a bum leg and Newman ain't so forked as he used to be.

AUSTIN NORTH WAS giving a bucking horse contest one time up where the Boosters of Billings built a penitentiary on the north side of Billings under the rims. It was never used for that purpose as the voters selected Deer Lodge as the penitentiary site. North bought the site and fixed it into a ball park. This contest was a local affair but open to all riders. I think there was eight riders including George and me. We was drawing for horses when a stranger wanted to enter the contest.

He had a few under the belt and was making a lot of noise. The judges informed him that anybody could ride with chaps and spurs on. He said, "Let's all take off our chaps and spurs and make it a real ride, the best man gets the grapes."

The crowd began to gather around and of course wanted to see the best show so they sided with the stranger. Some of the boys agreed to pull off their spurs, some never said anything. When he asked George what he was going to do, George eyed him and said, "Cowboy, these horses are plenty salty and you'll be lucky if you ride them at all. As for me, I won't take off my chaps or gut wrenches for nobody." The crowd laughed and that settled the argument.

The contest began and three local boys made good rides on good tough horses. The bragging rider was next and the announcer gave him a good talk. Everybody was all hopped up for they expected to see something extraordinary take place.

"Williams on a bucking horse."

He got a good bucking horse, you can bet on a bunch of cowhands to see to that.

The first jump looked pretty good, the crowd began to cheer. The second jump and he was in a lot of trouble, he got high in the saddle. The third jump he grabbed the saddle horn but it was too late, the cantle of the saddle hit his caboose and he sailed away like a kite. As he picked himself off the ground and looked to see where the horse went John Conway hollered at him, "They jobbed you, Boy, they greased the saddle horn on you." He'd lost his popularity.

George Williams didn't win many rodeo prizes. He learned to ride when you had to ride a bucker or walk in. He gave them all a business ride. He couldn't rake a horse with his spurs like some of the rodeo boys could but he never got throwed off. It was a hundred to one bet that he would ride any horse he climbed on.

He was a hardworking man, an honest square shooter. He didn't drink or gamble. He was always playing practical jokes. He was a tobacco chewing, swearing man. He used he-man cuss words with hair on them. He always called spurs "gut wrenches," his rope a "sheep hook," a mean horse was a "bucking son of a bitch." He had unprintable nicknames for every cowboy as was his. He never spoke of his wife being indisposed. It was always, "Babes is dragging a bush." For all that he was a diamond in the rough, his word was as good as gold and a man to tie to.

COWBOYS ARE great ones for jobbing each other and nothing delighted George Williams more than to job somebody. George and Billy Ogg was very good friends, they spent one winter together. They was supposed to be cutting cedar posts but I think they spent most of their time jobbing each other. Billy Ogg finally got the best of George. It happened this way.

George took up a homestead on Sand Creek near Pompey's Pillar. Now years before, there had been a sheep herder that was herding a bunch of bucks had killed himself on that location. The herder had left a note requesting that he be buried there. It was several days before his body was discovered and so the authorities buried him right there as he had requested, besides it saved a mighty disagreeable hauling job.

One spring after Williams took up his homestead he made a deal with Billy Ogg to have him make a log cabin while Williams was gone on the roundup for Walt Lee.

Billy Ogg knew that George was superstitious as hell so he thought he'd give George a little jobbing. His humor was a little gruesome, I'll admit, for he put the cabin right next to the grave of the sheepherder with the door opening just so anyone going in or out had to step on the grave.

George came back from the roundup to live his six months on the claim. He had lived there about three weeks when Billy saw him and asked if he ever heard or saw anything suspicious as he'd heard some of the cowboys say that Sand Creek was haunted. They had seen peculiar lights and heard funny noises. He didn't believe in ghosts and said that he didn't think the sheepherder would ever come back as he was tired of living or he wouldn't have gone harum scarum.

George was all ears as Billy knew he would be. He said he hadn't seen or heard anything unnatural. Right away he wanted to know where the herder was buried. Billy told him, "Over by the house somewhere, but the grave is all growed up with grass and would be hard to find." Having planted the seed of suspicion in George's mind, Billy left.

Shortly after Billy's visit George started to level the ground in front of the door. Just below the surface he struck a flat rock. He turned it over and there carved on it was the sheepherder's name and the day he died.

The next time Billy came to see George he saw a tent stretched on the far side of the claim from the cabin. He went over to it and there was George set up housekeeping and he knew his jobbing had worked.

He tried to convince George that it was a joke, that all he had to do was dig down and see that there was no body there.

George wasn't that curious. He lived in the tent until he proved up on his claim. Just as soon as he got his title he sold the place to Walt Lee.

Billy Ogg told me about it forty years or so later, not long before he died. He was still enjoying his joke. He said it was the only time he got the best of George Williams. He didn't say whether the grave was there or not, anyhow George Williams thought so and so did I.

IT'S GETTING SO now since about everyone has gone modern that you can't tell if anyone is home, for there is hardly a place where smoke is coming out of the chimney.

Not so long ago, I can remember when you drove up to a place, there was smoke coming out of the chimney, some flour sacks hanging on the line. There was a coffee grinder nailed against the wall for Arbuckle coffee and a well thumbed Montgomery Ward catalogue in a handy place for shopping. When the catalogue got out of date it was promoted to the back house.

These articles was all standard equipment for the camps and roundup wagons. These things, like the roundup cook, are memories of the past.

Most of the camp cooks and roundup cooks was generally men that had been cowboys all their life and had taken to cooking after they got too old to ride or had been crippled.

I remember riding up to a roundup camped on the Musselshell. The roundup cook was Al Mandel. He was a man fifty or fifty-five years old. He was a pretty good sized man, kind of sandy complexioned and minus one eye. He was a very good cook but plenty cranky. The cowboys used to call him "Sop Eye" when they was leaving camp and it didn't improve his disposition any.

Old Al had cooked for a lot of the big outfits in the early days and his cooking just couldn't be beat. Somebody asked him one time how he made such good coffee. He said, "I just put a lot of Arbuckle in the pot and boil the hell out of it."

After the big roundups began to break up, Al took up a claim on Blue Creek. Al used to cook for Nate Cooper during spring roundup and in haying season.

As a general rule most cooks are heavy drinkers and Al Mandel was no exception. Whenever he wasn't working, he was drinking. He stayed drunk as long as his money held out and 'til he couldn't bum another drink.

Now Nate Cooper never allowed any man to drink or have any liquor on his place but he had a soft spot in his heart for Al. He used to go in after Al when he thought he was broke. Cooper would sober Al up and give him a grub stake. Al would swear off liquor and would stay sober until he got in town again.

Al had one habit that he carried over from his early life. He always got up at 3 a.m. winter or summer. He got breakfast, then everyone sat around waiting for daylight. He always said, "One hour in the morning is worth three at night."

I was on a horse roundup one time with Nate Cooper. Al was cooking. There was talk around the campfire one night and the conversation turned to Al. Somebody asked Cooper where he got such a good cook.

Cooper had quite a sense of humor and he said, "I got him out of the Montgomery Ward catalogue."

The other fellow said, "I didn't know they sold cooks, but how did he get his eye put out?"

Cooper, with a perfectly straight face, said, "Well, when they put Al in the crate to ship him they run out of small nails and had to use a spike. It went through the boards and got Al's eye. But it don't seem to bother him from cooking any."

COWBOYS

IN THE OLD DAYS the winter was a pretty slack time for the cowboys. Most of them was let out of riding jobs after the fall roundup and as there wasn't many other jobs in the winter a lot of boys rode the grub line 'til spring.

Nobody considered them on the bum, just good hard working fellows out of a job. They was always welcome to hang out at the various ranches 'til the spring work opened up. If there was any work to do they pitched in and helped and more than paid for their grub. As far as that goes, their company was worth that.

I remember one winter when two cowboys drifted in to my ranch on Blue Creek to stick their feet under the table. One was Tex Fitchue, a Texas cowhand. He was a great rider, a teller of tall tales and a rawhide artist. He spent his spare time making rawhide hackamores, quirts and ropes. He made me a rawhide rope, eight strand, that was a dandy.

The other was Bob Catten. He was from the Ekalaka country where some of the saltiest cowboys hail from. He was better known as Powder River and was a good forked rider.

They had both rode in my shows and was good friends to tie to. They was typical cowboys, they put their heart in their work and in their drinking. There was no half way measures with either one. The trail wasn't too long, the bronc too tough for them to tackle.

One time I went to town with the lumber wagon. Tex and Powder River went along. They was celebrating. When I was ready to start home they told me to go on, they'd catch a ride back.

Sometime in the middle of the night, somebody woke me up and said one of my cowboys was laid out on the dugway and I'd better get him or he'd freeze to death. This fellow said he was so limber drunk he couldn't load him on his bronc.

I remember, I hitched up the bob sleigh and hurried to the rescue. I got about a half mile from the dugway and I seen my cowboys. Tex was staggering along with Powder River's feet clutched under his arms, dragging his body behind him. Powder

River had on a long overcoat but it wasn't doing him any good as it was spread out in back like a fan.

I loaded them in the bob sleigh and hauled them home. Powder River was all right in the morning except for a few frost bites and a sore back.

They said they'd missed their ride and the bright lights got to shining in their eyes and they thought they'd walk out. They misjudged the load they was packing and when Powder River's got too heavy and he laid it down, Tex went on to Conway's to get a rig to take him home. As it was Saturday night everybody was in town and there was no horses at the place so Tex went back and got him. While he was gone some superstitious soul saw Powder River laying stiffulcated by the road and went in and reported a dead man.

The authorities came out and made two searches for a victim of foul play before I could get word in the man was dead all right, but dead drunk.

I met Powder River in the Stockman about a year ago, so I guess he's still alive and kicking.

Tex joined with the Canadian army in World War I and was wounded in France and I think he probably died there for he sent word with Lawrence Osness, who was in the hospital too, that if he got back to give his regards to Bill Huntington for he thought he was going to cash in his chips.

JUST BECAUSE I'VE been spinning a few yarns about the happenings of fifty or sixty years ago don't mean I regard them as "good old days." Those times had a few advantages, it's true. Everyone knew everybody else. There wasn't any locks on the doors and you was always welcome, day or night, hungry or otherwise.

But it wasn't any particular fun to get up before daylight, feed and harness six or eight horses and take off with the wheels squeaking and groaning in the cold. Or saddle some old barnacle that would try to buck you off.

If you got sick it was a big dose of salts. For a cold in your chest, you was swabbed with coal oil and lard, maybe even skunk grease. If that didn't fix you, you fell heir to a mustard plaster. For cuts and bruises the standard remedy was turpentine. Most people kept a little liquor for snake bite but if it got used up and there was need for it, a fellow just spit tobacco juice on the wound and hoped for the best.

There wasn't any big white houses and red barns. Most everybody's spread was a one or two-room log shack, a corral, a small barn for a saddle horse, a big woodpile and a little building a short ways from the house, commonly called the back house. I want to tell you about the misadventure of one of those back houses.

I had bought a bunch of cattle in Billings and they was pretty wild. I got Casey Forrester to help me take them out to the ranch.

We got them down towards the old south bridge and they was giving us plenty of trouble. At the right of the road there was a cabin with a little building in the back.

As we tried to push them on the bridge, they scattered and we got them all back but one steer. He had his tail up headed for the brush on the other side of the cabin. As the steer plunged through the yard, Casey dropped a loop on it. The steer let a bawl out of him and run around the back house (old time term for outdoor privy), turning it over on its door.

The back house had no sooner hit the ground than a blood curdling scream came from inside. Casey jumped off his horse to rescue the trapped inmate but the steer wasn't in a cooperative frame of mind. As Casey lifted the house up about three feet, the steer made for Casey, and he had to drop the building. More screams from inside as Casey dodged away from the steer. I guess there must have been a sharp side on the thing for the rope broke and the steer ran for the rest of the herd.

I could see the whole show and hear the sound effects but was too busy watching the herd and holding my sides to lend any assistance.

Casey gave a mighty heave and set the building up right. It had no more than straightened up when the door flew open and a very pretty girl made a dash for the house. She didn't linger to thank her rescuer. Casey, his face a bright red, wasn't losing any time either getting to his horse.

It was sort of an unusual introduction but it must have been a good one for they got married later and had ten children the last I heard of them.

ABOUT 1899, the Fair Grounds in Billings, as I remember, was just north of the present North Park School between Eighteenth and Nineteenth street north and at that time was out of town.

At that time the racehorses was mostly just saddle horses from the surrounding country. They was not thoroughbreds with track records a yard long but they had their reputations among the cowboys.

There was always a lot of Indians with their racehorses too.

They rode their horses bareback. The Indians rode with their bodies all painted and only a breech clout or G string, as some called it. It wasn't always the fastest horse that came in, it was the Indian with the strongest arm, as they never stopped whipping from the word, "Go" 'til they got past the finish line. Everybody enjoyed the Indian races.

There wasn't many pumpkins or agriculture exhibits of course as there wasn't much farming. The main attraction was races. The people went big for relay races and there was a few sulky races. I remember one little pacing horse that belonged to Doc Clark was a great favorite and won most of the races. They called him Monty. Doc Clark had fetched him from Canada when he came here to doctor.

There was a peculiar character by the name of Jim Gaymond that always had some horses to run. He was a big raw boned man, stood about six foot four. He had a lot of hair that stuck up like a shock of hay on his head. His feet was so big that he used to cut the ends off his shoes in order to have room for his toes. His toe nails turned down like badger claws and his arms hung down to his knees. He was probably about fifty-five years old but plenty active.

He always had some running stock. He had one horse that was a quarter horse that was pretty good and he called him "Little Jim."

"Boy on a race horse."

Old Jim generally helped in the relay races and was a good hand. He would catch the running horses for a relay string. When the horse came in he would be up the track to about where the riders started to hold up to change horses. Old Jim would reach out with his long arm and grab his horse, run along beside the rider to the horse that the rider was going to take out next. When old Jim was running beside the horse he would throw more dirt with those toe nails than any horse there. That was half the fun of seeing the relay races.

Jim was always picking up some kid to ride his horses as he was too big to do it himself. I remember one such kid that Jim got. He was a limber jointed kid and he could ride pretty good. He acted like he had just come out of the sticks.

Jim had just matched a race and the boy was to ride the Little Jim horse. The boy had on a big floppy ten gallon hat that one of the cowboys had given him. It had seen a lot of honorable wear but the kid prized it a good deal and didn't seem to mind that it balanced on his ears.

The race got started okay and Jim's horse was a couple lengths ahead. It sure looked like they was running for blood and Jim had a cinch on that race when the calamity happened.

They was really fanning the breeze when the kid's old black hat blew off. He set back on his reins, jerked "Little Jim" to a stop, jumped off and got his hat, jumped back on the horse and started to race again although the other horse was just crossing the finish line.

Old Jim Gaymond was just jumping up and down, his hair was standing on end and he was frothing at the mouth yelling, "I lost fifty dollars that I had in my hand and my horse's reputation on account of an old slouch hat." He said a lot more but it wouldn't bear repeating.

The kid's only comment was that it was the only cowboy hat he'd ever had and he didn't want to lose it.

I KNEW QUITE a lot of old timers around Billings by the name of Smith. There was Horse Thief Smith, Red Eye Smith, Dog Thief Smith and Sheep Smith but this story is about Red Shirt Smith sometimes called Tex Smith. The real handle to his name is Bert.

He was born in Texas but grew up in the Indian Territory of Oklahoma. He came from the south to Montana with the 101 Wild West Show in about 1909. He was one of the show's best riders. He quit the show in Billings and got a job breaking horses for Johnny Conway.

That fall I was giving a contest in old Central Park at Billings. He entered the riding under the name of Tex Smith but he had on a bright red shirt and somebody called him "Red Shirt" and from then on everybody called him Red Shirt Smith. He won the riding contest.

Red Shirt was pretty forked at that time. Like all those southern boys he was a top roper. He really threw a wicked loop and hardly ever missed. He was no dally man—he always tied hard and fast. He won several roping contests in this country.

Red Shirt and his wife, a top lady bucking horse rider, wintered with us at my ranch on Blue Creek. George Williams and his wife spent the same winter with us. We was all young and full of zip.

We took in all the dances in the country. When it was cold and disagreeable we sure rode and roped some tough ones around the heating stove. We also caught a lot of wild horses, off the Crow Reservation.

Red Shirt said that he had run a lot of wild brush cattle in Oklahoma but he never had much experience in running wild horses. He said he would like to get close enough to get a shot at one with his rope. He would sure capture himself a wild horse.

In the spring after a pleasant winter we all felt pretty rollicky. Red Shirt was all hopped up about the wild horse stories George and I had been telling him all winter. We thought it was a good time to take a trip over on the Reservation and give them a run. Our saddle horses was in good condition for we had been feeding them hay and grain.

We went over on Woody about twenty five miles from the ranch. There was a line fence called the McCormick fence which was kind of a division fence between the sheep and cattle range. We located a bunch of about twenty five head. We thought if we had the fence on one side and could get them running alongside it, the three of us could handle them pretty good. For about five miles one of us stayed behind them and the other two stayed at the side to keep them running along the fence. We wanted to get them across Pryor Creek where we could corral them.

We done pretty well until we came to a jog in the fence. There we had a lot of trouble. Something had run into the fence and broke it and there was some loose wire. One of the wild horses got some wire caught in its tail and business picked up. Those horses scattered like a bunch of black birds. We was all pretty busy trying to get them together. After circling them, running hell for leather, we got them started again.

There was a washed out coulee that we had to go around as it was so deep we couldn't cross. That is where we spilt them. They split again and a very pretty paint stud ran between Red Shirt and Williams. Smith had his rope ready. When the stud went by him he made a throw.

The paint was really sailing when he hit the end of the rope. It knocked both horses down. Red Shirt just flew through space coming down in a cactus patch. You could hardly see for dust. Horses going in every direction. Smith's horse and the paint knocking each other down until the rope broke. The paint went running after the bunch with about ten feet of rope standing straight out behind him.

When Smith got up and we found he wasn't hurt we knew there was no more use that day to run them. He was kind of surprised that we didn't have any wild horses to bring home. I guess George and I hadn't seen fit, in our stories of catching wild horses, to tell him that was the case most of the time.

COWBOYS

I had a bunch of horses running on Pryor Mountain just west of Pryor Gap about thirty five miles from the ranch. It was a big day's ride to go over there and back. I had made that ride several times but this time I was riding a small horse and was afraid it was too big a trip for him to make it in one day.

Red Shirt and I left home early expecting to eat at a sheep camp. We didn't have any luck locating a sheep wagon. We planned on going on Sage Creek, stay with Mexican Tony overnight, get the horses and come home the next day. However, when we got to Sage Creek, Tony wasn't there. The shack was unlocked but there wasn't anything to eat in it.

It was about seven miles from Tony's up on the mountain where the horses run. We figured, with a lot of good luck, we could get the horses and get back to the head of Blue Creek where there was a small pasture and a place to eat.

We had good luck finding the horses but they was in with a bunch that was pretty wild. There was one old ridge running mare in the bunch that was a crazy old fool to handle. She tried to get away all the time.

We got off our horses and let them rest and graze for about an hour, then started the bunch of horses off the mountain. There was only about twenty head altogether. We noticed one big tall rangy brown horse in the bunch that looked like he might be a saddle horse as he had some white spots on his back that looked like saddle tracks.

We started the horses slow as we didn't want to get them running. We had a ridge for a ways, then there was a steep place. That old ridge running mare started down the steep mountain side on high. She was figuring on getting away.

When you are running wild horses you can't let them get too much of a start on you or they will get away. We made the bottom of the mountain but after we got down on the flat that old son of a gun was trying to get back to the mountain. We was plenty busy.

Just as we struck Cottonwood Creek she made a wild run to get back. Bert was running with her. As he turned her, his horse stepped on a rolling rock and fell head over heels.

I saw his horse go down. Bert looked about ten feet long sailing through the air. He had an awful fall, if he hadn't been tougher than whang leather it would have killed him. I saw him get up and knew he wasn't hurt too bad.

I was running those horses and didn't want to lose them. I headed them into the head of Cottonwood and had the luck to get them against a cut bank until Bert came leading his horse.

Bert's horse was so lame it could hardly walk, my horse was all in. That last run to get them in Cottonwood had played him plumb out. The other horses was willing to have a little rest too.

They was against a rimrock in a kind of a pocket. The only way they could get out was to come past us in a narrow canyon down a water wash. There was some small Cottonwood trees growing at the side of the wash.

Bert and I was in a bad fix, a long ways from nowhere and on foot.

Bert said, "I will slip up the canyon and tie the end of my rope to one of those cottonwood trees. When the brown horse comes by, I will drop my rope on him for I never can hold him a foot."

Bert worked up the canyon, tied his rope to a tree, made a hole in his rope and got all ready. I got on my played out horse and managed to get up close enough to get them turned down the water wash.

The old ridge runner was sure getting nervous. She was raring to get out of that rimrock trap. Here she came, the brown horse right behind her. I wasn't worrying that Bert wouldn't catch the horse for he just never missed, but I was afraid the brown horse might break the rope.

Bert made the catch. There was a little give in the cottonwood tree, the rope held and we had a horse. He had been handled sometime but he was a wampus cat not a saddle horse.

We fought him around for quite a while. We thought we would ride him double over about seven miles where I had some horses in my father-in-law's pasture.

Bert put his saddle on, I was going to ride behind. We couldn't get on until I took off my shirt and used it for a blindfold. Bert got on first, then he gave me a stirrup and took hold of my hand. I hit square behind the saddle and got a saddle string in each hand.

Bert pulled off the blind and said, "You spur him behind and I'll get him in the shoulder. We'll take all the buck out of him quick as we can."

We was all three doing our damnedest. I was just wondering how much longer I could stay on when the latigo broke. Bert, me and the saddle all tangled up and hit the ground. The last we saw of the horse, he was just hitting the high places for Pryor Mountain, with Bert's bridle on him.

We was in a heck of a fix, bunged up, a foot, tired and hungry. We had rode hard all day, hadn't had any dinner and we didn't know just what to do. If there was any way besides walking we was going to take it.

We finally decided to stay right there for the night. By morning my horse would be rested enough that I could ride him over to the pasture and get us a couple of fresh horses.

We used our saddles for pillows and the saddle blankets for beds but we didn't sleep too good for we was so hungry it seemed like our big guts was eating the little ones.

Next morning I went over and got fresh horses. In the night that old ridge runner had sneaked out of the horses. We picked the others up and got home that evening.

Later on Smith went over on East Fork of Pryor to build some corrals for Dan Cooper. He broke a bunch of horses for Charley Bair. I took a show south in 1913 and lost track of Red Shirt for a while. He rode inspection for cavalry horses for World War I. After the inspection he took up a place over in the Bull Mountains. When he left there I lost track of him again.

A short time ago Smith breezed through Billings. I was reading when I heard a knock at the door and opened it to find Red Shirt Smith. He sure looked in good health and was wearing a red shirt as always, though this one was quieter in color than the ones he wore in the old days.

I was sure surprised to see him. We had a very nice visit. We sure rode and roped a lot of tough ones.

ONE OF THE best ropers I have ever seen among the old time cowboys was Charley Binion. He had made several cattle drives from Texas. He was a typical Texas cowboy. What he didn't know about cattle and trail herds wasn't worth knowing.

As I remember him, he was tall, with grey hair and a Texas drawl in his speech. I never heard of him being anything but a honest hard working cowboy.

He was a tough old hand. I never saw many southern cowhands that could stand cold but Binion could take it. He never wore socks and in winter, he never wore overshoes. All he did to keep his feet warm was to take a piece of brown paper, grease it and wrap it around his bare feet and put on his boots. He'd ride all day in zero weather and never complain of getting cold.

He worked for several years around the Crow Reservation for the big cattle outfits. When he wasn't working, he generally made Hardin, Montana his stomping ground. Folks that knew Charley say he could ride by a cow on a lope and tell you what brand was on her. Some even went so far to say that he could tell even if the brand was on the other side.

Binion knew his cows as he had never done any other kind of work. His name mentioned to the cowboys meant "top hand."

He knew every privilege around a roundup wagon. If any cow puncher got out of line, Charley set him straight. He never had too much to say, in fact, he was kind of cranky. He seemed

COWBOYS

to think that everybody ought to know and do the right thing all the time whether they was old, young or indifferent.

He was an artist with a rope. I never saw him miss a throw.

He was the best. He had a fancy catch that he used on big stock. He would throw his rope over an animal's shoulder, catch the front legs and turn them right on their side. If you think it isn't hard to do, just try it.

Charley was living on the Porter Kennedy ranch east of Lodge Grass when he cashed in his chips. If there is a roundup where Charley went, I'll bet he's in it as top roper.

POWDER FACED TOM was a typical old cowboy, he done it all. He was a wonderful rider, bull dogger, and roper. He had a great sense of humor. He'd cowboyed in New Mexico, Oregon, Wyoming and Montana. He rode up north for the TV outfit for several years. I don't know what started him off riding for rodeos. He was a real rider but for some reason he didn't show off well on a bucking horse but I never seen him throwed off.

I had been touring the south with a Wild West show and was on my way home when I got tied up in Grand Island, Nebraska, due to the quarantine for hoof and mouth disease. I bought a restaurant and pool hall to run while waiting for the quarantine to get over.

One day a tough looking individual came into the restaurant to get a bowl of soup. My wife came to me and told me he looked like a cowboy down on his luck.

I took one look and recognized Powder Faced Tom underneath the whiskers, long hair, dirty shirt and runover boots. I went out to see what had happened to Tom as he'd always been a neat dresser.

It seems he'd been working for a wild west show that had gone broke in Alabama and he was beating his way north. We staked him to some clean clothes and a place to stay 'til he got a job riding out inspection horses at the sale yard. These horses was for the English government for World War I.

The job didn't last long but gave Tom a stake to get back to the sage brush country.

I didn't see Tom again for a few years, then one holiday season I ran into him and a bunch of cowboys in Bob Conway's Saloon. I remember there was George Williams, Danny Moore, the Powder River Kid, four or five other boys and myself.

There has been quite a change in the drinking of hard liquor since then. In those days nice ladies didn't go into a bar or saloon. Any female seen heisting a drink had a pretty shady reputation and was generally on the make.

Powder Faced Tom was kind of a homely fellow but he was full of the devil and would try anything for a joke. Anyway, he decked himself out in women's clothes with a pair of red stockings. His voice was kind of squeaky so he could imitate a woman's talk.

He got over in a corner at a table. He pulled up his skirt pretty high, reached down in his red stocking for a dime and demanded a couple sacks of Bull Durham from the bartender.

Everyone began craning their necks to get a look at that red stocking. Somebody passed out the word that it was Calamity Jane. A few boys in the bar knew Calamity but they kept still for they was curious as to what was a foot.

As soon as our imitation Calamity Jane knew he had everybody's attention he began a story about early days in Deadwood. Just as the story was getting good about Wild Bill Hickok, Calamity would lose her voice and call for a drink for herself and friends which was quickly served. As the story went on the pauses for a drink came oftener and the story got wilder.

It was sure getting good when a big, faced Irish man came in. He took a look at Powder Faced Tom telling the story and marched up behind Tom, grabbed his dress and yanked, bellowing, "You dirty spalpeen, many a drink I've had with Calamity Jane and I'll not have the likes of you making fun of her."

COWBOYS

He gave a mighty tug and just disrobed Powder Fac
who stood in his long john underwear and red stocking
made a dive for the back door and the last I saw of him he was
going down the alley looking like a picked chicken.

IN THE EARLY days there wasn't very many black cowpunchers in this northern country. In fact, I only knew of two or three. I want to tell you about the only black puncher that I knew well.

Tom Simms was a black cow puncher that came up the trail from Texas to Dodge City, Kansas with some of the first herds that moved to this northern country. I got acquainted with him about 1900. He was a likeable cuss and I used to like to hear him tell about those early drives and the hard times they had with the Indians and cattle thieves they came in contact with in Oklahoma Territory.

Tom had the reputation of being a good all around cowhand. He was a good bronc stomper and he broke a lot of horses for the different outfits in Wyoming and Montana. With a rope he was an artist. I want to tell you about the first drive he made as near as I can remember the way he told it to me.

After the Civil War, Tom's folks moved from Kentucky into Texas in the cow country. His father went to work on a cow outfit. As a boy, Tom was too busy around the ranch doing chores to get much experience as a cowhand. He had been out to the roundup a few times but he never had a saddle to ride.

The outfit his father was working for was going to deliver a bunch of steers to Dodge City. Tom wanted to go and as they was short handed they let him go along with the trail herd.

He said he was about eighteen years old, an ignorant black. He had his first pair of shoes about that time. He said those shoes was what they called plow shoes. They had soles about an inch thick and the heels was wide. They had buckles instead of laces and was made out of thick, rough leather.

"Tom Simms, cowboy."

COWBOYS

He naturally had big feet and going barefoot all his life let them spread out, he got the biggest pair of shoes he could get but they sure hurt his feet.

The cowboys had to have a saddle, a bed and a six-shooter.

The outfit furnished the horses and the ammunition. The outfit bought Tom a new saddle to make the drive. He said he sure was proud of it. It had two cinches, set down low on a horse's back and had a horn as big as a tin plate. It sure looked fine but when he put it on a horse his feet was so big he couldn't get his feet in the stirrups. He didn't want to tell the boss for fear he wouldn't let him go so he tied a rope in the stirrup straps.

He got along for a few days, then the rope began to hurt his feet. He thought he would try and make a pair of stirrups. He found some ash timber and cut an armful of light poles and the next three weeks he put in all his spare time trying to make stirrups. All the tools he had was an axe and a jack knife so he didn't have much luck.

The trail outfits carried a supply of horseshoes along with them so if a horse got sore footed it could be shod. Each cowboy had to shoe the horses in his string. Along the way, this outfit run out of horseshoes. The first blacksmith shop they come to they stopped to get more shoes. The foreman told Tom to get him a pair of stirrups made. The blacksmith took a look at the size of Tom's feet and said he didn't think he could make stirrups but he could make some large iron rings that would answer the purpose. Tom said he used those rings for five years.

The gnats, mosquitoes and flying ants caused them a lot of grief. Every night the cowboys had to shake out their beds to be sure they didn't have any scorpions in them. Long days in the sun on the trail, and the waddies all got sunburned until their faces was sore, especially their lips. The wind off the cattle mixed with alkali dust and what not was something awful and made their eyes sore. It was no wonder that when they got to Dodge City they really blowed the cork out and was spoiling to drink, shoot and fight.

Just as Tom was leaving for the drive, his mother came out to bid him good-bye. She had a bacon rind in her hand. She gave it to him and told him to rub it over his face every morning and it would keep the insects away and keep his face from chapping. He said it sure helped as he was never bothered like the white men.

After making several trips to Dodge City, Tom trailed into Nebraska and then to the Powder River country in Wyoming, from there he came to Montana. He worked on the Crow Reservation for several outfits.

Tom had a sense of humor, as a cowpoke he had lots of ability. I never heard of him being drunk or ever getting tough or in any kind of trouble. He called all his friends by their first names as Mr. Bert or Mr. Jack. He was liked and respected by all who knew him. When he got too old to ride, he ran a poker game but never played.

The last time I ever saw Tom was at Joliet, Montana. The coal miners' union was putting on a local rodeo, that must have been over thirty years ago. He was showing his age. He told me that he was going to Miles City. I heard that he died there.

WHEN I FIRST MET Bronc Savage his stomping ground was around Hardin, Montana. He had the reputation of being a good all around cowboy. He was a favorite among cowboys and a very honorable man. He was a fearless, reckless, happy-go-lucky cowboy.

He generally rode the rough string. It took a mighty tough horse to slip Bronc Savage. He was just as handy with his rope and always had a loop ready to catch a jack rabbit, coyote, calf or anything that was handy.

He was a good fellow and everybody liked him. Like most cowboys, he always had a good story or joke on somebody that he liked to tell. Bronc liked to celebrate when he went to town. He got on some pretty wild jags while he was celebrating.

Now there's fighting whiskey, laughing whiskey, crying whiskey, and riding and roping whiskey, depending on the nature and disposition and amount taken. Liquor is just sort of like dynamite, you never can quite predict the nature of its explosion. A few drinks puts one guy over in the corner to sleep it off, while the same amount makes another fellow think he can whip the world. I've heard that some of the liquor they used to serve in Hardin would make a cottontail rabbit fight a grizzly bear.

Bronc Savage was working for one of the cow outfits on the reservation. He made a trip into Hardin and was celebrating a little. He was riding his top rope horse. In the course of his spree he must have got some bragging whiskey.

Drunk or sober, Bronc was sure proud of his horse. He said he'd never seen anything too big for that old pony to stop.

Bronc wasn't over his jag when one of the cowboys of his outfit came in after him. They started to leave town. Bronc, as was his habit, was playing with his rope. As they passed the depot there was a passenger train going by.

Bronc saw the hand brake on the back end of the passenger train. He dabbed his rope on it. His horse set back to hold it. The train was a little too powerful. It jerked Bronc's horse down and broke the rope. Horse and Bronc rolled over in a ditch. The horse got up but Bronc had a broken hip. He walked with a limp from then on.

After that when he got juiced up and the cowboys was kidding him a little he'd say, "I'd have stopped the damn thing if my rope hadn't broke."

IN 1918 the Northern Pacific had just finished a branch railroad from Hesper siding to Rapelje, Montana. The country was just settling up with ranchers and wheat farmers. A man by the name of Gatewood and myself took a bunch of horses there to sell to the farmers. We dealt there for over a year and sold lots of horses and mules in that country.

I had come back to Billings on business. I happened to meet Max Zimmerman, an old friend and an old-timer, that owned a ranch west of town. The Zimmermans always handled cattle and horses. Max told me that the country around Molt where he run his horses was settling up and he wanted to sell all his horses that run in that country. He said if I would take them all he would make me a good deal. He said that he had gathered most of them and was holding them in the Cove pasture which was about twelve miles from Billings.

He had "Red" Dick Rains gathering them in. Red had just got in with a bunch when we went to look them over. There was about fifty head. Max wanted a thousand dollars for the lot. It was plenty cheap enough for them but there was some yearlings and colts in the bunch. I told Max I was buying them to sell and the farmers wanted to use them right away. Max saw my point and wanted to clean them out.

He was a man that liked to see bucking horses so he made me a proposition. He said I could have the bunch for seven hundred and fifty dollars if I would ride them all. We shook hands and it was a deal.

Max went to town to get the stock inspector to inspect them. When he came back he'd brought Bill Shirrian, another rider, two gallons of moonshine and a case of home brew beer. He said, as he didn't get much cash out of the deal, he wanted to get some fun. It was all right with me as some of those horses was pretty wild and rollicky. A little handling would cool them off.

After the inspection we started riding them. There was one wild mare in the bunch, probably eight or nine years old, and she was plenty wild and salty. The corral that we was riding in was a big old corral made partly of logs and wire, probably contained two acres. We couldn't get close enough to the mare to catch her in the corral and we was afraid that if we crowded her too close she would jump out and break the corral down.

We figured that we would leave her for the last ride. There was no one liked her looks so we drawed straws to see who would ride her. Red Rains was the unlucky guy. Red was a pretty salty bronc stomper. At that time, he would take a chance on any old ridge runner.

These horses was all range horses and had never been handled, no more than just branded. We would rope them by the front feet, throw them down, put a rope in the cinch of the saddle, throw it over their head and pull it under their belly and cinch it. Then we'd get on and ride them up. Sometimes we would just pull a rope around them and ride them without a saddle.

About two o'clock we had them all rode except the big blue ridge-running mare. We was all tired and thought we'd better have a rest and something to eat before we tackled her.

There was a big log house there that Max used for a cow camp. There was a phonograph in the house and plenty of chuck to cook. Max made some baking powder biscuits. I boiled some spuds with the skins on, fried some bacon and made some cow gravy and a pot of coffee. When we got that into us and a mixture of home brew and moonshine, someone started the music box. When it wasn't going, the boys was sure riding horses and joshing Red about the blue mare.

All at once someone seen the horses get out. We made a rush for the door, sure enough old Blue was in the lead making tracks. There was about four sections in the pasture and we didn't want them to scatter in it.

Max, Red Rains and I made a run for our saddle horses. We knew they was going to be hard to corral. We finally got around them and headed them in the right direction, when old Blue had a different notion.

Red went to turn them. He was riding a good filly chaser and was sailing down a long, sloping hill that was covered with those big flat cactus with thorns about two inches long. Red was really cutting the breeze when his horse fell head over heels. Red rolled about forty feet through the cactus.

The fall knocked the wind out of Red and he was kicking around trying to get some gas. Finally he got a little air and got on his feet. He was the funniest looking human I ever saw. His head looked like a porcupine. He had a million cactus in him. One was stuck right through his nose, a handful in his cheeks and his red hair looked like it was turning white.

Oh, what a mess! Max and I started pulling cactus out of Red. Every time we would pull out a cactus thorn a big drop of blood would follow it out and Red would holler. We finally got him down to the house and got his clothes off and got most of them out. Max told me that they pulled cactus out of Red for two weeks as there was a lot of them went in and broke off.

We was too busy taking care of Red to pay any more attention to the horses. Next morning I gathered them to take on to Rapelje. The blue mare had got out and gone. Several years afterwards I got her back in the horse roundup over in the Bull Mountains. I sold her to Leo Cramer for a bucker. He called her Calamity Jane.

I HELPED Johnny Conway take some horses into Billings. After we had put the horses in the stockyards, I stopped into Yegen's Store to buy a pair of overalls. One of the clerks told me that Pete Yegen wanted to see me.

That was a long time ago and Yegen's was the only big store in town. It was a store that any town could be proud of. They handled groceries, clothing and hardware. Their bank was in the west end of the store. They also bought and sold horses. The old store building don't look so big now but it sure looked big at that time. You could buy anything from a paper of pins to a freight wagon.

Yegen's warehouse was just across the street. You could always see several freight teams loading merchandise for the surrounding country as the Northern Pacific was the only railroad for miles.

When I went to the office, Mr. Yegen told me that sixteen of his work horses had got out of a pasture and strayed away. He said he'd heard of them on the reservation but the man he'd sent after them couldn't find them. Mr. Yegen said that the horses was all gentle broke stuff. He said he would pay me $5.00 a head if I would find them and deliver them at Billings. I told him I would try and find them.

It was in the fall of the year. The Antler cow outfit was just starting the roundup wagon to gather beef cattle. I heard some of the boys was in town celebrating so I went to the Owl Saloon to inquire if any of them had seen a gentle bunch of horses. They was having too good a time to remember anything about horses.

I met Johnny Bunko who was at that time working for Bill Cashen on the reservation. Bunko said he'd seen a bunch of horses on the East Fork of Pryor Creek a few days before. He said he hadn't paid much attention to them as that country was lousy with horses. He knew they wasn't wild horses because he had rode past them and they never run.

I stayed in town that night and went with the Antler cowboys to the roundup wagon that was camped on Pryor Creek. We got to the wagon about three o'clock. Nobody worked that evening, just set around and swapped stories.

They was joshing a new rider called Joe. In the Antler cavvy was a buckskin horse that they always put in a new rider's string, to job him. The buckskin was a real hard horse to ride and generally throwed his man. The buckskin had just bucked Joe off. Don't think a bunch of cow hands can't razz a plenty.

We was just eating supper when a young fellow rode up to the wagon and got off his horse. The cook poured him a cup of coffee, handed him a tin plate and told him to help himself. No one seemed to know him.

He was riding a good looking bay horse and had a good saddle. He looked like he was about twenty-five, about five foot nine, slim built and would weigh about a hundred and fifty pounds. He had a Scotch cap on, overalls and a canvas coat tied on the back of his saddle. On his feet he had one good looking boot and an old shoe. He was lame and limped pretty bad.

After supper the foreman asked him if he wanted a job. He said no, that he had mashed his foot and wasn't in any shape to do any hard range riding. He stayed all night.

In the morning the horse wrangler fetched in the saddle horses and put them in the rope corral. Someone said, "Catch the buckskin for Joe. Let's have another show."

It made Joe sore. He had had enough roasting. He said, "I'll ride him later but I don't feel so good this morning. I've got ten dollars that says there ain't a rooster in this bunch that can cowboy that horse."

They had about all been bucked off that buckskin and no one seemed to want that ten. The lame stranger spoke out, "I ain't got ten dollars but I'll bet you my saddle against ten dollars that I can uncork that yellow horse."

Joe said, "Fellow, you are crippled up pretty bad. I don't want to steal your money. It takes a man with two feet to ride that baby."

"Don't worry about my flat wheel," answered the stranger. "My saddle is worth forty dollars, that's a four to one bet or are you afraid you'll lose your money?"

"Not a damn bit," Joe answered, "only I hate to set you afoot, being lame, but if you want to lose your saddle, okay by me." Joe handed a ten dollar bill to the foreman.

They caught Buck and saddled him up. The only thing the stranger said was, "Someone ear down this old pony for it's hard for me to get on."

The foreman said, "All right, I'll ear him down. Let's get it over. We have a roundup to make."

Believe me, that buckskin horse was a real stem winder! He sure done his stuff. You could see after about four jumps that old Buck had nothing on that rider. He was on there to stay on top. Finally, Buck gave it up and trotted off. The stranger turned back to the rope corral, stepped off Buck and saddled his own horse. The foreman handed him the ten dollar bill.

He got on his horse, said, "So long. Thanks for everything."

As far as I know he was never heard of in this part of the country since then. He sure was a rider!

I'd seen a good show and went on over to East Fork that morning. I found the bunch of Yegen horses right where Bunko told me he had seen them. I delivered them to Pete Yegen that evening.

BULL MOUNTAINS used to be a big horse country. Until a few years ago, there was thousands of horses ranging in that country from the breaks of the Yellowstone to the Missouri River breaks. It was a big open country. You could ride for miles and miles and never see a wire fence. There was wild horses in that country before it was settled. Nobody seems to know where they came from.

Fifty to sixty years ago there was several big horse outfits that run their horses in that country. One of the big horse outfits was owned by the Ryan Brothers that branded the **R L**. John Chandler run lots of horses. There was an old-timer that had a ranch on Pease Bottom run horses there, I have forgotten his name. There was the **F U F** and many others. I ain't trying to give the history of Bull Mountains. I just want to tell of one of the wildest rides I ever saw that took place in that country.

It happened at the old **C A** pasture which was over forty miles north of Billings about thirty-five years ago. A bunch of the horsemen and cowboys got together and promoted a bucking horse contest. It was a long way from a town but there was a lot of people went to those contests for they was the real McCoy.

They didn't have any chutes to saddle in and they rode them right out in the big open space. They had judges but no one to pull the rider off and drop them in a pile of rocks or cactus. They figured if the cowboy could ride his horse he could get off alone.

There was no ten second whistle, they cowboyed them from start to finish. It was a real western old time exhibition where you could see cowboys riding in the rough.

I was running a bunch of cattle over in that country at the time of that particular ride. Horse Thief Smithie came by my spread and we went over to the **C A** together.

The riders that had gathered the bucking horses the day before was having quite a pow wow about an old outlaw, ridge running mare that was almost impossible to corral. Whenever she saw a man riding, she would take down some ridge and try her damnedest to get away. She had got in the bucking horse herd and they'd had an awful time getting the horses in the **C A** pasture. They hadn't corralled them for their saddle horses was about all in when they got to the pasture. They knew that they would have plenty help the next day as lots of the boys would come on horseback.

They was all mad at that old ridge runner and had drew straws to see who would ride her. A rider that hailed from the Powder River country, that had the moniker of Powder River Bob drew her. He had worked for the **R L** outfit when they was gathering their horses for the last clean-up.

Powder River said, "I just got a new saddle. I ain't going to put it on that old she devil. I'm afraid of losing it."

They decided that they would just tie a rope around her equator and Powder River would ride her Indian fashion. Don't think for a minute them Bull Mountain boys wasn't plenty salty. Anyone of them, had they drawed that old catamount would never have backed out, just took his chance.

There was about twenty hands went out to corral the bucking horses. They all knew that old ridge running mare would try to get away. She tried, but there was too many riders so she came with the bunch until they started into the corral.

Several of the boys had their ropes down, tied hard and fast expecting that old girl to stampede. All at once, here she came between Jim Steele and Jimmy Bryant. She couldn't have picked a worse place for both of them was top ropers.

She was a brown mare that weighed about eleven hundred pounds with a heavy long mane and long tail full of cockle burrs. Jim Steele got her by the front feet and she was down kicking and bawling. Someone got on her head and hollered for Powder River.

They tied a rope around her middle. They thought they'd better get the rope off her feet to avoid an accident. As soon as they released her feet, that old lady was flopping around trying to get up. Powder River saw that she was about to get loose. He made a run at her, grabbing at the rope, missed but got one hand in the mane.

That old mare was sure scared. She must have thought a mountain lion was on her back. Her eyes was plumb green. She let out the loudest snort I ever heard come out of a horse and started to buck.

That cowboy was grabbing at her with his spurs every jump to stay on. That old mare was scared crazy. At one time he was getting awful high and looked like he was a goner. He had a dead grip on that long tangled mane, his feet sticking straight up in the air. He was plenty forked for when she came down he still had her between his legs.

I wish I had the ability to describe that old ridge runner's action. She sure was a wampus cat and believe me, Powder River was making a salty ride.

The dust was flying. Her long tail, full of cockle burrs, big around as a bushel basket, was going up and down like a pump handle. She was sure trying to get rid of that thing on her back, tearing at her with its claws.

As crooked as she was bucking it didn't look like it was possible for her to hold her feet. Her mouth was wide open. She was bawling and kicking.

Finally she lost her feet and came down on her side. Powder River just managed to jump clear. That old mare never quit when she hit the ground. She just kept scrambling around, regained her feet and lit out a-running. My God, how she did go! I don't see how Powder River ever rode her.

I THINK Pete Cooper was the strongest man I ever knew. He was about six feet tall, slim built except he wasn't narrow hipped. He lived on the Cooper bottom between Brockway Coulee and the mouth of Blue Creek on the south side of the Yellowstone River, about eight miles from town. He was a half breed Indian. His father was a white man and I believe his mother was a full blooded Sioux Indian.

Pete raised a lot of wild hay and used to haul it into Billings and sell it to the livery stables as it was choice blue stem hay.

I'll never forget the time I saw how strong Pete really was. He was going into town with a load of hay. He had broke the reach of the wagon and pulled the front wheels out from under the hay rack.

I was going into town on horseback and stopped to see if I could help him. We talked the situation over and I told him I thought he would have to unload the hay to get the wheels back under the rack.

He thought that was too much work. He said he believed he could lift the load up if I could help him get it up on his shoulder. Then he would hold the load up while I rolled the front wheels back under the wagon so he could chain the reach together.

We got the rack up on his shoulder with Pete doing most of the lifting. When he got it on his shoulder the weight and the 2x4 cross piece which was setting on Pete's shoulder was hurting his shoulder.

He said if I would take his hat, which was an old floppy felt, and put it on his shoulder he could hold the load up while I rolled the wheels under it.

He lifted that whole front end of the wagon which had a ton or a ton and a half on it. I put the hat on his shoulder and he let the load down on it. He held that load while I pushed the front wheels back under and put the bolster in place so he could chain the reach together.

It took quite a while to get the front wheels under the wagon as Pete was holding the hay rack on the front end and I had to put the wheels in from the side and then turn the tongue around and place the bolster in the right position.

Pete never said a word all the time I was maneuvering the wheels. He was cross eyed and near sighted. The only sign of strain I saw was in Pete's eyes, they was bugging out.

When the hay rack settled back in place his eyes went back to normal. He hunched his shoulder a few times, straightened out his hat and put it on his head, then crawled under the wagon to chain the reach.

One time in the Montana Show House on Minnesota Avenue, Pete's strength got him in trouble.

In the Montana Show House fastened against the wall was a contraption to register how hard a fellow could hit it. It worked like a weighing machine. You just put a nickel in a slot and when you hit the leather pad the machine showed the number of pounds.

Pete and me was watching several fellows hitting the thing and they all seemed to be pretty good. I told Pete I'd put a nickel in and for him to show them up.

Pete grinned. I put the nickel in. He squared off and looked at it. He swung his arm around his head twice to kind of loosen up. Then he hit at that contraption with all he had.

Being near sighted and cross eyed, Pete didn't hit where he aimed. He missed the leather pad and hit the wall. The blow shook the building and Pete too. It broke his arm. We never did find out how hard he could hit for he always shied away from the machine after he swelled up.

WINTER USED to be a kind of a slow dismal time for the cowboys. Mostly cold hard work with little amusement to break up the monotony except poker games after the day's work was done. Most of the games was penny ante for cowboys seldom have much money. Of course I've seen some mighty big games in town when the sky was the limit but the most peculiar poker game I ever knowed about, the loser got the pot.

Now this poker game took place within a good hard day's ride from Billings. It had been a pretty stormy cold winter and the boys had had to stay pretty much on their home range to look after the cattle and hadn't got to town to let off steam. Except for a few kitchen sweats (kitchen dances) at some of the neighboring ranches, life was pretty tame for a while.

There was a family that lived in an out of the way place that was sort of unknown until one of the daughters named Nell, a girl of sixteen or seventeen, showed up at one of the dances. Their name might have been Smith or Jones but I will call them Doe. From that time on, theirs was a pretty popular place to the cowboys. They didn't seem to realize they was fooling around with penitentiary bait.

There was almost always a horse tied up at their gate. Nell never lacked for an escort for a horseback ride or a dance. She seemed to like them all. It didn't seem to make any difference to her who she went with, old or young, as long as he wore cowboy boots and a big hat.

Things went along that way for quite a spell and there was talk of her popularity, as there is bound to be, among the good ladies of the ranches with plainer looking and less popular daughters. The gossip must have reached the ears of old man Doe. He took a searching look at Nell's thickening figure, loaded up his old shotgun and headed for the cow camp.

The old man was a little slow in the head but once he got an idea he hung on to it. By the time he reached the cow camp he was in a hostile mood. He didn't say too much but he made it awfully plain that if the guilty party didn't do well by his Nell within a week he was going to take the first son of a bitch he seen and use his shotgun if he didn't marry the girl. He said he didn't care who he was either.

In the bunk house that night, so I heard, there was a big pow wow. Every one of them maintained he was innocent but they all agreed no man was safe from the law or the old man's shotgun until somebody married Nell and made an honest woman out of her.

They decided that since Nell never played any favorites they'd be square with her. They wrangled around trying to find an easy way out and finally decided to do it playing "freeze out poker," the loser marrying the girl.

There was four or five in the game. They took a box of matches to use as chips and they started to play. This was a game for blood and they played as they'd never played before. The game lasted all night and part of the next day. Finally one of the boys lost his last match. They all jumped up and shook his hand, congratulated him and promised they'd chip in on a wedding present.

It is doubtful if he was the guilty man as he was a little dried up cowboy, probably pushing sixty, but for all of that a right honorable man that paid his gambling debts in full.

He scarcely looked like a happy bridegroom as he saddled up and shagged off in the direction of the Doe's.

5: Mrs. Huntington

I MET Ella Daylong in Douglas, Wyoming, in 1891. She was working in a restaurant there. Her folks was camped down by the river. They had come from Missouri in a covered wagon. She was about sixteen, a very pretty girl about five feet two. She had beautiful brown curly hair that she wore in braids. Her cheeks was red and her blue eyes never missed seeing anything. She had a very kind, sunny disposition. I fell for her the first time I saw her.

I was just a rambling cowboy that had blowed in from the Lander country. I was only in Douglas about three months, then left for Montana. I didn't meet Ella again for over a year, then I met her again in Billings, Montana. We renewed our acquaintance and was married the following July 31, 1899, at Judge Frazier's home. She was eighteen, I was twenty-three.

I was breaking horses for W.B. Osten. Just before we was married, I had taken up a squatter's claim nine miles south of Billings. Neither of us was loaded with money.

I had been just a foot-loose and fancy-free cowboy and always thought if I was ever foolish enough to get married I'd like to go to Niagara Falls on my honeymoon. When I told Ella about Niagara Falls she said she'd rather settle for a hunting trip in the Bull Mountains (50 miles north of Billings).

However, when we got married, got our grub stake and a few necessities to start housekeeping I only had $1.35 in cash so had to postpone the thoughts of a honeymoon until later.

On the third of October we decided to take a deer hunt in the Bull Mountains as our honeymoon trip. Ella had her own horse, Indian, when we was married. He was a very nice gentle brown horse. She had traded a gold watch and five dollars to some Indians for him. I also had a horse I had bought from the Indians named Plenty Coups, but he wasn't gentle. He wasn't too mean but had a habit of trying to buck off his rider whenever the opportunity afforded. I had another bronc that I had just halter broke and rode a couple of times. I thought it would be a good time to gentle him as we had to have a packhorse to take our bed, tent and some groceries and fetch the game back if we got any.

We got all ready the evening before. We took some flour and baking powder, salt and pepper, some spuds, coffee and a side of bacon for grease, and a few cooking utensils. We put everything possible in sacks so if the pack got bucked off it wouldn't spoil our groceries.

We had quite a time next morning getting the stuff all packed on the horse and throwing a diamond hitch over the top. That old pony had to stand still as we had him tied to a big cottonwood tree with a blindfold over his eyes. He was just standing there trembling. We both knew he was going to explode as soon as we untied him and pulled the blind off.

After getting all set I untied the packhorse and got on my own bronc. I told Ella to jerk the blind off and get behind the tree and watch the show, when he got through trying to buck the pack off he'd be okay and we would get started.

I tied the packhorse's lead rope hard and fast around my saddle horn for I didn't want that cayuse to get away with our camp outfit. She pulled the blind and when that horse saw that pack setting on his back he just let a bawl out of him and went plumb nuts, bucking and bawling.

The horse I was riding, always looking for a chance to blow up, turned on all he had. I didn't get much pleasure out of the deal. I was too busy trying to stay on top. It took a little while but we finally got started.

The pack was riding pretty good but the bucking had loosened it up some. I figured it would stay for a few miles. We went about five miles and I knew we would have to stop and tighten up. We blindfolded him and fixed the pack. When I reached over and pulled off the blindfold we had another show but it didn't last so long.

We had to travel slow on account of the packhorse. We made Twenty Mile about three o'clock. On the flat we saw a bunch of sage hens. Ella rode over and shot two of them for our supper. It had started to snow and we never stopped for dinner as we wanted to get to the other side of Twenty Mile to camp at a spring where a trail led up on the mountain where there was a lot of deer.

Just before we got to the place we planned on camping we saw three deer standing on a little ridge about forty yards from us. We both started to get our rifles out. She jumped off her horse and shot. My horse was a little nervous and I had just got my rifle out of the scabbard when I saw the deer drop. It scared the packhorse and he began to try and get away. She shot again, there was another explosion. It was my two horses.

I had my gun in my hand and I don't know just what happened but it was plenty. The first thing I knew I was laying in a bunch of rock. The two horses was sailing down the coulee. I had my thumb out of place, my face was all scratched up and one eye was all black and my leg felt like it was broke.

As the horses ran down the coulee they connected with a pine tree, one on each side of it, knocking them both down. They both had enough and didn't want to go anywhere.

When Ella had shot the first time, it had knocked the deer down but it had jumped up and started to run. The second shot got him. She had hit him in the head just back of the horns. He was a large four point buck. We made camp, bled the buck and hung him in a tree.

We was plenty hungry after riding all day. Ella built a campfire and got supper. I wasn't feeling so hot. I have had some good meals in the course of my eighty years but I never had a meal that I enjoyed as much as I did that one. She made some baking powder biscuits in the Dutch oven, cooked one of the sage hens with some spuds cut in quarters nice and brown and a pot of coffee. It was fit for a king.

The next morning it was still snowing, a cold wet snow and the wind was blowing cold from the northwest. The packhorse stood out on the side hill with his lip hanging down and his neck twisted about forty degrees to the south. I don't know which one of us felt worse, me or that packhorse. After looking at the weather and the horses we decided to layover until the next day.

We was having a wonderful honeymoon. She put some water on the campfire so I could soak my thumb which was giving me a lot of grief. My eye was swelled shut and black as the inside of a stove pipe. My leg was so sore I could hardly step on it.

It cleared up in the night. The sun come over the mountain, looking like it was pure gold and about three times its normal size. There was two bunches of deer standing about fifty yards from our camp taking a gander at us but we had all the meat we could handle.

I went and drug the packhorse up between two trees and tied him up. He looked and acted pretty docile but I didn't feel like taking any chances. We got our camp outfit all ready to go and was ready to load the deer when we got in an argument. It was the first one we'd ever had.

I was going to cut the deer's head off as it was going to be hard to pack. She thought I had ought to leave the head on as the antlers was so pretty and it was the first deer she had ever killed. She said she'd killed wild turkeys, all kinds of wild chickens, bobcats, skunks and antelope. She won. I left the head on but it was hard to pack. We put all the camp equipment except the tent on the horse, then the deer with the tent over it all so it wouldn't show or smell, as most horses are scared of the smell of blood.

We made a brave start and got down the coulee about a quarter of a mile. We saw some "fool hens" (old term for any type of grouse) setting on a dry limb of a big pine tree. We stopped and looked them over. Ella decided that one would go good for dinner. I agreed but told her to wait to shoot one until I got down to the mouth of the coulee as I couldn't stand getting unloaded any more on one trip. She got the fool hen.

After getting down to the trail that run from Roundup to Billings we had good sailing. South of Twenty Mile we saw a lot of antelope. There must have been a hundred and fifty in one bunch, passed three bands of sheep and lots of wild horses. We camped at Twelve Mile to have some fool hen and coffee and give the packhorse a rest.

We had unpacked and was eating when a cowboy by the name of Tex came by and stopped and had dinner with us. When I introduced my wife to him he gave us both a good look over but never said anything about my beat up looks. He helped me pack the horse. I was just able to mount and as I was starting off, Tex said, "Bill, it looks like you sort of over-matched yourself." He grinned and started to ride away.

I was saying a few low words to Plenty Coups who was raring to go. I was kind of holding him up. He swung around and got the lead rope under his tail. He just naturally exploded and blew the cork out. He was swapping ends like an acrobat turning back-somersaults. I was trying to hold his head up and hit my sore thumb on the fork of the saddle. I saw I was slipping and rared back. The cantle of the saddle hit my suitcase and away I went into a sage brush about ten feet away. I wasn't hurt much as I lit on my head.

Tex and Ella had a good laugh at my expense, then Tex caught my horse. I took him on again but he had his buck out and we made it home without further incident.

As far as I was concerned, our honeymoon didn't go just the way we planned. I didn't mind so much getting bucked off but I knew that Tex would tell everybody he met that it looked as if Bill's wife had worked him over. It was a rugged honeymoon but we never forgot any part of it.

Another time, in the latter part of November there came a light snow so we thought we would go up in the Pryor

Mountains deer hunting. We went on horseback, taking a packhorse to fetch a deer back.

We had an old horse to carry the pack that I had traded for. We called him Porcupine as the hair on his back stuck straight up. He had short ears and was a freaky looking piece of horse flesh, lazy as sin. The only good feature he had as near as I could figure, was that he lead good. He must have been a Texas or Mexican horse as he had several brands on him that no one could read except maybe a Texan or a Mexican. He was so lazy and gentle we didn't think he would ever get scared or excited at anything.

When we got on the mountain there was quite a lot more snow and it was pretty cold. We saw lots of deer tracks but hadn't seen a deer that day. We built a campfire and warmed up. Then we staked our horses, rolled our bed in a place where I had scraped away the snow, had a snowball fight, cooked our supper and went to bed.

We had camped about a hundred yards from a spring on a level place close to a quaking asp grove. There was lots of pine timber on the mountain and I gathered a lot of wood to build a fire if we got cold.

Along in the night I woke up shivering. I nudged Ella and asked if she was cold. She said she was half frozen so I got up and built a fire. We both warmed up and went back to bed. We saw the reason we had got cold. The wind had blowed the tarp up and it had snowed on the bed.

We got up at daylight. As I was feeding the horses, I saw old Porcupine looking over at the quaking asp grove. I looked too, there was three deer just coming out of the quaking asps.

We had put the guns under the head of the bed in order to keep them dry. Ella was close to the bed and I told her to get the guns out as there was three deer. She saw them, hauled out the .30-30, took a quick shot and knocked a nice buck down. He floundered around, got up and run around the quaking asp grove where she couldn't see him.

Old Porcupine let the loudest snort out of him I ever heard. The old devil seemed scared to death. He was prancing around like a wild horse. You wouldn't have thought he had a lazy hair in his old hide. He had gone plumb crazy and I was afraid he would break his rope and get away.

I run over to quiet him down while Ella started around the quaking asp patch to see if she could get another shot at the deer. She came right back and said for me to take a knife and cut its throat as it was laying about fifty yards from where she had shot it. I went around and found it, cut its throat to bleed it, and dressed it while she got breakfast.

Old Porky must have smelled the blood for he was still snorting and trying to get away. He was sure having a hydrophobia fit, crazy as a loon.

We saddled up our horses and tied the blankets behind our saddles and put the packsaddle on old Porcupine. We put one heavy quilt on the packsaddle and left the tarp to tie over the buck so Porcupine wouldn't smell the blood. I was going to cut the head off the deer and leave it but again Ella wanted to save the head as it had such a pretty pair of horns. I left them on.

When we went to load the buck we couldn't get old Porcupine nowhere close to the deer so we blindfolded him and drug the deer up close to him but he was tearing around so we couldn't get it upon him. After working around a long time I finally threw him and tied him down. We put the deer on the packsaddle but had to let the horse up to get it tied good so it wouldn't slip. I knew whenever we pulled the blindfold off that old fool horse was sure going to blow up.

He was tired from being tied down. I let him up but tied his feet together so he couldn't tear around until I had the deer tied good. I put a squaw hitch on and pulled just as tight as we could to draw it up 'til it seemed like we would cut him in two. I knew there was a lot of give in the deer and it would loosen up.

When we got all ready I tied Porcupine hard and fast to my saddle horn. I got on my horse and told Ella to untie his feet, pull off the blindfold and get out of the way.

He had rested up and when she pulled the blindfold off and he could see, the pack business picked up. He went to bucking and bawling, making as much noise as a mad Texas steer. He bucked around me about three times. I was pretty busy keeping out of his way but I did see Ella having a good laugh.

My horse was scared, all at once they both hit the rope at the same time and busted the halter. Porcupine went down the side of the mountain with his mouth open bawling. He quit bucking and began to run. He lost his feet and turned over in the air and fell on his side.

He layed so still I thought he had broken his back. I rode up to him and jumped off to see if he was dead. He began to come out of it as he'd just had the wind knocked out of him. When he fell he had broken off one of the deer's horns.

I got my rope around his neck, tied it so Ella could hold him on one side, me on the other. He finally gave up and we got home just as the sun was going down.

DONOVAN & McCORMICK that run the first General Merchandise Store in Billings had a large wood yard and sold cedar posts and wood. At that time, everyone used wood or coal for fuel. I was living on Basin Creek where I had taken up a claim. There was quite a lot of cedar posts in the breaks and hills south of the Yellowstone River.

I had got out a load of posts for Donovan & McCormick. On my way into town I met Charlie Spear who used to run the Billings State Bank. Mr. Spear wanted me to fetch him a load of pitch pine, split up fine, to use for kindling.

I had a large wood pile at the ranch for winter. I fixed him up a nice load on the wagon. I was all hitched up and ready to

MRS. HUNTINGTON

start to town when a bunch of grouse lit in a cottonwood tree close to our cabin.

I hollered for my wife to fetch her gun and kill a grouse. We hadn't been married very long and didn't have any ice house to store anything and in the summer fresh meat was really a treat.

My team was gentle but kind of nervous. They was standing half asleep and I had the lines wrapped around the brake lever. I never thought they would try to run away.

She came out of the cabin with her .22 rifle. I pointed to the tree. I stood there like a stump beside the wagon with my mouth open watching her as I was proud of her shooting and hoped she wouldn't miss.

Crack went the rifle, down came a grouse and away went the horses with the load of wood flying in the air. That team was sure fanning the breeze. It was pretty rough country and it looked like there was a steady stream of that wood in the air.

"Run away."

They run up the creek a couple hundred yards making about 2.40 (old racetrack record) with the wood wagon. They crossed a coulee and started up on the other side. They hit a sideling (angled sideways) place, the wagon turned over with a big crash and as it rolled over the king bolt came out of the reach. The team was just flying with just the front wheels hitting the ground once in a while.

One horse was faster than the other one so they was running in a circle. After passing us a couple of times they began to slow down. When they finally run down I was able to catch them.

Oh, what a mess. The wagon box was all tore up and wood scattered all over the country. It took me all day to fix the wagon box and gather up the wood.

Anyway, we had meat for supper.

I HAVE HAD a lot of rough, tough rides in my time. In the early days they called me Basin Creek Bill the Bull Rider. I have rode a lot of rough horses, mules and bulls. One time I rode a bull buffalo at Columbia Gardens at Butte, Montana. But through all those tough rides I never had one to compare with a ride my wife gave me not too long after we was married.

I can't possibly explain how tough it was or how much I suffered. It was horrible and I can't understand how I ever survived it. I must have been tough in those days or it would have killed me.

We lived on Basin Creek about nine miles south of Billings. It had been nice weather right up to Christmas, then we had a three day rain that soaked the ground so it was good and muddy. There was a bunch of cattle went over the road and then it got cold and froze up. The country roads wasn't any too good in those early days and after they froze up it was horribly rough, especially if you was riding in a lumber wagon.

It was the day before New Year's in 1899. I had to go to town and was going in the lumber wagon. My wife went with

MRS. HUNTINGTON

me as she wanted to visit a lady friend that was sick, who lived at the edge of town. I told my wife to leave me in town and she could have the team to drive and to pick me up about four o'clock. I was to be watching for her in front of the Blue Grass Saloon.

It being New Year's Eve there was a lot of my friends celebrating. I never figured on getting jagged but we was having a rip roaring good time and I got too many under my belt. Consequently, I got paralyzed drunk.

My wife's two brothers was celebrating too, but used a little better judgment and was able to navigate. They watched to see her come and told her that I wasn't able to go home as I had a wonderful jag on and couldn't walk. They told her they would stay with me and put me to bed as soon as I was able to move.

She was plenty peeved. She didn't like drinking and she didn't like to see anyone drunk. She blowed up and told the boys that she would drive down the alley and for them to drag me out and throw me in the wagon and she would take me home where I belonged.

They done just that, and we was on our way home. It wasn't so bad until we got out of town. In the road where the cattle had made all the tracks it was really hell. I never suffered anything like it in my life, laying there in that wagon bed. She was really traveling. The rougher the road, the faster she drove. I was bouncing around in that wagon box like a gunny sack.

I was trying to get up. I would get about half way up, then the wagon would hit an extra big bump and down I would go. I was hollering, "Slow down for God's sake, you're killing me!"

She never paid any attention to me, just hit the horses another crack.

I got hold of the side of the wagon box and was just about to gain my feet. I fell and cracked myself on the bridge of the nose on the edge of the wagon box. I think that time I passed out. When I came out of that I tried it again and took a header, hitting my head on the floor boards and just gave up. I was hurting all over, I thought my time had come. After nine miles of that you can imagine about how I looked.

When we got home she unhitched the team, went in the house and built a fire. I tried to get up but no dice. I was bunged up so bad I just couldn't make it. She finally came out, took hold of my leg, give it a jerk and I fell in the yard. She drug me into the house and managed to get me on the bed. I was afraid to say a word. I thought that she might finish me up with a club. I just passed out.

When I came to, she was getting breakfast. She came over to the bed, gave me the once-over with her eyes and sat down on a chair and began to laugh.

I wasn't feeling exactly in a laughing mood and stood it as long as I could, then I asked her what the devil she was laughing at.

She never answered me, just walked over and got the looking glass and held it up in front of me.

I had two of the blackest eyes I ever saw. One ear had some dried blood on it. The side of my face was all scratched up and there was a couple of lumps on my head as big as hen eggs. My hair was standing on end. I was an unholy sight and my neck was so sore I couldn't turn my head. I told her that was bad enough but my back was paining me so bad I thought I must have some vertebras out of place and I would probably be crippled for life if I didn't die.

I think that worried her a little for she went and got the liniment bottle and rubbed my back. She said, "Your back is straight and okay. You just bruised it." She slapped me on the rump with her hand and said, "You are all right. I don't care if you take a drink or two, but I want you to make me a promise and keep it. When I go to town with you I don't want you to get drunk and disgrace me."

I promised for I knew I couldn't take her treatment for drunks. We lived together almost forty-nine years. She never had to take me home again or never saw me again when I couldn't navigate under my own power.

MRS. HUNTINGTON

IT WAS IN October in 1900 I hauled a load of freight from Billings to Lewistown. I had a six-horse team pulling two wagons that was loaded with fanning machines used to blow away the chaff from grain. The weather was good and though we had a baby about four months old my wife wanted to go with me. She figured the freight wagon was too rough for the baby so she drove along with a single buggy.

She took her .22 rifle along to kill grouse and sage hens for us to eat on the way. She was a very good shot and hardly ever missed. She always shot them in the head so as not to mess up the meat.

We went by Flat Willow Creek and through the Judith Gap as that was the best road. It took us five days to get there. The weather was fine except for two windy days.

Lewistown at that time was an inland town and wasn't very big, probably five hundred people lived there. We had good luck on the road and had a lot of fun as my wife was a western raised girl and loved the outdoor life.

We got in Lewistown about two o'clock in the afternoon. I unloaded my freight and camped that night near the brewery. We decided that we would come back over the mountains as it was closer. We planned to camp there one day and see if we could get a deer as there was lots of them in the mountains.

We got an early start as we wanted to get on the mountains to a nice camping place known as the Box Springs where there was lots of deer.

Coming along the road we passed by a field of oats all shocked. I thought they would be pretty nice to feed the horses that night and I wouldn't have to turn them loose to graze. I got over the fence and appropriated a shock.

We got to Box Springs late in the afternoon, stretched the tent, put up the sheet iron stove and built a fire, for it was kind of cold for the baby. It looked like snow.

It snowed about two inches that night. I told my wife it was a dandy day to get a deer and took my .30-30 and started out. I hadn't gone over a quarter of a mile when I saw three deer but didn't get a shot at them as they was too far away. There was deer tracks everywhere and I thought I would surely get one. I walked 'til about noon and no luck so started back for camp, tired and hungry.

My wife asked me if I got a deer. I told her no, that I had just had a long walk for nothing. "Well," she said "I got one."

I was surprised as I knew she couldn't leave the baby to get out and hunt. I wanted to know where it was. She pointed to a tree right near camp and sure enough, there hung a nice three point buck. She said she had noticed the horses looking over that way and looked to see what had caught their attention. There stood the deer. She had got her .22 and killed it. While the baby slept, she bled it, dressed it, pulled it up in a tree and there it hung, ready to go in the wagon.

When I was paid for hauling the freight it came to a little over a hundred dollars which I put in my billfold and put the billfold in my inside coat pocket. We was feeling pretty good about the deer, when for some reason I felt for my billfold. It was gone! We began to figure where I could have lost it.

When we left Lewistown we had crossed a creek. I had stopped to let the horses drink. The wheel team was checked up so I had walked on the wagon tongue and unchecked them. I might have lost it there. If I had, the water was swift and it would have floated away. On the other hand I might have lost it when I crawled through the fence after the oats.

We talked about going back and hunting for it but it clouded up and snowed again, about four more inches. We decided it was just too bad but there wasn't any use trying to find that billfold. My wife always felt that those free oats cost us plenty. But it was a good trip, even if it didn't pay off.

I HAVE SEEN some awfully good shots in my time but I never saw any person I thought could beat my wife shooting a rifle. I don't mean trick shooting—I mean good, straight, off-hand shooting at any kind of a target. I don't think that anybody would say I am bragging if they had seen her shoot.

She was a wonderful homemaker, whether home was in a camp under a cottonwood tree or in a house, and made everyone welcome. She was never too busy or too tired to cook a meal for a hungry person. She could nurse the sick and many a time helped sew up a wire-cut man or horse.

She was a true pioneer. She came to Montana from Missouri in a covered wagon when she was about eleven or twelve. Her father didn't stay long that first trip but headed back for Missouri. Two years later they made the long, slow trip again. They only had one team and wagon, so was heavy loaded. My wife, her two older brothers and her father walked most of the time to save the team all they could.

They had a .38 Winchester rifle and a reloading outfit so it didn't cost so much for ammunition. They depended on that rifle for meat as they traveled.

They took turns carrying the gun. Anyone of them that didn't shoot a grouse or sage hen in the head lost the gun to the next one. She said she used to miss on purpose so she wouldn't have to carry the gun. Her father and two brothers was wonderful rifle shots too.

She was a good rider and knew cows as few cowboys do, a fairly good roper, she could catch her own horses. She did a half hitching stunt in our shows. She would catch me around the neck, then half hitch both my arms, then I would jump up and she would half hitch my feet. When she had me all tied up she would jerk me over and there I was until someone untied me.

She never rode bucking horses. I remember one time on the show, one of the cowgirl bucking horse riders asked her why she didn't ride bucking horses as she could do everything else. My wife looked the girl right in the eye and said, "After me doctoring you for a week, you ask me such a foolish question. Anyway, one fool in the family is enough." I guess she meant me.

When I took my show south she used to shoot on exhibition. I offered a hundred dollars for anyone that could beat her shooting but no one ever did, though a lot of people tried.

She shot potatoes off my head, even empty twenty-two shells off my head at probably fifty or sixty feet. She would shoot ashes off a cigarette and I would have people in the audience mark a penny or dime and then I would hold it in my fingers for her to shoot the mark.

A person working before a crowd has to cultivate a deaf ear so that they never hear either the applause or the boos, just go on with their act in an unconcerned manner. I never knew my wife to ever acknowledge in any way that she heard her audience but once.

It was in Oklahoma. She was doing her shooting act, apparently not hearing or seeing anything but the target in front of the shooting blackboard. There was a loud-mouthed drunk in the audience. He was shooting off his face about her act. He kept saying it was all a fake—that she was using mercury instead of bullets, that there was a spring in the cigar that flicked off the ashes of the cigar and making other insulting remarks.

It was all I could do to keep from stopping and pushing his face in but my wife ignored him until he stuck his face, which had a cigar in it, alongside of her shooting board and said, "She can't shoot the ashes off a real cigar."

I guess she had been hoping for a break like that for she cut his cigar in two with a quick shot. The drunk like to broke his neck jerking it away from the shooting board. The crowd was well pleased to see the drunk put in his place, laughed and applauded her while the drunk slunk out of the show. She kept right on as if nothing had happened but she had a mighty pleased look on her face.

6: Freighting

IN 1899 WHEN I was married it took a lot more scrambling around to make a buck than it does these days. I had taken up a piece of land and broken out a bunch of horses. I thought as I was a married man I'd have to settle down and do some other kind of work.

I traded my bronc saddle off for a lumber wagon. It was a pretty good wagon but it had an old rickety box. I had looked at some lumber to make a new box but just didn't have the cash to buy it.

I think it was Labor Day, anyway we drove into town. The Woodman Lodge was putting on a celebration. There was a few foot races, the band played some music and someone made a spiel, then they put on the main event, which was the wheelbarrow race around the block.

The celebration was on the south side of the track starting at the big Yegen Department and Grocery Store at the corner of 28th Street and Minnesota Avenue. At that time there was only two big general all around stores in Billings, Yegen's and Donovan & McCormick's which was on 29th Street and Montana Avenue.

The Donovan & McCormick Store had a lot of new wheelbarrows on display out in front of their store. The committee of the celebration had managed for the use of them for the race.

Everyone that was going to run in the race went over and got a wheelbarrow and rolled it over in front of Yegen's store at the corner of 28th Street and lined up. There was twelve or fifteen of us all raring to get the $10.00 for the one that won the race.

E.W. Keene, a young carpenter started the race by shooting a gun in the air. Most of the town had turned out for the celebration and they was yelling and applauding as we started off.

We ran south to First Avenue, then east to 27th Street, north to Minnesota, then finished at the Yegen store.

At that time there wasn't any paving on the streets. They was just packed dirt cut up with deep ruts by the heavy freight wagons that hauled supplies from the Yegen store to the surrounding inland country. A wheelbarrow with only one small iron wheel didn't roll so easy over those ruts.

It is a long ways around a city block. Some of the racers only made it to the first corner. We was to run in the street, but some took to the sidewalk. We was strung out like a bunch of cattle on the trail.

I needed that ten dollars and was out to get it, if I could. I could hear my wife hollering, "Come on, Will!" I came in first but there had been so much corner cutting and running on the sidewalk that the judges decided to make it fair, the race would have to be run over.

Most of the runners had had enough and didn't start the second time but there was some fresh ones who took their place. There was a lot of excitement over the second race and some bets made.

I didn't want to run again as I knew how far it was around the block but hated to quit after making the long run and beating once.

We lined up again and Keene wasted another cartridge. We never broke any speed records, but we did our damnedest on a rough road. I took the lead and kept it just nosing out a fresh man.

I really earned that ten dollars. I never was so exhausted in my life and was sore for a week over that run.

When they paid me I went over to the lumber yard and bought enough lumber to make me a new wagon box. That

FREIGHTING

evening when we got home I told my wife that I'd rather ride a hundred head of bucking horses than run that race over.

No doubt, there is other old timers that remember that endurance wheelbarrow race.

THE FIRST freighting I ever done was in 1900 when the Burlington ran a branch road from Toluca through Pryor Gap into Wyoming. It was in the fall when I started to haul freight. I rigged up a six horse team, then a little later I put on another four horse team and freighted all winter.

I hauled mostly to the main commissary camp in the Pryor Gap where they was cutting a tunnel through the mountain. It was a large camp. They used horses and mules for all the construction work. You have no idea how much material it takes to build a railroad. Just the hay and grain to feed the work stock when hauled forty miles is quite a big thing besides the material to build a cook house and dining room, shacks for the men to sleep in. They had to make a place to store the powder and dynamite. There was big tents to put the grain, groceries, cement, pig iron, dump carts and light rail used in the tunnel and cuts.

All of the stuff for the camps was loaded out of Billings. There was a lot of freight teams on the road, some of them was six, eight and ten horse teams drove with a jerk line. They was called string teams.

There was a lot of camps along the railroad grade but most of the freight went direct to the main camp in Pryor Gap called the McShane Commissary which was forty miles south of Billings.

In February there was about fifteen railroaders took down with smallpox. Some of them died. They was just throwed in the grade and covered up with scrapers. Someone reported it and the authorities got after the company, made them dig them out and give them a decent burial.

Billings got the smallpox and was quarantined. The town had a guard on the two bridges. All the freighters had to get examined and vaccinated. Their loads was fumigated and they had to have a pass to get in or out of town.

One real hard trip I remember well. I had an Irishman by the name of Nels Stranahan driving the four horses on one wagon. I was skinning a six-horse team with two wagons.

We was loaded with cast iron culvert pipes. The big pipes weighed fifty-six hundred apiece and we could only load one on a wagon. The pipes had a big bell on one end. We had to load the bell on the back end of the wagon so it wouldn't be hard to unload. When we wanted to unload, we would hitch a team with a chain around the bell and pull it off behind the wagon.

The smaller pipes just weighed about a ton and we could put two pipes on a wagon. It was a bad load as the pipes was long and the load was all on the back end of the wagon. We had to chain it good or the pipes would slip and there was danger of spilling the load. We always tried to load according to road conditions.

We loaded one evening, the road was frozen hard and was good for a heavy load. That night there came a big storm. The wind blew hard and drifted the snow bad. For those conditions, we had overloaded. Nels had a big pipe on his four-horse wagon and I had a big pipe and two small pipes for my six horses.

We only made about twelve miles as the low places was drifted full. We would have to shovel through the drifts where it was deep. We'd get stuck and have to drop the trail wagon.

It had quit blowing and the temperature was somewhere near thirty below zero. The horses had long icicles on their noses. You could see the warm air coming out of their lungs freeze in the air. It looked like grey smoke from a locomotive.

Shovel snow, whip and cuss got us to Doc Wells' road house about dark. We was tired, hungry and half froze to death. We took care of the horses, stretched our tent, got supper and went in the road house to spill a little hot air. We played cards with a

FREIGHTING

couple more freighters for a quart of Old Crow. We won. We kept it for morning for we knew we would need it next day.

We had eight miles all up grade and one long hard hill. After we got up on the flat there was a lot of snow. It was hard going. We had to rest the horses pretty often. It was a bitter cold day, even colder than the day before. The only place we had to ride was astride a big cast iron pipe. When we got up the long, hard, steep hill we took a good shot out of the quart bottle.

I was cold and I just couldn't ride that cold pipe. I was walking but Stranahan was still riding the pipe. I was in the lead and was cold even while walking. I stopped and went to Stranahan's wagon. He was just about all in. I jerked him off the pipe and roughed him around for about half an hour. We finally got started. If I hadn't got him off that pipe he would have froze to death. He said he didn't feel cold but when he got to walking he was shaking all over.

We made about twelve miles that day. We camped on Powder Creek as there was a choke cherry patch there and it offered some protection for the horses. We stretched the tent, shoveled the snow out of it, built a fire in the camp stove and had supper. We finished the bottle and went to bed.

It was nice and warm in the tent but as soon as the fire went out it was plenty cold. Stranahan must have got cold for he nudged me and said, "Bill, you better pull your feet in, they're sticking out of the bed."

I moved my feet, they was warm. I looked at the foot of the bed and saw his feet sticking out from under the covers. I told him, "You better pull your own feet in if you don't want them to freeze."

He raised up and looked, discovered that he had made a mistake and pulled his feet under the covers. They was so cold that he had no feeling in them.

We had a few frost bites from the trip but kept on freighting though I can't say there was any pleasure in it or very much money.

[Freight cost]

"Red Eye Smith's hog ranch" was one of the worst places on the road to Pryor Gap. He had two black wenches to get the money the railroaders carried. They usually got the customers drunk and rolled them. When the customers complained, Smith always said they'd spent their money. He said, "Everybody gets a square deal at Smith's." He settled any beef they had after that by pulling a gun and running them off.

Any freighter that happened to unhitch too close to Smith's and didn't watch his load found it was much lighter at Pryor Gap than when he left Billings. In fact, it happened to me once.

I was loaded with canned goods on my trail wagon. I had dropped my trail wagon about a half a mile from camp as the road was awful bad and Smith's hog ranch was at the only water for a camp. It was late and I didn't go back for it until morning. My load seemed to pull lighter next morning but I thought it was because my team was fresh and the ground frozen.

When I got to Pryor Gap, I found out why it pulled easier. About half the cases on my load had been emptied and the empty boxes had been nailed up and left in their original position.

I knew where the stuff had gone but had no way of proving it, besides I didn't want to look down old Smith's gun.

A freighter with a good six-horse team, pulling two wagons on a forty-mile trip loaded one way, took about four days. It paid about ten dollars or a little over a day. Out of that came the expense of the trip, at least twelve dollars for hay and grain and the man's expenses.

There was a lot of men going back and forth between Billings and Pryor Gap to work on the railroad. It was said there was a thousand men working on the road. Anyway there was a lot of them going back and forth. The railroad hired two outfits to haul the man wagons. Felix Clark and Charlie Litsinger was the drivers. Their wagons had seats for the men. The railroad paid a dollar apiece for the men's transportation to the Gap. The men had to pay their own way back to town.

FREIGHTING

The railroad made small shacks for the railroad stiffs to sleep in and fed them in a big tent. When the cook's triangle was sounded, there was a regular stampede to get at the first table. One time a fellow broke his arm in the wild scramble to get his feet under the table first.

When I first started to freight my partner and I made the mistake of rolling our bed out in an empty bunk in one of those shacks.

We scratched all the way to Billings. Stranahan, who was with me, said we must have caught the itch. We had, but it was nice healthy gray backs (lice). We had to boil our clothes and our beds. After that we took time to pitch our tent at a good safe distance from the railroad camp.

I don't believe those shacks was any lousier than any other railroad camp but it's the honest to God's truth, if you looked close at the goods in the commissary that was for sale, you could see gray backs waiting for a customer. I've heard that lumber camps in those days was just as bad and the gray backs got as big as snapping turtles.

There was another road house about twelve miles out of Billings. It wasn't as tough as Smith's. It was run by a man called Doc Wells. Although there was several fights and one killing, it was a decent place compared to Smith's.

There was a bartender at Doc Wells' that was a bluffer but quite harmless if you knew him. Any time any argument started, it was his habit to pull out a big .45 from behind the bar and threaten the customers.

It generally stopped the argument. He pulled it one time too often. It was a bad mistake and his last.

THERE WAS a young fellow from Terre Haute, Indiana, came to Billings to see Nels Stranahan. I got pretty well acquainted with him. He wasn't loaded with money and was hunting a job. His name was Seth Dix.

Seth got a job with Casey Forrester. He was a nervous man, a hell of a good worker, and seemed to be honest. However, he did handle his liquor pretty reckless. He was sort of an adventurous man. I guess the east was too tame for him and he came west to grow up with the country. He'd probably heard and read a lot of stories about how rough and tough the west was. Like a good many pilgrims of the time he believed them all.

He worked about three months for Casey. At the end of that time there was kind of a slack time and nothing much to do. Red Eye Smith came to Casey's ranch and asked if he could get a man to do some rough carpenter work for a few days. It was arranged for Dix to go help Smith.

Smith was on his way to Billings and Dix went with him. Casey told Dix as they left, to go to his brother's jewelry store and get his (Casey's) gun and fetch it out to him, as they went by, on their way out to Smith's.

Smith and Dix stayed all night in town and came back the next day pretty well jagged up. When they came back, Casey was gone and his door was locked so Dix kept the gun with him.

They went on to Smith's place and Dix did the carpenter work. When he got through, Smith was taking him back to Casey's.

They stopped at Doc Well's road house to get a drink. There was bad blood between Red Eye Smith and Doc Well's bartender. They'd had some quarrels but it had never got beyond fighting words.

When they went in Seth Dix bought himself and Smith a drink. There was an argument over the change with the bartender. Dix told the bartender he didn't get enough money back.

The bartender reached under the bar and got his .45 and told Dix he would give him his change out of it.

Dix had Casey's gun in his hip pocket. It was a .32 automatic. At the sight of the .45 in the bartender's hand Dix reached for the gun in his pocket and let the bartender have it. He shot him three times. Then he went and gave himself up to the law.

As Dix was a stranger in the country and was with Red Eye Smith, a lot of people figured it was a put up job. I know in my own mind that wasn't so.

Dix didn't have any money to hire a lawyer so the court appointed one. I believe I could have put up a better defense myself. Anyway Dix got thirty years at Deer Lodge, and served twenty of it before he was pardoned.

He was convicted mostly because he happened to be with Red Eye Smith and had a gun on him. It wasn't a fair trial according to the code of the west.

I REMEMBER WHEN bicycles had a great big wheel in front and a little wheel in back and was a mighty awkward affair. I remember, too, the first tandem bicycle I ever saw. It was in Greeley, Colorado. A couple of missionaries, little chunky fellows, was traveling through the country on it. I think more people came to see their bicycle than came to hear their message. Like everything else the designs have improved.

People used to have a lot of fun taking off on a picnic or excursions and for a while everyone's ambition was to have a new bicycle.

However popular bicycles was with the people, they was quite an irritation to the horses. I was hauling freight out of Billings in the early days and had a pretty snuffy six-horse team. I stopped at Platte's blacksmith shop on the south side. I put the brakes on and left the team standing while I went in to get a rough lock chain fixed.

While I was talking to the blacksmith, I heard the damnedest commotion, horse snorting and chains rattling. I knowed something was wrong with my outfit.

The horses was all snorting, bucking, kicking and striking, scrambled up in a heap. One of them had a foot through a wheel of a bicycle and was hog wild.

"Two missionaries on a bike."

When I got the horses quieted down and rescued the remains of the bicycle, there was just the bent handle bars and the rims of the wheels.

The bicycle rider came rolling out of the scramble. He'd lost his hat, most of his pants and a little hide. He was awful scared and began apologizing for running smack into the middle of my team.

I told him the team wasn't hurt but it looked like he'd need a new bicycle. I always wondered if he didn't shy at the next freight team he met.

Another bicycle episode I'll never forget happened on Blue Creek. It was on a Sunday, in the early part of the summer. A rain storm had washed a ditch across the road and everyone had to make a little detour around it across a little cactus flat.

A young couple, that I took to be unmarried, was on their bicycles enjoying a nice outing. I was horseback on a hill just

FREIGHTING

above them hunting a cow and they never saw me. As far as that goes, I don't believe they'd have seen or heard a brass band.

When they came to the detour, which was pretty rough, they never slacked up their speed, just followed the tracks. They ought to have been paying more attention to the road.

First one bicycle and then the other turned a houlee hand (houlihan) into a big patch of cactus. The girl gave some blood curdling squawls and the guy said some he-man words. He was the luckiest, he'd only picked up a few but the girl's rear end looked like a porcupine's.

They pulled cactus a while and started to get back on the bicycles but some of the cactus had went through their clothes and broke off. There wasn't any setting 'til they got them out.

It was an embarrassing situation for them and I didn't think I'd better show myself. Every time he pulled a cactus out she'd scream.

The last I saw of them she was flat on her stomach, her skirts raised and he was pulling cactus.

AROUND 1901 I was digging a basement for the city jail and fire department on the corner of 28th Street, west of where the Northern Hotel is now. I read in the paper where they wanted teams at Red Lodge to haul coal from Bear Creek to Red Lodge.

It sounded good as it was an all winter job. I rigged up two four-horse teams and went up to haul coal. It was in the fall and the first two weeks done all right but they put on too many teams. The mine was new and they was having trouble and couldn't get the coal out fast enough to keep the coal haulers busy. That was before they had the railroad into Bear Creek.

It was a bad road over the mountain. There was several miles up hill, then you just fell off the mountain into Red Lodge. When it got cold and the snow got deep, it was a bear of a job.

The coal haulers all bought their hay and grain from a man by the name of Weaver that run the livery stable. He had some kind of a deal with the mine as they only paid off once a month. We could get all the feed we needed on time. He sold us good baled timothy hay but it was pretty high priced. We always paid our grocery bill and rent first, then if we didn't have enough left to pay the hay and grain bill Weaver would say, "Everything is all right, let it go until next pay day."

When you got in debt to Weaver, you never got out. About the time you seemed to be doing pretty good something would happen in the mine and you would have to lay off a while. Then it would snow and storm. The road would drift and we couldn't get through for a while. Weaver would never kick. He would sell you all the hay and grain you wanted and say, "You will make it up next month." If any poor devil quit, Weaver would attach his outfit and take it for a fraction of its value.

He had us all stuck, for the scheme was to never let us get out of debt so we could leave. We got wise to how we was being gypped but couldn't do anything about it. Some couldn't get away because they couldn't raise the money to pay Weaver, others thought that just as soon as they got even they would quit.

It was a tough job after a storm and it stormed a lot. The wind would drift the snow. Sometimes snow would push ahead of your wagon until you got stuck, then you would have to shovel out. When you got up the mountain and started down it was steep and generally icy. Your horses had to be sharp shod to stand up and at the top you had to rough lock to keep your wagon from skidding and running over your team.

One time the snow was awful bad and I thought that a bob sled would be just the thing. I borrowed a bob sled from Bill Greenough and put on a whale of a load. I got along fine until I got to the hill coming down into Red Lodge.

It was steep, slippery and crooked. The rough lock didn't hold on the ice and the horses couldn't hold back the load. I was going about a mile a minute when I hit the curve. The sled skidded and the wagon box with the coal went down the hill. I

FREIGHTING

was holding on the lines like grim death when the wagon box and coal left the sled. The horses pulled me in the clear.

There they was, going down that mountain on high for when the wagon box tipped off the sled it made an awful racket. When I hit the snow bank they jerked the lines through my hands. How they did go but they never left the road. They just sailed down that mountain, crossed Rock Creek, swung west and made a circle for about a half a mile. They was going so fast that they couldn't stop any sooner. They ran up to the barn where I was keeping them and stopped. The bob sled was still with them and nothing seemed to be hurt. When the load hit, a piece flew up and hit me. I had a piece of coal sticking in my jaw.

There was lots of trouble on the road, someone stuck in a drift or brakes slipping. You could see a load of coal in trouble most any time. The coal haulers could take the grief but fighting their way to the mine and finding no coal to haul was the worst to take.

A fellow by the name of Frank Collier was hauling coal. He was from Billings, too, and was boarding with me. We was plenty sick of the job. Frank had one of his horses cut its ankle with a shoe coming down the mountain.

Frank was sore and he said, "Bill, let's bunch this job. Day after tomorrow is pay day, we're gypped and we have put in over three months of hard work. We can load our stuff about midnight and be out of the county by daylight. They'll never know we have left for two or three days. We are just about out of hay and grain and we don't want to get in any deeper to Weaver. If you have enough feed to last us to Billings we can raise the money to get in the clear with Weaver. If he smells something, he will attach our outfits. Let's beat him to the punch. Let your wife take the seven o'clock train in the morning and we'll pull out tonight. It's about sixty miles and we can make it by late tomorrow night."

We done just that. We left our checks to pay the grocery bill and rent and made our fade-away. We wrote back to Weaver

[...]m our check was still there and to take his cut out of it [...] know the amount we still owed him and we would [...] soon as we could. We stalled him off for a couple of weeks just to worry him, then sent him a check.

SOME PEOPLE are so superstitious they won't start a job on Friday nor sleep in a hotel room numbered 13. Others carry a rabbit foot for good luck or a charm of some kind to keep the hoodoo away. I have noticed through a long life of experience that the ones that never had any superstitions was the ones that had an easy job without much danger attached to it.

As for myself I don't mind admitting that I never had any use for a damn black cat. It always seemed to me if a black cat appeared that it was an omen of bad luck and it most always proved out true.

I remember one time when I was freighting from Billings, over to the Musselshell when a black cat dealt me plenty of grief. I was freighting supplies for the Milwaukee railroad contractors.

It was late in the fall and we'd had no rain. The road, such as it was, was in good shape. Rube Poor and I started out with heavy loads. Rube had a six-horse outfit and I had an eight-horse team. There was a little spring about fifteen miles from Billings to the left of the road. Not many freighters stopped there so the feed was good. We made that spring the first day. It rained like the devil that night.

The night before we left Billings, Rube had been celebrating a little. I was too busy driving my eight horses to pay much attention to Rube during the day but I noticed as we made camp he wasn't feeling so happy. During the night I could hear Rube tearing around but it was raining and so dark I couldn't see what he was doing and I was too tired to care.

Next morning I asked him what he was prowling around in the rain for. He said he'd heard a cat in his load and he was trying to find it. I wanted to josh him a little and asked him what brand of liquor he'd been drinking in Billings for I'd heard of fellows seeing butterflies, pink elephants and snakes, and that the last freighter I'd been camped with had seen a grasshopper setting on a fence playing a bull fiddle, but never heard of anyone chasing cats before.

When we went to get our horses there was three gone. It took a while to find them sloshing around in the mud. It gave us a late start and it seemed as though everything was going wrong. It had stopped raining but the roads was all soaked up and the coulees had run water.

Between Twenty Mile and Thirty Mile there is a bad gumbo flat and one low nasty bog hole. It was good and boggy that day. We stopped when we got there and looked it over and it didn't look good but we had to try and cross.

While we was off our wagons discussing the best place to get through, Rube said to me, "Bill, you may think I'm hearing things but I know there is a damn cat in my load."

He was in the lead and when he hit about the middle of the bog hole his wagon just seemed to drop to the hubs. As his wagon stopped a black cat jumped from somewhere out of his load. It lit at the side of the road and took off into the sagebrush with its tail all fuzzed up.

Rube looked at the cat and then at me and he said, "I knew there was a cat in my load but I didn't know it was a black one. He sure put the gyp on this trip . . ."

Rube's load was really stuck. We hooked my eight horses in the lead of his six and by a lot of sawing and pulling and profane language we got it through the mud hole.

Before I started through I dropped my trail wagon and hooked his six on ahead. I guess I must have been throwing too much leather, hoping to jump it through, for the reach snapped in two. It was quite a job to fix the reach in the mud hole, but we finally got it done and got through.

While we was working getting the wagons through the mud hole somehow that cat managed to get in my load without our seeing him but no sooner had we got started down the road than I heard him yowl. When we got to camp we unloaded and made sure that damn cat didn't go on with us. Bad luck followed us all the way over and back to Billings. Among the many mishaps, one of my horses got sick and we had to lay over to doctor him up.

Now maybe the black cat didn't cause all our bad luck, maybe it was just coincidence.

WHEN THE temperature drops way below zero, it makes me think of the old days when everyone put up ice. There wasn't any artificial ice plants or automatic refrigerators in those days. If anyone wanted ice for the following summer he got out and got it in below zero weather. Most everybody got their ice from the Yellowstone River and stored it in large ice houses along the river.

As soon as it got cold enough for the river to freeze over everyone got ready for the ice harvest. It was a very disagreeable job but about the only work there was in the winter. It didn't take much equipment. A team of horses, an ice rack fourteen feet long, a pair of tongs, plenty of warm clothes and a lot of guts and you was ready to put up ice. The colder it was, the better for the ice man for the ice was better and you didn't get so wet unless you fell in the river as some of them always did.

The river isn't the best place to get ice as it freezes uneven. A lake is the best place if there is one handy. When there was snow on the ice as there generally was, it had to be scraped off. Then there was an ice plow pulled by a team that they used to mark the ice and then they would sock it down in the ice to cut it on the mark. Sometimes they sawed the ice. They had to be careful to mark it straight so the ice cakes would be the same size.

When it was all ready to go in the ice house there was a long wooden trough that reached up into the top of the ice house. In the top of the ice house there was a pulley and an iron frame that had a couple of prongs on it that was put back of the ice. A horse was hitched to a long rope attached to the pulley and about ten cakes at a time was pulled into the ice house. They weighed about a hundred fifty pounds apiece.

It took several men in the ice house, especially if it was a big ice house. They set the ice cakes on end just like bricks as close together as possible. If there was some uneven cakes they had a spud bar to even them up. They generally placed the ice four or five inches from the wall, packed sawdust all around it and over the top to keep the air out. The ice house had to have a drain to take care of any water that melted from the ice.

I remember one time we was putting up ice for Pete Yegen. The weather turned warm. He had a big crew working and wanted to get through while the ice was good. He had a large platform built on the edge of the river and a trough to pull the ice upon the platform. The wagons would back up to the platform and men would the push the ice in the back of the wagon. Several wagons could load at the same time. On account of the weather turning warm the water raised so we couldn't load at the platform. We had to go up the river about thirty yards and drive out on the ice to load. It was dangerous, but Yegen wanted to get his ice house filled that day.

The ice was thick but when you got loaded the ice would pop and make a lot of noise. There was a team broke through but we got them out without too much trouble: The only casualty was Mr. Yegen. He stepped in an air hole in the ice and got a cold bath.

I had a very heavy team, a Percheron stallion and a large Percheron mare. They weighed right at 3,500 pounds and was worth a lot of money. I was worried that they would break through the ice but didn't want to be the first one to quit for all the teamsters was scared. I was doing a lot of business with Yegen Brothers and I knew that if anyone quit the whole crew would quit. I was sweating blood every time I drove out on the ice. Anyway, we got the job done and the ice house filled. We was all glad to be finished.

When I got home tired from wrestling those 150-pound cakes of ice my wife took me in our bedroom to show me the new lace curtains she'd hung at the windows at the head of our bed. I admired them and went to bed early.

In the night I had a nightmare, dream or something as I hadn't had a drink for three months. I thought that my nice stallion had broke through the ice. I grabbed him by the tail and was pulling him out of the river when my wife shook me and woke me up. She wanted to know what I was doing upon my knees in the middle of the bed tearing up her new curtains. I told her I was sorry about the curtains but I'd sure pulled a good horse out of the river.

7: Indians

THE CROW RESERVATION has always been one of the best grazing lands in the state of Montana. It has mountains, plains and lots of water. It may not have as much grass as the Big Hole country but it has the advantage of winter grazing. In the early days no one ever fed hay or any other feed to cattle in the winter.

The cattleman, as he pays his grass lease, can remember when it only cost five cents an acre. A few years later the Indians decided they wanted ten cents an acre. The stockmen figured it was too high but they needed the grass so they paid ten cents but did a little figuring and rented every other section. Since there wasn't any fences they couldn't help it if the cattle trespassed a little. They got by for a while.

Then the Indian Agent done a little figuring too. So the land was divided into units and the stockman had to pay for all the acres in a unit or lose his lease.

Any way you look at it, the cow business has had lots of ups and downs. Just about the time a cowman thinks he's got the world by the tail on a downhill pull, along comes a dry summer, a hard winter and low prices and all he's got left in the spring is a depleted cattle herd and a big debt.

While the reservation was still unfenced and they still held big roundups, a lot of things happened that never got in print.

I remember one time, there was a roundup on the reservation. The foreman sent a couple of cowboys out to kill a beef. The foreman told them to poison the offal to see if they could get rid of some coyotes, wolves and magpies.

They killed the beef quite a ways from camp and put a lot of strychnine on the parts they left. In those days the Indians seemed to have a nose like a coyote, they could smell guts a long ways away and always came to get their share.

Until about that time, they hadn't been putting poison out to get varmints. One of the cowboys rode over to see if it was effective.

Well, he found it had worked all right. There was several magpies, a coyote and a big buck Indian. I guess the Indian was having a raw lunch.

There was quite a pow wow at the roundup that night. They figured it was strictly an accident as there was no Indian camp close so they decided to just keep quiet about the whole affair.

That wasn't the end of the matter however, for next morning a squaw came to the roundup camp and demanded "money" because her buck was dead. She said, "Beef heap killum."

They didn't want any trouble with the Indians so they all pitched in all the money they had to make a collection. It amounted to fifteen or twenty dollars which they gave to the squaw. She seemed satisfied with the deal and went over and piled brush and rocks over the dead buck and went on her way.

The cowboys was paid their part of the collection by the cow outfit and that was the end of the whole affair. I never heard any more of it.

ONE TIME a couple of Jew peddlers stopped at the ranch to buy some chickens. The chickens came to twelve dollars. Before they settled for the chickens they brought out a lot of stuff they wanted to sell. In the stuff was some cheap jewelry, rings with glass sets, beads and side combs with sets.

My wife wanted money for the chickens as she didn't want any of the stuff. I got a hunch that the stuff would trade good with the Indians. We picked out a pair of side combs, a couple of rings and a string of beads. The Jews wanted four dollars but that was way too much. I told them I'd give two dollars and if

INDIANS   181

that wasn't enough, to turn the chickens loose and get to hell up the road. They paid up.

A few days later, I had been out hunting horses and as I passed by the horse corrals noticed quite a few Indians camped at the water there. They had quite a lot of loose horses with them.

Our house was about a quarter of a mile from the horse corrals. In a little while I told my wife to put on the stuff we got from the Jews and maybe we could get a horse trade.

There was several tepees stretched and the Indians was getting supper on camp fires. The horses was grazing around close to camp. There was a little, thin, ragged looking, pinto mare. She was a bay and white pinto with black ears. She was pretty the way she was but I knew that if she was fat she would be a beauty.

There was one camp that was off from the others. The Indians around it looked a little different to me than the other Indians. I took them to be Sioux Indians. There was a real tall old buck who was thin and gaunt and crippled in one leg, a big fat squaw, two young squaws probably fifteen and sixteen and a little buck about ten years old.

"Indians camped at water hole."

I asked one of the Indians who owned the little paint mare. He pointed to the tepee where the old man was.

I went to their tepee and said, "How Kola," which is Sioux for hello.

He answered me back in Sioux.

I asked him who owned the paint. He pointed to the squaw and said, "Squaw pony."

I tried to talk to her but didn't have much luck as she either couldn't talk or wouldn't.

I said, "How much?"

The oldest girl and the squaw talked in Sioux and finally the girl said, "Twenty-five dollars."

I answered her, "Too much."

The young squaw was good looking with pretty, large, brown eyes, white even teeth and had two long braids hanging below her waist. She just stood tall and straight never saying a word or batting an eye, with no more expression in her face than a cedar post.

I had noticed the old squaw looking at the side combs in my wife's hair. I took ten silver dollars out of my pocket, laid them on the ground, pulled the side combs out of my wife's hair, put them on the silver dollars, turned to the young squaw and said, "Swap?"

She never said a word, just stood there dumb.

Then I made out like I was mad, pulled the rings off my wife's finger and piled them on top of the side combs and silver.

The old squaw took the side combs, looked at the five glass sets in their sides, then she looked at the rings. The old squaw and the girl talked but my Sioux language was limited to just a few words and signs. They was looking for more money but that was all the silver I had.

I said, "Swap?" I didn't get no reply so picked up the stuff and went on back to the ranch. As we was going back Ella said, "That's one of the prettiest Indian ponies I've ever seen."

I told her, "Maybe we will get her yet. They will stop in the morning and try to get more money. You just see. If they do, you take the young squaw down to the garden and give her some garden stuff to sweeten her up a little. She can talk as good as we can but she won't. I think she will talk when you get her alone. Don't say nothing about trading. When you get back I will try to trade with them."

The string of beads we'd got from the Jew peddler must have been made for a little girl as they was too short to go around an adult's neck. When we got home, Ella decided to restring the beads. She had an Indian bead that was about two inches long that she had found at an old Indian camp grounds near Laramie, Wyoming, when she was a small girl coming from Missouri with her family in a covered wagon. She put this bead in the center of the string.

Ella said that she and her brother was looking for arrow heads. They found a few broken ones and was scratching around when she found what appeared to be a rounded stone about two inches long. She wiped it off on her dress and it was a hard, black rock with gold specks on it.

She took it back to her father to show him. They scrubbed it off and found there was a hole in it. One side was flat and the other side rounded. On the rounded side there was carved a little Indian tepee on each end of the bead and an Indian head in the center of the bead. The Indian head had a war bonnet with feathers. The tepees and the Indian head was very small. Whoever carved them in that hard, black rock must have been a wonderful artist as they was just perfect.

The next morning the Indians stopped. The Indian boy was riding the paint pony bareback with just a loop in her mouth. Ella took the girl to the garden to give her some vegetables. While in the garden the girl visited with Ella. She told Ella she had gone to school but didn't like to talk when there was other Indians present.

After they put the vegetables in the Indians' wagon, I started to try trading. We had gathered up a little more change. I piled the silver up, put the side combs and rings on the pile, then Ella went in the house and got the string of beads and put them on the pile.

The old squaw picked up the string of beads, looked at the Indian bead and said something to the buck He looked at the bead and they talked back and forth, then had the girls look. There was more talk, then the old squaw nodded her head and said, "Swap!"

She took one side comb and stuck it in the oldest girl's hair, the other one in the youngest girl's hair. She put the two rings on her fingers and the beads around her neck, gave the small change to the little buck and the ten silver dollars to the old buck and then they started on their way to town.

AT ONE TIME the government was trying to make farmers out of the Crow Indians on the Crow Reservation. A boss farmer was appointed. There was several big pow wows held to get the Indians interested in farming. The government issued the Indians plows, wagons, harness, mowing machines. In fact, they was issued most anything they wanted if they would agree to start farming. A lot of Indians agreed, just to get the new stuff.

I lived close to the reservation and had plenty of chances to observe their actions. Whenever the Indians took a notion to plow, mow some hay or haul a load of wood, when they got through with the job or got tired of it they would just unhitch and throw the harness down and turn the team loose. You could see harness throwed down most anywhere, mowers in the field, hay rakes under about every choke cherry patch.

One old Indian broke his wagon and used his hay rake for a buggy until he wore it out. They never greased their machinery. When they broke anything they would tell the boss farmer and get a new outfit.

INDIANS

Indians was great hands to trade or sell their stuff. If they needed a little money you could buy a wagon or most any kind of machinery for five dollars as they had no ideas what the stuff was worth. After the Indian had sold his wagon or what not he would go to the boss farmer or agent and say, "Want new wagon."

The agent would want to know what had happened to the one he had.

The Indian would say, "Gone, me no savvy. Maybe so white man ketchum."

When the Burlington was putting the railroad through Pryor Gap I was one of the freighters.

I used to break horses on the trips as it was a good place to break a horse in a string team. I would hitch him up, tie him on the chain and he couldn't do much only throw a fit or two. He would soon learn to follow the leaders as he had lots of company. When I got a horse broke I could sell him pretty good, for work horses was in demand.

I bought seven head of horses at a sale cheap. There was four of them that was supposed to be broke stuff. One pair was worth what I paid for the bunch. Three head was unbroke but had a little too much age. The other pair had been spoiled. They could kick the soda out of a biscuit. I named them Satan and Dynamite.

They gave me plenty grief. The first time I drove those two snakes I hitched them together. I had them on the tongue, called the wheel team. They got to kicking. They throwed a regular hydrophobia fit, broke the wagon tongue and kicked each other until I thought they would kill each other.

Dynamite got the best of the battle, for after their spasm was over, Satan was lame in three legs and I had to leave him. Dynamite made the trip but he didn't look very good when he got back. I left him and took Satan even if he was still limping. That's the way I worked them for several trips. I wanted to get them together, and finally I got them going after their little show.

I was hauling baled hay and oats. I would load the lead wagon with baled hay. Satan and Dynamite couldn't do much damage kicking those bales of hay. I had those horses well named but didn't always call them by their right names when they throwed a kicking spasm. I just can't tell you how ornery those horses was.

I was over on Pryor Creek about twelve miles from the Gap. It was the first time that I had ever drove them that far without several kicking spells. I thought that they was giving up when something started them off. Dynamite got straddle of the tongue and business picked up. After the spasm was over Dynamite had tore up the harness pretty bad and I didn't have anything to fix it with so I could go on.

I saw an Indian's harness hanging on a wire fence and made an even trade with him. He wasn't there and I didn't want to cheat him. My harness was a leather harness a little worse for wear. The Indian's was a chain harness.

I passed that place for the next three months and the harness was still hanging on the fence. I guess he liked them, anyhow I was satisfied.

WHEN I WAS freighting and when the Indians used to camp at the ranch on their way to town, I had plenty of opportunity to observe some of their peculiarities.

There was an Indian family that had their tepee on Pryor Creek along the freight road. It was a handy place to water my freight team and I often stopped and visited with them as they could talk a little.

They was real blanket Indians and had several children, all little squaws. It didn't look like a very prosperous setup so I made it a point to clean my grub box out and give them any extra grub I had on hand.

I cannot remember the buck's name but it seems to me it was Big Ant or Big Bird or something like that. One time I looked at all the little squaws running around the tepee and mentioned that he had a big family.

He looked pretty disgusted and said, "Heap sh—! Too many squaws. No good. Me want um little bucks."

After the railroad was finished Big Ant, or whatever his name was, felt like I was his friend. He always camped at my ranch on his way to and from Billings.

One trip he stopped looking pretty glum. They had just had another squaw papoose. My wife went to see it. The squaw, whose name I never knew, had a talk with my wife which amused us quite a bit.

The squaw said, "Me no savvy. All time have squaw papoose. My man heap mad. He want buck, I want buck. Me no ketchum, all time squaw. Heap sh—! Buck say he go to Sioux reservation get squaw, have um boy. Maybe so, you savvy. You tell um. How make um boy?"

That was the last time they stopped and I had about forgotten them until one day I saw her in Crow Agency about a year later. She said, "How" and I said, "How" to her.

She stood and stared at me for quite a while. I thought she had something to say so I waited. She finally said, "You see um Big Ant?"

I shook my head, "No."

She said, "Big Ant, gone long time. Me no savvy. Maybe so drown in Big Horn. Maybe so ketchum another squaw."

Several months went by before I saw her again. I happened to be riding on Pryor Creek and rode by their place. I saw there was a fire in front of the tepee and rode over to pass the time of day with them.

Big Ant was setting on a cottonwood log smoking a pipe. He acted real glad to see me. As I shook his hand I said, "Long time me no see."

He looked at me quite a little while, then he said, "Me go Sioux reservation to ketchum young squaw. Me no ketchum. Me come back. All same, heap good. My squaw ketchum little buck.

Heap good!" He acted real happy as he said, "You come, me show."

We went into the tepee to see the little buck. He was laying on a blanket on the floor of the tepee. He was surrounded by toys and had a bear claw necklace around his neck.

But what made my eyes pop was the baby. It was a good looking baby with fair skin, blue eyes and light hair. I figured maybe it was an adopted baby as the Indians are great on adopting other children. I asked, "Where you ketchum?"

He said, "Squaw say maybe so Charlie Bair's sheepherder, maybe so Billings policeman. All same. My squaw, my papoose. Maybe so grow up be policeman. Maybe so grow up be chief. Maybe so be good horse thief. All same. Heap good."

JUST BEFORE they started to do any blasting on the tunnel a bear got into one of Charlie Bair's sheep bands and killed a lot of sheep. About daylight the sheepherder heard a commotion in his bunch of sheep and he run over to the bed ground to see what was disturbing them. There he run into a big she bear with a couple of cubs. She was just knocking over sheep like they was ten pins in the bowling alley.

The herder took a shot at her and scared her off. Before the herder had scared her off, she had killed about a hundred and fifty sheep.

When the camp tender came next day and saw the casualties he reported it to the foreman. The foreman went to the subagency at Pryor and told the agent of the loss of the sheep.

He told the agent that if he would send out a bunch of Indians to kill the bear the company would pay a hundred dollars for the bear's carcass.

There was a bunch of Indians went bear hunting. They did a lot of riding around, had a lot of pow wows and sign language confabs but they didn't get the bear. Maybe, they hadn't lost any bears. I don't know.

At that time there wasn't any heavy machinery. Everything was done by horses. I had been hauling baled hay, grain, dump cars and light rails to be used making the tunnel through the mountain.

The contractors was getting ready to open the hole for the tunnel. They had been drilling holes for about a week to put dynamite and joint powder in. They was figuring on tearing a big hole out of the side of the mountain and wasn't stingy with the explosives.

There was a lot of canyons and deep coulees alongside of the mountain. They had to have a lot of large culverts to put in so the water running down the coulees wouldn't wash out the track. This trip out, the loading boss told me he would have to load my trail wagon with a culvert. It was round, about three feet high, sixteen feet long and weighed 5,600 pounds. I think it was the first one hauled out to the grade.

There was an Indian camp along the road on Pryor Creek. I knew one of the Indians that was camped there. His name was Joe Child In Mouth. He could talk a little English. He saw me coming and come to beg some tobacco. I stopped to rest my teams while I visited with Joe.

Now on my trail wagon I had my sheet iron camp stove setting in the mouth of the culvert but a length of stove pipe stuck out. My bed was crowded in along by the stove kind of covering it and in the back end of the pipe I had some bales of hay.

Joe Child In Mouth looked at the culvert and I guess he couldn't figure out what it was so he pointed his finger at it and said, "No savvy."

I made some signs and said, "Heap big gun."

By that time some more Indians had gathered around. They was talking Indian and making lots of signs I didn't understand. I started figuring I had pulled a pretty good joke on the Indians.

The next day as I came back, three Indian bucks and Joe came out to the road and wanted some more tobacco. We was standing there visiting when the tunnel gang touched off the big charge in the mountain.

We was about seven miles from it. It was a terrible explosion. Black smoke, rocks and dirt went into the air. At that distance it jarred the earth.

The Indian bucks just stood there with their mouths open.

Squaws, papooses and other Indians came running out of their tepees pointing at the cloud of smoke, dirt, rocks and whatnot in the air a quarter of a mile high.

One Indian buck said, "Heap sh—, me no savvy."

Joe Child In Mouth said to me, "Shoot um big gun. Maybe so kill um bear."

THE OLD-TIME Indians was a peculiar people. If they took a liking to you they would do a lot of nice things for you. They never forgot a favor nor never forgot an enemy. They had sun worshippers, rain makers and medicine men. The medicine men doctored the people and the horses. I don't know what cures they used on people but they would tie feathers and bright colored rags in the horse's mane and tail for medicine.

They liked dogs but hadn't any use for cats. They liked to prophecy the weather. I remember one time I was at Pryor Agency. It was in the fall. There was an old Indian there that I knew. He could speak English pretty well. I asked him what kind of a winter we was going to have.

He said "Heap cold, heap snow, lots of ponies freeze. Prairie dog got lots of dirt built up around holes."

When I lived on Blue Creek around 1900 the road from Pryor Agency went right by my ranch. I got acquainted with a lot of the Indians.

There was an Indian by the name of Joe Child In Mouth came to the ranch one day. It was in the fall and was a cold, rainy day. The roads was bad and his team was tired out. I let him stay all night in the bunk house. He could talk but his squaw couldn't or wouldn't.

She had something the matter with her arm and it was paining her something awful. Joe came over to the house and said his squaw's arm was sick and wanted to know if we had any medicine.

My wife and I went to the bunkhouse to look at the squaw's arm. There was no sore or anything so my wife figured it must be rheumatism. She thought a mustard plaster might ease the pain a little. She made a mustard plaster and bound it on the squaw's arm.

We was just going to bed when Joe came over and said the medicine was making the arm sicker. We went and took the mustard plaster off. It was sure smoking. My wife had thought the squaw would take it off when it got too hot. In the morning she went to see how the squaw was getting along. Through Joe she learned the pain was gone but the arm was blistered. They soon left for Pryor.

In about three weeks Joe and his wife came along again. They gave my wife a very nice pony. It was broke to ride and nice and gentle. Joe said, "Heap good medicine, squaw's arm all right."

We kept the pony staked out around the house to use to get the cows in. We had him about two weeks when another Indian, White Man, came along. He saw the pony and said, "My pony, me take."

We didn't like to lose the pony but didn't want to have any trouble so let White Man take it. The next time I saw Joe Child In Mouth I told him that White Man had claimed the pony and took it.

Joe said, "Him no understand, me fix um. He my brother in law. I marry his sister. He marry my sister. His pony my pony, my pony his pony. All same. Me fix um. You get um pony back."

The next time Joe came along he fetched another pony and said, "My pony, you keep. White Man no understand. Him sister, him pony. Him no savvy. Heap good medicine. Heap sh—!"

We thought everything was settled okay, but then one day White Man came along and fetched the pony that he had taken and said, "You keep, me no savvy, medicine heap good."

When Joe came along again I told him that White Man had fetched the other pony back and now I had two ponies.

He said, "Heap good, you keep. White Man's squaw had big jaw, awful sick. Me take medicine your squaw put on my squaw's arm, put it on White Man's squaw's jaw. Hide all come off but it take away big jaw. White Man afraid big jaw come back if he don't take pony back. All same, heap good."

It must have been a year later. Joe stopped at the ranch. He said, "Medicine heap good, cure squaw, cure horse, cure dog. Maybe so your squaw fix um. It getting little, I show."

He went over to the wagon and fetched out the remains of the mustard plaster. It was filthy dirty and was drawed up not much bigger than your hand. In fact, it looked like a cow chip.

My wife fixed up another mustard plaster and told him when he wanted to use it to soak it in warm water. I think she showed him how to make the medicine. He left her a pair of beaded moccasins and went on with his "heap good medicine."

I WANT TO tell you about an experience that an early day banker had with an Indian. I heard the story told and knowing the Indian ways and peculiarities got quite a chuckle out of it.

It happened before the west end of the reservation was throwed open. There was an Indian that lived on the Boulder or the Clark's Fork, I have forgotten which. But, anyway, he had a good piece of land, a small bunch of cattle and a lot of ponies. He had a very nice bottom of wild hay land which he used to rent for ten cents an acre to a sheepman.

At that time hay was worth about ten dollars a ton. The Indian got smart and thought he would put up the hay and make money selling it.

In those early days the Indians didn't savvy a check. If you done any business with them you had to show money and the most of them wanted it in silver dollars as they didn't savvy paper money either.

There was a small bank opened up in Joliet. The Indian heard that it was a place that the white men got money. He thought he would see if he could get some money to buy a mower and a rake to put up hay with. He could talk a little and through signs and motions make you understand what he wanted.

He went in the bank and up to the cashier's window. He told the cashier he wanted to get some money.

The cashier thought perhaps the Indian had a check and said, "Show paper."

The Indian shook his head, "No paper, want money."

The cashier pointed to the back end of the bank where the banker had his private office. The Indian went back and told the banker, "Me want money buy cut cut and scratch scratch. Make um hay."

The banker hadn't been in the habit of loaning money to Indians and was turning over the problem of a loan when a rancher came into the bank and seeing the Indian said, "How."

The banker took the rancher aside and asked about the Indian's financial state. The rancher said that he was considered a pretty honest Indian and had a lot of land, a lot of horses and some cattle.

So finally, the banker decided he would lend the Indian the money, about two hundred dollars, and take a mortgage on his horses and cattle. There was lots of questions of "How many horses, how many cattle, how much hay you put up? When you pay back?" There was a lot of signs and grunts connected with the mortgage before the Indian put his X on it.

The Indian got his money and bought a mower and rake.

That was the last the banker saw him until he sold his hay. Then he came in and paid off his mortgage.

The next year the Indian did pretty well. He had sold his hay and some ponies and had some money he wanted to put in the bank. The banker was very pleased.

The Indian asked the banker, "How many ponies you got?"

The banker said, "I haven't got any ponies."

The Indian asked, "How many cattle you got?"

The banker shook his head and said, "I haven't got any cattle."

The Indian said, "You got bank, me take mortgage on bank." The banker tried to make it clear to the Indian how the bank worked. He said, "You don't need any mortgage. You leave money, we give you paper. You can come in and get your money any time. We are good, honest people."

The Indian replied, "Me no savvy. Me want mortgage or me no leave money. Me want money back or bank. Me honest but you want money or ponies and cattle. No give mortgage on bank me no leave money. Heap sh—! Me no savvy white man's money house."

NOT MANY of the older Crow Indians could talk English. They could say a few words and then they would use sign language. The squaws would never talk at all to you if there was other Indians around.

At that time you hardly ever saw a squaw with a dress or pair of shoes on. They wore a blanket for a dress and moccasins on their feet. The bucks wore long hair braided down their back.

The Crows have always been a peaceable tribe and friendly to white people. They had a reputation for stealing horses and from what the old-timers said, they was plenty good at it. A good horse thief among the Indians was highly respected.

INDIANS

There was quite a lot of Indians that was allotted land on Pryor Creek. They did most of their trading at Pryor Sub Agency about thirty miles south of Billings. There was a commissary store there. The government used to give the Indians rations there every month. About all the heavy business the Indians done in Billings at that time was to take in any shows that happened to be coming through.

I never had them touch anything around the ranch. A lot of their ways was funny to us.

They just camped and minded their own business. They traveled in wagons with their families. They must have liked dogs for they generally had several following behind their wagons.

One evening about five o'clock there was an Indian wagon pulled in. The buck came over to the house. It was cold and stormy. It had rained first, then turned into a wet snow. He looked cold and wet so I asked him in to warm up.

An Indian is funny. If he has anything to tell you he don't come right out and tell you but generally looks things over and takes his time.

The buck sat down by the stove and warmed up. He had been in warming up for about fifteen or twenty minutes and I thought he was alone. Finally, he said, "Squaw heap sick in wapatotsy (wagon)."

At that time there had been some smallpox around the reservation. I was kind of worried and asked him what was the matter with her.

He said "Maybe so have papoose."

I told my wife what he had said. We thought we would go out and ask the squaw to come in and warm up too. We put on our coats and went out to the Indian's wagon.

It was a little too late. She had just had a papoose in the wagon. My wife pulled off her coat and wrapped the baby in it and run in the house with it.

I built a fire in the bunk house and drove the Indian's team right up to the door of the bunk house to get the squaw inside. I called the buck to help me take her out of the wagon.

He said something to her that I couldn't understand. She got out of the wagon and walked in the bunk house. She was a little wobbly but she made it all right.

My wife washed the baby and told me to go see if they had any clothes for it. I asked the squaw for some clothes but all she gave me was a blanket. They was real blanket Indians.

I took the blanket to my wife. She wrapped the papoose in it and laid it on the bed. She got one of her own outing flannel night gowns and cut it up and made the little papoose a gown. She found some flour sacks for diapers. When she had it dressed like a baby should be, she wrapped it in the blanket and took it to the bunk house for its first feed.

The next morning the Indians went on into Billings with their brand new papoose.

ONE TIME an Indian stopped at the camping place, made his camp, then came over to the house. He said to us, "Squaw heap sick. Me take to Medicine Man in Billings. Pony, heap tired, me camp. Me buy some bread, some milk, maybe so two potatoes." He gave my wife thirty-five cents.

My wife had just baked some apple pies. She got the stuff together that the Indian wanted and, on account of the squaw being sick, put in half a pie.

The Indian reached for the pie and began to eat it saying, "Squaw too sick. No eat um. Me like. Me eat."

That evening as I went to get the milk cows that was in a pasture by the corrals, the Indian saw me and came over to me. He said, "Come see squaw. Heap sick."

He had a tepee stretched. The squaw was laying on the bed in the tepee. She sure looked awful sick to me. Her face was all swelled up and broke out. It looked like to me she might have smallpox.

When I got back to the house I told my wife I thought the squaw might have smallpox. We figured we ought to get word to the authorities to quarantine them or they might scatter smallpox over the whole country.

Before we could do anything, next morning the Indian stopped at the gate all loaded up on his way to town. He wanted to sell me a pony. He was driving an old rickety wagon and leading a couple of poor horses behind the wagon and had three dogs following behind.

The two horses that he was leading didn't look very good to me. One was a small brown Indian digger that didn't look like he was worth anything, only for some kid to learn to ride on. The other was a cream colored horse that was just skin and bones with a big pie on his back (saddle sore). He looked like he'd had a lot of riding. After I looked him over I saw that he was pretty well built and, if the Indian hadn't broken his heart, with some meat on he'd be a good looking horse.

I gave him ten dollars for both horses. I told him I'd give him a letter to give to a friend of mine and he would get a medicine man for his squaw.

I wrote a note to Jim Webb, the sheriff, explaining I thought the squaw had smallpox. I gave the note to the Indian and told him to go to the court house and give the letter to Jim Webb, if Jim wasn't there to show the letter to someone there and they would get him a medicine man.

The Indian said, "Heap good. Maybe so squaw get well," and started for town.

The next time I went to town I went to the sheriff's office to find out what the squaw had. Webb told me it was smallpox and they was quarantined, that the squaw was getting better and would be alright.

I did all right with the Indian horses but it took a little time. When he got fat, the little brown horse brought fifteen dollars for a kid pony. I doctored the cream colored horse's back, put some shoes on his sore feet and turned him in a good pasture. He got rested up and fat. He was a very good horse, gentle and kind with plenty of life. He was no Indian broke horse as he had Seth Tripp's brand on, that had a ranch on the Dryhead.

I had asked the Indian where he'd got him when I'd seen the brand and he'd said, "Me get horse from Mexican Tony, live on Sage Creek. Me get paper from Tony. Me no steal horse."

I kept the horse about a year and sold him to a man at Bridger for $35.00. I'd got rid of the horses when the Indian came again and camped by my corrals.

He came to the house, handed my wife thirty-five cents again and wanted some bread, milk and potatoes. He wanted some more pie but he didn't know how to say it. He took a stick and drawed a circle on the ground, then marked through the circle and said, "Heap good." He was out of luck that time as she didn't have any pies baked.

I asked him how his squaw was and he said, "Squaw, heap sick." He stretched his arms out in front of his stomach as far as he could reach and said, "Heap big. Can't hardly sit in wagon box. All time make grunt. I think pretty soon ketchum papoose, maybe so two. Me no savvy. Heap big. You give me letter to Medicine Man. Him fix um. Me no savvy. Heap shaw!"

I gave him a letter but didn't know how much good it would do. In a few days I was in Billings and saw the Indian. He gave me back the letter saying, "Me no see um Medicine Man. Squaw, ketchum papoose on way to town. All same. Heap good, ketchum little buck."

THERE WAS A half breed woman named Lula that lived on a piece of the reservation that had been throwed open south of Billings. She wasn't too good looking, being a little cross eyed but she had something! She never lacked men in her life. I knew her well as she lived just across the road from my wife and me for a while.

She was married to a man called Scar Face Davis the first time. Scar Face was quite a hustler but he didn't have too good a reputation. I always thought he stole a cow from me but I couldn't prove it.

Scar Face Davis and Lula lived together a while. They got along pretty good until Scar Face fell for a good looking white woman named Molly D.

Scar Face bought Molly D. a lot of presents and Lula didn't like it. They fought around a while until they split their blankets and Lula got a divorce.

Lula married another man by the name of Davis but no relation to Scar Face Davis.

Molly D. went away for a while so Scar Face turned his attentions back to Lula. He visited her several times when her husband number two was away from home. Naturally number two didn't like it and there was bad blood between the two Davis's.

When Scar Face went a-courting he took his Winchester with him for company. One day he made a visit at the wrong time. The other Davis was home.

There was some fighting talk and both was heeled for such an occasion. I was away at the time but heard the story told several different ways. No matter how it was told, the ending was always the same.

The two Davis's shot it out. Both was killed. Scar Face used his Winchester and I believe the other Davis had a shotgun.

Lula was pretty upset. Loving both men and losing them at the same time. She had them put in different coffins but buried them in the same grave on her allotment on the reservation.

After a few years my wife and I ran across Lula with a small child. My wife remarked to her, "Lula, I didn't know you was married again."

She said, "I'm not, this kid is mine but its father is a coyote as he won't own his own kid."

Then she told us her story.

She was awfully lonesome after the two Davis's was dead. She took up with another man that I will call Bill Doe. This Bill promised to marry her. They had a love affair and Bill left the country for a time.

While Bill was gone Lula had a baby. When he returned, Lula went to show him the baby and take up the marriage proposition.

Bill saw Lula and the baby coming. She said he took off running like a scared coyote.

Bill of this story is an old-timer that I know. He is quite respectable now and runs a business in Billings. I am not telling his name as he is bigger than I am.

JIM DAYLONG, my father-in-law, came to Montana the hard way, in a covered wagon, over sixty years ago. There was three children by his first wife, Millard about fifteen, Ella about thirteen and Perry about ten, the second wife and two or three small children in one wagon. They was so heavy loaded that Jim and the older children walked most of the time.

They had a lot of hardships on that trip; a prairie fire that nearly burned them up, dry camps without water, hail and rain storms, crossing rivers and streams that had no bridges. The wolves killed one of their horses between Douglas and Buffalo, Wyoming. They was stranded for several days while Jim went to Buffalo and bought a horse, taking all their money.

They came to Billings but for some reason Jim decided to go back to Wyoming. They was traveling through the Crow Reservation on the Little Big Horn when one of their horses got sick and they had to stop near an Indian camp ground where several Indians was camped.

The Indians came over to where the Daylongs was camped to see what was going on. They tried to help doctor the horse with their medicine. They tied calico strings of various colors in the horse's mane and tail, sang and danced around it. Their medicine didn't do any good for the horse died.

At that time a white man had to have permission to be on the reservation. The bucks all wore their hair in long braids. They had beaded vests with elk teeth on them and eagle feathers in their hair. The squaws wore blankets tucked down around their middles with a butcher knife in a leather scabbard hanging on their belts. Their fingers was covered with brass rings.

The Crow Indians was a friendly people and liked to be with each other. If they traveled, several families went together. When they camped permanently there was always several tepees at a camping spot. They liked to run horse races, foot races, throw arrows, play shinney and have all kinds of dances.

The government was trying to get the Indians to give up their old ways and adopt the white man's way of living. The Indians was allotted land and the government hired carpenters to build them houses. Once a month there was an Issue Day. On Issue Day, the Indians received clothing, shoes, blankets, groceries, wagons, harness and machinery to work the ground if they wanted it.

At the time Jim Daylong stopped on the reservation, the government had built several houses for the Indians. The houses was all done except the doors and windows hadn't been put in. The carpenters had made more money selling fire water to the Indians than building houses so they had all been fired before they finished.

While Jim was camped there trying to get another horse an Indian policeman that could talk a little asked Jim if he could fix the houses. Jim told the policeman he could, but that he didn't have a permit to be on the reservation and showed the policeman his carpenter tools.

The policeman told Jim the Agency wasn't far, that he was going there and would try to fix it with the agent for Jim to have a permit to work and stay on the reservation. Which he did.

Jim had a lot of funny experiences while finishing those houses and making new ones. The funniest experience he had was not connected with his carpentry but when he was called to do a little home doctoring.

Jim was making a house for an Indian somewhere near Wyola on the Little Big Horn. There was a pretty good sized Indian camp there including an Indian policeman and his squaw. About once a week the policeman and his squaw would go away on a visit. While they was gone a couple of Indians riding horseback and leading a packhorse would go out hunting. They never came back until after dark. Next morning all the Indians had fresh beef.

There was an old couple in the camp. They was both large. The buck was the largest as he had a great big paunch. He wore a pair of soldier's pants with a belt to keep them up. You couldn't see the belt except in back as his big loose paunch hung over it almost to his knees.

One morning after the Indians had been hunting, the buck got awful sick. The squaw had pulled his bed out of the tent in order to have more room to work on him. The buck was bloated up big as a hay rack and seemed to be in a lot of pain.

The squaw was down on her knees with her hands doubled up into fists. She would put her fist in his stomach, then push down with all her might, twisting her fist, then reverse with the other fist. The buck would groan and would make a lot of noise like a heavy horse. His eyes was sticking out like a wild steer's on the fight.

It was a mighty amusing sight to the Daylongs. They didn't want to offend the Indians so they stayed in their tent and peeped out through the tent flaps.

Finally, the squaw saw she wasn't getting any results so she got up on his paunch and began to walk up and down. She still didn't get the desired results. Indians gathered around the sick buck's bed. Some of the squaws was beginning to hum the death chant.

INDIANS

The Indian policeman came over to the Daylong tent. The Indian said to Jim, "You come, you fix. Him belly heap big. Pretty soon bust. Maybe so you stick knife in belly like stick cow."

Jim had about half a pound of salts in a can, that he had to give a horse. He took the can, filled it with warm water and gave it to the Indian policeman. Jim told him, "Sick buck, drink it all heap quick."

By the time the policeman got back to the sick buck, the squaw had given up and stood hacking her fingers with a butcher knife to show her grief.

Well, the salts did the business. In a little while the sick buck rolled his eyes, gave a grunt or two and made for the nearest brush patch. The other Indians muttered, "Heap good," and went off about their business.

LIVING SO CLOSE to the Indians, the Daylong family had lots of opportunity to learn their ways.

The few squaws that could talk English at that time wouldn't if there was other Indians present. One time the lack of an interpreter almost got Jim into trouble.

It seemed like every Indian had a reason for wanting his house finished first. At first Jim tried to please all the Indians but then he saw they just wanted a house. They got some furniture from the government, invited the rest of the Indians in to see it, then lived in their tepees.

Jim was working on a house. An old couple whose tepee was old and leaked wanted their house fixed right away. Jim tried to make them understand he would finish the one he was working on and do theirs next.

The buck was in a hurry for the house and decided he would fix it himself. He hung blankets up for windows. The door was too small for the opening without the door sills and jams that a carpenter puts in.

The buck got a couple of logs, stood them in the doorway so he could lean the door against the logs from the inside. When he got the door and windows fixed to his satisfaction he called his squaw to see the cabin.

She was short and wide, a very big little woman. She had a big smile on her face when she went to look at the cabin, but it soon turned to a scowl for that door hole looked pretty small to that old girl. She tried it but it was "no dice," she couldn't get through the door hole. She walked slowly back to the tepee looking pretty glum.

The buck, too, looked pretty disgusted. He said, "Heap sh—," and went over to Jim again and said, "You fix. Me no savvy."

Jim put the windows in the old Indian's house and was ready to hang the door. He looked at the door opening and was a little skeptical whether the squaw could get through an ordinary door. He thought he ought to measure her to be sure.

He put his rule in his hip pocket and started over to the tepee to measure the squaw.

The old buck was sitting out by the house smoking a pipe admiring the windows. The squaw was in their tepee sitting on the bed combing her hair with a fine comb. When she combed out a louse, she would catch it with her fingers, put it in her mouth and crack it with her teeth.

Jim tried to tell her what he wanted but she couldn't understand. He pointed at the house, then pointed at her, spreading his hands wide apart. She just sat there combing her hair as if he wasn't there.

He stood there a while making motions, trying to make her understand he wanted to measure her rear end as that was her widest part. When he saw that she was just going to ignore him, he took his ruler out of his pocket and took a hold of her arm to pull her up.

She got up alright, with a big knife in her hand. Jim made tracks out of there fast. The old buck just kept smoking his pipe and looking at the windows in his house.

Jim then went to the Indian policeman, who could talk, and explained his difficulty. The Indian policeman went over to the tepee with Jim and explained what Jim wanted. She stood up then and let Jim measure her width.

He cut the doorway a little wider. When the buck saw that his squaw could go in and out without any trouble, he looked at Jim and said, "Heap good, squaw no have to live in tepee."

COULSON WAS located about where the Fair Grounds is now. When the Northern Pacific Railroad was built the town moved closer to the depot and was renamed Billings. My father-in-law, Jim Daylong was living with his family in one of the houses built in original Coulson so this incident happened a long time ago.

Jim Daylong was a stout, healthy man until he was about fifty years old, then he took down with rheumatism. He was suffering a lot from the pain. He had the doctor. The doctor said to bathe him in hot water to relieve the pain. The doctoring wasn't doing him any good as he was getting worse and suffering a lot. He got so bad he couldn't turn over.

The family had a pow wow and decided they would take the old man to Thermopolis to the Hot Springs for they had heard it was a sure cure for rheumatism. It was a distance of about two hundred miles by wagon for there was no railroad to Thermopolis at that time.

The two oldest boys came to my place to make preparations for the trip. We got together and built a wagon box for traveling. We put some bows and canvas over the wagon box.

When they was ready to start for Thermopolis, the boys carried the old man out on the mattress and springs and slid it in the wagon box.

They went through Pryor Sub Agency, through Pryor Gap, over on Sage Creek and up the valley until they struck the Big Horn River that went through Thermopolis.

INDIANS

The road was rough. They couldn't make much over twenty miles a day and sometimes not that much. The old man suffered plenty. By that time, he wasn't able to feed himself.

About half way to Thermopolis the old man was so bad and they did not have any way to give him a hot tub bath to relieve the pain. The boys thought they'd give him a steam both and maybe it would help. They had seen the Indians taking sweat baths along Pryor Creek. It gave them their idea.

The Indians take some small willow poles and bend them in a half circle, sticking both ends in the ground making a round hogan. It is usually close to a creek or river. They cover the willows with hides, canvas or blankets to keep heat in the sweat tepee. They heat some rocks, roll them in the sweat tepee, then get a bucket of water. The Indians take an old cow tail, dip it in the water and sprinkle the hot rocks. The sweat tepee fills with steam. The Indians stay in the sweat tepee until they are sweating all over, then they run out in their birthday clothes and jump in the cold water. The Indians call this "Heap Good Medicine."

The Daylong boys did about the same thing, only they dug a hole in the ground and set a tub of water in the hole. They put the bed springs over the water with the old man on it.

They heated rocks on the campfire and dropped them in the water. They was doing alright and the old man was getting a wonderful steam bath.

They had just one big black rock left. It was red hot when they rolled it in the tub. It exploded with a tremendous loud report. The explosion threw the old man up in the air.

It scared them all pretty bad. The kids all ran and Mrs. Daylong tripped over the wagon tongue and fell down.

The explosion threw the old man about fifteen feet from the sweat tepee. He wasn't hurt from the explosion, mostly scared. He couldn't move but he could talk. He lay there groaning, cussing the boys, the rheumatism and the sweat bath.

They went on to Thermopolis, though the old man was suffering from the jolt of the wagon he wouldn't consider another steam bath.

As soon as they got to Thermopolis, they began giving him the hot baths. He started to get better right away. In two weeks he could walk with two canes. He was taking baths and drinking a lot of that hot spring water. After he was there about seven weeks he was climbing the high hills around the hot springs.

When they started home he wouldn't ride in the wagon, said the team was too slow. He walked all the way home.

Jim died about fifteen years or so after that trip. He never had rheumatism again or an Indian steam bath.

8: Sheep Business

ABOUT FIFTY to sixty years ago sheep was big business in the northwest. They used to start in Utah and Idaho and trail through Wyoming down as far as Rawlins. It was called the desert country. There wasn't much water so they went down in the fall and back in the spring so the sheep could eat snow to quench their thirst as a sheep doesn't require much water. On the sheep wagons, they kept a barrel on each side full of melted snow water. There was practically no grass, just white sage.

Two men, a team, a saddle horse and three or four dogs went with a band of sheep usually about three thousand head. The dogs was the most important part for they couldn't have moved the sheep without them. That was just winter range.

In a storm or windy weather they tried to find a sheltered place and stayed there until the weather cleared, but ordinarily they moved a little ways each day to keep the sheep on fresh pasture. In spite of the distances they traveled the sheep came through in good shape. Prices wasn't so good but the sheepmen seemed to make good money as they had very little expense.

The sheepherders as a general rule was a queer lot. They knew sheep and little else. After herding sheep for three or four years, if they was all right when they started herding, they was touched in the head by then. Some of them got so dirty you wouldn't go in his wagon while others was so clean he wouldn't let you in. Most of them abided by the unwritten range law of feeding you.

They all got a faraway look in their eye and an empty expression on their face just like the sheep and would hardly talk to a stranger. So many went off their beam that in later years a law was made that required the owners of the sheep to take a herder into town every six months. I don't think the law did much good as the herder just got drunk and blew his wages, then went back to his little moveable home on the range.

In the spring they worked the bands towards a shearing pen. Shearing started about the twenty fifth of May. A great many made for Stoner, Wyoming. It was on the railroad and there was plenty of water. That was before the day of machine plants and the shearers used blades.

A good shearer would shear around a hundred head. He got about ten cents a sheep. Sheep shearing is dirty hard labor at best and when they used blades it was a man killer, but the shearers made big money. After they began to shear by machine a good shearer could do about two hundred and fifty sheep.

The best man I ever knew was Ira Ellis. He sheared three hundred and twelve sheep one day and was out of the pen by four o'clock. He was a champion. He broke the world's record for thirty days in a shearing pen in Chicago, I've forgotten the year. It seemed like he could shear a sheep in the time it took for an ordinary man to catch one, throw it and let it up. I believe the most he sheared was 337 in nine hours and fifteen minutes.

He gave them what he called the bloody blow. He started at the hind leg and went plumb to the head in one stroke. His clippers was cutting wool all the time. When he turned his sheep loose it was a good clean job, no tags left and his sheep was never cut.

In shearing sheep they put the band in a big corral. There was two alley ways to fill the pens holding twelve to fourteen sheep leading from it. One was for the sheep to be sheared and the other was to let the sheep that was sheared out into what was called the catch pen where they was branded with paint.

When a man in a pen caught his last sheep, he hollered, "Sheep out." Then the wrangler counted them out and tallied them on a tab at the gate and refilled his pen. The shearer always counted his strings that he tied his wool with. That way the sheep was counted twice in case there was a dispute or mistake.

Generally there was about four wranglers and a sheep dog that did more work than all of them. Then there was the wool sackers, two men to throw the fleeces at him, a wool tromper for about every ten shearers. The wool sacks weighed all the way from two hundred and fifty to four hundred pounds depending on how good the wool tromper was and the quality of the wool for fine wool weighs heavier than coarse. The wool sacks was piled in long ricks and covered with canvas until it was freighted to the railroad. There wasn't any easy job around a shearing pen.

At sheep shearing time the wool had to be hauled to the railroad. I have seen a half a mile of string teams strung out, waiting in line to be unloaded at the wool house in Billings.

After freighting wool, I saw that a shearing plant was a good place to make money as I could get all the wool hauling, the shearing of the sheep, the sacking of the wool and run the boarding house for the shearers.

I put my first shearing pen on what was called Post Pile Creek about fifteen miles south of Billings. There was a lot of sheep in that country. Gus Barth had five big bands running in the Duck Creek country, Jimmy Ash had several bands running on Cottonwood and Duck Creek. Then there was Johnny and Jimmy Ross on the head of Blue Creek country, John Clanton with several bands, Frank Summers with a lot of sheep and several others, besides there was a lot of drifting bands. I caught them as they was going through the country because of the short freighting cost.

I ran several shearing plants all over that country until the country settled up with dry land farmers.

I put in one of the first machine plants. They was a good deal faster. The hotter the day the easier the sheep shear. There is a lot of grease in wool and when it is a cool day, the grease is hard. Some of the sheepmen used to use sweat sheds to get the sheep real hot.

They enclosed the sheep in a tight shed, packed as close together as possible. When you would open the door of the shed, the smell was awful and the fumes just about put your eyes out.

Well I remember one bad break I got one year. There was a lot of sheep over in the Musselshell country. I was talking to a sheep man by the name of Sam Church that had several bands of sheep in that country. He said that if I would put a shearing pen over on Carpenter Creek I'd get all the sheep in that part of the country.

Carpenter Creek runs into the Musselshell not far from Wolf Springs. I went over and saw a lot of sheepmen and booked them up, then put a shearing plant on Carpenter Creek.

I had a pen on Cottonwood about thirty miles from Billings. I figured that by starting the Carpenter plant on the Musselshell early I would finish shearing them out, then move on to Cottonwood.

Just after starting the Carpenter Creek plant, we got a bunch of scabby sheep. They quarantined a lot of that country. I could only shear scabby sheep that was quarantined, then I had to burn the plant.

It rained a lot that spring and we had to lay off in the wet weather. I cleaned up the scab sheep and was to start shearing at the Cottonwood plant the fifth of June, only three days off and about ninety miles away.

I had to take the shearers to Roundup where they could take the stage to Billings so didn't get started to move until afternoon. We only got on our way about fifteen miles.

It rained most all night and the road was bad and forty five miles to Billings where I had to pick up the shearers and get a load of groceries, then thirty miles to Cottonwood.

We started early but it was twelve o'clock that night before we got into Billings. Sturm and Drake had a store on Montana Avenue. I went to Sturm's house and got him out of bed. I told him my troubles and that I wanted a four-horse load of groceries. It was two o'clock by the time we got the wagon loaded.

I had to rest my teams a while. We got on the road about six that morning. We got into Cottonwood about three in the afternoon. We got the cook tent set up, had supper for twenty four men that night and started shearing sheep in the morning.

SHEEP HERDERS are a peculiar class of people. After a man goes to herding sheep and stays with it for a year, he will hardly ever take another kind of job if he can get a herding job. Like the miner who likes to work underground, the herder likes sheep and likes to be with them.

I have met some very nice sheep herders, some that was well educated. I never could figure out why they got a little queer after they had herded a few years, whether it was from being alone so much or whether it was the smell of the sheep that affected them. There is a bad odor to the sheep when they get hot.

A sheep herder is generally very good to his dogs. The sheep dog gets to know as much as the herder about sheep. I have seen herders talk to their dogs and the dog would look at the herder and then go and do exactly what he had been told.

I know of an instance at Douglas, Wyoming. One night in a bad blizzard, the sheep left the bed ground. The herder tried to hold them but the storm was blowing so hard that they split in two bunches. The herder sent his dog around ahead of them to turn them but the dog couldn't turn them against the wind. The dog stayed with the sheep until the next day when the wind quit blowing, then fetched them into camp. The herder got his bunch in a coulee out of the wind and camped, then went back to his wagon. A herder always hangs a lantern in his camp wagon. He had froze his ears, fingers and feet. When the dog fetched his bunch in, the herder fed him and sent him out to hunt the bunch the herder had had. He fetched them in just before dark, he was sore footed and tired out.

I knew of another case where the herder froze to death, but they found the dog holding the sheep.

There was an old Scotchman that used to herd. He was a buggery looking fellow and quite old. He always had a shock of whiskers all over his face, long hair and dirty ragged clothes. When he wasn't with a band of sheep he was drunk. His language was pretty rough, though he was supposed to have a wonderful education. He always looked so wild that everyone called him "Scotty, the Bugger." He had the reputation of being an awful good sheep herder and a trainer of sheep dogs. When he wasn't talking to the dogs, he was talking to himself.

He was herding sheep over on Basin Creek one time when he came upon a scarecrow. It had been there a long time and the rain had washed the clothes on it and they looked fairly clean. A camp tender saw Scotty walk around it a time or two and say, "Good morning me boy, you look nice and clean this fine mornin' and I believe you are dressed better than me and I'll just trade clothes with you." Which he proceeded to do!

Scotty always used two dogs. He worked one and rested the other. Scotty got sick and died while herding. When the camp tender found him it looked like he had been dead several days. One dog was guarding Scotty and the other was out tending the sheep.

In the early days those old time sheep herders that was herding on the open range in all kinds of weather went through plenty of hardship. They froze in the winter and was plagued in the summer by wood ticks, flies, rattle snakes and varmints.

If it hadn't been for the companionship of those wonderful sheep dogs they couldn't have stood it.

THERE WAS a man by the name of Joe Poor, who came to Billings from South Dakota in a covered wagon. He had a boy about sixteen with him and they was looking for work. I was haying and put them both to work.

SHEEP BUSINESS

They had a very pretty collie dog named Fanny and three puppies with them. When the Poors left their covered wagon, Fanny stayed and watched the wagon. Believe me, she took care of things while they was gone. Fanny was so smart that I asked for one of her pups.

Joe gave me a pup and I called him Kaiser. He grew to be one of the smartest and best dogs I ever had anything to do with. He had a keen instinct. I don't think he understood everything we'd say, but he watched while we talked to him and understood enough to do what we wanted done.

I was living on Blue Creek at that time and raised quite a lot of alfalfa hay. The fall that I got Kaiser, I sold my hay to a sheepman. The herder had his camp wagon about a quarter of a mile from our house. When the weather wasn't too bad, during the winter, he would take the sheep out to graze on the hills.

The herder had a wonderful sheep dog that had never done anything but herd sheep. The herder liked our pup and asked me if I would let him train the pup for a sheep dog. I let him have the pup for the winter. By spring he was a good sheep dog. That herder and his sheep dog together had taught Kaiser plenty.

That year I put up a shearing plant and used Kaiser around the pens. He turned out to be the best corral dog I ever saw work in a sheep corral. He did more than two men.

There is one lane from the wooly corral to the shearing pen and one lane where you turn the sheared sheep out to another corral until all of a band is sheared. The main thing is to always have plenty sheep in the wooly lane so when you turn a pen of sheared sheep out there will be plenty sheep to fill the shearer's pens again without having to wait for sheep.

Kaiser took care of that job without any talking to. When the wooly alley began to get short of sheep, he would cut out enough sheep to fill the alley and lay down behind them and never leave the alley except to fill the lane.

He hardly ever barked in the corral. Once in a while he'd give a couple of barks if he got dry. Someone would take him a tin of water, but he would never leave the head of the alley as long as there was a sheep in the lanes.

After sheep shearing was over he was just as good a ranch dog as he was a sheep dog and kept all the varmints away. You could say, "Listen, Kaiser, I hear a coyote."

That dog would cock his head on one side and listen, then he'd stand on his hind legs and sniff the air and if you was on a hill he would go all around it to be sure nothing was around, then he'd come to you and wag his tail as if to say, "You must be mistaken."

We had a little girl about four years old, whenever she was out of the house he was always with her. He used to play ball with her. She would throw the ball and he would run to get the ball and fetch it back to her. Sometimes, we used to put a blindfold over his eyes and then hide the ball. He would hunt until he found the ball, then he would take it to her.

We had a couple of milk cows. They ran in a large pasture and someone always had to go after them every evening. I took Kaiser with me a few times after the cows. One evening I told Kaiser to get the cows. Away he went. In a little while he came back bringing the cows. After that, every evening he went out and found the cows and fetched them in.

My wife wanted some ducks so she bought some duck eggs and put them under a setting hen. When the little ducks hatched my wife kept them shut up until they got big enough to get around good. It wasn't long after she turned them out with the hen until they found the creek.

The hen and Kaiser had a bad time then. The hen was clucking along the creek and Kaiser was trying to get the little ducks out of the water. He would push a little duck out of the creek with his nose, then try to get another one out while the first one was getting back. He liked little chickens and such, and was being mighty careful not to hurt them.

My wife was watching the hen and the dog and helped him get them out of the water and into their little pen. After the ducks got pretty good sized the old hen never paid any attention to the ducks when they got in the water, but every evening Kaiser drove the ducks and the hen to their coop and waited until someone came to shut them up.

One time I was cutting brush along the creek, Kaiser was with me. After a while I missed him. In a little while he came out of the brush, barked at me and looked over in the brush. I thought maybe he had seen a skunk or porcupine.

I went over to see what he wanted to show me and found five little rabbits all piled on a little bunch of grass. I looked them over and found that none of them was hurt. I hunted around to find where he had got them and found their nest under a fallen cottonwood log. I put them back in their nest. Kaiser wagged his tail and left them alone, he just wanted to show them to me.

He was a wonderful watch dog, not cross but if anyone came to the ranch he didn't know, he always got between them and our little girl. If he thought they was getting too close or too familiar he would show his teeth and growl. He never paid any attention to any of the neighbors but one man who was a German.

The German came to our place quite often. I always had to watch the dog as he always growled at the German and I was afraid the dog might bite him. My wife noticed the dog's actions and said she didn't like the looks of him either. Many years later the man was arrested as a spy for the Germans in World War I.

When I sold the ranch and moved into town. Kaiser didn't seem to like being idle. He never left the yard but acted lonesome and had a faraway look in his eyes as if he was looking for the open spaces.

We hadn't been in town very long when one morning Kaiser was missing. We searched the town for him. I put an ad in the paper offering a $50.00 reward for his return but never got any trace of him.

We was gone for two years with the Wild West Show. After we came back, I was over north of Billings hunting horses. I rode up to the ranch and there was Kaiser. He saw me coming and came to meet me.

He was the happiest dog I ever saw. I was riding my pet horse Hornet that had been raised on the ranch. The dog smelled the horse's feet and when the horse put his nose down to smell him, the dog licked his nose and ran all around him, barking like he'd met his long lost friend. When I got off to pet him he whirled and barked, ran around me and licked my hands.

The man said, "That dog must know you. I never saw him act that way with anyone else."

I told him, "He ought to know me. I raised him and he's my dog. When he disappeared two years ago he had a license tag on his collar. I advertised and done everything I could at the time to find him. Where did you get him?"

The man said he'd bought a bunch of sheep in Billings and as he was taking them home the dog came to him and helped with the sheep. He said he was the best dog he'd ever seen and would like to buy him.

I told him I wouldn't sell Kaiser and was going to take him home with me. If Kaiser didn't want to stay in town and came back to him, he could keep him.

When I got home with Kaiser following me, there was a joyous reunion. Kaiser seemed so happy to see all the family. He played ball with the girls and acted as if he'd never been away. In a few days he seemed to be lonesome and one day he was gone. He just couldn't stand a life of idleness.

WHEN OLD TIMERS get together sooner or later some funny story of the past comes into the conversation. That's the way it was not long ago when I was visiting with Mike Savarcey. We got a chuckle out of the antics of some cowboys and a sheep herder and I'll pass the story on to you.

SHEEP BUSINESS

It took place a long time ago when the cowboys and sheep herders was making whoopee. There was always a distinction between the two. They seldom mingled for the cowboys didn't like the sheep herders and the herders had no love for the cowboys.

The cowboys rode a good horse on the range, went places and was free while a herder went a foot and could never leave his band of sheep. He stayed alone all the time and naturally got a little queer in the head for his dog was his only companion.

Whenever a herder went to town he always took his dog. There used to be a saloon on the south side of town on Minnesota Avenue where they had a shed to keep the sheep herders' dogs while they was in town. It was a kind of headquarters. They could eat and drink in the saloon and that was what they wanted to do most.

I have known sheep herders that came to town with six or seven hundred dollars and in a week it was all gone. Some painted lady would get him to stay with her, in the morning he was minus his roll or else the bartender would give him a drink out of the black bottle, drag him in the back room, relieve him of his dough. Then the herder would go back to his "home on the range," a sheep wagon and a bunch of woolies, for another year or so.

Mike was telling me about a herder that had been rolled a time or two and thought he'd try a different stunt. He thought he'd pretend to be a cowboy and have some fun.

Before he came to Billings he sent to Montgomery Wards and got a ten gallon hat, a pair of pretty high heeled boots, some California pants (heavy-weight wool pants favored by many cowboys) and a pair of crooked shank spurs to drag along the sidewalk to draw attention to himself.

He passed as a cowboy all right on the south side for a while as the real cowboys only played the south side after dark.

The hangout for the cowboys was Bob Nix's saloon. Clay Jolly used to be bartender and gambler there.

Old Boar Cat Williams, a foreman from the N Bar, had come to town with a bunch of his cowboys to celebrate. They was in Bob Nix's taking a drink when the sheep herder dressed in his Montgomery Ward clothes came in. He didn't realize it, but he had got in the wrong pew. Those cowboys could smell a sheep herder a mile away.

He walked right up to the bar, ordered a whiskey straight from Clay. He was in a real expansive mood and bought drinks for everybody. He said he was just down from a riding job in Canada and wanted to get acquainted. He had quite a line, in fact, it was pretty raw.

He wasn't fooling that bunch any. They knew he wasn't a cowhand and thought they'd have a little fun with him.

After taking a few drinks part of them went over to a table and sat down and began looking "the Canadian cowboy" over. Boar Cat said, "I think he looks and smells like a damn sheep herder off from his range. Can't you see the wool around his eyes?"

While they was talking, a cowboy from the Bird Head outfit came in and joined them. He took a look at the fellow they was discussing and said, "I'll be damned, that fellow is one of Charlie Bair's sheep herders. What's he doing in here?"

That lit the fuse. They decided to have a kangaroo court and try this guy for "impersonating his betters."

The court was set up right then and there with judge and lawyers. The case was argued out, the Bird Head puncher was witness for the prosecution. Undoubtedly it was a prejudiced court. The verdict was "guilty" and the sentence, a chapping.

They rolled in a whiskey barrel, laid the unhappy sheep herder across it and applied the chaps with vigor. Then they fined him, drinks for the house. That was the end of his cowboy career.

IT MUST HAVE been about 1899. I was hunting horses on Blue Creek, about twenty miles south of Billings, I rode over to a spring to get a drink. As I got close to the spring I saw there was a camp there. I rode over to the camp and made the acquaintance of Mr. Logan, Mrs. Logan and their three children Tom, Dick and Fay.

I visited a while and Mr. Logan asked me to have dinner with them. He told me they was going to Red Lodge for some kind of gathering, I have forgotten what it was. Anyway, they was musicians and was going to play there. He said the trip was more for pleasure and an outing than anything else. The kids all had a saddle horse apiece while Mr. and Mrs. Logan rode in the wagon.

In after years I got to know them well. Tom Logan ran cattle in the Sand Creek neighborhood until he passed away several years ago. Mr. Logan died in Billings. Fay married and went to the coast. Dick Logan was manager of the Billings Airport. I sort of lost track of Mrs. Logan, if she is still living she is a pretty old lady.

Several years after I had met them, Mr. Logan was running a bunch of sheep on Cottonwood Creek, north of the Pryor Mountains. It was along in June. I took a bunch of sheep shearers over to the shearing pens on Cottonwood Creek. We was going to start shearing about the tenth of June. Mr. Logan had his bunch of ewes and lambs on the creek just above the shearing plant.

Cottonwood Creek isn't a very long creek but it has a lot of coulees running into it and it drains a lot of territory. The country around it stands on end, it has a lot of fall.

It had been a dry spring until about that time. It had been very hot, clouds would roll up but it couldn't seem to rain. Sheep like to graze out early in the morning as soon as they can see to graze. When it begins to get hot they will come in on water and lay in the shade until it gets cool in the evening.

This particular day was a beastly hot day. The sheep had drank and camped along the creek for a half a mile in small bunches forty-five or even a hundred in a bunch, as there was about twenty-five hundred head of ewes in the band. The herder had gone to his wagon to get some dinner. He saw some black clouds at the head of the creek but had no idea that it was raining there.

It began to rain a little, the herder went up the creek to move the sheep out of the bottom. He would drive a bunch out away from the creek, but just as soon as he'd leave to move another bunch, back to the shade would go the other bunch. I just can't tell you how hard it is to move a bunch of sheep on a hot day after they have camped in some shade.

The herder heard a loud roaring noise and looked up to see a wall of water, brush, sticks and logs about ten feet high rushing down the creek. When it hit those ewes and lambs, it was just too bad. It just rolled them up in a bunch and took the most of them into the Yellowstone River.

As the flood roared down the creek, the sheep shearers went out to the creek to watch as the sheep, logs and brush boiled by. In among the tangled debris it looked like there was a man. Somebody yelled, "There goes the herder." But there was nothing we could do.

Later when the flood went down we saw the herder. He told us what we had seen was a scarecrow that he had put up to keep the coyotes away from the sheep.

I was there and saw the casualties of that flood. There was probably five hundred head that the water didn't get. It was a pitiful sight, ewes running around bleating for their lambs and the lambs bleating for their mothers.

After the water ran off there must have been five hundred head that had got stuck in the logs and brush and washed out on the low places. Mr. Logan went to Billings and got a crew of men to skin them out. After a couple of days they began to get ripe and there was an awful smell. I didn't think we could shear there as it was horrible as most of the dead sheep was close to the shearing pens.

The skinning crew left the pelts where they had skinned them. They was going to start hauling the pelts the next day and kill the orphan lambs that was bleating around starving to death.

About eleven o'clock the next day another cloud burst came and it was worse than the first one. It took all the pelts, carcasses and most of the little lambs and washed them all in the river.

The herder saved the ewes the first flood left as he had them out on the hills. Mr. Logan took a big loss, about two thousand sheep and most of his lamb crop.

SCOTCHMEN AS A RULE are very good sheepmen and very good herders. Johnny and Jimmy Ross was Scotchmen from the old country. They went to Wyoming and herded sheep there until they saved enough money to buy a small band of sheep. Then one of the Ross brothers herded their band while the other one worked as foreman for a large sheep outfit to take care of their expenses.

Neither one of the Ross brothers had any education. Johnny could just write his name after a fashion, Jimmy signed with an X. They couldn't read or write but they could count to a hundred. They would count sheep with their hands, five at a time. When they got to a hundred they made a mark and when they was through they counted the marks. Johnny did most of the business because he could sign his name.

They came to Montana with two large bands of sheep and settled on the head of Blue Creek about twenty miles south of Billings. I got acquainted with them in about 1899. They both took up claims and hired me to fence their claims. That was the first fence that was built on the head of the creek. At that time, there was just a few ranches in that part of the country and they was along the creek. The rest of the country was free open range.

The Ross brothers ran sheep there for several years. When the country began to settle up, they cut their herds down to one band. Jimmy Ross stayed up on the creek and took care of the sheep while Johnny went to Billings and got in the saloon business.

After Johnny went to Billings he married a very popular young woman by the name of Bates. She was working as a singer and entertainer in the old Topic Saloon and Show Shop which was south of the tracks on Minnesota Avenue. Johnny was very proud of her popularity and was heard to say, "I am proud of her, boy, all the high muckity mucks buys champagne for Bates."

Johnny Ross was a good looking man about five foot seven inches tall, rather on the fair order, but not too light and weighed about a hundred and forty pounds. He had just enough Scotch brogue to sound comical. Johnny was naturally crooked. He would rather cheat a man out of five dollars than to get twenty dollars honestly. He was a good mixer and you couldn't help but like him even if you knew he was crooked as a dog's hind leg.

When Johnny went in the saloon business on the south side of the track he made his saloon to fit the needs of sheepmen and herders. He made a place for the herders to keep their dogs for in those days, a herder always took his dog with him wherever he went. Ross also had a place where they could leave their war sack and bed. If a sheepmen wanted a herder, he went to Johnny Ross's as the sheep herders all hung around close to their dogs.

At that time most of the herders was Scotchmen and when they came to town they would head for Johnny Ross's place so they could leave their dog and belongings while they did a little celebrating. Johnny would meet them and shake hands and say, "Boy, I'm glad to see you, come up and have a drink on the house." Then he would wave his hand to all the bar flies in the saloon and say, "Everyone come up and have a drink. This is a particular friend of mine." The bar would be lined. Then someone else would treat the house.

The sheepherder naturally would think that he ought to buy a round as he was an honored guest. The herder would offer to buy a round, if Johnny would cash his check. Most of the herders' checks would be all the way from a hundred to five hundred dollars depending on how long he had been herding.

Johnny would take his check and say, "Boy, that is too much money for you to carry around with you, someone might rob you. I don't want to see you lose your money, man. Sign your name on the check and I will give you all the money you need. Here is twenty dollars, that is enough to spend, if you need some more you can get it."

Johnny would then tell the bartender to give the sheep herder anything he needed, money, drinks or credit. By that time, a few more drinks had made the rounds and the crowd was getting to make a lot of noise. Ross would tell them to go into the back room and have all the fun they wanted as the waiter would take care of them.

When they got to the back room, anything went. If the herder didn't get drunk before he spent the twenty dollars, he would get a shot out of the "black bottle" which settled him for several hours. When the herder passed out the bar bums knew there was no more free drinks and would drift away.

When the herder came out of his trance he found himself in the middle of an awful mess—cards and whiskey bottles all over the floor, tables and chairs turned over and himself with a blank memory of events and a head that felt like a keg of nails. He'd go to the bar for a drink to help his head and ask for his money.

Johnny would say "Boy, you spent all your check last night, if I had been here I would have stopped you. I tried to take care of you but you went wild ordering drinks. Your crowd all got drunk and raised particular hell. You made so much noise the police just about pinched the house. Didn't you see all the mess you made?"

The herder would hang around for a day or so and when he went back to his job, Johnny would give him a pint of liquor and some advice. "Now when you come in again, Boy, come and see me and don't be such a bloody fool and spend all your money in one night."

JOHN CLANTON an old time sheepman was quite a character. He was nicknamed Slop John as he used to haul the slop from the restaurants to fed his pigs. He was a very smart man, done lots of business but had no education. He raised a nice family, two girls and a boy. His son Albert lives on a ranch on Blue Creek.

Clanton had several bands of sheep and a ranch that bordered the west side of Billings, now known as Clanton Heights. There was a homestead just east of the Clanton place, just about where Pioneer Park is at the present. Clanton told me that it was traded for a saddle worth about thirty dollars. Well, even at that it fetched more than Long Island which was bought for less than twenty-five dollars' worth of beads and some treaty talks, from the Indians.

Clanton was a very busy man, always on the go between his ranches and his various bands of sheep. Before the country settled up he ran his sheep on Blue Creek.

The panic of 1910 killed John Clanton. He was getting along in years. He had put in most of his life working hard, scheming and managing. He told me he had went through two bad panics and he just couldn't stand to go through another one. Two days later he was dead by his own hand.

When I ran the sheep shearing plant on Basin Creek, John Clanton used to have his sheep sheared there. He was always losing his horses or having some kind of trouble. When he came to shear that year he had a spring wagon loaded with a lot of sheep pelts, lamp black, turpentine, coal oil, some red paint to brand the sheep, a bed and some wool sacks.

When his sheep was sheared he wanted me to haul his spring wagon into Billings for him as he had lost his team of horses. I told him to tie it on back of my wool wagon, which he did. He had a lot of junk tied on it. It wasn't a heavy load just bulky.

There was several coulees that had to be crossed, they wasn't very deep but was pretty steep. I never paid any attention how he tied on but supposed that he had tied his wagon secure as it was about ten miles into Billings. Clanton was setting on the spring wagon on top of the load of junk.

We got over the first coulee okay. The second one was a little worse. As we crossed the second one, just before the spring wagon got to the top it broke the rope that it was tied with and ran back into the coulee and tipped over.

Millard Daylong was driving my four-horse team. He saw Clanton break loose. We stopped and ran back as soon as we could get off the wool wagon.

The spring wagon had turned bottom side up with Clanton underneath the load. We both grabbed the wagon and turned it over. There was Clanton with his head sticking in a bucket of red paint, trying to get the bucket off his head. Millard put his foot on Clanton's shoulder, got a good hold on the bucket and gave it a jerk. The bucket came off with considerable hair and skin.

He was an awful looking specimen of humanity with red paint all over his hair, face and clothes. His ears was full. We got a wool sack and tried to wipe it off. It was real heavy paint and he began to holler as it was hurting him pretty bad.

We got the coal oil and tried that. It done pretty good, it cut the paint off his hair, but he couldn't stand the rough sack on his face. We told him that when we got to the creek maybe we could do a better job.

When we got to the creek we gave him another working over. We had used all the coal oil so we tried the turpentine. John looked a little better but was moaning and taking on about his eyes. He said he was blind as a bat, couldn't see a thing.

He moaned all the way to town. When we got there I told him I'd take him to Doctor Clark and he would fix him up. He kept saying, "I'm ruined, I'm ruined, I'm blind and my head and face feels like it is all burned to hell. I wouldn't be surprised if my hair all comes out."

Millard and I didn't look so good either with red paint all over us from the wool sack mixed with coal oil and turpentine and mud from the creek.

Clanton was all right in a few days. Mostly he just needed cleaning up.

I WAS RUNNING a shearing pen on Basin Creek about nine miles south of Billings. It was a good spot except for two reasons. It was too close to town and too easy to get booze.

I had two four-horse teams that made a trip with a load of wool every day. The shearers was always giving the teamsters money to fetch liquor to the shearing pen. I didn't like it but there wasn't much I could do about it. I had spoke to the captain of the shearing crew about it and about all he said about the liquor in camp was that it might come in pretty handy if one of the sheep shearers got rattlesnake bit. Then an accident happened and I decided that liquor and shearing sheep wouldn't mix to any advantage.

My wife was cooking for the shearing camp. She had a younger sister by the name of Estelle helping her. On this particular day Estelle had been subpoenaed to appear on a divorce case and I had to take her to Billings.

It had rained in the night and there was water still in the low places in the road. I had bought a nice small rubber-tired single buggy for my wife and was using it for the trip to town.

We had gone about a mile from the shearing plant when we met one of the lead teams from the wool wagon coming up the road on a dead run dragging a pair of stretchers. I knew something had happened and said to myself, "Booze!" And I was plenty mad.

My wife had sent in for a big grocery order and the shearers had sent in for wet goods. I got the story out of the teamsters later.

The teamsters had sampled the wet goods too frequently and matched a horse race with the wool wagons. They was racing in a road that was pretty narrow, a wire fence on one side and hills on the other side. As they came to a narrow place it was pretty sideling and one of the wool wagons turned over with all the groceries into a large mud puddle.

When I came along with the buggy and saw just what had happened I was just boiling and I thought to myself I'd fire them right where they was and fetch a couple of men from town to drive the wagons on to camp.

When I went to pass the wool wagon I had to get up the hill where it was pretty steep. The horse I was driving was scared of the tipped over wagon and went up the hill a little too far. One of the upper wheels hit a sagebrush and went over, dumping Estelle and me right in the mud hole with the groceries.

Estelle weighed about a hundred and eighty pounds and she lit right on top of me in the mud. She laughed and laughed at the way I looked as I jumped up and grabbed the buggy and set it right side up.

I was so damn mad and embarrassed that I never even looked at the men, wagons or groceries in the mud but just drove on into town.

That was the last of the wet goods. I told the teamsters if they ever fetched any more liquor for the shearers I'd fire them and if I ever knew of them taking a drink when they was hauling wool they would get the can tied on them. I also made it plain to the shearers that there was to be no more liquor in camp. If they wanted to drink they had to go to town to do it.

MILLARD DAYLONG and I was going in a wagon by the old south bridge on the Yellowstone River. Going up the road, Millard spied a big, new, black ten gallon hat. He got out, tried it on and it just fit him. We thought that it had been lost by some drunken Indians that was on their way back to the reservation. Millard put the hat on and we went on in to town.

At Bob Conway's Saloon we met a sheepherder that was pretty well juiced up. He'd spent all his money and was trying to sell his horse. I needed a horse but all the money I had was two and a half and Millard was broke.

The sheepherder kept eyeing Millard's black hat. Millard got me to one side and said, "Bill, I believe we could get that sheepherder a little drunker and we could trade this hat for his horse and go fifty-fifty on it."

It looked like a good gamble so we went out to see the horse which was in John Clanton's pasture just on the other side of where the Billings Senior High School is now.

It was a grey horse that weighed somewhere about a thousand pounds. He was fat and looked pretty good from a distance. We decided to skin that sheepherder out of his horse.

We went back to Conway's and we bought the sheepherder drinks until the $2.50 was almost gone. Whiskey was only fifteen cents a drink. The sheepherder was feeling mighty good. Millard took the black hat off his head and put it on the sheepherder's head saying, "God, you look good in that hat. Makes you look like a cowboy."

The herder took the hat off, looked it over and put it back on his head. Millard knew then it was time to trade. He said, "I think a lot of this hat. I just bought it but it looks so good on you that you ought to have it. I'll tell you what I'll do, I'll trade you this hat for your horse."

The sheepherder took the hat off again, admired it, then put it back on and said, "Buy me one more drink and it's a trade."

I spent my last half a dollar for drinks and the trade was made. My money was all gone. Millard and I was pretty well jagged and thought we had got the best of a sheepherder. We went home as it was too late to get the horse by that time.

Next day we went after the horse. We went in the wagon. We just took a rope as it was a small pasture, we thought we could just run the horse up in a corner of the fence and throw a rope on him. Which we did.

When the rope tightened on that old pony's neck he snorted and sure threw a whing ding. He started running and bucking across the pasture, dragging me. Millard grabbed on the end of the rope. The horse drug us both to the end of the pasture, then stopped long enough for Millard to tie the rope around a post. The horse threw another fit. Our hands was all rope burned so we thought the post would hold him.

When the horse took a run and hit the end of the rope it threw him and broke the post. He got up and made another run and snapped off about fifteen more posts. That took quite a lot of the bugs out of him so we managed to get him tied to the back of the wagon, although he was kicking and striking all the time.

While we was dragging the horse home we wondered if we had beat that sheepherder any for the horse didn't look so good on close inspection. One hip was knocked down. He had little, mean, pig eyes and the disposition of a mountain lion.

When we got him home he was so mean to strike that we threw him down to put a halter on him. I looked in his mouth and seen that he was about ten years old. We decided he was an outlaw and completely spoiled. Millard wanted no part of him.

I called the horse Sampson. He was the meanest horse I ever tried to break. I tried to break him to ride. I rode him in a round corral. He bucked until he played out, then run alongside of the corral to try to drag me off. I saw there was no use trying to make a saddle horse of him so I thought I'd break him to work.

He was a wampus cat all right. The first time I hitched him to the wagon he just about kicked everything apart and broke the tongue out of the wagon. I was about as stubborn as he was mean. I made up my mind I'd make him work or kill him.

I got him so I could work him but I pretty near had to kill him to do it. Every time you got close to him he'd strike or kick at you. For two weeks, when I'd get one tug unhooked, he'd start to bucking, kicking and bawling. He didn't stop until he got the harness all bucked off, even the collar.

He would work but he never got gentle. He broke up more stuff and caused me a lot of grief. I'd have been a lot better off if I'd taken him out and shot him.

GEORGE WILLIAMS and I was riding on the Crow Reservation. We was hunting horses that had strayed away from their owners and had a reward on them, at the same time gathering some of my own horses that had strayed over in that country.

We never thought about carrying grub along in those day as there was lots of cattle roundup wagons and sheep wagons where we could eat. No one ever turned a rider down for a meal. They was glad to have company and hear any news that was going around the country.

The most of the sheepherders was awfully glad to see someone and visit with them as sometimes they wouldn't see a man other than the camp tender for several weeks at a time. The camp tender would only come to their camp about once a week to move their wagon and bring them supplies.

We had rode for two days and hadn't found a stray. We had seen a lot of wild horses but it was almost impossible to look at them, for as soon as they saw you or got wind of you, they'd start running. We wasn't riding for wild horses that trip so we left them alone.

It was tiresome riding all day, seeing lots of stock but not a stray with a reward. We had rode Fly Creek Basin where lots of horses was running, then Woody and over to Bill Cashen's ranch on Beauvais.

Going into Cashen's we run into a team of horses that belonged to Jimmie Ash, a sheepman that run his sheep on Duck Creek. They was a camp team that Jimmie Ash used to move the sheep camps. There was a twenty-five dollar reward on the team so that made George and me feel a little better.

We stayed all night at Cashen's. Bill Cashen told me about seeing a gentle buckskin mare with a yearling and a little colt. The mare was branded ⌒ S (Lazy J Reverse 2) which was my brand. She was running about five miles north and east of Cashen's. The mare had been gone two years, I was anxious to get her.

We went over next morning to get the mare and her colts. In the bunch the mare was running with, there was a saddle horse that belonged to Frank Summers, a sheepman that lived in Billings. It was a nice gentle bay horse and there was a ten dollar reward on him. We felt like we was beginning to hit pay dirt.

We drove the bunch over to Bill Cashen's corral and cut out the bay and my mare and colts. Our horses was tired so we got fresh horses from Cashen. We rode that country and found a saddle horse belonging to Jimmy Ross, who had a ranch on Blue Creek. The Ross horse had a reward of $7.50. We run the bunch of horses he was running with up against a rimrock and roped him as we didn't want to take the bunch into the corral.

That night we stopped at a sheep camp. We had made a long ride. We hadn't had any dinner and was plenty hungry. We spied the sheep wagon just before sun down. The sheepherder hadn't got in yet.

We hobbled our horses, then went in the sheep wagon and cooked up a big feed. George said, "Let's josh the sheepherder a little."

It was already to eat and on the table when the sheepherder came to the wagon. Before the sheepherder had time to say anything George said to him, "Hello, fellow, come right in and eat. We didn't expect company or we'd a made a pie but come right in. Make yourself to home. We sure like company."

The sheepherder looked kind of surprised. I guess he thought he'd got to the wrong wagon or was going nuts or either we was and he didn't know just which.

He came in and set down. The only thing he said was, "You're pretty good cooks."

When we was through eating, George told the herder to get over on the bed and set while we washed the dishes. When we was through with the dishes, George picked up an extra bed roll that was in the wagon and started for the door. He said to the sheepherder, "You just sleep in the bunk, we'll roll out our beds outside."

It was just breaking day when the sheepherder called us. It didn't seem like we'd been in bed over an hour. He had breakfast all ready.

George was still keeping up the pretense that the sheepherder was our guest and thanked him for cooking breakfast. He told him we didn't know he wanted to get up so early or we'd rolled out sooner.

The sheepherder didn't say much, but when we got ready to leave he said, "Who the hell do you think you sons of bitches are?"

9: Rustlers and Killers

IT HAS ALWAYS been amusing to hear the different stories that have been told about the Hole in the Wall country in Wyoming. Some said it was a big country in the mountains. The mountains enclosed a basin that was surrounded with steep rim rocks, impossible to get into only through a hole in the rocks that was always guarded.

There was stories that said the Wild Bunch, as they was called, had a regular village where they kept their families, that they lived like kings off the loot from their crimes. If there was a killing happened anywhere and the killer made a get-away, gossip always said the killer went to the Hole-in-the-Wall.

No one I ever talked to knew how the Hole-in-the-Wall got its name. To get to the Hole-in-the-Wall you rode twelve or fifteen miles west of Kaycee through a shallow, narrow valley to the Middle Fork. You come to a red canyon just wide enough for the Middle Fork and a trail. That was the entrance of the Hole-in-the-Wall.

Just beyond the short canyon of the Middle Fork you are in an entirely different country. The Hole-in-the-Wall is a big, rolling range country. The low hills that surround it can be ridden over from the north, south or west.

During the 1890s and early 1900s, the Hole-in-the-Wall was plenty tough. When the Montana stockmen made war on the rustlers on the Little Missouri a lot of them made for the Hole-in-the-Wall. Horse and cattle rustling got too slow so they got to robbing banks and holding up trains.

They got by for quite a while as the country wasn't too thickly settled. When a train was held up, by the time it was reported and a posse raised, the hold-up men would be miles away disbanded and scattered. There was miles and miles of open country with no communications. Of course every robbery that was committed was layed to the Wild Bunch from the Hole-in-the-Wall. If all the people of the Dakotas, Wyoming and Montana that was accused of being in there had made the Hole-in-the-Wall their headquarters it would have been a crowded place.

When I was in Lander, Wyoming, quite a few of the Hole-in-the-Wall outlaws used to come there and gamble or stick around for a few days. Tom O'Day was a well known character. He was a cowpuncher and worked in that country before he joined the Wild Bunch. I was well acquainted with him. He was working on the roundup as a "rep" on the Wind River. The nights was pretty chilly. His bed was pretty skimpy and so was mine. We doubled up and slept together for perhaps ten days.

He was a hard worker and a nice man to talk to. You would never have believed he was a leader of the gang. Later he was arrested at Cheyenne. He was too game to talk and though they never proved anything on him, he was convicted on circumstantial evidence and sentenced to six years, which he served. I have heard that he turned straight when he got out.

There was a fellow that was called Butch that tended bar occasionally at Slick Bernard's Saloon. I believe he was Butch Cassidy, anyway, he was well liked.

They used to tell a story about Butch. It seems he was arrested and taken to Cheyenne. He got a good lawyer who was pretty expensive. The law tried Butch but didn't have enough evidence to convict him. When the judge dismissed the case he made Butch agree to leave the State of Wyoming and never come back.

Butch made his way into Montana, robbed an N. P. train, sent the money to pay the lawyer, then left the country to join up with his friends in South America.

Though Butch Cassidy never killed a man there was plenty in that bunch had a lot of notches on their guns. Harve Logan,

RUSTLERS AND KILLERS

sometimes known as Kid Curry, had the reputation of killing nine men. He was undoubtedly the leader of the tough gang. Some of his right hand men was Flat Nose George, Harry Longabaugh or the Sun Dance Kid, the Roberts brothers, Tom and George Jones and Ben Kilpatrick, known as the Tall Texan.

About the time the gang was operating there was a lot of hard feelings between the big cattlemen and the small ranchers and nesters. The big outfits tried to keep that country from settling up and even went so far as to have several nesters killed or chased out of the country.

The outlaws worked on the big outfits and left the little fellows alone. Naturally, the little ranchers didn't grieve any when they heard the big outfits had cattle stolen. If they suspicioned who did the stealing they kept still.

Like all outlaw bands, they robbed one train too many. The government got on their trail so hard that they disbanded. Some was killed, some joined "The Rough Riders" in the Spanish American War and others made their way to South America.

I'VE NEVER LIVED in a cow country yet that there wasn't some talk of rustling. While a beef now and then disappears most of the talk comes from some lazy son of a gun that doesn't want to take the trouble to ride the coulee heads and the bog holes.

On the Crow Reservation there used to be a big outfit that wasn't popular with the small outfits and undoubtedly lost quite a few head furnishing the winter meat for those small ranchers. The big outfit had no kick a-coming as it was a well known fact that its roundup wagon always killed a stray and was pretty apt to pick up any odd cows and throw them off of their home range, let them raise a few calves which the outfit branded as their own, then gather them up and sell a car load, letting the money eventually get to the rightful owner.

Now a fellow that was short a milk cow calf after the wagon passed just felt it was his duty to keep the score even so when he needed a piece of meat you can guess whose stuff he butchered.

The big outfit got all indignant and offered a thousand dollars reward for the arrest and conviction of anyone rustling their beef. That sort of tickled the folks around and it seemed to put a spicy flavor to the meat. They ate a little extra beef on general principles.

The reward didn't catch any rustlers so the cow outfit thought it would try another method. It put four cows with great big slick calves in the territory they thought they'd lost the most beef. They hired a special deputy to keep an eye on the slicks and arrest anyone he caught molesting them.

Of course they'd no more than hit the range until it was well advertised up and down the creek by a "cowboy Paul Revere" that there was a trap waiting for any guy with a long rope and a hot iron.

The deputy kept his lonely vigil for two or three months. More beef disappeared than ever before but those slicks was as safe as if they'd been kept in a church yard. It was a big joke to the cowboys. Never did two or three get together but what they plotted ways and means to get the slicks and make the deputy look ridiculous.

Finally they couldn't stand it any longer. Two or three of them got pretty well juiced up, so I heard, and decided the time was ripe—the deputy had held down a soft job long enough.

Now the deputy was camped in a little shack with a small fenced-in horse pasture. He went out one morning to catch his horse but somehow his horse was missing. He spent the day trying to find it on foot but had no luck. However, the next morning his horse had got back in the pasture. He saddled up and went right out on the range. The cows was bawling but their slick calves was gone.

The deputy went to Billings and got some reinforcements and they went snooping around the ranches of the most likely suspects.

Sure enough they came to a place that had four nice freshly butchered calves hanging up on the lean-to of the house.

The deputies chased the bawling cows up to the dead calves but the cows was bug eyed and excited from the smell of the blood. They sniffed a time or two and went high tailing it back to the place where they had evidently lost their calves and continued their bawling.

The law and the cow outfit had forgotten one little important fact, a cow won't claim a butchered calf. There was a lot of fellows around that part of the country with a satisfied smirk on their mugs at the mention of a certain unhappy John Law.

ONE TIME a bunch of us was gathering some horses off the Crow Reservation. It was cold and rainy and we couldn't do much riding. We was setting around the campfire shivering, hating the thought of crawling into a wet bed. Nobody had much to say. We was too miserable.

We was just about ready to go bye bye when one of the boys that had been to town rode in. He was well lit up and staggered to the campfire with a quart of whiskey in each hand. He was as welcome as Santa Claus in an orphan asylum.

All thoughts of crawling into wet beds just evaporated. There are several brands of whiskey. I cannot remember looking at the label but from the stories that was hatched that night, it must have been talking whiskey.

The prize story as I remember was told by a Wyoming cowboy. He swore it was the truth but as to that I cannot say. This was his story.

There was a little Irish cowboy named Smith that lived in Wyoming somewhere near the Greybull River. He was getting on the shady side of life and had accumulated a little bunch of dogies.

This Smith was a witty little Irishman. He always had a twinkle in his eye and a witty comeback to any story. He was a hospitable cuss, always glad to share his meals and bed. He always entertained his visitors with some good salty stories. He was a good all around fellow and everybody liked him. He was counted honest, though he seemed to be accumulating a lot of dogie calves.

Smith was seen driving an old granny cow across the Greybull River to where there was a lot of other cattle. One curious soul asked Smith why he did it. Smith said he didn't have any bull. The incident tickled Smith and he just had to tell somebody about it.

This old granny cow that Smith had was one of those cows that are just crazy for a calf. Every cow man has had one like that. They let any calf suck them and generally have two or three calves hanging around them. They claim them all and let them suck.

"Smith's cow bringing calf across the Greybull!"

RUSTLERS AND KILLERS

When Smith would throw the cow across the river the first thing she would do was hunt up a calf that wasn't getting too much milk. As soon as she found a calf that would follow her she would take it back across the river to Smith's for he always fed her a little grain.

In two or three weeks Smith would shut that calf up, let old granny's bag get full of milk and take her across the river again. She never failed to bring a calf back. In the course of a summer she accumulated several calves. Smith said she wasn't much to look at but she was a damn good hustler.

I WAS BREAKING OUT a bunch of horses for Peggy Osten on his ranch south of Billings. The country and the people was all new to me but naturally, being raised in a range country, I noticed things that was a little out of the ordinary of honest ranching.

At that time there wasn't any fences except for a few small pastures. On Blue Creek there was a few settlers along the creek. These people had taken up their places on squatter's rights. There had been an early survey of the country but the survey wasn't accepted by the government.

There was lots of horses, cattle and sheep. There was quarrels between the horsemen and cattlemen and the sheepmen. Gus Barth, a sheepman, had his sheep wagons burned up. There was some gun action and a man or two got killed but that has always been the case where there was free grass and lots of stock. There was always thieves, brand blotchers, mavericking and crooked stuff pulled off.

The incident that I am telling wasn't what you would call stealing but both parties knew the horses didn't belong to them, even if they was slicks.

One of them lived on the Clark Fork. His name was Simms, I believe. He had a notch or two filed on his gun barrel and from what I heard of him, he was plenty tough. Most of the time he carried a gun belted around his middle.

At the time I am speaking of, he was gathering horses on the reservation and in fact, all over the country, from Hart Mountain to the Big Horn Mountains. He had some range horses running on the reservation which gave him an excuse for being there, but the stuff that he was getting was unbranded. He had pretty good luck. He gathered somewhere around a hundred head. He put them in a small pasture belonging to Jimmy Ash over on Duck Creek about twenty miles south of Billings. Simms went into Billings either to celebrate or get some provisions, I don't know which, or maybe for both reasons.

Now the other party, we will call him John Doe for he is still living in this country was working for Osten. John Doe must have known Simms was doing a little too well in the horse gathering business. While Simms was in town celebrating his good fortune, John Doe slipped the horses out of the pasture and brought them over to Osten's.

I heard later that he took about half of them and then I heard that he took all of them. I don't know which story is true but this I do know, there was between fifty and sixty horses of various ages put in the Osten corral while I was gone and they all had fresh brands and not Osten's either and there was no old brands on them.

It was just getting dark when I got to the ranch and saw the horses in the corral. The branding fire was still smoldering, as if someone had poured water on it. The corral was a couple of hundred yards from the house but you couldn't see the corral from the house.

The next morning when I went to the corral, John was already there. I was setting outside of a small board shack fixing a stirrup strap on my saddle that I had broke the day before. John was doing something in the shack when Simms rode up to the corral and looked at the horses. He saw me in front of the shack fixing my saddle and rode over to where I was.

RUSTLERS AND KILLERS

He began asking me whose horses those was in the corral and who put them in there. I told him I didn't know as I had been riding up on Blue Creek and they was in the corral when I got back. I told him I hadn't been working there long and knew nothing about the business.

He said, "I am going to take them out, they are my horses." Simms wasn't ten feet from the shack when John Doe stepped out of the door with a big .45 aimed at Simms' belly.

He said, "See that coulee with the trail. Hit it and keep going if you want to stay healthy and don't look back or I'll fill you so full of holes you won't hold buttermilk."

Simms said, "I ain't got no gun on."

John said, "You are lucky. Get going." Simms did. After he had gone John throwed the horses out on the creek and let them drink for the pasture was rough when you got out of the creek bottom. The horse wrangler, Jerky Bill by name, held the horses in the pasture out of sight that day. The next morning the horses and John Doe was gone and Jerky Bill was in bed.

"Riders sitting under their horses."

That day while I was riding a colt up on the bench I saw someone over on a high divide. When he saw me he rode over to where I was. It was Simms. He had a gun at side and a rifle in a scabbard tied on his saddle. He looked plenty hostile.

He wanted to know what John had done with the horses. I told him I didn't know but the horses and John was gone when I got up, that they must have left in the night. He asked me how long I had been working for the spread. I told him again I'd been there only a week or so and was not acquainted yet with the people or much of the country as I had just landed.

Simms was a man of few words but when he rode off I had the feeling there was a shooting scrape in the making. For a long time after that Simms and John Doe rode around the country armed to the teeth but it is my notion that they was careful not to meet. Anyway, nothing ever came out of the deal but a bad stink.

A MAN THAT gives his life doing his duty gets a big newspaper story and is called a hero. Everybody talks about him for a few days and then he's forgotten. Sometimes a status or fountain is raised in his honor. So it was with Jim Webb.

Jim Webb worked for the 79 cow outfit for quite a while. He was a salty forked cow hand, a very nice individual. Everybody liked and respected him.

He was appointed stock inspector in the early 1900s. He was very efficient and made quite a reputation for himself. Then he was elected sheriff of Yellowstone County in 1906.

I remember one time, just before the election, I was in the Owl Saloon. A bunch of the nominees for office was buying drinks for the crowd when Jim Webb came in.

Someone said, "There is the next sheriff. Buy us a drink, Jim."

Jim wasn't a drinking man. He said, "I may be elected sheriff and I may not be but I ain't going to buy any votes with liquor." And he didn't.

I was personally acquainted with Webb, in fact, I worked with him when he was stock inspector. I thought a lot of him.

He had lots of savvy and plenty guts. He wasn't afraid of the devil himself. Jim Webb was a determined man and I think he had a little too much confidence in himself that made him a little careless. He was no chair warmer. When there was a job to be done he did it himself and didn't have the court house full of deputies.

He had a warrant for a sheepherder with a bad reputation that was working for the Woolfolk & Richardson sheep outfit on the Musselshell. This herder, William Buckfourd, was wanted for horse stealing. He was originally from Canada. He'd been a Mounted Police but got in some kind of trouble and crossed the border into Montana ahead of two Mounties.

Jim went to Richardson's and asked where he could find the herder. Mr. Richardson was a real old man and not very well so he hitched up a light spring wagon and took Jim over to the sheep camp.

When they got to the camp, the sheepherder was washing some clothes in a tub beside the wagon. Webb and Richardson got down and Webb told the herder he had a warrant for his arrest. The herder asked what the charges was and on being told it was horse stealing, said it was all a mistake and he could prove he was innocent. He asked Webb if he could go into the sheep wagon and change his clothes. Webb told him he could.

He went in the wagon and took a .30-30 that was in there and came to the door with it cocked. He pointed it at Webb and said, "Throw up your hands, both of you," and shot once between Webb and Richardson.

Richardson threw up his hands but Webb stood looking at the herder. He repeated, "Get them up." Whether Jim went for his six-shooter or not is hard to tell but the herder let Jim have a fatal bullet. He threatened old man Richardson and then left. That was March 24, 1908.

Richardson sent word to Billings that the sheriff had been killed. I think Jack Herfford was deputy at that time. Anyway a posse was organized. I know that Walt Lee and other salty friends of Webb was in the party. They was plenty mad.

The posse went over to the Musselshell at the mouth of Willow Creek. They met another herder who said he thought the fugitive herder was in a sheep wagon close by.

They went to the wagon, surrounded it and hollered for the herder to come out. He looked out the door with a rifle in his hand. They told him to drop his gun and come out with his hands in the air and give himself up.

He answered with a shot and slammed the door. The posse tore loose at him and shot the wagon full of holes and finally killed their man through the canvas.

They held a pow wow and decided to bury the sheepherder near where he was killed. However, the story that was told around the campfires was there was an old abandoned well close, and they didn't have any tools for digging, so they just heaved him in and threw a lot of rocks in on him to hold him down.

They rode back to Billings feeling they'd done a good job and saved the county a lot of expense. The coroner spoiled their good feeling for he had to inspect the corpse and said they would have to bring the killer's body in.

There was a lot of moaning around the court house as they knowed how hard it would be to heave the rocks out of the well, but they got it done.

Old man Richardson never got over the shock of Webb's killing and died not long afterwards.

It seemed like the whole country turned out for Webb's funeral. The court house and all the business houses closed down for a couple hours. One of the deputy sheriffs led Webb's beautiful bay horse with Webb's empty saddle on it to the grave yard. You may have seen the fountain at 2nd and 27th Street erected to Jim Webb's memory.

RUSTLERS AND KILLERS

TIM RIORDON, an old-time cowpuncher and wild catcher, used to live around Billings. He was well liked. He was a small man, weighed perhaps one hundred thirty or one hundred thirty-five pounds. He was a typical little Irishman. Tim was knowed for his reckless riding when chasing wild horses. There was a lot of fellows chased wild horses but Tim fetched them in.

One time he was running a bunch of wild horses around Two Leggins, he'd run them pretty near all day. He finally got them up on the Blue Creek divide about twenty-five miles south of Billings. His horse was getting awfully tired but Tim was determined to get those horses. He reached down and uncinched the saddle and let it drop while he held on to the mane, in order to relieve his horse of the weight of the saddle.

He was riding an awfully good horse. It seemed like when Tim left his saddle it put some new life in his horse. Anyway he corralled the horses in the old Bar K corrals at the fork of Blue Creek. He was the only man I ever knew or heard about that throwed his saddle away and corralled a bunch of wild horses bareback.

Tim married a woman in Billings and they went to Nevada. After a time Tim came back. I heard that he and his wife was having trouble. Tim went to tending bar for Bob Conway at the Mint Saloon, I think it was called, anyway it was between 26th and 27th south of the tracks on Minnesota Avenue. There was a rooming house above the saloon.

I had given a show in Central Park west of town. It was late when we got through the show. I thought I'd get supper before I took the horses home. It was dark and it started to rain. I was afraid of spilling the bucking horses.

I saw Tim while I was having supper. He told me he had a room upstairs. He said he was on night shift and wouldn't be through until twelve, but for me to use his room and he gave me the key, as we was good friends. I was tired and went to bed early. As I was expecting Tim in around midnight I didn't lock the door. In those days I was a pretty light sleeper. About eleven o'clock I heard someone gently open the door. It was a front room and the street lights showed through the curtains. I thought it was Tim coming in. But as soon as the person got in the room I could see it was a woman. She had kind of a light dress on. She had her right hand in the front of her dress.

I didn't know what to say, but I wanted her to know it wasn't Tim in the bed so I said, "Is that you, Tim?"

She stood there an instant and I said again, "Is that you, Tim?" She immediately whirled and left the room, closing the door after her. I got up and locked the door. Tim never showed up that night and I didn't get to see him the next morning before I left town. The incident just sort of slipped my mind.

Outside the show grounds at Central Park, there was a saloon and Sundays Tim used to tend bar there. The following Sunday after I stayed in Tim's room, Mrs. Riordon came to the saloon and told Tim to come out as she wanted to talk to him. She waited for him at the door. Tim passed her and was walking ahead of her. She called his name and as he turned she shot and killed him.

I never knowed Mrs. Riordon but she looked to me like the same woman that slipped into Tim's room that night. I always have believed she had a gun in her hand, anyway she had something.

They turned her loose. I could never understand why. I never told of my experience as Tim was dead and I couldn't swear for sure who it was.

After Tim's killing I figured it was a good thing I slept with one eye open when I was in a strange bed.

ONE OF THE most cold blooded murders was the uncalled for killing of Roy McClaren, a cowboy that was shot in the back by Jim Meddles.

RUSTLERS AND KILLERS

I knew them both. Roy McClaren was a very nice man. He worked for Nate Cooper that used to run a spread on Blue Creek. Roy used to break horses to ride. He was a very good hand, never abused a horse. Roy had the reputation of getting along with horses and handling them in a way that they hardly ever bucked when he rode them. I rode with him for several years on the horse roundups. I never saw him ill tempered or hard to get along with. All the boys liked Roy and I never heard of him starting a quarrel or argument with anyone.

Jim Meddles worked over on the Dryhead for a horseman by the name of Barry. I didn't know him too well. He was altogether a different kind of a man than Roy. He always carried a gun and used to drink lots of hard liquor. When he got plastered he was quarrelsome and mean.

The main road to Dryhead went right by my ranch and often Barry or his men stopped overnight with me. One time Meddles come by on horseback on his way to Dryhead. He was carrying a considerable jag. There was a can full of coal oil by the back door. He shot it full of holes, then wanted to stay all night as it was evening. I was away riding so my wife sent him to the bunk house.

Next morning I told Jim that I didn't like any shooting around my house and from then on I wanted him to pass up my place. He said he just done the shooting because he was full of liquor.

At the time of the killing they was both working for Barry. He had sent Meddles, Roy, and a boy by the name of St. John, Barry's stepson I think, in for supplies, a distance of about sixty miles. They had a camp outfit. Roy had a saddle horse with the outfit. If I remember right, Roy came with Meddles and the boy as he wanted to get some new clothes.

They stopped at Conway's on the way to Billings. An argument started. I heard two or three of the cowboys say it started over Meddles beating a horse over the head. They had a fight and Roy licked the hell out of Meddles. They went on in to town the next morning.

I was going in to town when I met Roy horseback on his way out. He stopped and visited. He told me of the fight at Conway's and said he hated to go back to Dryhead with the mean son of a gun as he was getting drunk.

I told him not to go back but to winter with me. He said he might come back and do that but he felt responsible for the St. John kid and the load as Meddles was apt to do anything. He was going to wait at my place until they came along. Which he did.

They camped that night at Pryor Creek near the old shearing pen. This is the way I heard the story of the killing as it came out in court.

Meddles was taking care of the horses and Roy was cooking supper on a campfire. Meddles had a six-shooter laying in the front of the wagon. When he took the nose bags off the horses he put them in the front of the wagon. Roy was taking the coffee pot off the fire with his back to him. Meddles picked up his gun and shot Roy in the back and he fell into the fire.

"Roy fell in the fire."

RUSTLERS AND KILLERS

Meddles told the St. John boy he'd sure kill him if he ever told anybody. Meddles drug Roy over to the old shearing pen and covered his body with some brush and trash that was there. Then he went on to Dryhead. He told them he'd left Roy in town, he thought he could come when he wanted to as he had his horse.

Someone riding by the shearing pens saw a bunch of magpies around it and went over to see what was there. He found Roy's body. He reported it to the authorities. They traced Roy's movements and found out about his trip with Meddles. When they arrested Meddles the boy told the details of the killing.

Justice slipped up somewhere for he only got a long prison term. I know he didn't even serve all his term. They should have hung the cold blooded son of a gun.

I THINK HIS first name was Bill but I never heard him called anything but Smithie. Later on he was nicknamed Horse Thief Smithie. I don't know how he come by the name Horse Thief as he was never convicted of stealing any horses.

He was a full blooded Irishman. He always had a good story to tell or a witty saying to fit any occasion. He was a good, hard worker, a good roper, rider and all around stock hand. Smithie had a weakness for hard liquor and would go on some long benders.

Smithie got in some trouble one time while on a prolonged drinking bout. I don't know just what it was, anyhow he got sent to the county jail to do some time.

George Hubbard, the sheriff at the time, said Smithie was a good fellow and didn't have much more time to serve so they ought to make him a trusty.

One morning a deputy sheriff told Smithie that they was making a trusty out of him. He said for Smithie to take a couple buckets out and get some coal.

Smithie had been in quite a while and when he got outside it was a nice warm day, the birds was singing and he got spring fever right away. Smithie was just like a range horse that had been kept in a barn all winter. He wanted to see wide open spaces.

He started to the coal house to get the coal but when he saw the window where they put the coal in, temptation got the best of him. He set his coal buckets down and eased himself out the window and made off for the rim rocks.

His absence wasn't noticed for a little while, then the deputy seen him going for the rim rocks on a high lope. At that time there was a rope ladder that people used to climb the rims. Before the deputy got there, Smithie had pulled the rope ladder up and headed for parts unknown.

But not for long, as Smithie had a girl just as Irish as he was. He came back to see her one dark night. Her old man tipped off the sheriff that Smithie was down seeing his daughter. So George Hubbard went down to get him. Pat, the girl's father, got a change of heart when he got home and he wanted to warn Smithie.

He said, "Smithie, my boy, I had a dream last night, I saw you sitting with Anne in the parlor, and Sheriff Hubbard is coming after you."

About that time somebody rapped at the front door. Smithie made a dash for the back door and run right into George Hubbard. He was arrested and put in the klink to serve his time out. In about a week George told him to take the coal buckets and get some coal.

Smithie said, "I'll be damned if I do. I don't dare trust myself, if one of those buckets touched my leg. It would scare me and I might stampede again."

It tickled George Hubbard so that he turned Smithie loose. Smithie came to my ranch in Bull Mountains some twenty-five years later. He was on his way home from a big bender. He was awful sick, seeing pink elephants and snakes. He told me he thought he was going to die.

I was alone at the time and I was afraid to leave him for fear he might pass out. The only thing I knowed to do was to get him some liquor to sober up on. When I thought it was safe to leave him, I saddled up and went over to a moonshiner's and got a pint. I fed it to Smithie in small doses. In a couple days he was well enough to go home.

In two or three weeks I saw him again. He said, "I was sure sick and I thought I was sure going to see the Pearly Gates. Bill, I want to make you a proposition. If you die before I do, I will get you some flowers. If I die first, you get me some."

We both laughed and shook hands on it. About six years after that pact, Smithie died from a heart attack. He got the flowers.

GATLEY WAS A peculiar individual. He came into this part of the country in the early 1900s. He had two sisters with him. They took up homesteads near Pompeys Pillar and bought up some other land. Then there was several women, supposed to be relatives, that took up places next to him. It made a nice big spread.

Some people said he came from Canada, some said he came from other places, but I don't think that anyone really knew where he came from. He had plenty money and spent a lot of it improving those places with buildings, fences and equipment.

I was slightly acquainted with Gatley but from what I knew of him he was honorable, his word was good, and whatever he done was inside the law. Several of the ranchers was sore at him because he had taken up land that they had been using as free range. Gatley never asked any favors, nor gave any. He done everything on a money basis. He paid everything with cash. I have heard that he never gave a check, just paid out the long green.

George Williams and Billy Ogg had places near Gatley and worked for him a lot. They both swore that Gatley had his money buried in the hills near Sand Creek. George told me that one time Gatley went to pay some money to them for some work they had done. He got it out of a satchel that looked like it had been buried. When he completed the deal in the bunk house he started out the door with his satchel, got on his horse and said as he left, "I'll be back before long and don't either of you sons of bitches follow me." And he patted his gun as he said it. Billy Ogg told me the same thing years later.

After having quarrels with different ranchers over fencing the range, he buckled on a gun and wore it all the time. He put a big sign on the gate that said, "IF YOU WANT TO SEE ME COME TO THE RANCH AND STATE YOUR BUSINESS. NO TRESPASSING ALLOWED OTHERWISE."

I heard that a pretty salty cowman, Walt Lee by name, paid no attention to the sign and went in to Gatley's pasture looking for stock. He came out at the business end of Gatley's gun. Nobody ever crowded Gatley after that.

Gatley wasn't no bluffer, he had plenty of guts and was more than willing to back them up. I always liked Gatley and knowing the people, the country and the times felt he had to be tough to hold his own.

The only time I ever knew Gatley to fight with his fists happened in the Owl Saloon. He didn't have his gun on as usual for a policeman had made him take it off.

He and Tom Logan had had some quarrels but had never settled them as Tom was a nice respectable young rancher that never carried a gun. I don't know what their trouble was but when Tom caught Gatley in the Owl Saloon without his gun, Tom knocked the hell out of him. As Gatley got up and was washing the blood off he snapped his teeth together and said, "Tom Logan, just remember this, don't ever hit me again. I don't fight that way." I never heard of them having any trouble after that.

RUSTLERS AND KILLERS

Gatley had some serious trouble with an ex-Texas cowpuncher named Dutch Ed. This Dutch Ed was a big man, weighed perhaps a hundred eighty pounds and was a fighting fool. When he was drinking, he was mean. He was a gunman, too. He would pick a fight just to keep in practice and keep his reputation up. He worked as a roundup cook for several of the big outfits and was known as a surly tough individual. He got a contract with Gatley to cut and deliver fence posts at so much a post.

There was an argument over the settlement of the posts, anyway, they was in a pool hall and I don't remember if it was in Pompeys Pillar or Huntley but they pulled their guns and shot at the same time. Their aim was good for they was both killed.

Billy Ogg who saw it all told me Dutch Ed died instantly but Gatley lived long enough to say he'd like to see his sister or send her word and then passed out before he could leave a message.

Billy Ogg and George Williams always thought Gatley wanted to tell where his money was cached. They said that for quite a while after Gatley's death, the gate to the Gatley place was locked and they had seen the Gatley sisters prowling around the hills as if they was looking for something.

THERE ARE PEOPLE that have been raised right, educated and lived an honorable life, then all at once, bang, they rob a bank, kill someone or do some outrageous thing that horrifies their parents and friends. Such was the case with Norton Mosier and Jim Grady some forty five or forty six years ago.

I was well acquainted with the Mosier family. They lived on a ranch on the Yellowstone River about a mile west of the old south bridge. I did a lot of business with Norton's father. Mr. Mosier was an honorable man, Mrs. Mosier was a very nice person. The two sisters was nice, they was good musicians and was very popular. Norton was a tall nice looking young fellow, a good rider and well liked.

I had a speaking acquaintance with Jim Grady who lived with his mother at Fourth Avenue and South Thirty First Street. Jim Grady hadn't been married very long to a very nice looking girl. I had seen her several times but was not acquainted with her.

Both Mosier and Grady seemed to be very nice young men with lots of friends and was both raised in Montana, both of them came from good homes.

I could never understand why those two boys ever pulled a stunt such as they did, there was no cause for it. They went in the Owl Saloon, in Billings, with handkerchiefs over their faces, a sawed-off shotgun in their hands and held up the roulette wheel which was at the back end of the Owl Saloon.

The man that was running the roulette wheel recognized them and thinking they was joking called them by name and asked who they was trying to fool. When they pointed the shotgun at his middle and scooped up the money, he knew it was the real thing.

As they went out the back door they ran right into a policeman, Haggerty I think his name was, who was coming down the alley. Whether he tried to stop them or whether they saw him and got scared, I don't know. Anyway, the one of them that had the gun shot Haggerty in the stomach and for good measure gave him the other barrel and then made their get away.

I have heard that Grady did the killing and I have heard that Mosier did it. But anyway, they killed an officer that was thought a lot of. Haggerty had a lot of friends. His death caused a lot of commotion.

Mosier went home and told his folks that he was in some trouble and that he was taking a saddle horse and leaving. When they asked him what he had done he only said, "You'll find out soon enough."

He rode off then on a little, brown, one-eyed horse. Mosier was caught over in Wyoming, fetched back and put in jail. Jim Grady was still on the dodge.

RUSTLERS AND KILLERS

Sheriff George Hubbard layed for Grady at his mother's place and after a few nights Grady slipped in. Hubbard went in the house to make the arrest. As he opened the door Grady and him had a mix up. Grady got hold of Hubbard's gun arm and in the fracas Hubbard got shot in the arm and Grady got away.

There was quite a reward out for Grady. Seven hundred and fifty dollars, if I remember right. After several days a woman friend turned Grady in for the reward money, which she got. He was put in jail.

It was suspected by a good many people that she gave the money to Grady for a getaway stake and then smuggled in saw blades and arranged for horses to be handy. Anyway, they had friends on the outside for they sawed their way out of jail and got away.

I saw the bars they sawed and it has always been a mystery to me how they got out of their cells for it was the main part of the jail that they broke out of.

Alkali Ike, who lived on North Twenty Sixth Street reported he had a couple of saddle horses stolen that night. I am satisfied they was the horses used in the getaway.

I lived in Billings, at the time, on North Twenty Fifth Street just across from Ike's place. About two days after Ike's horses and Mosier and Grady disappeared, the horses came back. I heard something in my hay real early in the morning and went out to see what it was. It was Ike's horses and they looked like they had had a long, hard ride. I took them over and put them in Ike's yard.

Mosier and Grady have never been heard of since though I am positive they headed for Bull Mountains, for a rancher at Blazed Tree gave them fresh horses, not knowing they was on the dodge.

George Hubbard thought that Grady would try to get in touch with his wife or mother. He put a twenty four hour guard on Mrs. Grady and Grady's mother.

Young Mrs. Grady had a friend that lived across the street. Pretty near every day Mrs. Grady would run over and visit an hour or so. The officers that was keeping tab on Mrs. Grady never thought she could get away as they watched the house all the time she was visiting.

The lot on which the friend's house was located was level until the back end of the lot. Then there was a second bench where there was an old ditch running along the bank about five feet lower than the upper bench.

One evening just about twilight Mrs. Grady ran over to visit her friend. She had on just a calico dress, slippers, and was bareheaded. The officer in charge didn't think she'd go far in that rig and, I suppose, he was a little careless. He waited for perhaps a couple of hours and when she didn't show up he went to the house and asked for her.

The friend seemed quite surprised to see the officer. She told him that Mrs. Grady had been gone for quite a while. A search of the house was made but the bird had flown. That was the last time anyone ever saw or heard of Jim Grady's wife.

An old cowpuncher, that has cashed in his chips since then, told me about fifteen years ago that he had heard of Jim Grady in South America. I have never heard of Norton Mosier.

THE WINTER of 1921-22, I was wintering on Elbow Creek between Fromberg and Joliet, Montana. It was a tough cold winter after a dry summer plagued by grasshoppers.

Hay went up to thirty five and forty dollars a ton and there wasn't much hay to be had at that price. Cattle had gone down to about twenty-five dollars a head. Money was like chicken teeth. There just wasn't any, especially if you only had to give cattle for security.

I had managed for about fifty tons of hay for a hundred head of cattle. There was quite a lot of pasture land, about three sections and some open range. I thought I could get through the winter if I wintered all the dry stuff on pasture.

It was a rough hilly country with lots of coulees and a mountain ridge on the south side. On the north side, down in the Rock Creek valley there was a herd law district. Whenever any stock strayed in the valley some farmer would shut them up and charge whatever he felt like. You had to pay cash before you could get them back. Some of those people was sure unreasonable. There was a fence around the pasture I had rented but it hadn't been kept up and most of it was laying on the ground. Believe me, I was plenty busy keeping the cattle from getting out in the herd district.

As I said before, it was a cold hard winter. There was about two feet of snow and generally a freezing wind coming down that canyon from off the Red Lodge Mountains. The temperatures was all the way from ten degrees below zero to forty below. The snow drifted bad and if you wasn't on a ridge where the wind had blowed the snow off you was liable to get your horse down in a drift most anywhere.

It was about the middle of February. It had been cold weather for about six weeks. In those six weeks, I don't think there was a night that was over ten below zero. The snow kept piling in the coulees until some of them had snow at least twenty-five feet deep. The only grass available that the cattle could get was on the ridges where the wind had blowed the snow off.

It was sure hard to get around through the frozen, drifted snow. Every step a saddle horse took he would break through that frozen crusted snow. You was lucky if you made a mile an hour unless you was on a ridge and you couldn't stay on a ridge all the time.

One real cold day, it must have been thirty below, I went about two miles where there was a short ridge off the mountains. I could see my dry bunch of about thirty-five head all scattered along the ridge. It was about two o'clock. There was a cloud in the northwest rolling and tumbling around. It didn't look good to me. I started back to camp and got there around about four when the storm broke.

It began to snow, the wind picked up and started drifting. In a little while you couldn't see ten feet. The wind blew all night. It was an awful storm. In the morning it cleared and the wind went down but it was awful cold. I was plenty worried about the dry stuff.

I got started pretty early to look for them. I went over to see if they was on the ridge where I left them. They was gone and the wind had covered their tracks. I didn't know which way they had gone but guessed they'd headed for the herd district and I rode in that direction.

I followed a ridge and just before I got to the bottom of it I could see a bunch of cattle in a corral eating a load of hay. I thought they looked like mine but I wasn't sure. I watched them a little while until I spotted a big brindle steer that was one of my markers.

It was late in the afternoon. I'd been up since before daylight fighting my way through the snow drifts looking for signs of those cattle. I hadn't had any dinner and I was colder than hell and mighty discouraged about that time. I had found my cattle but I didn't have any money to bail them out. I was a stranger to that country and knew better than to go down to that farmer with a hard luck story. I thought there must be some way if I could just put my head to working.

I rode back out of sight to where I'd seen a pitch log. I built a fire and thawed out while my saddle horse rested. My thoughts was going around in circles. I couldn't leave the rest of my cattle to go to Billings to raise some money so I'd have to rescue them some other way. It came to my mind that I hadn't seen a dog and I was sure hoping that farmer didn't have one.

I guess I must have huddled around that fire until about midnight. Then I went quietly down to inspect the farmer's corral. It still was a gloomy situation. There was a log chain

RUSTLERS AND KILLERS

around the gate fastened by a padlock. I was just about ready to give up the ghost when I noticed the hinges on the gate was black smith made, the kind you can lift out of their sockets.

I tried to lift the gate but there wasn't enough of Willie so I found a cedar post and was able to pry it up. I swung it around, got on my horse and silently worked those cattle out to the trail. Then I slipped back, turned the gate around and set it back on its hinges.

The cattle, with their bellies full of hay, was ready to go home. They followed my horse's tracks back to the end of the ridge.

It was just breaking day when I got into my camp. I was dead tired, hungry, sleepy and cold, but I would have liked to have seen that farmer's face when he went out to feed those cattle.

A BIG SHIPMENT of cattle had come from the south and had been unloaded. There was several southern cowboys along with the cattle to trail them from Billings to the northern part of the state.

The cowboys with the cattle was taking the town in. One particular would-be tough had got juiced up over in the south side of town in the red light district. He seemed to get a lot of amusement out of seeing people dance.

He made several town people do a jig by pointing a big six-shooter at them. He got by as he was spending his money right and left and everybody was drinking.

On the north side of town they didn't go for that kind of stuff. Potter and Vale ran a pretty decent place. Potter was an old cow puncher and the cowboys used to patronize his bar a great deal.

Potter and Vale had an old Texas cowpuncher tending bar. He didn't take any tough stuff from anybody. He was a good bartender, polite and nice to everybody but they couldn't pull off anything on him.

This tough hombre had got away with a lot of tough stuff the night before so he thought he would come over on the north side of town and see if there was any good dancers there. Of course everybody in town had heard about him and had him pegged for what he was.

When he came into Potter and Vale's, he sized everybody up. He asked Tex, the bartender, if there was any good dancers around.

Tex told him that all the dancers hung around on the other side of the tracks, that if he wanted to see them dance he'd better go back over there.

The tough hombre pulled his six-shooter out of his scabbard, whirled it around his index finger, put it back in the scabbard and swaggered up to the bar. He began to shoot off his mouth saying, "I'm a rooting, shooting son of a bitch from Texas. I'm a big bad wolf and this is my night to howl."

Then he looked at Tex and said, "I will have a little poison on the house."

Tex reached for a whiskey glass but came up with a big .44. He aimed it at the tough hombre's middle and said, "I know you are a rooting, tooting son of a bitch, but I don't think you ever saw Texas. Just haul your big carcass out of that back door and howl with the alley dogs. Don't come back in here or I will learn you a new step. Get going and don't make any passes or you won't be able to dance."

Mr. Tough Guy slunk out and that was the last Billings heard of him.

10: Horse Breaking and Filly Chasing

WHEN I FIRST came to the country and went to work for Peggy Osten, I made my first ride on the head of Blue Creek with Packsaddle Ben Greenough, Osten's foreman. I thought as I looked the country over, this is a stockman's paradise.

We rode through a bunch of Nate Cooper's brood mares and colts. The mares weighed all the way from 1,400 to 1,600 pounds. There was some of the prettiest Shire colts a man ever laid eyes on. There was cattle and horses everywhere and farther on the Crow Reservation there was sheep and Indian horses everywhere you looked.

You could tell the Indian horses as far as you could see them. They was all colors of the rainbow. They didn't mix with the other horses much as they was a kind of a breed of their own, small and tough as rawhide.

Nate Cooper's horse ranch was up pretty well toward the head of Blue Creek. There are two forks of the creek, his buildings and big corrals was situated at the forks. Later, I lived about eight miles down the creek.

That was a great range, grass up to your stirrups. Cooper's was the only ranch on the upper creek, farther down on the lower end of the creek there was a few ranches. The Crow Reservation was on the east and south. There, there was no ranches, no wire fences, just a big open country for miles and miles.

In the spring of the year toward the last of May or the first of June, Nate used to round up his horses to brand the colts and cut all the two-year-old stud colts. I had some horses that ran on the same range. He always told me when he was going to make the roundup.

I would go up to his ranch and stay there until we gathered all the horses, worked them and turned them out. It took several days.

Nate Cooper was a large man. He must have weighed over two hundred pounds. He always rode a good horse with plenty size and action. Nate was a great horseman, he could ride a horse farther than any man of his size I ever rode with. I rode with him gathering horses all day many times and never saw him come in riding a played out horse.

Cooper was an early riser. He sure never layed on the bed ground in the morning. He used to say that one early hour is better than two late ones. I used to think that he over did it. It was very common for him to get up at two or three o'clock in the morning and sit around waiting for daylight.

One spring I went to his ranch and took a rider with me. That was before Cooper was married and he was batching.

He always kept a saddle horse staked out to jingle the horses in out of the pasture. This morning he got up and as usual it was still dark. He rousted me out of bed to get the saddle horses in while he got breakfast. He said that the jingle horse was staked down by the corral.

I stumbled around in the dark toward the corral and found a horse tied to a big hind wheel of a wagon. He acted pretty snuffy but that was the only horse I could find in the dark so I took him into the corral and saddled him up. He was hard to saddle but I finally got it on him.

When I stepped on him I could tell that he'd never been rode. He sure tried to throw me off. He bucked into the corral and about tore my pants off. I had a time getting him out to the saddle horses. He ran through a choke cherry patch and skinned my face all up. When I started the horses they went right for the corral and he followed them in.

I had been gone a long time. When I got to the house Nate asked, "What kept you so long, did you get lost?"

I told him that I'd had to break that horse to ride before I got the horses.

He laughed and said "You got the wrong horse, Bill, there is a gentle horse just over the raise. I had Tom halter break that bronc yesterday. He had him tied on the wagon wheel to break it to stake out. I forgot to tell you."

It was just breaking day and was foggy out. By the time the fog raised so we could see, Cooper decided it was too late to make the ride. We put it off until the next morning and I finished breaking out the bronc.

OSTEN WAS QUITE a horse trader. At that time, there was lots of horses in the country. A horse was just a horse to Osten. For a few dollars in boot, he would trade for any kind of a horse.

He got a very nice looking bay horse (that was spoiled) in a trade. He knew there was something wrong with the horse but didn't know what it was. He thought he was probably a hard bucking horse but none at the ranch had tried to ride it.

I was breaking out a bunch of green colts right off the range. Osten cut the spoiled horse in with them. One morning I thought I would try him out.

He wasn't hard to saddle. I was extra careful for I didn't know what to expect. He acted like he wanted to kick more than anything. When I stepped on him he seemed to be alright, never moved. I let him stand for a while, then started him and he never acted like he wanted to buck. I rode him around the corral a few times. He reined pretty good.

I knew there was something wrong with him but couldn't figure out what it was. There are a lot of horses that won't buck in a corral but as soon as they get out in the open they will turn it on. This horse didn't act any different when he was turned out. He was a little nervous and wanted to go places. I gave him a pretty good ride. He seemed to be alright, but I was careful. I was beginning to think he was okay outside of being nervous.

When I got back to the corral and stepped off, I found out what was wrong with the horse. As I swung off and hit the ground, the horse jumped and kicked at me with both feet, then tried to run away. I was hanging on but he was trying to kick me every jump. I expected every kind of a trick but that one. I had found out what made him a trading horse.

I tried everything that I could think of to break him of that trick. I tried cheeking him, pulling his head around and getting off as far ahead of him as I could so he couldn't reach me with those hind feet.

It was all the same, he went hog wild swinging his head, kicking and trying to get away. I had to let go when I hit the ground and no fooling around. He wasn't kicking for fun. He was sure trying to get me.

I tried another stunt. I fixed a leather blind on my bridle so I could drop it over his eyes. I rode him in the corral, dropped the blind down so he couldn't see and stepped off. That was the worst of all. He just went crazy, running and kicking blind. It was a small corral and I had a time keeping out of his way. Everywhere I ran, his rear end seemed to be there—whirling and kicking. He liked to have kicked the corral down. I was so busy keeping out of the way that I couldn't get out of the corral. He never quit until the blind came off.

Osten was there and had shut the gate when I rode in. He saw the whole show. He laughed and said, "Just keep trying, Bill, he will quit that stunt after a while. Don't try it in the corral anymore. Just look at that corral, it's all tore to hell."

That horse had me buffaloed. I have seen riders that hated to get on. It was just the reverse with me, I hated to get off.

The last time I rode him I tied my rope around his neck, then made a loop and dropped it on a post at the end of the corral. I jumped off and ran to get out of the way. He did the same thing, kicked at me and run. When he hit the end of the rope, it turned him over. I had enough of that rough stuff.

Osten said he would trade him to Mexican Tony and maybe the horse would kick his head off as Tony had given him a cheating the last time they had traded.

WHEN I BOUGHT my ranch on Blue Creek it had previously been a horse ranch. It had a nice set of corrals. I made good use of them when breaking saddle horses for the different cow outfits. George Williams and I used to contract to break a bunch of horses at so much a head.

Well I remember a bunch of horses we broke for a man by the name of Bonameezer. He was an Austrian. I heard he had some sort of a title in the old country. Anyway he had a ranch on Pryor Creek and run his cattle on the reservation. He sent word to me that he had thirty-five geldings he wanted broke to ride.

George and I went over to see him and take the horses home if we could make a satisfactory arrangement. Which we did.

Bonameezer was a large man, probably weighed two hundred thirty five pounds or more. He was no horseman, usually rode an old work mare around the place. He had a very nice horse in the bunch that he wanted broke for his own use. He wanted this horse broke good and gentle so it would stand perfectly still while he got on.

He said he would pay me twenty five dollars to break that horse. As we was getting ten dollars per head for the rest of them I could afford to put a lot of extra work on that particular horse.

He was a beautiful brown horse and had a nice disposition. He was well broke to lead and weighed close to twelve hundred pounds with plenty of action.

He was an awful nice horse and I took a lot of pains with him. He never did buck, I really liked him. I used to feed him sugar and he would follow me around the corral. I could catch him anywhere without roping him. I rode him around the corral with just a rope around his neck. I could crawl under his belly, pick up all his feet and slide off over his hips. I got on him fifteen or twenty times a day and he never moved. He learned to rein good and I got him so I could open gates without getting off. I thought he was just perfect.

They was all nice horses to break except one **RL**. He was a rascal to buck but finally gave it up. Before we delivered the horses I cleaned the brown horse all up, pulled his tail, cut his fore top and the long hairs round his legs. He sure looked fine and I was proud of the job I had done on him.

Bonameezer and his crew was having dinner when we got there, we corralled the horses. He invited us in to join them and began talking about the horses. I can't say I exactly dislocated my arm patting myself on the back but I let them all know in a general way that I considered myself a pretty fair horse breaker. Before I got through with my story I got the subject changed by one of the boys. I guess he thought I was doing a little too much bragging.

Jim Frazer was the foreman. He wanted us to ride them all out to see how good they was broke. I guess he wanted to check up on the loose talk he'd heard at the dinner table.

We rode them all leaving the brown horse until last. Then I got on him bareback, rode him around, then saddled him to show off again. I asked Bonameezer to try him. Bonameezer's suitcase was so big he couldn't put it in my saddle so he told one of his men to put his saddle on the horse.

Jim Frazer threw Bonameezer's saddle on the brown. He never moved while Bonameezer climbed up. As I said before he was a big man and instead of swinging up and easing himself into the saddle he just dropped into it, ka-plunk.

He landed in the saddle, then the brown horse let a snort out of him and just left the earth. The second jump and Bonameezer went up in the air. When he came down it was with a thud that about knocked all the dust out of the corral. The brown horse just kept bucking around the corral jumping over Bonameezer who was trying to get out of there.

I never was so surprised in my life as when that horse started to buck. I just stood there paralyzed with my mouth hanging open. The rest of them just beat their sides laughing. George Williams made the little remark that old Bonameezer's feet must stink like hell to touch off the horse like he did.

It was quite a situation. Mrs. Bonameezer who had come to see the horses was crying, the boys was laughing, the horse was bucking like an outlaw and Bonameezer was cursing me and the horse in Austrian, then in American.

Brownie finally ran out of gas and stopped. He stood trembling with his eyes bugged out and acted scared to death. I went up to him, petted his head and neck and finally got hold of the latigo, uncinched the saddle and pulled it off.

I began to smell skunk. I knew that horse had been jobbed. When I got the saddle off I looked at his back and saw some cactus thorns sticking in it. Then I looked at the saddle blanket. Inside of the fold of the blanket there was a big cactus.

Bonameezer was outside of the corral still trembling, his face red, still blabbing. I showed him the cactus and the blanket. He didn't feel any happier to know that one of his men had jobbed him.

He paid us for the horses and we went home. Jim Frazer told me afterwards that the brown horse was one of the best horses he ever rode but Bonameezer never tried to ride him again.

MOST EVERYONE around Billings has heard of Charley Bair. Around 1900 he had most of the Crow Reservation leased. He was supposed to have more sheep than any other individual. He used one end of the reservation for cattle, as cattle and sheep don't get along on the same range.

He came to my ranch one time and made a deal with George Williams and myself to break a bunch of saddle horses. He had bought the horses in the fall and they was supposed to be all green broke. What I mean by green broke is just rode a time or two and then turned out for the winter.

When they got the horses up for the spring roundup they was a lot worse to handle than if they had never been rode. If you start breaking a horse and don't ride him much he just seems to get smart and mean. He knows what's coming when you lay a saddle on him, and is all ready to throw you off.

Now most cowboys are good riders on the range but when it comes to riding a real pitching horse, they can't get the job done. Some of the best hands I ever knew that worked on the range all their life couldn't or wouldn't ride a mean bucking, salty horse.

On the big spreads they most all had what they called a rough string. It was made up of horses that was poorly broke or naturally mean. They had never got over trying to slip a rider. The outfits got a bronc rider to ride them and payed him a little more money than the other cowboys.

In this bunch of about thirty head that Bair got us to take the stretch out of their backs was some real bucking horses. They was all good sized, five and six years old.

Ernie Cardwell, who was working on the roundup, told me that the first few days after they started the roundup there was bucking horses all over the range with saddles on. They had slipped their packs and got away with their saddles.

They gathered them up and sent Sam Taggert, Bair's foreman, over to Conway's corrals for George and me to break them from bucking.

There is one thing I want to say about Charley Bair. He always paid good. He wasn't cheap in his dealings. He expected a good job and he paid good.

We sure earned our money for them horses was big, stout and fat. They had bucked off several men and they really was tough. We tried at first to get them off without bucking but it was no dice. They was really a spoiled bunch of horses. Every time you rode one of them, you had to have your riding clothes on. Then you wondered if you was going to stay on top or buck off.

HORSE BREAKING AND FILLY CHASING

In breaking horses, the best way is to treat them good. Pet them and let them know that you ain't going to hurt them. Get their confidence and never let them buck with you if you can keep from it. If a horse throws you off once he will try it again as a horse is an intelligent animal.

On the other hand if he is naturally mean or spoiled you have to conquer him. If petting him won't do it you just have to knock it out of him the best way you can.

There has been many a good horse spoiled on account of some ill tempered man, who didn't have as much sense as a horse, had abused him. I always did think that a man had to have a little more sense than a horse to break them.

Horses are a great deal like people. They have different dispositions and different peculiarities. I am going to describe a few of those Bair horses as the most of them was hard to manage.

There was a bay horse that we named Snip as he had a white spot on the end of his nose. He was a beautiful piece of horse flesh, perfectly built, nervous and quick as a flash. He seemed to have been rode more than the rest of the horses.

He had a real bad trick. When you saddled him he would stand still and quiver all over. He was plenty nervous. When you started to get on he would never move until you went to throw your leg over the cantle of the saddle. Then he would jump, quick as a cat, right towards you. With one foot in the stirrup and the other in the air you was off balance. The first thing you knew you was laying on the ground and he was gone with your saddle.

We had a lot of trouble to break him of that. As a general rule, a horse will jump away from you. He broke out to be a very good, gentle horse.

There was a buckskin colored horse with a black stripe down his back that was the meanest one. He was sure a devil. He would try to kick or strike you. When you was on him he would reach around and grab your leg with his teeth. We used to put a feed bag on his head to keep him from grazing on our legs. He was a tough one but when he gave up he made a wonderful roping horse and became as gentle as a house cat.

There was a black horse that we named Charley Bair. He was a big horse for a saddle horse. He must have weighed close to twelve hundred pounds but had plenty of action. He was built on the blocky order. He had a wide, heavy muscled chest but fairly long active legs. Most horses that are heavy bodied have short legs.

He was a bucking fool. He was not disagreeable to handle or a bit mean. You could saddle him up just like any gentle saddle horse. He would straddle his front feet out wide, get his hind feet under, pretty well forward. He would seem to brace himself and never make a move as much as to say, "Go ahead and do what you want to. I'll throw you off."

If you had any sporting blood in you, you naturally liked the Charley Bair horse. I never saw another horse like him. Oh boy, he was hard to ride! He would start to romping with you and you would wonder if he was ever going to quit. Whenever he got out of gas he would freeze right there until he got his wind, then go through another spasm. He didn't care when you got off or on, he never moved until he was ready.

We would relay him. When he stopped bucking, the one that was on him would get off and the other one would get on. One time we thought we would both ride him. George had taken the first round so I got on behind, to my sorrow. I wrapped the saddle strings around my hands. George was going to work on his front end and I on his back end.

The horse, Charley Bair, was sure doing his stuff. A string broke, I landed against the corral fence about ten feet away.

He sure was a likeable horse. He never tried to hurt you, just bucked you off. He never would buck with an empty saddle. If he unloaded you he would never run away. He sure was a grand sport.

We got him a going but we never broke him from bucking. He'd be all right until some old boy would get rough with him, then he would buck his rider off. Charley Bair used to take him to the local shows and enter him as a bucker. He was a good one too and dirtied many a cowboy's back.

WHILE GEORGE WILLIAMS and I was breaking horses for Charley Bair, we was handling them in the old corrals on Blue Creek known as the Johnny Conway Spread.

George Williams was a tobacco chewing man. He ran out of chewing tobacco one day and said, "Let's ride into town on a couple of these snakes. I have to have some chewing tobacco and it will be a good ride for these broncs."

We picked out a couple of salty horses to ride into town. When we got there we tied them to a telegraph pole back of the Dark Horse Corral and Livery Stable that was run by Jeff Brewer.

As we walked by the board corral back of the stable we saw a man saddling a horse in the corral. It was a bronc, as he had a hind leg pulled up to put the saddle on. The horse acted pretty salty so we stopped to take a gander. It had rained the day before and the corral was pretty nasty. It had some holes full of water and manure.

George Williams had a great sense of humor. It tickled him to see someone bucked off, then he liked to josh them. Just as this young man started to step on the horse, George hollered at him and asked if he had any message to leave.

The rider turned and looked at George and said, "Oh, go to hell."

When he finally stepped on that old pony, things really began to happen. He exploded like a real bomb shell, bucking around water holes. That old boy was sure trying to ride that horse. It was bucking straight for a water hole but just as it got to it, he threw on the brakes and whirled back. The rider went on, head first, into the muck hole and turned over right in the middle of it on his back.

He sure was a comical sight as he got up, green all over. He had lost his hat and was wiping the manure out of his face and hair with his hands.

George and I was having a big laugh at his expense. George hollered, "Cowboy, you forgot to keep the horse between your legs but you found a good place to light."

The stranger didn't seem to enjoy us. He stood there and cussed us, then told George, "You can't ride that horse one jump."

We had had our fun and the stranger was getting too familiar. So we went on our way laughing. George got his tobacco and we went into Bob Conway's Saloon. We was having a few drinks at the bar when George punched me in the ribs with his elbow. I looked up and saw the rider coming up to have a drink. He looked like he already had one too many. We both began to laugh but never said anything to him.

He came over to us and said, "You guys think you are damn smart. I got fifty dollars that says neither one of you can ride that horse."

There was several in the saloon and they went into a huddle by the bar to get an ear full. George told him to forget his mad, that either one of us could kick hell out of that horse but to come and have a drink with us.

He had the drink but was still jawing about whether we could ride his horse. One word fetched on another.

We was all beginning to feel good. He got pretty rough. The drinks was working in me and I told him that I could ride the old pony that threw him off, on a packsaddle.

He really did have a fit then. He threw fifty dollars on the bar and said, "You afraid to take that bet?"

I told him I didn't have fifty dollars on me, just twenty-two. He said that I had made a fifty-dollar talk and that I was a damn coward if I didn't cover his bet.

Bob Conway was standing there. He said, "Bill, if you're short, I'll stake you to the rest of the bet."

HORSE BREAKING AND FILLY CHASING

I told him I wouldn't ride the horse in the slippery corral. We would take him out of the city limits and ride him in the open. We made the bet and Jeff Brewer was the stake holder.

Next morning George and I rode into town and got a packsaddle. It had a big wide cinch, just right to hang a pair of spurs in. We rustled an old soogan to throw on top of it. We lead the horse over on the flat just north of where the sugar factory now stands.

There was a good sized crowd had heard about the bet and came to see the results. A cowboy by the name of Tom Teagardner that worked for Nate Cooper helped George put the packsaddle on.

As there is no stirrups on a packsaddle, they helped me mount. They turned him loose with nothing on his head.

I reached down with my spurs, got a good hold in that cinch and a handful of mane. We had it out. He was a good tough bucking horse. I was scared the first few jumps as he got my head to popping but recovered myself.

There was a ditch that used to run along the bench there. The horse went to jump the ditch and fell in it. The fall didn't hurt me any but the horse was laying in the ditch and couldn't get up without some help.

The judges said they was satisfied with the ride and turned over the money to me.

UNTIL ABOUT 1915, Miles City, Montana, was one of the largest shipping places for horses in the northwest. The country around there was lousy with horses. They used to hold big horse sales. Horsemen and dealers came from all over the United States to Miles City to buy western horses.

One of the big horse outfits was owned by the Ryan brothers that branded the **RL**. It was one of the oldest horse outfits in the country. They ran thousands of horses north of the Yellowstone River. Their horses ranged for a hundred and fifty miles west and north to the Missouri breaks on the north and all through the Bull Mountains.

Their saddle horses was mostly light stuff, well bred, for saddle horses and driving teams. I had an old timer tell me that the Ryan brothers turned loose on the range at one time, one hundred head of two and three year old well bred stallions.

Their horses got plenty wild as there wasn't a wire fence outside of small saddle horse pastures in that whole country. Of course that was before the tractor and automobile when people raised horses for transportation and farm work.

Horse raising was a good business in the west at that time. There wasn't much expense as they ranged them on free grass summer and winter. About all they had to do was brand the colts every year.

A horse can eat more and get along on less than any animal I know anything about. They can paw snow and find grass. They can get along without water in the winter if there is snow on the ground. I don't know how the pioneers could ever have settled this country if it hadn't been for old Dobbin.

When the farmers began to use tractors for farm work and Fords for stages and to go across country, horses began to get cheap. The country was settling up and there wasn't free range any more. The horse men saw the horse had lost his job so they began to sell out as fast as they could.

The **RL** outfit gathered their horses in about 1910. I helped gather some of them and they was hard to handle.

There was a horse roundup in Bull Mountains. The **RL** wagon was camped on Carpenter Creek. George Williams, Horse Thief Smith and myself was working with the horse roundup. We helped deliver the **RL** horses over to what was called the Junction. I have forgotten whether we corralled at the Junction or at Bull Mountain.

These **RL** horses was wild and we had a lot of trouble. It was a mixed bunch of about six hundred head. The little colts got

HORSE BREAKING AND FILLY CHASING 277

tired and lagged behind while the geldings and dry stuff got in the lead and tried to get away.

We had to have a couple of riders in the lead to hold them bunched up for if some of those ridge runners got to running we would be liable to lose them.

"There was bucking horses packing saddles all over the range."

The horses was to be shipped from the stock yards that was on the south bank of the Yellowstone River. We crossed the river just a short ways from the old ferry that was just west of Pease Bottom.

The river wasn't too high but it swam the horses for about thirty yards. The current was pretty strong and we had a hard time getting the horses to take to the water.

There was a great many little colts in the bunch. We had to be careful not to get too many in a bunch so if they would get to milling they wouldn't drown the little colts. We got about fifty head started across, then kept them going.

It is quite a sight to see a bunch of mares and colts cross a deep river. The colt will get just as close as it can to its mother's side and bob along beside her like a cork.

There was seven of us swam the horses across the river, George Williams, Horse Thief Smith, Snapper Gunyon, Henry Grearson, two boys whose names I have forgotten and myself. It was none too many. We lost four colts that was pretty young and one mare that started back, got in the channel, then tried to get back to the herd. She played out and drowned.

I don't believe that there is any of the hands alive outside of myself that was in that horse drive. I heard that Grearson died at Forsyth, Montana. George Williams passed away in Burbank, California. Horse Thief Smith cashed in his chips in Billings. I have heard that Snapper Gunyon died. The other two must be dead for they was past middle age at that time.

IN 1923, I WAS RUNNING CATTLE at Pickett Springs in the Bull Mountains about forty miles northeast of Billings. One time a friend of mine that lived about ten miles north and east of me came to the ranch and stayed all night as he was gathering his horses.

Smithie wanted me to help him gather his horses. I had a couple of mares out with unbranded colts so thought it would be a good chance to get them. Smithie had some horses that run over on Railroad Creek so he decided we would ride that country first.

There was lots of badgers in that country. When you was riding Railroad Creek you had to watch out for the badger holes. If you was running horses you was liable to have your horse step in a badger hole any time and get a bad fall.

While we was riding along visiting, Smithie told me that before he came to Montana he used to live in Colorado. He said there was lots of badgers there. He said they was a peculiar animal, if they heard you coming and was near their hole they would back down in their hole with just enough of their head out to see you. If you was real close they would back down all the way in the hole, but would always come up after you passed to have another look. He said you could snare a badger if you would make a small loop and slip it down in the mouth of the hole. He and a friend had caught a lot of them that way in Colorado.

We was riding down a cow trail when we saw a badger. Smithie asked me, "You want to snare him, Bill?"

I'd roped about everything but a badger so I said, "Sure, I'll try."

Smithie said, "When we get about a hundred yards from the hole, you stop, the badger will go down the hole. Fix your loop down in the hole while I ride past aways. I'll come back, when the badger hears me coming back, he will come up to see what's coming. Give him a jerk and pull him out of the hole for if he gets all the way down a horse can't pull him out."

I fixed a small loop as soon as I could, and got out to the end of the rope so the badger wouldn't see me. Sure enough, Smithie's plan worked. When Mr. Badger stuck his head out, I jerked him clear out of the hole. He was sure putting on a show trying to get away. I was taking up on my rope to keep the slack out so he wouldn't get away.

I got the badger up to about ten or twelve feet from me and he was getting mad. He made a kind of a spitting noise and made a dive at me. I went to step back, hit a sage brush and fell down. I managed to roll over a time or two to keep the rope tight. Smithie was having a good laugh at my expense.

He got off his horse to gather some rocks to throw at the badger to kill it as neither of us carried a gun. The badger saw Smithie and started at him. I let some slack in the rope. It was Smithie's time to run. Just before the badger got to him I stopped it. I was doing the laughing then.

Smithie could only find a few small rocks and wasn't having any luck hitting the badger. I told him to get on his horse and hold the badger while I rode up on the ridge where there was some timber to get a club.

Smithie's horse was afraid but finally I got the rope to him. His horse went to bucking. That old pony was sure doing his stuff and Smithie was in a lot of trouble.

Smithie was a busy man right then trying to stay on top. He tried to make a dally around the horn of the saddle just as his horse made a dodging whirl. The badger was going the other way. Smithie took a dive and came near to landing on top of the badger.

I saw the rope was coming off the badger and made a run for the rope. I was too slow. The badger was in high gear making for his hole.

The fall didn't hurt Smith much, just knocked the wind out of him and he got a rope burn on his hand. When he got his gas he said, "That damn horse has been trying to buck me off for a year. He had to catch me at a disadvantage to get it done."

We went on with our horse hunting. We run into our stuff in a bunch of about fifty head. We corralled them and cut our stuff. Smithie had six colts and I had two. There was one slick mare yearling. That night we played seven-up to see which one got her. Smithie won.

HORSE BREAKING AND FILLY CHASING

HARRY RAMSEY had about twenty horses and a mule in a pasture near Bridger. They got out of the pasture and was heard of on the reservation near Woody Creek. Ramsey wanted George Williams and me to get his horses for him and deliver them to Billings.

We started from my ranch about five o'clock in the morning. It was a long ride for one day, if we had good luck in finding the horses, if not, we would have to sleep out. It was warm weather so that didn't make any difference to us. There was lots of sheep wagons on the range and you could always eat at one of Charley Bair's sheep wagons.

We got over on Woody about ten o'clock and looked on the head of the creek. There was three bands of Indian horses and a bunch of wild horses but no Ramsey horses. We thought we would ride down Woody, and if the horses wasn't there we would swing over in Fly Creek Basin.

We stopped at a sheep camp and had our dinner. We asked the herder if he had seen a small bunch of horses with a mule in the bunch watering in the creek.

He told us he had seen such a bunch about four days before. They had gone south as he had seen them going up the Woody Divide.

He told us about seeing a loose horse with a saddle on. He had seen him the night before about a mile from his camp but the horse had been hanging around about a week. The herder said he thought at first it was the camp tender's horse but he had seen the camp tender. The camp tender had seen the horse and tried to look it over. The horse was spooky and he couldn't get close to it.

We was curious. We thought we ought to look the horse over, see what he was branded and take the saddle off as the cinch would make a bad sore if the saddle was left on too long.

We run onto the horse. He acted pretty wild and run when he saw us coming. He seemed to be kind of sore or stiff. We worked him over against a rim rock. We both got our ropes ready. We worked him along the rim rock until we came to a place where it circled in.

George got on one side, me on the other. We kept closing up on him until he finally broke back. George threw at him, missed his head but caught the saddle horn.

The horse was running fast. When he hit the end of the rope, it broke the cinch of the saddle on the loose horse. Williams had a saddle on the end of the rope but the horse was running down the flat.

Everything happened so quick that neither one of us saw the brand on the horse, if he had a brand on. We didn't know where the horse came from as he had been there a week. There was nothing more we could do about it. The saddle cinch was bloody and mattery. It had rotted the cinch so it broke easy.

We never did find out how that horse happened to be in that country. The horse never had a hackamore or bridle on. Someone may have saddled him, tied him up and he pulled back, broke whatever he was tied with and got away. Anyway, it must have been a relief to that horse to get that saddle off.

It was a good saddle, not too old, made in Miles City. When we had looked the saddle over, we left it.

We had rode hard all day. Late in the afternoon when we was about seven miles this side of Beauvais, we met a camp tender that I knowed. He said he had seen the horses about two miles from where we was. He told us there was a sheep wagon about a half a mile away with an extra bed in it. He said there was plenty grass for our horses as he had just moved the wagon that day.

We was tired and our horses was tireder than we was. We went over to the sheep wagon and had supper ready when the herder got there. We stayed all night.

Next morning we rode over and found the horses. When we rode up to them, the mule came out to meet us. He trotted around us with his tail sticking up in the air and swinging his head.

George said, "That damn mule will look good carrying that saddle."

It was a gentle bunch of horses and didn't give us any trouble. We drove them back to where we left the saddle. We drove them back up in the circle of the rimrocks. George said, "Catch the mule, Bill. I think we can have a little fun."

I caught the mule. He was well halter broke and had a few collar marks on him. He was a little kinkey to get the saddle on. We pulled up a hind leg, blindfolded him and put the saddle on.

George said, "Wait a minute, Bill. I want to get some of that skunk brush and tie in his tail so he'll give us a good show."

After twisting some of the brush in the mule's tail, we turned him loose. When the mule saw that saddle on his back, moved and saw the brush on his tail, he let a bawl out of him and began to buck and kick at the brush on his tail. He sure put on a good show for a little while. When the brush came loose from his tail he quieted down and we got on our way.

We delivered the horses at the Ramsey Sale Barn just as it was getting dark.

I HAD GOT ACQUAINTED with an Englishman by the name of Berry. He had a spread on the Big Horn River close to the Dryhead where he was running quite a lot of horses. Berry was quite a promoter. At one time, he did some placer mining for gold in the canyon of the Big Horn River. It was common talk that he was getting quite a lot of gold. I don't know if it was true or not, anyway, he had a big dredge that I never could figure out how it got lowered in the river.

I met him in Billings sometime after Christmas one evening almost fifty years ago. He wanted me to take a message and some money to his wife at his ranch as he had to make a business trip to New York. He didn't have time to go to the ranch before his trip. He said he would send her a letter to Kane, Wyoming, but the snow was so bad in the mountains that he didn't think she would get the mail from there for some time. Anyhow, he hired me to take a letter over to the ranch.

He wanted me to start early the next morning. It was about seventy-five miles to the Berry ranch. It would take me two days on a good horse, with good luck, to make the trip on account of the snow being so deep.

About daylight, I met him in the lobby of the Grand Hotel. As he gave me a letter and a big envelope containing paper money, he asked, "Have you a good pocket to carry this in?"

I said, "Yes," and put it in my inside coat pocket.

I had a sourdough, sheep-lined, canvas coat for a top coat, a pair of leather chaps, wool underclothes. I wore a hat as I never liked a cap but had a big silk handkerchief to tie over my ears and face. A pair of overshoes and some warm mittens had me all fixed up for a long, cold ride.

"Horses crossing the river."

Mr. Berry came out of the hotel to see me off. He looked at my saddle horse and said, "That don't look like a very good horse for a trip in the mountains."

I told him, "No, this is just a colt I have been breaking. I have a good, tough, rollicky blue roan at the ranch that tries to buck me off every time I ride him. I'll change horses when I pass the ranch." Then I started on a damn rough trip.

The first day was the easiest as the snow wasn't too bad on this side of the mountain. There was only one place to stop, that was at the Phelps, afterwards known as the Will James, ranch. That was the first time I saw the Phelps boys, Frank and Bud. They was just school age. Their folks had a special room fixed for a school room and a teacher hired to teach them.

Before I started out in the morning Mr. Phelps directed me as he had been up that way a few days before. That second day was plenty rough. I had my horse down in the drifts several times. There had been a fresh snow since Mr. Phelps had been up there and on account of it I couldn't tell when I was running into a coulee or where there was a cut. I had to guess and guess right.

It was a bright, clear day. The sun shining on the snow just about put my eyes out. After going a while I came to an old dry tree. I got some limbs and built a fire. I thawed out, then stuck the burned ends in the snow, then I used the charcoal to black my face all over so I wouldn't go snow blind.

When I got pretty near the top of the mountain I could see a track once in a while. Following Mr. Phelps' directions, an occasional track and guessing, I got on the divide.

Some places on that mountain was solid rock wall, then it would break up with a sharp ridge going down the mountain. I couldn't follow the road as it was drifted full of snow. Those ridges was all steep. I rode and looked at all of them and finally decided on one and started down.

Oh, boy, it was steep and slippery. My horse wasn't moving his feet at all, just slipping on all four. Finally, we slid to a place where it was drifted and was going so fast that we lit in about a six foot snow bank. My horse lost his feet.

There we was about half way down the mountain stuck in a snow bank and the horse couldn't get out. One good thing, the snow wasn't crusted.

I tromped and kicked and throwed snow with my hands. I took off my sheepskin coat as it was too bulky to work in. I guess I must have been working an hour before I got the horse out of that drift.

I saw that I could get around that drift by going to the left. I put on my sheepskin coat and was ready to start on when I happened to think about the money and the letter.

I felt for it and it was gone. Believe me, I was scared. I remembered I had felt it just before I'd started down the mountain. I figured that I must have lost it right there in that drift.

I went to digging snow again. I was sure worried and didn't know whether I would ever find it or not. I was just about played out when I found it in the snow right where I had taken my sheepskin off. It must of worked out coming down the mountain.

After more slipping and sliding I finally got down the divide. There wasn't so much snow over the divide and over at the Berry ranch there wasn't no snow to speak of.

My horse acted tired, I was riding him in a walk. About a quarter of a mile from Berry's gate where the road ran down to his ranch, I saw a wire puzzle laying in the road. I got off and picked it up.

I was tired and threw one leg over the saddle horn and was just looking the puzzle over. I put it in my pocket and went to throw my leg back over the horn.

I guess old Blue thought I was getting too familiar with him. Anyway, he throwed his head down and turned on a real good job of bucking. I wasn't expecting anything like that and hadn't got my foot in the stirrup. About three jumps and I was standing on my head in the road but I still had one rein in my hand.

I got back on and went on to the ranch. I sure was glad to hand Mrs. Berry the letter and the money.

DURING THE Boer War, the English government sent buyers over to the United States to buy cavalry horses to use in the war. They bought horses all over the western states. At Billings, the receiving place for the horses was at Johnny Conway's ranch.

There was thousands of horses in Montana at that time. At Conway's ranch all the horses that was brought in was rode for the English inspection. The horses had to be five years old, all solid colors, no greys, whites or pintos, and sound. Of course, many of the horses brought to the inspection was rejected.

John Ramsey, a horse dealer and one of the first sheriffs of Yellowstone County, turned in a lot of horses at the Conway ranch, the rejected ones he was holding in a pasture up by Columbus. When the English was through buying horses, Ramsey had over forty head of horses in the pasture.

He got word that the horses had got out of the pasture. Mr. Ramsey sent a man up to find the horses and fetch them to Billings where he was having a sale in the Northern Pacific Stock Yards. After hunting that country for about two weeks the rider came back and said he couldn't find them or even hear of them and thought that the horses must have been stolen and run out of the country.

Mr. Ramsey came to my ranch on Basin Creek to ask me if I might have heard of the horses as he knew I rode the range a lot. He wanted to hire me to hunt the horses. He said there was forty-one head, some of them broken and a small sorrel mule in the bunch. As there wasn't many mules in the country, somebody ought to have noticed the mule.

I told him I'd like to go but I had just sold Dave Fratt all the saddle horses I had and just had two colts to ride that I was breaking out.

Ramsey said, "If you will try to find my horses I will stake you to a good saddle horse. I will give you a dollar and a half a head if you find them or pay you three dollars a day if you will take a hunt for them. I'll tell you one thing, they aren't around Columbus. I bought some of them over in the Big Horn Basin and I rather think they went that way."

He had come to the ranch in a light spring wagon. He said, "Throw your saddle in and you can go in with me and ride the horse back."

When we got to Mr. Ramsey's sale barn there was about twenty-five horses in the corral with the saddle horse. One of them must have kicked the saddle horse for he was dragging a hind leg. Mr. Ramsey was quite put out as that was the only good saddle horse he had on hand.

I noticed a very nice looking sorrel horse in the bunch that had some saddle tracks on him and asked Mr. Ramsey if he wasn't a saddle horse.

Mr. Ramsey said he looked like an awful good horse but his bronc scratcher had tried to ride him and the sorrel threw him twice so he'd given him up. Mr. Ramsey said, "Basin Creek, do you think you can ride that horse?"

I told him I thought maybe I could but if he was a bucking horse he wouldn't be much good to go hunting horses on but undoubtedly the horse had been used some to have those saddle marks on him.

Ramsey said, "If you think you can ride the sorrel, try him out and if you can get it done, ride him after the horses and I'll make you a present of him."

The sorrel looked like $50.00 worth of horse flesh to me, if I could ride him, so I said I'd try him.

We caught the sorrel and he didn't act a bit mean, just a little touchy. He never bothered when I put the saddle on him, just stood all spraddled out. I had seen a few horses that acted that way and I knew that he was going to give me a hard ride.

He never moved when I stepped on, just froze there. I let him stand a little while, then tried to rein him around. Nothing doing, he wouldn't move a bit. I grabbed him in the shoulders with both spurs.

Oh boy! He made a balloon ascension, came down with his mouth wide open. He let an awful bawl out of him. He was sure mad. He done his stuff twice around that large corral. I got pretty high, lost a stirrup and pulled everything on that saddle I could get hold of. He sure had me bucked off several times but didn't quite lose me.

He hit the middle of the corral and froze down again with his legs spraddled out. He was getting his gas for another try and believe me, I was taking some too.

I knew I never could ride that sorrel catamount and spur him after he was rested up. I told the foreman to hit him on the rump with his rope. We sure went around again but this time I reached down with my gut wrenches and fastened them in the cinch. I knew that he wouldn't throw me unless a spur slipped.

Finally, he had enough and I had too much. He broke into a long trot around the corral. They opened the gate and I started horse hunting.

As I was crossing the south bridge I met Tom Rule that lived on Blue Water, and asked him if he'd seen a bunch of horses with a small sorrel mule in the bunch. He'd seen them about three weeks before on the head of Blue Water and they had been working east.

I rode over on the Dryhead and met a hand. He said he'd seen a bunch of horses with a mule that morning hung up against Berry's pasture fence.

I rode on to Berry's, stayed all night, picked up the horses and started back to Billings. There was only twenty-seven head in the bunch at Berry's. Mr. Ramsey got the rest of the horses over near Hart Mountain that fall in the horse roundup.

That sorrel horse never romped with me again. He was a good horse. I sold him to O'Donnell for eighty dollars.

LOOKING OVER a *45 Years Ago* column in the *Billings Gazette*, I saw where Charley Bair's White racing steamer, "Whistling Billy," was matched for a race with Barney Oldfield. I do not know how that race came out but I want to tell you of a race Bair and I had.

I have heard that Charley Bair was the first conductor on the passenger train that traveled between Billings and Butte. He went into the sheep business on the Crow Reservation. At one time he run a lot of cattle. After leaving the reservation he went over in the Musselshell country and developed a large ranch there.

Charley Bair was a great financier. His ability was outstanding in keeping his sheep and other numerous businesses going. He had quite a sense of humor. Bair enjoyed a good joke and always had a good joke to tell. He was a good sport. He always played the Billings Fair and liked any kind of rodeos.

I was very well acquainted with him. I broke a bunch of horses for him. I took a bunch of sheep shearers over on Hay Creek and sheared out 7,500 head of sheep for him.

At that time there was only a few cars and the roads was so bad, and the country so rough, that he couldn't get around with a car. He had two teams of well bred driving horses that he drove on a mountain made light spring wagon called a buck board. And believe me, those horses could really get over the ground. He kept them well grained and he sure was proud of them drivers.

I had a buckskin saddle mare that I used to run wild horses with. I was just like Bair, I was plenty proud of her. I don't know whether she had good breeding or not as I had bought her out of a bunch of range horses and broke her. She was fast, had lots of wind. I had done quite a lot of bragging on her.

We was on Hay Creek at the sheep shearing plant about twenty-eight or thirty miles from Billings. Mr. Bair was going to Billings on some business and I was going in too as I had been subpoenaed on a trial. I was going to ride Maud, the buckskin mare, pride of my heart. Bair was driving in, with his best driving team.

He said, "Bill, how would you like to have a race to Billings? I would like to show you the difference between a good driving team and a saddle horse."

The sheep shearers began to hurrah me. I hated to back down, then I began to drum my head. So I said, "For how much?"

He said, "Oh, fifty dollars, just to make it interesting."

"Okay," I said, "the first one into Billings gets the dough."

His reply was, "All right, we will make the finish at the Grand Hotel and no beefing."

It caused quite a lot of excitement among the sheep shearers and there was quite a lot of betting on the race.

When we started I took the lead as Maud was nervous and wanted to go. I let her go because I didn't want her to fret charging around. I kept the lead for about a mile and a half with Bair about two hundred yards behind. I knew that I was setting the pace too fast so when I came to a place where I could cut off a little I took the short cut while Bair went around. I wanted him in the lead as it was pretty rough on the cut off.

When we got to Pryor Creek, he was a good half a mile ahead. Oh Lord, how that team was going. I wouldn't have given a plugged nickel for the chances of me winning that race. Maud wasn't showing any weakness but I knew at the speed we was going that she could never hold out. I had a "hole card" that was pretty good.

I knew when we struck Wet Creek that there was a cut off of four or five miles. Bair would have to go about thirteen miles while I would have to go about eight to the south bridge across the Yellowstone River. I would come in from the east of the bridge while he would come in from the west. He had to make the loop around Blue Creek.

I figured we would not be too far apart as it was fast driving around the road for him. I couldn't make as fast a time as he could as I was going through rough country. I figured the race would have to be won from the bridge on into Billings.

When I got to the bridge, Bair wasn't in sight. I was worried, I was wondering whether he had crossed the bridge or hadn't got there yet.

As I was crossing the bridge I saw a lot of dust flying. It was Bair coming around the dugway, about a half a mile away. How that team was coming.

I didn't lose any more time, I was sure riding for town. I kept looking back, he was gaining on me. I was saving a little in Maud for the finish.

I sure needed it. When we hit town I could make the corners a little faster. I was giving Maud all she had. When I got to the Grand Hotel, Bair was just half a block behind me.

Bair would have beat me easy but he got held up at the dugway as there was a bunch of sheep crossing the dugway when he got there. He couldn't get through until the sheep was out of the way. It caused him a fifteen or twenty minute delay.

Anyway, I got to the Grand Hotel first, that was the bet.

I WAS GATHERING some of my horses. I'd rode all day and corralled all I'd found at Cooper's corral as it was the only corral in that country. I stayed all night as I hadn't found all the horses I was looking for.

Tim Riordon was an old-timer at the ranch and had been riding for Cooper. He told me that they had gathered some of my horses off the reservation with some of Cooper's horses. In the bunch there was a buckskin horse with my brand that looked like he was a broke horse and two mares with unbranded colts. Tim said he'd seen the bunch of horses that mine was running with the day before and they was only about two miles from there.

HORSE BREAKING AND FILLY CHASING

The buckskin horse had been gone about two years. I had bought him from Joe Poor. Joe had told me that the buckskin was a good saddle horse but he was plenty hard to ride if he wasn't used regular.

I rode over and got the horses that evening to have them with the ones I'd already gathered. I thought I could find the others by noon the next day and go home.

I had rode my horse hard that day. I thought I'd ride the buckskin to hunt the other horses and have my saddle horse rested to take them all home.

I knew from what Joe Poor told me about the buckskin horse, that after running with a bunch of range horses he was going to be rough to ride. He was thin when I bought him. I got him cheap and turned him out without riding him.

It was just beginning to get light when we had all saddled up ready to go. The buckskin was hard to mount. When I reached up to get hold of the saddle horn, he was gone. I tried a couple of times but couldn't make it, so Nate said, "I'll ear him down for you, Bill, so you get a good seat for I think you are going to need it."

Nate got the buckskin by both ears and jabbed his nose on the ground. Nate Cooper was the best ear down man I ever seen. He weighed over 200 pounds, was stout as a bear and really knew his stuff. I stepped on that old pony, he just quivered.

Nate said, "Take your time. Get set and holler when you're ready."

When I got settled in the saddle I hollered, "Turn him loose!" Oh, boy, that buckskin was good. I rode him but he was the kind of a horse that you didn't know whether you was going to ride or not. He was a romping cuss. I thought I was a goner several times but just managed to stay on top and that was all.

I was riding him in a large corral. After he done his stuff I run him around the corral several times. Tim opened the gate and we went to the hills on high. When he got the wild hairs out of his nose, the buckskin was okay.

I found the horses and fetched them in. The corral was in the pasture. The gate was open and I had no trouble but stopped to shut the gate so the horses wouldn't get out when I went to corral them. It took me a little while to shut the gate and the horses got about 200 yards ahead of me going right down the creek.

There was quite a wide flat on each side of the creek and a prairie dog town on the flat. The horses crossed the creek and started east up a trail. The gate was open on that side of the pasture. I cut over to try to head them from getting out the gate. My horse was running his best when he picked up a prairie dog hole.

I never could remember him falling with me but I woke up about a half a mile from where I remembered running the horses. As near as I could figure, my foot must have hung in the stirrup and he was kicking me while I drug. He must have kicked me once square in the face as he left the print of his foot on my face. My nose was broken, my knee was throwed out of place and my head was scratched and cut all over.

"Dragged."

I must have lay where my foot came loose about three hours in the hot sun. I think what fetched me to was that my nose had bled and the blood had dried in my nose and I was choking. There was a million flies on my head and face.

The horse went on running, hit the four-wire fence and cut himself awful bad. Duey, a red head that was riding for Cooper, saw the horse all cut up and came to see what had happened to me. He found me about the time I regained my senses. I couldn't walk or ride so he went back and got a spring wagon and took me home.

The buckskin horse died. I thought I was going to. I didn't look very good, head swelled up, both eyes black, nose broke, chin cut through to the bone, knee out of place, skinned and bruised all over. I've got some of the scars from that fall to this day.

MONTANA WAS OVER-RUN with wild horses. Most every crazy cow puncher that got out of a job would have a yen to try to capture a bunch of them. Those cowboys took some desperate chances running them over rough country, across prairie dog towns where there was dog holes for a horse to fall and break a leg and roll his rider in a bunch of rocks or in a cactus patch.

George Williams and I was two of those Loco Birds that used to think it was sport to run wild horses. Sometimes we got a bunch but more times they got away.

I remember one time we was both out of a job and decided that we would go over on the Crow Reservation where there was thousands of wild horses. Our plan was to get a bunch, break them out and sell them.

We took a packhorse loaded with our bed and some grub. We was riding our top filly chasers and was determined to capture a bunch of wild horses. It was dry and a lot of the water holes had dried up. Most of the wild horses was watering on Two Leggins.

We staked the packhorse and rode up on a point to watch the wild horses come in to water. They would come in on the run. The water was down in a deep wash in water holes. There would always be one horse that would stay up on top as a sentinel. If he saw or heard or smelled anything unnatural he would let out a loud snort and away they would go on a dead run for the rough country where it was impossible to catch them.

The wind was in the east and we was west of the water where they couldn't catch our scent. We had our saddle horses just over the point out of sight and we layed on the point where the wild horses couldn't see us. We watched several bunches come in and water and then away they would go again.

They all had to go into the deep wash at a certain place where there was a trail, then go down the wash about three hundred yards to the water hole. Below the water hole about a quarter of a mile there was another trail into the wash that went out on the other side. When the horses was in the wash they couldn't get out for a long ways only through them two trails as they was about ten feet deep.

We lay there figuring how to get close enough to them to keep them from getting in the rough country to the south. We finally decided that we would take a chance after a bunch had just watered. George would get down in the water wash and I would stay out of sight until another bunch came into water. When they got in the wash I would make a run in behind them and George would be ahead of them. We would have them trapped in about a half a mile of the wash where they couldn't get out.

He could spook them so they would run toward me and then I could spook them back. That way we thought that we could give them a lot of grief and tire them so we could handle them when we let them out. We had them running back and forth about two hours. They would try to go up the sides of the wash. It looked like sometimes one would make it but then it would fall back.

HORSE BREAKING AND FILLY CHASING

There was about thirty head in the bunch. They was sure crazy scared horses, their eyes bugging out, head and tails up, snorting, trying to get away. They was running from one trail to the other and back again.

There was a lot of loose rock in the wash. George's horse either bruised a foot on the rocks or strained a tendon, anyway, he went lame and could hardly travel.

In the wild bunch there was a **7-7** saddle horse. You could tell he was a broke horse from the saddle tracks on his back. There was a bend in the wash and we got the horses in the bend. George and I could holler to each other. George said he was going to try to rope the saddle horse. There was nothing else to do. His horse was in bad shape.

We worked up as close to them as we could. The horses got to milling around and started to pass George. The **7-7** and a wild pinto stud was running neck and neck. George threw at the **7-7** and caught them both but the saddle horse got out of the rope.

When the wild horse hit the end of the rope both horses was knocked down. The rest of the horses stampeded down the wash. I couldn't leave George to follow them, so they got away.

I threw my rope on the wild horse too, as he was jerking the lame horse something awful. When we got him throwed and tied down George said, "Here's where I ride a wild horse."

We took George's saddle and put it on him and pulled the cinch under him and got the saddle cinched. I tied my rope in the ring of the hackamore on the wild horse and tied it on my saddle horn hard and fast as we didn't want him to get away.

George got on the saddle with one foot in the stirrup ready to catch the other when he got up. I was careful when I untied his feet so he could get up as I wanted to get on my horse before he got up. Luck was with me for I was on my horse before he got up. He sure threw some nasty whing dings with George.

We was doing pretty good until just before we got out of the wash. That pinto throwed hydrophobia fit and broke the hackamore where the ring was tied in it. He was loose and he sure went down the wash on a dead run. When he came to the trail out of the wash, out he went into the wide open spaces.

I made a hole in my rope but I couldn't get close enough to catch him. George began to pull him and it slowed him up enough for me to get a throw at him.

I caught the saddle horn and when he hit the end of the rope it just busted the cinch on George's saddle. I had the saddle and George but the wild pinto stud was still going the last time I saw him.

RED SHIRT BERT SMITH and I was over on Woody Creek hunting horses. That was a long time ago.

There is a long ridge that starts off Pryor Mountain that comes down into a valley. We saw dust on the ridge and thought it was a bunch of wild horses coming to water. We watched the dust and finally saw a rider behind them. Those old ponies was sure coming down the divide, their manes and tails blowing in the breeze.

There was a cut bank corral about four miles from there and we figured that the cowboy was making for it. When the horses came off the ridge, Bert and I spread out so the horses would go between us. Our horses was fresh. We could help the cowboy handle the wild bunch for his horse was losing ground. If a bunch of wild horses gets too much of a start, you never catch them.

He saw that we was going to help him and stopped to give his horse some wind and a little rest. We whipped them right up the ridge to him and he fetched them back to us.

They had run a long ways and was getting winded. We never let them get any wind. We just crowded them all the time. By the time we got them to the cut bank corral they was all out of gas and we had them in the corral before they really knew it.

Wild horses are hard to catch, no fooling. Get them in a flat country, they just out run you. In a rough country they will go places that a saddle horse, carrying a heavy stock saddle and a man, can't follow. If you do get them close to a corral they are scared to death and will scatter like a bunch of blackbirds. You just have to out-smart them.

At the cut bank corral where we corralled them, there was a deep canyon that came out of the mountains. In fact, it was a deep water wash probably fifteen feet wide. In the spring at high water time when the water rushed off the mountains it had cut a gorge ten to fifteen feet deep. At the bottom of the wash where it came into the valley, it wasn't too steep. If you got wild horses started up the water wash there was no way for them to get out. There was a sharp turn in the wash where it made a circle back down to the creek. Some cowboy had built a wire gate in the wash. When the horses got in the circle all you had to do was shut the gate.

The gate was made of barb wire about four inches apart with poles about ten feet high nailed up and down. There was about an acre of ground in the circle with a cut bank straight up about twelve to fifteen feet high all around it.

When we had the horses in the corral and the gate shut, we set down and had a visit. Red Shirt knew the rider and introduced us. He was Bronc Savage. I'd heard a lot about him but that was the first time I met him. I noticed he had a kind of hitch in his get along.

We rested a while, then looked the bunch of horses over. They was mostly mares, some colts, yearlings, two year olds and one very nice looking bay horse. Bronc said there wasn't anything in the bunch he wanted except the bay horse which belonged to him. He said he had got him out of a wild bunch, broke him to ride and made a rope horse out of him. He'd turned him loose with the saddle horses in the fall but he'd got out and come back to his old range and picked up with the wild bunch.

Bronc went in the corral and roped the bay horse. Then Bert and I caught a couple of very pretty pinto two-year-olds. Those old mares wasn't any good to us and we didn't want them. We tied the colts down and turned the rest loose.

We put war bridles on the paint colts and broke them to lead on our way home. Later Red Shirt traded me a rawhide hackamore for my paint. The following year he broke them out.

STURM & DRAKE had a sale barn and corrals on 15th Street and Second Avenue North in Billings. Sturm hired me to go to Bridger about sixty miles to help his foreman, A.B. Todd, get a bunch of horses and bring them to the corrals.

We was both riding good horses when we started from Billings. We went by the head of Blue Creek and Cottonwood Creek. When we got to Bridger and looked the horses over in the corral there, we knew we was up against a bad deal.

As near as I remember, there was about sixty head, a mixed bunch of horses. There was about twenty head of wild snakes, probably about fifteen head of range horses, the rest was work stuff with some heavy mares and young colts. There was one big old mare with a young colt that kicked everything that got close to her. The wild ones acted scared and crazy, running around the corral trying to find a place to get out. The range horses wasn't so bad but they was everything but gentle.

We rode up one day and stayed in Bridger so we could get a good early start. We knew we would need all the daylight to get them to the head of Blue Creek where there was a pasture to put them in overnight, a distance of about thirty-five miles.

We had pretty good luck for about three or four miles out of Bridger as there was a fence on one side of the road. Todd was riding in the lead as I wanted to work on the big old mare with the young colt, with the end of my rope to take some of the fight out of her. When she saw you coming she would lay her ears back, begin to switch her tail and kick.

When we hit the open country we began to have a lot of trouble. Them snakes wanted to get away and we couldn't keep them bunched. They stampeded right toward Pryor Mountain with Todd riding hell for leather after them. I just bid them good bye. All I could see was a cloud of dust once in a while until they finally dropped over a ridge out of sight.

I turned the rest of the horses up against a rim rock and waited for Todd to show up. After what seemed like an hour, I saw dust and Todd was fetching them back. I rode out to turn them up against the rim rock to get them bunched again. Just before they got close to me I saw that Todd's horse had gone lame.

My horse was fresh so I took to them and finally managed to get them bunched with the other horses. When Todd's horse limped up I knew we was in a bad fix as there wasn't any saddle horses in that bunch. There was one horse that had a scar on his nose. We thought maybe he had been rode. Todd was a top hand but no bronc stomper so it was up to me to try and find some horse to ride.

I shook my rope out, made a good hole in it and worked up to the horse with the scar. I knew I had to make a sure catch. It was just good luck he happened to be in the gentle bunch. When I got close enough to make a throw, I snared him. When the rope hit him he throwed a fit but before he knowed what happened, I had him far enough from the horses not to bother them much.

He was halter broke all right, but I don't think he'd ever been rode. We pulled a hind leg up and cut a piece out of my saddle blanket and blindfolded him. I took my saddle and put it on him. Todd put his saddle on my horse and snubbed up the bronc for me to get on. I told him to pull the blind off as soon as I hit the saddle and be ready to ride because those wild horses would stampede again when the bronc started doing his stuff.

When Todd pulled the blind, that old pony unwound. He sure turned an awful dose for me and started right for the bunch of horses. The bunch of snakes saw him coming and started for Pryor Mountain again, Todd after them. I was plenty busy. When I did have time to look all I saw was a big dust. I wasn't worried for I had run lots of wild horses on that horse and never spilt them.

My worries was right there for the rest of the horses had split up and one bunch was headed for Bridger, some of the work horses and the old kicking mare was still there. The colt was sucking when the mare saw me coming and began to switch her tail. As I came up to her, she unwound and kicked the bronc in the stomach. He didn't seem to like it, saw the bunch going toward Bridger and took after them. That suited me as I wanted to get them stopped.

When I did finally catch up to them he run right in the bunch but I couldn't get him ahead of them, to head them off. I had to fight him quite a while before I could get them turned. I could see a cloud of dust that was Todd and his bunch of snakes coming in the other direction.

With a lot of trouble we got them together. In the course of the day I had to catch and ride two more broncs. We run them and fought them all day and just about dark we got them in the pasture on Blue Creek. We was sure hungry, tired and sleepy. I honestly believe Todd rode close to a hundred miles that day and I rode three green bucking horses. I don't know who was the tiredest, Todd or me.

We had to sleep out that night on our saddle blankets, no supper, no breakfast. In the morning I had another bronc to ride. We was only about twenty miles from Billings. We made it in about noon.

11: Bucking Horses

GEORGE WILLIAMS and I was giving riding contests and shows at Central Park in Billings. That was before the big rodeos started. There was roping and riding contests but not like today's rodeos where it is done in a big way.

We had a few good bucking horses and at that time there was lots of horses in the country. With a little advertising we could always get outside bucking horses brought in to be rode. We thought we would manage for more bucking horses as it looked like we could make good money taking in the fairs.

There was lots of wild horses in the country. George said, "Let's catch some wild horses, they ought to make good bucking horses."

After running our saddle horses almost to death, we caught several bunches of wild horses. They didn't work out, for when we handled the wild horses, halter broke them and rode them a couple times, the horses abused themselves so much that they just gave up and wouldn't buck any more.

Some of them would be scared so bad that they would just stampede and run away. They was no good for bucking horses and plenty dangerous to ride as they might pick up a hole and fall down or run over a cut bank or through a wire fence.

When the wild horse idea didn't produce any bucking horses we watched the sale yards and got a few. We traded for any bad horse we heard about. We got an awful good bucking horse from Charley Bair and a good one from George Sturm.

One of the best bucking horses I ever bought, cheap, I got off the Crow Reservation. I bought him from an Indian but the horse wasn't an Indian raised horse.

He was a cream colored horse with a mixture of sorrel and had a dark streak running from his mane to his tail. When the sun shone on him, he glistened to a gold color. He was very well built, weighed about eleven hundred fifty pounds and had a lot of action.

An Indian rider by the name of Shobe Daylight stopped at my ranch one night and told me about the horse. Shobe said that I could get the horse cheap as none of the Indians had been able to ride him. The horse had bucked off an Indian and got away with his saddle. It was about a month before they found the horse. It had picked up with a bunch of gentle Indian horses south of Hardin.

The Indians caught the horse and took the saddle off, then turned him back on the range. The saddle cinch had made big sores on the horse and the hair had come off. When the sores healed the hair had come in white. The horse was still running with the gentle bunch of Indian horses that was easy to corral.

The Indian that owned the horse lived south of Hardin so George and I went to take a look at the horse. We corralled the bunch of horses and dropped a rope on the bucker. He was fat and pretty and was well rope broke. He wasn't a mean horse that wanted to strike you or kick you. He had just been spoiled to ride.

The Indian, whose name I've forgotten, said he'd got the horse off a white man who was leading him behind a wagon. The Indian had traded a mare for the horse. The Indian wanted twenty-five dollars for the horse: I offered him fifteen and he took it and we had a horse.

We got back with the horse from Hardin on a Thursday. We was giving a bucking contest on Sunday. George said, "Bill, we ought to ride that son of a gun out before Sunday to see how he performs. I'll play you a game of seven-up to see who rides him in the morning."

We started a game of seven-up. We was six and six. George bid three and I bid four on a deuce and jack. George didn't have a trump so I made high, low, jack and game. It was George's ride.

The horse was sure afraid of a saddle. When he saw the saddle laying in the corral he just went crazy.

We had to blindfold him to get anywhere close to him with the saddle. When we got a sack tied over his eyes, he just froze down and never moved, just stood all spraddled out, quivering.

He never moved until I pulled the blind off. When he saw daylight he sure went to town with his head between his legs, bawling worse than any bawling, bucking horse I ever heard. He sure made an awful noise and was giving George a tough ride.

I knew that he was a bucking horse that was hard to ride and a good one for a good bawling horse always makes a hit with a crowd. When the horse gave it up and George got down, George said, "Bill, that's the hardest horse I've rode in two years. We sure got a wampus cat."

We named the horse, "Wampus Cat." Sunday, at the contest, Wampus Cat bucked off a long legged black man that had just blowed in from Texas. He made a fairly good ride for several jumps and then sailed away.

I bucked Wampus Cat for two years and he dirtied many a rider's back. I had him up to Missoula when he showed signs of giving up. I rode him without spurs. He gave a half hearted jump or two and I pulled him around a few times. That was it. He was through as a bucker.

We was careful with him and he turned out to be a good saddle horse. I finally sold him to Frank O'Donald a stock man, for eighty-five dollars.

I WAS PUTTING ON a Wild West Show at old Central Park west of Billings for the Fourth of July. I went up on the head of Blue Creek, which was about fifteen miles from my ranch, to gather a bunch of bucking horses. Tommy Rorick was helping me. We had rode until about two-thirty in the afternoon and had gathered all the horses except a few head that was running on the head of Duck Creek.

We corralled them in John Miller's corral on the head of Blue Creek. Our saddle horses was just about played out. In gathering, we had picked up a gentle horse of mine and a stray horse that looked like a saddle horse as he had his tail trimmed and had a small bump on his back that undoubtedly had been made with a saddle.

Tommy wasn't no bronc stomper so I told Tommy to ride my horse as I knew he was a good gentle horse and the stray acted pretty snakey. I figured the stray would rag a little but had no idea he was the wampus cat that he turned out to be.

He was a very pretty horse, seal brown colored, well built, quick as a cat, with a pretty intelligent head and a Roman nose. He probably weighed about 1,050 pounds. I'd never have picked him for a bucking horse. He acted plenty ornery when I roped him. We had to pull up a hind leg before we could saddle him.

When we got him saddled I looked him over again. I could just see red in his eyes and I knew there was a hard ride coming. I had one of those ear bridles that you pull over one ear without a throat strap.

I'd told Tommy to open the gate and get on his horse. When I stepped on the brown he sure turned on a dose. The first time around the corral he didn't see the gate. He had his head down with his mouth open bawling like a Texas steer. I was plenty busy. I had a new saddle, it was stiff and slippery. I was pulling on the bridle reins plenty hard. It seemed to loosen the ear strap. The head stall came off and he jumped on it, pulling the reins out of my hand.

There we was out on a dog town flat, full of dog holes. By that time I had both hands full, Grandma in one hand and a bunch of mane in the other. Tommy was hollering, "Stay with him," but his horse wasn't fast enough to keep up.

I was doing my damnedest to stay on and the horse was doing his, to get me off. I have rode a lot of bucking horses and I have bucked off a lot of times but I never rode a horse before or since that I thought that I was going every jump and still rode him. I pulled a hand full of mane out and thought I sure was a goner but Grandma saved me until I got another hold of mane.

By that time Tommy caught up with us and he strung out and run about fifty yards, then blowed the plug out and made a balloon ascension. I was trying so hard to ride that hurricane that I never thought of quitting him. He'd buck and do his damnedest to unload me until Tommy would catch up, then he would break out and run a ways and do it all over again.

He bucked through a plum thicket and scratched my hands and face but he was getting some scratches too, so I guess we was both glad to get out of there. He left my hat hanging on a plum tree.

We finally got him headed for the Bar K horse corrals and finally got him in. The Bar K corral was about five miles from where we started. He'd bucked most of the way.

Dan Cooper, a salty hand, was at the ranch. When he saw the horse I was riding he said I had plenty of guts to try to ride that horse as he was a tough son of a gun (as if I hadn't found that out). Dan said that about three weeks before that he had run across the horse carrying a saddle and turned him loose. Dan told me who he belonged to but I've forgotten the man's name. The owner had got a bronc snapper to break him but he'd thrown him off and run around with the saddle on for a week or ten days. The owner wanted to trade him off.

I knew from that ride he was a bucking horse and traded a good unbroke horse for him. I named him Duck Creek. He was a great bucking horse. He made a reputation for himself. When I left Billings with a Wild West Show, I put a hundred dollars on his head for anyone that could give him a contest ride. Many a good rider took a setting at him but I never had to pay the hundred dollars. Many of the old-timers around this western country remember old Duck Creek.

I AIN'T ONE of the old coffee coolers that think the old-time riders was better than the riders of today. I can't see much difference. A top rider is liable to ride any horse and then a top bucking horse is liable to slip any rider.

I've heard a lot of folks say that the bucking horses are trained, that the men who ride them know what they will do and so they are ready for their tricks. All I can say is that those folks just don't know horses.

A horse is a pretty wise animal. A smart horse can be trained to do most any kind of a job. A bucking horse gets educated too. A rider on him is using his spurs a-plenty and it hurts the horse so he wants to get the rider off as soon as possible. The horse does every stunt he knows to throw the rider.

In the early days when I owned a bunch of good bucking horses, a lot of them wasn't bucked out over a dozen times a year. When a horse bucked a rider off he'd try the same thing over and naturally educated hisself to unload a rider whenever he could.

A green colt is twice as easy for a cowboy to ride as one of those self-educated buckers that comes out of a chute kicking over his head, whirling and doing anything to get that thing off from his back that is raking him with a pair of gut wrenches.

I bought a very pretty grey, two-year-old mare with a bunch of horses that I got from Si Cooper. I paid $8.00 a head for them. The first time I rode the grey mare was when she was a four year old at old Central Park. She was such a good bucking animal that I never tried to break her from bucking.

She weighed about 1,100 pounds and was a bear kitty to ride. She had a bad habit of throwing the boys off and kicking at them while they was in the air. She never happened to hurt anyone serious but she connected with a lot of the boys. I called her Cow In The Woods.

As a five year old, Cow In The Woods had a black, chunky colt. It never seemed to slow her up a bit. We named the colt Steamboat.

Whenever the mare was bucked out, we had a big horse collar that we stretched over the colt's back and turned him out behind his mother. The crowd used to get a big kick out of seeing little Steamboat buck the horse collar off, then stick up his head and tail and run to his mother.

When he got to be a four year old, Steamboat was a blocky chunk that weighed about 1350 and was plenty hard to ride. He was well halter broke. You could feed him oats out of your hand but whenever he saw you pick up a saddle, business picked up.

He was plenty mean to saddle as he knew what was going to happen. He got so he would throw himself down and we could hardly saddle him when we didn't use a chute without an awful lot of trouble.

He would strike, bite or kick. We just had to catch his front feet and blindfold him to get a saddle on him. He always done his best to lose his rider and generally did if they wasn't a plumb top rider. I finally traded him off when I had to travel without a chute. He was just too much trouble to saddle.

The second colt Cow In The Woods had turned out to be a bucker too. He was a grey that we called Bull In the Woods. He was the best crowd getter I ever had. When he was rode he used to put his head down between his front feet with his mouth wide open, bawling like a mad bull. I never heard a horse that could make as much noise as he could. We always opened the show with him as he made so much noise that the people wanted to see what was causing all the commotion inside the canvas.

Cow In The Woods had two more colts. The third one broke out into a nice saddle horse that could run like a streak. I sold it to Stuart Pope, a racehorse man.

The fourth colt was a roan mare that through some mishap got a hip knocked down. I never handled her at all but she raised seven colts that all went into our bucking horse string.

ONE YEAR, just a week or so before Labor Day we got three outside horses that was sure salty. I can't remember who brought in two of the horses but one, a sorrel, was brought in by Dan Cooper. Dan was a real honest to God cowpuncher that knew bucking horses and had a ranch on the East Fork of Pryor Creek.

Anyway, George Williams rode one of the outside horses, Matt Gross rode one and a Texas rider called Texas Bud got the Cooper horse.

Oh, boy, that sorrel horse was a stem winder! He done it all and throwed Texas Bud about the fourth jump. The sorrel never quit bucking. He seemed to be trying to throw the saddle off too and had the stirrups cracking together in the air above the saddle. He won the prize for being the best bucker fetched in, easy.

After the show a bunch of us was at Bob Conway's saloon talking over the day's show and especially about the sorrel bucking horse. One of the riders said he'd like to see Williams take a seat on him. George said that he would, on Labor Day.

There was a man from Big Timber in the bunch and he said he didn't believe Williams could ride the sorrel. Williams kind of bristled up at that and told him, "Money talks. I'll bet you some folding money that I can ride the sorrel horse."

There was some rag chewing. The Big Timber man had about two drinks too many. He said, "I ain't got any betting money with me but I got a real outlaw horse at Big Timber that I'll bet a hundred dollars you can't ride."

George told him to bring the horse down on Labor Day and his hundred dollars with him. The Big Timber man answered, "I'll be here with my horse and plenty money to back him."

A lot of people heard the talk and it soon got around town and was a boost for the Labor Day show. George and I had a thousand hand bills made too, advertising the coming ride of the Big Timber Outlaw.

BUCKING HORSES

Labor Day was a nice, clear, warm day. There was a lot of Indians in town. They had fetched in a horse for us to ride. Somebody else had brought in two big snuffy bulls to be rode. We had a good crowd, everything was fine except the Big Timber man and his outlaw horse hadn't showed up.

We had an Indian race, a matched race, a free for all saddle horse race, a roping contest and rode about thirty bucking horses. The crowd seemed to be getting a big kick out of the show.

When the bucking horse contest started and several of the riders had been throwed, the crowd began yelling for the Big Timber Outlaw.

I didn't know what to do. I'd advertised in good faith that we'd ride the Big Timber Outlaw so I told George we'd have to put in one of our horses and no one would know the difference as no one knew what the Big Timber Outlaw looked like.

I had a very pretty five year old black mare with four white legs up to her knees and a white face. We had bucked her out a few times the year before and she was a bucking fool. She had slipped the last two riders before she was turned out. I hadn't found her that spring and figured she had winter killed.

Just before Labor Day, Nate Cooper had found her with some of his horses that had strayed over on Hart Mountain and brought her home. She hadn't been rode at for nearly a year and was fat and rollicky. I didn't think anyone would remember her so we picked her to take the place of the Big Timber Outlaw.

Ben Ford was announcing for us. I put him wise to stall the crowd, for I kept hoping the Big Timber man would show up. Ben made quite a talk and told the crowd that Williams would ride the Big Timber Outlaw as soon as the contest was over and from the looks of the animal he thought Williams would have a tough time staying on top.

I had told the chute men to have the black mare all saddled and ready to come out when the last contest horse was rode.

Ben Ford was in front of the grandstand and announced, "George Williams on the Big Timber Outlaw. Here they come!"

The black mare was a real bucker. She came out of the chute wild with her head down between her front legs, mouth wide open, tongue hanging out, bawling like a Texas cow on the fight. She was a crooked, fast pitcher that showed her belly to the grandstand like she was proud of it. She was about the fastest sunfisher I ever saw rode. It looked like she was going to come down on her side every jump but somehow she kept her feet under her.

George did a fine job of riding. The crowd gave them plenty of applause. They got their money's worth in that one ride. No one caught on that the black mare was mine. A lot of people told me that she was the best bucker that had ever been rode in Central Park. After that, we always called the black mare "The Big Timber Outlaw."

ONE FALL, I turned fifteen head of bucking horses on the head of Blue Creek to winter. Sometime about the middle of the following June, George Williams and I went out to gather them for a show we was going to give at old Central Park on the Fourth of July. We was having a lot of trouble finding them as they had split up.

Tom Logan, that was working with Walt Lee on the roundup, sent word to us that there was a bunch of our horses with a wild bunch in the Fly Creek Basin. Tom said that the roundup was just about over and if we would come to the wagon on Fly Creek, the roundup crew would help us get our horses separated from the wild bunch.

Wild horses was almost impossible to corral and we would need some extra help so we went over to the roundup wagon on Fly Creek. It was just good luck that we got there at the right time as they had made their last roundup that day. The bunch of horses we wanted was ranging about three miles from where the wagon was camped.

We knew all the cowboys that was working on that roundup. Walt Lee was the roundup boss. Tom Logan, Walt Lee and George Williams had ranches close together on Sand Creek. Being neighbors and good friends of course they all wanted to help us get our bucking horses.

Walt Lee said he thought the easiest way to get the horses was to take the cavvy of saddle horses with us and then for some of us to slip around the wild bunch and head them for the saddle horses. If some of the riders would stop along the way they could lane the wild bunch through to the cavvy. Maybe we could split the wild horses off, but if we couldn't, there was an old corral about five miles away where we could corral them.

There was twelve of us left the wagon to get those horses and they was all good hands. I don't remember all their names for it was a long time ago but the ones that I do remember was Eddie O'Donnell, Johnny Bunko, Tex Fitchue, Billy Ogg, Tom Logan, Walt Lee, George Williams and myself. I believe they are all dead now but Johnny Bunko and me.

The scheme worked. We got the wild horses mixed with the gentle horses. We had a lot of running and trouble with the wild bunch as they tried to get away but there was too many riders. We was relaying them all the time on fresh horses.

After we got the bunches together, we milled them around a while. The wild horses was always in the lead. Finally, we got the wild ones cut off from the other horses and let them go.

Among the bucking horses was a buckskin horse branded **7-7**. Tom Logan said it belonged to a nester that lived on the Yellowstone who wanted ten dollars for the horse. Tom said that we ought to have the horse as he was a good bucking horse. Tom said the horse had bucked a rider off and had carried a saddle for about three months until he and Billy Ogg had roped the horse to take the saddle off. The horse had fought them like a bear. I gave Tom ten dollars to give the nester and took the **7-7** horse with the bucking horses.

The **7-7** horse was a dark colored buckskin with a black streak running from his mane to the root of his tail, weighed about 1,100 pounds. He had a long dish-faced head with short ears. His two small, bead black eyes stuck too close together in his ugly head shone like shoe buttons.

That was one of the meanest, orneriest, most disagreeable pieces of horse flesh that I ever came in contact with. He was nine or ten years old and a real honest to John outlaw and the most dangerous horse I ever saw. There was no bluffing with him, he just tried to kill you.

He was halter broke and you could lead him—if you could get a halter on him, but you had to throw him down to get a halter on him. When you would rope him, he would turn around with his head toward you. If you would try to touch his head or neck he would strike at you, then whirl and kick at you.

George Williams rode him that Fourth of July at Central Park. That **7-7** was a devil on four legs. He done it all, but at that time, I don't think there was a horse in Montana that could throw George Williams off.

When the horse saw that he couldn't unload his pack, he reached around with his mouth wide open and grabbed the leg of George's chaps. He was whirling and bucking, pulling at George's leg. I knew if he pulled George off he'd jump in George's middle and tromp him to death. If I remember right, Tom Logan helped me pick up the horse. Tom got hold of the **7-7**'s halter rope and pulled while I pounded him on the nose with my rope to make him let go of George's leg.

We gave shows and riding contests that summer and fall throughout the state. I never rode the **7-7** horse and I wouldn't ask anyone else to ride him for he was such a mean devil that if he ever did slip a rider, I knew he would jump on the cowboy and stomp him to death. As far as that goes, no one but George wanted him for he'd snap his teeth at you just like a mean dog.

George Williams seemed to like to ride that horse. I wanted to take that **7-7** outlaw out and shoot it for he was a man killer but George said, "No, I'll ride the son of a bitch but I'll fix him so he can't bite me."

George fastened a couple of heavy pieces of leather at the side of the horse's halter and tied them under his chin so he could get his wind but couldn't open his mouth.

That 7-7 horse just naturally hated a man. When he found out he couldn't bite Williams or throw him off, the horse got smart and would only make three or four jumps, then whirl around, jump up in the air and fall on his side.

That 7-7 horse made a great show and the crowds liked to see his performance but that last stunt was too dangerous. I knew sooner or later, if I kept him, he would hurt or kill somebody so I got rid of him.

AT ONE TIME, in the early 1900s George Williams was called "The Champion Bronc Rider of Montana." I had rode with George in a good many rides. There was always a little feeling between George and me as to who was the best rider.

George was working on the reservation at the time we decided to see which of us was the best rider. He was to bring in some horses from the reservation and I was to fetch some horses in from Blue Creek. He would ride the ones I brought in. We would split the gate receipts 50-50 but wanted a decision as to which of us was the best rider.

We arranged for the contest to be held at Austin North Park in the north part of Billings under the rimrocks where the penitentiary was built but never used.

The contest was on a Sunday, we had a nice crowd. We had brought in quite a few extra bucking horses. We paid the boys that wanted to ride mount money so as not to conflict with the contest between Williams and me. The horses all did their stuff and there was a couple of boys throwed.

In the contest we was to ride three horses apiece. Johnny Conway and Tommy Logan was two of the judges, the other one I have forgotten. George rode the first horse, a good bucking horse and got a good hand.

Frank O'Donald, a friend of mine, came and told me to look out for a jobbing on the Star horse as he had overheard some loose talk. He said that Walt Lee was waving a large roll of bills betting that I wouldn't ride the Star horse.

The first horse I rode was a bay mare. She was a whirlwind. A whirling dodger that was hard to ride but I got it done and got a good hand.

George's second horse was a bay horse that belonged to me. He was a straight away bucker that didn't give much show. My second horse was a buckskin owned by Billy Ogg from Sand Creek. It was a good showy horse that was easy to ride. I thought I had a little the best of the riding that far.

George's last horse was a horse that I had been bucking for two years. He was a good horse and George didn't do anything but ride him. It looked like he was giving George a bad time.

I want to say a few words in regard to the Star horse that was my third horse. He was undoubtedly the best bucking horse there that day. He was raised by E.R. Clark on Pryor Creek that branded the star brand ☆. Clark had sold him to Jim Boyd. Star had throwed many a cowboy including Johnny Lee, a noted salty rider. Jim Boyd said George had taken a setting at him and got slipped off. I asked George about it years later but he denied it.

We both had our friends and there was a lot of rooting and betting on both sides. The decision all layed on the Star horse. If I made a good ride on him it looked like my decision.

I was sure feeling good that day and wanted to beat George. I had my riding clothes on and a lot of luck or Star would have slipped his pack.

Star ran about fifty yards. I grabbed him in the shoulder with my spurs. He just made a balloon ascension. I fell back on my reins and they flew over my shoulder. Naturally, all riders use their reins for a balance. When the reins flew over my shoulder I knew someone had cut the rawhide loop where the reins was snapped into the hackamore.

The cantle of the saddle hit me in the caboose and I started for Mars, but had the presence of mind to throw my legs back. There was plenty of daylight under me as my spurs hit the skirt of the saddle. I was pretty well forward. Luck was with me for I never lost my stirrups. I grabbed a handful of mane, got straightened up and made a good ride.

Star was a nervy horse and hard to catch. After he got his fill of bucking he started running and dodging the holes and big rocks around the foot of the rimrocks.

Tom Logan was catching the bucking horses. He had a hard time catching me as there was nothing to get hold of with the reins gone. Both horses was about run down before Tom made connections with me. While we was running around dodging the rocks and holes some little boy was heard to say, "Gee, Bill is getting a good old ride."

I was one mad rider when I got back to the judges and showed my hackamore shank with the fresh cut in it. The judges wouldn't make a decision on the ride as I had disqualified by getting the mane. They called off all bets and called it a tie contest on the first two rides.

I do not know to this day who cut those reins but there was a lot of fights that day over the decision of the judges.

12: Wild West Shows

IN THE EARLY days of Billings, Central Park was located west of town just north of the present underpass of the N. P. Railroad. It was owned and managed by Frank Savarcey that used to run one of the show shops on the south side. Billings was small and Central Park was the first place to offer outside amusements. There was picnics, ball games, horse races and lots of Wild West contests and shows held there.

George Williams and myself was putting on a contest when flying machines was just new. There was a man traveling with one for exhibition purposes. He framed up with us to give a contest at Central Park and he would exhibit his machine. Everybody wanted to see the flying machine and we turned a large crowd.

He had done a lot of advertising and everybody thought he was going to fly and wanted to see it fly. He didn't do any flying. He would start the engine going and it would make a lot of noise. It was the main attraction. Every once in a while he would gun the engine and everyone that wasn't around it would think that it was going to take off and fly. I don't know to this day if it could really fly or not but the only flying that day was done by the cowboys as we had a salty lot of wild horses and four bulls.

The bulls put on a battle royal that appealed to the crowd. There was some cottonwood trees on the inside of the high board fence that enclosed the park. The trees wasn't too big but everyone that was big enough to climb had a man in it to get a better view. The bulls was fighting on the south side of the enclosure. All of a sudden one bull got the best of another one. He raked him in the ribs with his horn. The defeated bull let a bawl out of him and started to run with the winner hooking him in the rear end. He hit a tree and the man in it fell out and landed astride of the second bull.

He wasn't a bull rider and didn't stay on long. He hit the ground a running. He never looked back. The cowboys was a hollering, "Look out, he's a coming." The bull wasn't after him or anywhere near him. That man really was running, almost flying expecting every jump to be hit by the bull. When he got to the corral he just fell down and passed out.

A man whose name I have forgotten and Jesse Brewer that used to run the Dark Horse Livery Stable on the south side had trotting horses. They was going to have a sulky race to open the show. As it was a short circle track, they was to go around the track three times.

Jesse was going to drive his horse but he had so many drinks aboard we wouldn't let him. He had a good looking young woman with him and she wanted to drive. Jesse said if he couldn't drive to let her as she was a good driver and had drove the horse lots of times. So after an argument we let her drive and she made a great show.

She was a very good looking woman perhaps twenty five or thirty years old. She had pretty red hair. She had a very pretty light blue dress on. She tucked her gown around her legs and got her feet braced in the side of the sulky. She was driving a long legged good looking brown horse, her opponent was driving a very pretty sorrel mare. Everybody was all hepped up to see the race.

They came trotting up slowly in front of the grand stand. The judge hollered "go" and they was off. The lady took the lead and the farther they went the farther she beat.

The first time around the track the wind had blew her gown up around her waist exposing a very pretty pair of legs encased in blue silk stockings and a pair of red panties. When she passed the grand stand the male part of the audience gave her a big hand.

That brown horse had his head right up in the air and she was holding onto the reins like grim death. Seemed the farther he went the faster he got. The second round the brown was really going, her hair had come down and was flying in the breeze. She was a good hundred yards in the lead. The third round she was half way around the track ahead. Everybody was a cheering, even the airplane let out a few snorts.

The crowd went hog wild. I don't know if it was her good horsemanship, the red pants or whether it was her personality. Anyway, she wasn't through. Her opponent immediately left the track but she made another round.

There wasn't any applause this time for the crowd saw that she couldn't stop her horse. She didn't seem to be frightened. She just held him in the middle of the track. A couple cowboys saw her difficulty and got on each side of the track, closed in and stopped the horse on the fifth round. The cowboys helped her out of the sulky. The folds of her gown dropped and she made a polite little bow to the audience and got another round of applause.

I ain't going to say much about the contest. George Williams won the bronc riding. John Lanahan rode two bulls and I rode the other two. A free for all horse race which Bill Shirran won closed the afternoon contests.

SOME OF THE boys that made their first appearance in our Wild West Show went on to be world's champions. There was Montana Jack Ray, that turned out to be the world's champion trick and fancy roper. Pinky Gist world's champion bull dogger, others that I could mention that made their mark in the rodeo world.

We had some salty horse races. They wasn't thoroughbred horses but saddle horses. They caused lots of excitement and betting and sometimes a fight or two but the people enjoyed them.

One time we had a balloon ascension that made a hit. The man that went up in the balloon hung by his legs with his head down, then worked on a trapeze while the balloon was rising. He had three dogs that had parachutes tied to them that he dropped from the balloon.

The first time Pinky Gist came to our show and wanted to take a part, we volunteered his services as a horse thief and promptly hung him. We thought we had it fixed so it was a "safe stunt" but we hadn't reckoned on the horse getting scared.

Pinky was running his horse down the arena with a bunch of cowboys after him. Tex Jones roped him and drug him over to a tree. Tex threw his rope over a tree limb and started to pull Pinky up. The limb bent down and scared Tex's rope horse. It stampeded pulling Pinky over the top of the limb and drug him off a couple hundred yards before Tex could get the horse stopped.

Pinky must have hit his head on the limb. He was limp as a dish rag. We was sure scared, we thought he was dead. We poured water on him and fanned him with no results. Finally, when we'd just about give him up, Bull Riding Scotty put a whiskey bottle in Pinky's mouth and forced a little whiskey down his throat. Pinky coughed, blew a few bubbles out of his nose and managed to stagger up. The crowd went wild, they thought it was part of the act.

There was always a lot of Indians came to the shows for I let them in free if they came horseback. We generally made up an Indian race or two. One time there was a Sioux Indian that was visiting the Crows. He wanted ten dollars to ride on exhibition dressed only in war paint, a war bonnet and a breech clout. I thought it would make a hit so agreed.

We had a tent stretched by the corrals for changing clothes or any kind of emergency. While the Indian was in the tent getting painted for the ride, a windy cowpuncher by the name of Ben Ford gave quite a spiel.

WILD WEST SHOWS

He said, "Chief Buffalo Nickel, a Sioux Indian is going to ride for your approval. He is going to show you how the Indians ride on the Sioux Reservation in South Dakota."

The Indian came out of the tent all painted up with just a breech clout and a band full of feathers around his head. He danced around in a circle and the rest of the Indians gave him a few war whoops.

The horse was all ready in the chute. We never gave that Indian a pet to ride but a good salty bucking horse. About the second jump the Indian got pretty high. When he came down he had the saddle horn under the breech clout. A couple more jumps and the breech clout tore loose. About the same time the war bonnet came off. Then down came Chief Buffalo Nickel. He rolled over a few times, then got up and ran for the tent with only war paint on and that was pretty well smeared.

"A couple of more jumps and the breech clout tore loose."

IT WAS A SPECIAL occasion, I think it might have been Labor Day. The show consisted of races, bucking bulls and bucking horses. It really was a wild show.

We opened with a free for all horse race. There was about fifteen entries for a ten dollar purse. It was a quarter mile circle track. It had rained the day before and was still slippery.

Doc Dennis, a well known character entered the race. He was wearing a big ten gallon hat that looked like a parasol, a beaded vest and he had a pair of big tapaderos on his stirrups that pretty near touched the ground. Doc got away in the lead. His tapaderos was a flopping and the mud a flying.

When he came around the turn his horse hit a greasy spot. Doc's horse fell, all you could see was Doc's hat and tapaderos flying in the air. Then all the other horses ran over him before he could get up. He was tough, he lost a little hide but mostly he was just muddied up.

We had four big bulls in a corral. They got to fighting and we turned them out as we didn't want them to tear the corral down. They kept right on fighting and got under the grand stand. Frank Savarcey had a lemonade stand on the shady side of the grand stand.

The bulls went right through the lemonade stand and turned the barrel of lemonade over and knocked the counter down. Four by fours was a cracking, bulls a bawling, people boiling out of the grand stand, Old Diego Frank grabbed an axe and was after the bulls yelling, "God damneddy! God damneddy! I kill the God damneddy bulls!"

I don't know if he got in a slash or not as I was too busy laughing to see. The bulls came out just as the crowd got out of the grand stand. They met almost head on. The people rushed back for the grand stand. We didn't have to chase the bulls out as Savarcey and his axe done it for us.

The bull fight didn't take any of the buck out of the bulls, in fact, it just warmed them up. George Williams rode one with a saddle. This one was called the "Lamey bull" and he was awfully mean. He busted the cinch and George and saddle sailed off.

I rode the next bull, I did okay until he bucked into the other bulls. They started to fight and chase him. I was scared to stay on and I didn't dare to get off. Everybody was cheering the bulls.

The bucking horses had an extra kink in their back that day, too. A good many of the local boys around Billings was riding. One in particular was Earl Talcott. Everybody used to say he was raised on a horse with a rope in his hand. He drew a good forked horse called "Bull in the Woods" that had bucked off a lot of the boys.

This old pony was plenty tough and he was bothering Earl. Earl didn't reach for the saddle horn but it looked like he might have been reaching for the back of the saddle. His shirt tail was out fanning the breeze and he got the shirt instead of the saddle and pulled it up right over his head. It must have helped steady him for he got straightened up in the saddle and made a good ride.

We had caught a coyote for the occasion and we took it out in the middle of the arena and turned it loose for the boys to rope. Several boys missed their loop but Earl didn't miss. When Earl made his throw he had the coyote on the end of his loop.

WE HAD TWO young boys named Shirran that used to ride with us. They was cousins, about fifteen years old and was pure blooded Scotchmen. One was fair and the other was dark. We called Bill, Black Scotty and George, White Scotty. They was the ridingest kids I ever saw. Both boys' mothers had died when the boys was quite small.

Bill was the smallest but the best rider. We used to advertise him as the "Kid Champion" as we never had many men that could out ride Black Scotty. He put me in mind of a tom cat when he was riding for he was a pawing, scratching kid and never afraid of no bucking horse. For a long time we gave them light horses and not too tough but after a while they would ride most any horse.

The Shirran boys and the O'Donnell boys was great friends. The O'Donnells ran lots of horses and cattle. The O'Donnell boys and the Shirran boys started to ride calves, then yearlings. From then on they branched out to cows, steers, horses and bulls, whatever was handy. I don't know if Mr. O'Donnell knew what was going on or not but the Shirran and O'Donnell boys was salty riders.

Anyway, this story is about the Shirran boys, Bill in particular. We would take the stirrups up for them and if the saddle was too big we would roll up a coat and tie it in front of them in the saddle so there wasn't too much room in it.

I remember one time when White Scotty was going to ride. I saw him fixing the coat on the saddle. I never paid much attention to him as he knew how we fixed it. Whitey got bucked off and I couldn't figure out why as the horse didn't buck half as hard as a lot he'd rode. Then Whitey gave the reason.

He thought that if he tied a rock to each side of the coat it would stay in place better. When the horse went to bucking the rocks stretched the coat and worked a little loose and them rocks began to pound his legs. He could hardly walk for a week.

I honestly believe if Black Scotty had kept it up when he got a little older, he would have made one of the world's champion riders, but at that time there wasn't many rodeos and not much money in the riding game.

BILL WENT OVER on the Crow Reservation working as a cowboy for some of the big outfits for several years. When Bill was about eighteen maybe twenty, there was a rodeo over on Pryor Creek. It was at that rodeo Bill made one of the greatest rides on one of the best bucking horses that I ever saw.

The horse was a very pretty big white horse owned by the McDowell boys, who had a rodeo string of bucking horses. They called the horse Butterfly. He was a large horse, probably weighed fourteen hundred pounds and built like a fire horse. He bucked off many a champion rider and whenever a cowboy drew Butterfly's number he knew he had a salty horse. There wasn't too many that rode him.

This rodeo at Pryor was a small local affair and the riders all refused to take a setting on Butterfly so the McDowells cut him out and wanted someone to ride him on exhibition for a purse. Bill Shirran said he'd take a setting on him. Bill asked me to help him saddle Butterfly up and pick him up after he got through pitching.

There was a big crowd from Billings including the Billings band. Most everybody knew the horse and was rooting for Bill. One of the McDowells led Butterfly in front of the crowd while a purse was made up of about eighty five dollars.

There was a little discussion as how the money was to be split between them, whether Bill would get the money if he rode the horse or the McDowells get it if Bill was throwed. They both wanted all the grapes so I suggested they split 50-50 and they agreed.

Just before Bill was ready to ride, my wife who thought an awful lot of Bill, brought him one of my fancy shirts and said, "I want you to wear this shirt. I made it and I think it is lucky. Its back has never been dirtied and I don't think you will dirty it either. I wish you luck."

He took it and said, "I'll do my best, Mrs. Huntington." We saddled Butterfly with no trouble. He was a nice horse to handle, never fought you but was always ready and I never heard or saw him misfire. Bill got a good seat and they turned him loose.

I was right behind him when he blew up. I had a rope in my hand and I swung it out so he would buck up the track. How he did buck up that track, almost hit the fence, dodged back away from it and bucked into a bunch of Indian horses and knocked one down. That probably slowed him a little but he did a wonderful job and Bill made a good honest scratching ride. The crowd went wild with applause for Bill and the band began to play, "The Old Grey Mare."

After the ride Bill gave me back my shirt saying with pride, "Well, I didn't dirty the back."

I REMEMBER one time in the early days when a big red bull came walking right down the middle of Montana Avenue. Every once in a while he saw something that he didn't like and would stop, lash his tail, paw dirt and let out a rumbling bawl that sounded like distant thunder. He was a scarey looking individual that weighed perhaps 1,700 pounds with bristles sticking up on his neck and a pair of wicked looking horns.

A lot of people knew that bull and gave him a clean right of way. As long as he wasn't molested, he wouldn't take you, just go until he found what he was hunting for. It was generally the town cow herd.

The bull belonged to a rancher named Lamey that lived west of Billings. He kept his milk cows and work horses in a pasture. Most all farmers around there had a few milk cows but hardly any of them owned a bull. When they needed a bull they went to Lamey's place and borrowed his bull. When they was through with the bull they took it home.

It spoiled the bull. He got so he did his own visiting without any help. He was so big and stout with hide an inch thick that he would just push over a wire fence and go wherever he wanted to. Of course, the farmers didn't want him as a visitor very often and they got to abusing the bull to make him leave.

Abuse made the bull mean. Finally, he got to be an individual character and came and went where he pleased. After he had been on a rampage for a while he would go back to his own pasture. He had visited the town herd a few times but that was the first time he had ever taken in Montana Avenue.

Everybody that met the bull was afraid of him. They began to call the police to do something with the bull. The police didn't have no way to handle a big fighting bull. They thought that was a cowboy job.

Walt Lee, a stockman, had just fetched some livestock into the stock yards. George Williams, Tom Logan and Johnny Bunko was helping Lee in with the stock. The police asked them to drive the bull out of town before he did some real damage as they didn't want to kill him.

By the time the cowboys got ready to take the bull out of town he'd got about on 26th Street. There was only a few lumber shacks on the street. The bull saw the cowboys coming and began to paw dirt, ring his tail and bellow.

Those four hands was pretty salty cowboys. Walt Lee suggested they draw straws to see which one would ride the bull. They drew straws and George Williams got the short straw. He said, "I never rode a bull but I think I can get the job done."

They roped the bull, threw him down and got George's saddle on him. George got on after the boys had untied the bull's feet. As the bull was getting up, Walt Lee hit him over the back with a hard twist rope.

He didn't like that kind of treatment and oh boy, that big bull really done things. George was doing pretty well until his cinch busted and spilled him and the saddle.

There was a pretty good sized crowd accumulated to see what was going on, but no one except the cowboys got very close to the bull. He was bucking right toward them and they was scrambling to get out of the way.

There was a black woman out in her yard watching the show. The bull saw her and made a run at her as she started to run into the house. She just grabbed the screen door and got inside. It was a close shave for the screen door was still partially open when the bull hit it and took it off with him on his horns. He was running, bucking and kicking at the screen door. When it finally fell off, he didn't need to be drove out of town, he was leaving it as fast as he could. I never heard of him ever coming into Billings after that.

Afterwards, we got him into Central Park to ride with three other bulls. He tore the chute down, whipped the other bulls. They got to fighting under the grand stand and tipped over the lemonade barrel and just raised the dickens.

Old Dago Frank got in under the grand stand with a double bit axe and slashed around with it and chased the bulls out of there. Then the old red bull made a mad charge at Tom Logan's horse. He ripped him open so his guts was showing. Tom had to have a veterinary sew up the horse but it lived.

I don't know whatever became of the Lamey bull. He was around and then he wasn't. He'd got so mean I think that someone probably shot him.

JOLIET USED TO BE a pretty sporty little town. At one time it had a good race track, and several buildings used for a fair in the fall. One year I went there to pull a show at the fair. The racehorses was all there and we was all raring to go. It started to rain about four in the afternoon the day before the show and rained nearly all night. Though it cleared up in the morning there was water all over the track and was too muddy to have any entertainment that day.

The women folk of the town had made a lot of lace work, sweaters, shirts and what not to sell to raise some money for some good purpose, I don't remember what it was. Anyway, they wasn't doing much good selling their stuff as everyone was feeling blue over the rain.

I had a rider with me at the time by the name of Ben Ford. He was a trick rider, Roman stand rider, relay rider and a good bronc rider. He was also a good spieler.

Ben saw that the women was pretty discouraged so he said if they'd make it an auction he'd get their stuff sold. We all began to boost for the women, Ben acting as auctioneer.

When he'd got everything sold Ben said he would ride a bucking horse and while it was bucking reach down and get some mud and put it into the bronc's ear. All he wanted was to take up a collection big enough to buy a jug of whiskey. Just enough to give all the boys a drink.

That sounded good to the crowd as everybody craved a little excitement. They took up a collection and someone went after the jug and a couple boys went after a bucker.

Ben was going to ride in an abandoned livery stable yard. There was a well there. The grass had grown up around its edge and turned down in the hole. If you didn't know it was there you could hardly see it.

The bronc and the jug arrived about the same time. Ben took a big drink and turned the jug over to the crowd. It seemed like everybody in town was there to see Ben ride. There was a lot of joshing going on. We saddled his bronc, when he got all set he hollered, "Turn him loose." I was hazing for Ben.

The horse had given three or four jumps when Ben went down for the mud. The horse was going straight for the well. As it got close it saw the hole and dodged sideways. Ben went head first in the well, plumb out of sight.

I was sure scared and ran my horse over to the well and hollered, "Ben, are you hurt?"

He answered, "Hell no, throw me down a rope and pull me up."

I untied my saddle rope and dropped it down the well and hauled him out with my saddle horse. He was a sight—mud and water all over him.

Everyone stood in his tracks and never said a word as they was afraid he was hurt.

When Ben came up out of the well he had one hand full of mud. He said to the people, "Folks, I had to go down so far to get the mud that I just couldn't get up in time to make connections."

RED LODGE, MONTANA, used to be a hot little mining town. I remember back in 1900 when Lamport was mayor and John

Weaver ran the livery and sale stable. Alcott, I think ran the lumber yard, was champion seven-up player and took on all players at $150.00 a game. The railroad coal mine was running full blast with a night shift. There was a lot of teams hauling timber out of the mountains for props for the mine, and they used little mules to haul coal out of the mines.

There wasn't any railroad at the Bear Creek mine so they hauled the coal in wagons over the mountain to Red Lodge where it was shipped all over the country. At that time the miners was about all Finns and they had a Finn newspaper in town. There was a good pay roll as everyone was working. It was also a good stock country and on pay day it used to sizzle with heat.

Red Lodge used to have a fair every year. The fairgrounds was in the lower end of town. There was a half mile race track and some stables. They used to have some good races and quite a lot of exhibits.

One year I framed up with the fair management and took some bucking horses up there for a bucking horse contest. There was quite a lot of stock fetched in from around Red Lodge as there was a prize for the best bucking horse. There was some good ones, too. Red Lodge has always been noted for her good riders and I know the reason. They raise them big mountain bred horses there that are plenty salty and the boys learn to ride them. They just have to be good to stay on top.

Three boys that hailed from around Red Lodge, George Williams, Ben Ford, a Texas rider who went by the name of Texas Bud and myself entered the contest. At that time they used to call me Basin Creek Bill. There was no other bareback riders there so I rode two mules and a bull on exhibition.

In the contest we had all rode one horse apiece. Ben Ford bucked off and a Red Lodge boy lost his seat. Williams rode his second horse. As he was unsaddling, the horse whirled and kicked him on the ankle. His ankle swelled up so bad that we had to cut his boot to get his foot out, so he was out of the contest. The next rider was a Red Lodge bronc stomper. His horse fell over backward and caught him. Some of the cowboys got on the horse's head and held him down until we got the boy loose from the saddle.

I told them to uncinch the saddle and pull the saddle off and I would ride him up with a hand full of mane, which I did. He bucked right toward the grand stand. We was riding in the infield, as he went to jump over the fence onto the racetrack he hit his front feet on the top rail and turned a somersault. I don't know just how it happened but I hit on my feet. As he jumped up and ran I threw him a kiss with my hand. The crowd gave me a big hand.

I won the contest but what I didn't like was that the winner had to ride an **RL** outlaw horse that everybody around Red Lodge was proud of. He had slipped a lot of good riders.

He was a very nice looking bay horse with a white strip in his face. He belonged to Arthur Dake that lived at Bear Creek. I had heard so much about him that I didn't know whether I could ride him or not. I hated to get throwed after winning the contest.

He wasn't a bad horse to saddle and was easy to mount. When he blew up there was something doing. You knew that you wasn't sitting on a rocking chair. He had made about four jumps when he hit the gate that went to the race track. He fell on his side. I threw my leg up behind the saddle as he went down. He sort of slid his head under the gate and couldn't get up. Some of the boys got hold of the gate and got it clear. I rode him up and we had it again. Finally he gave it up and started to run.

Arthur Dake was the pick-up man and he was riding a very nice grey horse. As I got off the **RL** on behind Arthur Dake I accidentally hit his horse in the flank with my spur. He forgot he was a gentle horse and turned on a dose. He threw Arthur Dake on one side of him and me on the other side to the amusement of a big bunch of miners that was sitting out in the infield around a keg of beer.

IN 1908 OR 1909 I took thirty head of bucking horses to Red Lodge to give a bucking horse contest. It was in the late summer. It was a holiday of some kind, but I have forgotten just what it was, anyway, the miners was celebrating. There was some horse racing as well as the bucking contest.

I took five bronc scratchers from Billings and there always was a lot of good riders that lived around Red Lodge. We was camped at the fairgrounds. In the evening before the ride, a man came to camp and said, "I have a horse running in the fairgrounds pasture. He has been there all summer and I can't corral him. I'll give some of you cowboys ten dollars if you will rope him for me."

We agreed to catch his horse for $10.00 if he would let us ride him as he looked like he would be a good bucking horse. He was a nice looking horse, plenty wild, weighed about 1,300 pounds. He was with three other horses and was a "bunch quitter."

Four of us went to get him. There was a corral in the pasture but that old outlaw wouldn't go in the corral. We ran him into a corner and scattered out with our ropes ready to catch him.

When he came out of that corner, he came out on high.

None of the other boys got close enough to throw at him. He came by me and I dabbed it on him. Boy, business picked up.

When he hit the end of that rope it threw my horse right in a bunch of boulders. The wild horse also hit the ground and rolled plumb over. The fall threw my knee out of joint and bent my thumb back against my wrist, but we had the horse.

He got up first and every time my horse would try to get on his feet the wild horse would jerk him down. Finally, one of the boys threw his rope on the wild horse and took all the run out of him.

I was laying on the ground with all the wind knocked out of me. The boys pulled my knee into place, then pulled my thumb in. Oh Lord, how that thumb did hurt me. I'd had my knee threw out of place several times before and it didn't hurt so bad to pull it in.

I thought that I had ought to go see a doctor about my thumb so George Williams and I went into Red Lodge. The Doc looked at it and said that it was in place and there wasn't anything to do only get some liniment and rub it on.

We got some liniment and started to camp when we met a man that George knew and stopped to visit. While they was visiting I thought I would put some liniment on my thumb. It was just getting dark. I dropped the cork to the liniment bottle and couldn't find it.

When I went to get on my horse I was sore and stiff. I had the bottle in my right hand so I hooked my elbow around the horn so as not to hurt my thumb. As I started to get on the horse shied and I got a big slug of liniment in both eyes.

I couldn't see. I thought I was going to be stone blind. After a little while, I could see but my eyes hurt something awful.

After a miserable night hurting so bad I couldn't sleep I was in no shape to ride in a contest.

We had advertised for outside stock to ride. There was a big white faced steer fetched in to be rode and I was the only bull rider in the bunch.

The man that fetched in the steer was taking on and said that he was demanding the reward money that I had advertised. I tried to explain to him that I wasn't in any shape to ride but didn't want to give up fifty dollars for not getting the steer rode. I tried to get some of the other boys to ride him but they didn't want him. Finally, I told the man I'd give the steer a ride.

At the time of that ride, there wasn't bareback riding. There had been a few bulls rode with a saddle. Anyhow, if there was any rode bareback I never saw one rode or ever heard of one rode with just a rope tied around his equator. A bull's back is different than a horse's back and a saddle just don't fit a bull or steer. That's why the boys didn't want to tackle the steer.

There is no use describing the contest rides. George Williams won first money. A local boy and Ben Ford tied for second.

I rode the white faced steer on exhibition. Boy, he was a bear cat to ride and he was on the fight. I don't know how I ever rode that baby. He never bucked like a steer. He just swapped ends like a horse. When I was leaving the chute someone poured hokey-pokey all over his rump.

I saw I couldn't ride him stiff legged so I had to keep grabbing him with my spurs to stay on. I slipped my knee out of place and hurt my thumb. I would have quit him, he was punishing me so bad, but I was scared he would hook me so I just kept trying to ride him.

The crowd was helping me all they could and the cowboys was hollering, "Stay a long time!"

I would have given that fifty dollars gladly to have been on the ground. After damn near killing me, the steer finally quit bucking and one of the cowboys roped him so he could get me off.

I HAD A PRETTY GOOD STRING of bucking horses and made a trip to the western part of the state. I put on shows at Livingston, Bozeman, Deer Lodge and Missoula, then went up the Bitter Root Valley to take in the Indian Pow Wow at Hamilton. At one time that country was reservation and the Blackfoot and Flathead Indians used to go there every fall and have a celebration. They put on dances, ran horses and had all kinds of Indian games. A lot of people attended these celebrations.

I had a group of good riders with me. George Williams, Horse Thief Smith, Gale Downing, Harry Jones, Bill Harper, I don't remember the rest of their names but they was all good riders. It was getting late in the fall and I was breaking up my show to come back to my ranch on Blue Creek, so we only stayed there about a week.

A lot of funny things happened on that trip, too many to mention.

I had my horse named "Duck Creek" with the spread. I was offering a hundred dollars to any outside rider that could ride him.

One of the Indians came over to my show and wanted to ride Duck Creek. We told him we'd be glad to have him try. It was announced at the Indian dance that night that he was going to try for the hundred dollars. A lot of Indians came to the show to see him ride.

The Indian had an old saddle so I told him he had better borrow one of the cowboy's saddles as his didn't look very stout. He said that he would rather ride his own saddle. We saddled Duck Creek up for the Indian, gave him a good seat and asked him if he was all ready.

Duck Creek was a peculiar bucking horse. Most horses are the worst to ride the first three jumps. Duck Creek started kind of slow, but after a few jumps he would really go to town. When that horse unwound he certainly done it all fast and furious. He was pitching toward the back entrance of the canvas when he unloaded the Indian. He threw him over his head and was bucking right behind the Indian who was running to get out of his way.

Then, the old saddle came off and flew up in the air scattering pieces like a busted feather bed. The Indian went under the side wall and kept going. We gathered the saddle up and threw it in a pile thinking that he would come after it but he never showed up. No other Indian wanted to try for that hundred dollars.

There was a cowboy there by the name of Bill Smith who was counted as a good rider. The people around Hamilton was pretty proud of him. He had won first prize at a contest in Butte. He was a pretty good sized man, perhaps weighed a hundred eighty five pounds.

He declared himself, and said, "I will take a sitting on your horse in tomorrow's show." The next day Smith was there. You could tell he was a good bronc snapper by the saddle and outfit he had. He fetched a good sized crowd that had plenty of folding money to bet that Smith would ride our horse. In fact, I was just a little worried myself, but made a fifty dollar bet and all my cowboys made wagers for we was all proud of Duck Creek.

We saddled Duck Creek and Smith got mounted. He had a heavy quirt on his wrist and wanted to know if he could use it. I told him "yes" but if he hit the horse over the head all bets was off and I wouldn't pay him the hundred dollars. He said, "Okay."

Duck Creek jumped three or four times and Smith hit him down the flank with his quirt. Duck Creek wasn't used to anything like that. It looked like he turned back through himself. There was just a black streak in the air. He really blew up and when the dust kind of settled, so you could see, Smith was on the ground.

I will say one thing for Bill Smith, he was a thoroughbred. He went in front of the grand stand and said, "Folks, that is the best bucking horse I ever straddled, he threw me slick, fair and decent."

We had a sign painted on the front of our show that read, "Will give $100.00 for any animal you can lead, drag or drive in this canvas that we can't ride."

A man was driving a mule team with his family in the wagon when he noticed the sign. He stopped them and came over to the ticket booth where my wife was selling tickets. He pointed up to the sign and wanted to know if that included mules. She said that it did. He said, "I have a bucking mule and I would like a chance on that hundred dollars."

She asked him where his mule was at. He said, "He's hitched up to my wagon."

She told him to have his family go into the show and for him to unhitch the mule and take him to the back end of the canvas and she would have the manager meet him there. He said he was in too big a hurry for the family to get out. He just unhitched one mule and left the other one hitched to the wagon. I met him at the back as he lead the mule in.

He was a man of few words. He said he wanted to get him rode immediately as he was in a hurry. He wanted to know who was going to pay the hundred dollars, also who was the mule rider.

I told him he'd get his money right away if we didn't get him rode, that I was the mule rider.

He looked me over and grinned as if he could feel that hundred dollars in his pocket.

When that mule moved around I knew he was going to be hard to ride. He had led him in with the blind bridle. We put a blind fold on him and a rope around his equator. One of the boys gave me a leg up, then pulled the bridle and blind off at the same time. There was a mule into the air. About the second jump he kicked both of my spurs off and one of the heels of my boots off. I was some surprised but riding like grim death. I thought, here goes a hundred bucks.

If you have ever rode with just a rope tied around a slippery mule and with no spurs to help you balance you can figure how busy I was. That mule almost had me bucked off a dozen times, but seemed like he would kind of catch me on the next jump.

I have rode lots of mules but never rode one that gave me such a ride. It seemed like I was riding a big rubber ball. I sure was glad when that mule began to slow up bucking and started to run. I was afraid to quit him when he quit bucking, afraid he would kick me. The pick up man finally got close enough to pull me off.

I asked the mule man if he was satisfied. He said, "Yep, that's the first time he was ever rode, but I was right close to that hundred dollars several times."

He took the mule out to his wagon, hitched up and drove off. I think the crowd enjoyed that ride way better than I did.

WE WAS SHOWING in Bozeman when a young man, looking a little worse for wear, asked me for a job with the show. I asked what he could do for he was dirty, ragged and definitely on the bum.

He said that he never had traveled with a show, but he would do anything to help out. He said he was hungry and would work for his board until he learned enough to be worth something to me.

There was something about him that I liked so I sent him over to the chuck wagon and told the cook to fill him up. Even after he got a feed in him he still wanted to go along with us.

I told him he could stick around, we'd find something he could do. We hustled a pair of overalls, a clean shirt. One of the punchers cut his hair. It sure made a big improvement in his looks. Somebody asked him if he was a bronc scratcher or what kind of a stunt he had. He said, "I can't do nothing much, I'm just a hobo."

After that his name was, "Hobo." I don't remember that he ever told us what his name was. He was quite a character. In the evenings he entertained us with stories about his bumming experiences. One that I got quite a kick out of was the following, as near like he told it, as I can remember.

He said he went to a place and asked a lady for a hand out. She fixed him a nice lunch, put it in a paper bag and gave it to him. As he was going out of the gate she hollered to him and asked if he would help her son carry a trunk upstairs. He said he set his lunch down and helped the boy with the trunk and then went to get his lunch. He got outside just in time to see a big red dog gulping it down. He stood looking at the dog, not knowing just what to do. The lady happened to look out and see the dog at the lunch sack. She called Hobo back and said she had nothing else to make a lunch out of so she gave him a dollar. He still had the dollar and showed it to us. He said that dollar had kept him out of jail many times. They used to "vag" all the bums and put them in jail. The law couldn't vag anybody if he had a dollar.

He wasn't a bad roustabout. He did have one bad habit, he hated to get up in the morning. The cowboys cured him of that habit in Missoula. The treatment was a little rough but effective.

Hobo slept in the same tent as the cowboys. Every morning they would have to roll him over a few times before they could get him awake and then it didn't always get him out of bed.

We was showing at River Side Park about two miles out of Missoula. It was Labor Day and it seemed like all of Missoula was headed for the park for entertainment. The street cars going to the park was just loaded down. We had our canvas all stretched and ready to go. A big black cloud was coming up so we decided to show early in case it rained.

I missed Hobo as I wanted him to tend the canvas curtains. One of the boys said he was still sleeping as they couldn't get him up for breakfast.

I sent George Williams and Harry Jones to go get him up. George was always quite a jobber and always carried a bottle of "hokey-pokey" in his pocket just in case he got a chance to use it.

While they was gone to get Hobo, the spieler began telling the crowd to get their tickets early and avoid the rush. People was starting to buy their tickets when I heard an awful commotion. I looked up to see what was happening. There came Hobo running, really sailing from the tent toward a big water tank that set about forty yards from the entrance of the show. All he had on was a calico shirt and the tail was standing straight out. He grabbed ahold of the top of the tank, dived his head in the water. His naked hind end was exposed to the crowd. He pulled his head out and then stuck it into the water again. On his way to the tank he almost ran over a woman wheeling a baby carriage. She yelled, "Crazy man." The crowd took up the cry.

The water must have cleared Hobo's head for he took a look at the crowd closing in on him and his own lack of clothes and headed for the brush as hard as he could go with the crowd in full pursuit.

They might have caught him but there was a loud clap of thunder and the wind blew a big gust and it started to rain. In about five minutes our tent blew down and most of the other concessions. Everybody got soaked to the skin. It cleared up in a little while and we put up our tent and gave a show to a pretty small crowd.

Hobo didn't show up until it was dark. A sorry looking sight he was. The mosquitoes had just about ate him up. He never did know he was jobbed for George had just poured the "hokey-pokey" on his head and left. When the stuff began to work he didn't know what was the matter and sort of went loco.

There is a funny thing about "hokey-pokey," it sets animals crazy for a few minutes. You put it on a man's head he goes wild. If you pour some on the back of your hand it doesn't bother any, it just feels cold. It only works on hair. It's harmless, the effects last just a short time. It doesn't leave a sign of any kind to show where it has been.

The cowboys solemnly asked Hobo if he had those fits often. He said that was the first time he'd ever had anything like that happen to him. He said he was sleeping and when he woke up he felt like someone was boring a hole in his head with a dull brace and bit. They told him they thought it was caused by sleeping too long in the sun. I don't know if he wised up after that, anyway he didn't take any chances of laying in the sun too long. No one ever had to call him to get up again.

IT WAS AROUND 1911. I was at Butte, Montana, making a western moving picture for Forsyth and McGillis. We was showing in Columbia Gardens, charging admission while the cameras was taking pictures of the various events.

I had a pretty forked bunch of riders, good horses and a bunch of spayed cows that was really hard to ride. My riders was all proud of their reputations and when the director of the picture company wanted someone to buck off a bucking animal none of them would agree to do it. They said they'd been hired to ride not to get their back dirtied.

It was up to me. I told the director that I had a bucking whirling cow that I would buck off of for the picture. She wasn't hard to buck off but hard to stay on top.

I rode the cow out a few jumps, then caught her just right in a whirl and sailed over her head. It looked like the real McCoy.

Next, the director wanted a picture of a cowboy riding a buffalo. None of my riders had ever rode a buffalo. I had rode bulls and a lot of steers but had never rode a buffalo and didn't want to either but finally agreed to try and ride one for the picture.

There was all kinds of wild animals in Columbia Gardens at that time, among them was a bunch of buffalo. We got permission to ride one of them.

We ran three buffalo in the corral that had a chute at one end of it. We had been riding out of that chute. It was a good stout chute and I thought it would hold anything.

After a time we got a big buffalo bull that must have weighed close to a ton in the chute. When we slammed the gate on that buffalo bull he got scared and mad.

He began to use his horns and weight against the sides of the chute. The planks began to give away and it wasn't long before he had it all tore down and he was on the fight a-plenty.

That night we made another chute strong enough to hold a buffalo. We made it out of three-inch hardwood planks and put some rings in the floor to tie his head down until we could get a riding rig on him.

They was taking the picture of the buffalo ride after the regular show as we was afraid the buffalo might get into the crowd and hurt or kill somebody. The camera men was all ready and we got the buffalo in the chute.

When I got on the chute ready to ride and looked down at the buffalo bull, he looked as big as a load of hay. His eyes was red and he was snorting and a-pawing. Oh, boy, he was sure mad and on the fight. I'd about as soon have hugged a grizzly bear as got down on him.

After we got his head tied down close to the plank floor he couldn't do much. I got a good seat on him.

When they opened the chute gate, he just made a balloon ascension and started for the buffalo pens which was about fifty yards from the chute. He wasn't too hard to ride after the first two jumps as he was running and bucking straight toward the other buffalo.

I thought he would turn when he got to the fence. It was a hardwood plank fence made to hold buffalo with the posts set in concrete. That buffalo bull charged right into that plank fence. It held but made a loud cracking noise.

I went straight up in the air about fifteen feet. The buffalo bull was setting on his tail back of me when I landed. I beat him up and made a run and got away.

When the bull got up he made another charge at the fence in the same place and busted a hole through it and got in with the other buffalo.

For some reason, they didn't get a good picture of that ride. The director wanted to have me ride him again. I positively refused. The pictures we made was all good except the buffalo bull ride. It showed here in Billings as late as 1915.

TWO OF THE BUFFALO BULLS at Columbia Gardens matched themselves a fight. I had never seen buffalo fight so watched until the fight was over and believe me, there was plenty action in that fight.

When the fight first started, the buffalo bulls pawed dirt, bawled, sniffed and snorted around and made a lot of commotion. One would hook at the other and he would dodge out of the way. The other one would try to get in a hook, then they would paw dirt and back up.

WILD WEST SHOWS

There was a big half breed buffalo cow that was agitating the fight. She would get behind one of the bulls and give him a hook in the rear end and then she would go to the other one and give him a rake too, with her horns. The buffalo bulls never paid much attention to the cow as they was too busy watching one another.

They sparred around for quite a while, then they locked horns and really got to fighting. I can't begin to tell how mad and fearful they looked with their tails high in the air and their eyes all red. I have seen a lot of bull fights but never saw a bull with such speed and action as those buffalo had.

The half breed buffalo cow would run around them when they stopped to spar and hook the first one she got close to and they would go again.

One would get the other one going backwards. They would dodge and turn trying to hook the other one in the shoulder or side.

They was fighting in a large corral. There was about fifty people watching the fight and three moving picture cameras taking pictures of it.

I can't describe the many maneuvers those bulls went through, whirling around trying to get the advantage. One bull was two or three hundred pounds heavier than the other which gave him a little advantage over the lighter bull.

Several times I saw them in a tangle when they met head on that the heavier bull had the other bull's front feet off the ground. He would try to whirl and hook the lighter bull but the lighter bull was plenty fast and always dodged and met him head on.

It didn't seem to hurt them when they was slamming their heads together but it shook the ground around them. If one got the advantage, he caught the other in the shoulder or ribs and gave him a rake with his sharp horns. The bull that got the rake would let out a loud bawl and put on speed until he could whirl and lock horns again.

They was raising so much dust, at times you could hardly see them. It was fast and exciting. Lots of buffalo hair was flying in the air, and it was anybody's guess which buffalo bull would win.

They fought and fought. When they got tired they would back up to catch their wind and eye one another, watching for the other one to make a move.

Finally, the heaviest bull got his horn in the lighter bull's shoulder, then hit him in the rear end with all he had. It turned the lighter bull plumb over. That settled the fight. The lighter bull had had enough and retreated. They was both bloody and scratched all over. They had fought three hours and twenty minutes.

13: Iowa

WE HAD BEEN giving a show at the State Fair at Minneapolis. We had a contract at Sioux City, Iowa, but due to a train wreck we got in a day late and couldn't fill our contract so only gave exhibition rides in front of the grandstand. We loaded up and was shipping to Norfolk, Nebraska, to give a show there. It was a long train ride and no way to get anything to eat on the caboose.

I had quite a lot of money in my money belt, quite a bit of it was silver that I hadn't had time to change into bills. It was too heavy to wear so I took out a couple dollars, handed the belt to George Williams to hold while I went to buy some lunch.

I asked the conductor if I had time. He said the train hadn't been checked out and if I'd hurry he thought I had plenty of time. It was about two hundred yards to the restaurant in the exchange building, at the stock yards.

I had to wait several minutes while they was preparing the lunch. The train was just whistling out as I got out the door. I made a run for it. The train was going slow and I was going fast, for a ways I gained on it but then it picked up speed as I was slowing down. I could see Williams and Armstrong motioning at me to come on. I chased it about a hundred yards, then sat down all blowed out. There I was with thirty cents in cash, a paper sack of sandwiches, stranded in Sioux City, my show on its way. I was in one heck of a fix and no way to fix it. My head began to spin a little for a way to make a few dollars right quick. There was a big sale yard close where they was selling horses, mules and cattle. I made my way over to it thinking I might pick up a few dollars.

I seen the auctioneer and asked him if I could ride a horse in the sales arena for a collection. He referred me to the manager who said it would be all right to do it when they stopped selling horses and began selling cattle. He asked me where my outfit was. I told him that my outfit was on the train and that I was trying to make enough money to catch up with it. I said, "All I need is ten feet of rope and I can ride anything in these corrals." It was taking in a lot of territory but I was desperate and would have tried anything.

He looked me over and said, "Fellow, you're either a rider or a damn fool."

I told him if I didn't ride any animal they gave me I'd give him the money in the collection. He said it was okay for me to ride.

When there was kind of a recess in the sale ring, they put in the chute a big, old, wild, snakey, grey mare. Her tail drug the ground and her mane was long and tangley.

The auctioneer announced there was a cowboy that was broke and in distress was going to make an exhibition ride using ten feet of rope for a saddle. He said, "He is going to earn his money if he rides this animal."

As they was making up a purse, I was putting the rope around the horse. The old mare was giving a good ballyhoo for she sure was jumping, kicking and bawling in the chute.

I was afraid of getting hurt in the chute so I told the gateman to jerk the gate wide open when I hollered ready.

When the gate opened, the old mare came out bucking and bawling and switching ends. She was plenty tough, it wasn't like setting in a rocking chair. She lost her feet and fell a couple times but I rode her up and down. When she quit bucking and began to run around I jumped off and threw a kiss at her.

The audience, made up of livestock buyers and sellers, threw money in the ring at me. I thanked them and told them I'd like to ride a bull or mule. I did, later. After three rides I counted the collection. It amounted to forty-seven dollars.

I took the passenger train and headed for Norfolk. It beat the freight that had my show on it. I was waiting for the boys when it pulled in.

Williams knew I was broke so he thought I'd beat my way on the passenger train. After I told my story and showed the money, he was all for leaving me every time we pulled away on a train after that.

IN 1909, I TOOK a bunch of bucking horses and steers to the Minnesota State Fair at Minneapolis to work in the Wild West Show that the Fair Association was putting on. After the Fair was over I thought I would give a few rides down through that country to see if it would be profitable to take a Wild West Show there the next year.

George Williams and some other riders was with me. We made the Sioux City Fair, then went east into Iowa. At that time, most of the entertainment seemed to be baseball. Most every town had a ball park. As we had gone to Minneapolis to ride for the fair, we didn't have any canvas with us to ride in but figured we could ride in the ball parks.

We had a trick rider and fancy roper with us and George and I did most of the riding. In one Fair town, a man joined us that had five trained horses. The man with the horses told us about a town, I have forgotten the name, where they was playing off a ball game series. Each town had won a game and was going to playoff the tie. If we could get together with the baseball park man where the tie was to be played off there was a chance to pick up some good money.

Me and the horseman went to see the ball park manager. The charge to see the ball game was thirty-five cents. We wanted him to charge fifty cents and go 50-50 on the receipts. The manager thought that was too big a cut so we finally settled for a third of the receipts and would show before and after the ball game. One ticket was good for the whole performance.

The ball park wasn't in too big a town, perhaps two thousand lived there, but that ball park was a real money maker. It was fixed up nice with flowers and trees and had a big grandstand with bleachers on each end of it. There was a half a mile track on the outside of the baseball diamond where they had trotting races.

The manager of the ball park said he had a bucking mule that he'd got off a show the year before. The mule was well known and we could have him to ride. We got some special hand bills printed and passed them all around advertising the extra attraction at the ball game.

The day of the ball game was a nice day. I don't know where the people all came from but there was 3,100 tickets sold. We started our show at ten o'clock but just done rope spinning, rode a couple of bucking horses and the horseman worked out his educated horses. We was holding off for the late show.

The ball game was to start at one. At fifteen minutes before one the seats was all full and the manager of the park suggested that while we was waiting for the ball game to start, it would be a good time to ride his mule.

He lead the mule up in front of the grandstand and got a lot of applause. The mule was a small brown mule that wouldn't weigh over 800 pounds. He had a slim body and low wethers but was plenty active. That mule knew what a saddle was and didn't want that saddle on his back.

He sure fought us. We couldn't get close to that hard tail with the saddle. We had to blindfold him and just about tie him down to get the saddle on. Then the saddle was just too big for that little mule and we couldn't cinch him very tight.

George got on and we pulled the blindfold off the mule. That little brown mule turned on an awful dose. About the fourth jump, off come the saddle and George right over his head.

The people sure got a big kick out of the exhibition. The manager announced we would try the mule again after the ball game, which was ready to start. It was a good game. The score was 4 to 2 in favor of the town nine.

Near the grandstand was a long kind of a shed where they kept pop, candy, popcorn, ice cream and balloons. The back side away from the grandstand was boarded up but the front side was open with a long plank seat where people could get pop, ice cream or what not. There was an opening about five feet wide in the middle where the pop boys got their pop out of a big galvanized tank that was filled with pop, ice and water to carry up in the grandstand.

After the ball game everyone began hollering, "Ride the mule."

I was to ride him that time. On account of him being so small around the equator, I just tied a rope around him. He was sure cutting up. We blindfolded him until I could get on. George gave me a leg up and the park man was to pull the blindfold off when I got ahold of the rope

That mule was raring to go. He was right in front of the opening of the pop stand. The blindfold stuck and as the man was trying to pull it off the mule kept backing away from the man and backed right in the opening of the pop stand.

He backed into a bunch of balloons. When the balloons touched his legs that mule kicked at them with all he had. The blind came off, the balloons began to fly around in all directions and break, then the mule knocked the popcorn over.

He was one scared mule. He was bucking and bawling and making quite a wreck of things. Stuff began to fall from the wall. He was kicking at everything that fell and trying to dodge the balloons.

I didn't feel so good myself, dodging the pop cases that was piled against the wall while hanging onto that damn mule like grim death wondering what next.

Finally the mule saw the gap in the wall where he'd backed in the pop stand. He got through it in high gear and bucked several revolutions in front of the grandstand before he started to run down the track. He started to make a quick turn and fell down. I was glad for a chance to quit him.

Talk about a crowd going crazy, that one did. They was hollering, laughing and jumping up and down. We finished out the show but nothing pleased them like the mule doing his stuff in the pop stand.

IT WAS LATE IN THE FALL but the weather was good so we was in Iowa about a month. We showed in several places but it has been so long ago I have forgotten the names of the places. We met a lot of nice people.

However, there was one small town that wasn't friendly. They charged us too much for a license, too much for the show grounds and didn't want us to charge fifty cents for a show ticket.

We was going to give a two-day show. We advertised that we would give a free pass to anyone that brought in a mean animal they wanted rode.

The first day was a cloudy, cold day. We didn't have too much of a crowd. However, a man brought a brown horse in for us to ride.

There had been some western horses shipped into the country during the summer, among them was the brown horse. He was spoiled before the farmer got him. The farmer couldn't work him or ride him. All the horse would do was just buck, kick and run away. The horse had a bad reputation. Most of the people that came to the show that day came to see the local horse rode.

I wanted to draw a better crowd next day so I told my riders that I wanted whoever drew the brown horse to buck off and we would agree to try the horse again.

George Williams, who had the reputation of riding anything that wore hair that he could put a saddle on, said, "I'll ride the horse but if he bucks me off, it will be on the square. I learned to ride, not buck off."

None of the other boys wanted to buck off so it was up to me. I wised the spieler that I was going to get pitched off and for him to tell the people what a great rider I was. I thought it would please the people to see me hit the dirt and they would come to see the horse do it again.

We had all done our stuff in the show. I was to ride the brown horse as the last act. He was well halter broke and wasn't too hard to saddle. I got on and waved my hand at the crowd. The horse had plenty of action but he wasn't a hard horse to ride.

I rode about five jumps, leaned back in the saddle and let the cantle hit me on the caboose and went sailing through the air. I hit the ground rolling over and over. I stalled a little like I was hurt, then got up, shook the dirt off my clothes and limped off, to the amusement of the crowd.

Iowa was dry but the drug stores done a land office business selling alcohol. It was Saturday night and there was a lot of people in town. A lot of them was showing the effects of hard liquor. Everywhere we went they would laugh and make some cracks about my riding ability.

It began to get under my hide and I said to George, "Heck, as long as we have jobbed them to get a crowd, let's go on through with it and do a good job."

We got a bottle of alcohol and poured it all out except enough to smell and filled the bottle with water. I pretended I was awful drunk and George was taking care of me. Every little while I'd take a big drink out of the bottle so everyone could see me.

Every time anyone said anything to me I'd brag and say that I would ride that old pony for money, marbles or chalk. I took a few more drinks out of my bottle and pulled a roll of bills out of my pocket and said, "I made it riding, I'll bet it all on my riding."

George made me put the money back in my pocket and tried to get me to go back to camp, saying, "Bill, you're too jagged up, better keep your money in your pocket."

I was really putting on a drunken act. I kept saying, "These farmers think I can't ride. I'll show them, money talks with me."

I pulled my roll out again and waved it around. One young fellow wanted to bet me five dollars. I told him that was chicken feed, I wanted to bet money, that he'd better keep that five to buy candy for his girl.

The crowd was getting pretty sore at me and my drunken talk. They pooled their money and one came over and said, "If you want to bet $75.00 that you can ride that horse tomorrow, here it is. If you don't want to bet, put that roll in your pocket and leave it there."

We didn't want to seem too eager so George said, "Fellow, my pardner is a pretty good rider but he's pretty well lit up. You better keep your money, you might lose it."

They was just about ready to mob us so we finally took the money and put it in the hands of the Justice of the Peace, who was carrying a star.

George told him, "If we lose it we will never squawk, if we win it we want it without a squawk. All we want is three honest men for judges and we'll abide by the judges' decision."

We had a good crowd and they seemed to be getting a kick out of the show. We had selected three men for the judges. Some of the farmers wanted to raise their bets and they got their money called.

When it was time to ride the brown horse, I told George to stick close to the stake holder and get the money as soon as the judges made the decision and to have a saddle horse ready so I could get out of there after the ride, for I knew there was going to be some mad farmers and they was liable to take me apart.

We lead the horse right in front of the grandstand and saddled him up. George eared him while I stepped on.

He was a showy pitching horse. He sun fished a little, then bucked straight ahead. I was getting a lot of applause. After I had the most of the hard bucking out of him, I slammed a spur in the cinch, reached over his head, pulled the halter off and threw it away.

There wasn't any kick on the ride or the judges' decision. The stake holder gave George the money but they knew they had been jobbed. They looked for me but I was long gone.

14: With the Carnival

IN 1913, I JOINED UP my Wild West Show with a carnival called "The Campbell United Shows." It was a large affair supposed to carry a thousand people. It just showed in the large towns and at Fairs and usually stayed a week at a place. At that time, towns in the west was small and shipping costs was pretty high. In the deal I made with Campbell, he was to furnish transportation, pay showing licenses, furnish the band, show grounds and lights as he had a light plant.

I figured that if I could make a little money and get in the east where the towns was closer together I could pull out for myself if I didn't make good with the carnival. All the experience I'd had at that time was in contests and giving shows in the west where everything was on the square. I had always figured to give the people their money's worth, have a good time, make friends and a little money. I thought a carnival would be right up my alley.

I soon changed my mind. There was a few square people on that show. One show in particular that was clean was the Negro Minstrel. The people that run the various rides was okay. For the most part, there was all in one bunch cheap, crooked, dirty grafters, pick pockets, short changing artists, thieving rotten dope fiends, holdup men and every other degraded son of creation tied up with that carnival. Campbell, I think, was worst of all for he knew what was going on and you can bet he got his cut out of every crooked deal.

Riding from Billings to Sheridan, Wyoming, with my family, some of the cowboys and cowgirls, seventeen Indians, among the carnival people I knew, in that church, we had got in the wrong pew. A lot of the carnival people was drunk, using bad language, quarreling and fighting, others bragging of how they had trimmed some sucker.

I had enough of that bunch right then. I told Campbell that he would have to furnish us a coach to ourselves or he could leave us. After much arguing he agreed but said it would be hard to keep the other people out of it. I told him I would tend to that end of it. We wrote a sign, "Only Wild West People Permitted" and hung it on the coach. I put a cow puncher at each door with a big six-shooter. They got the idea and we had no trouble keeping to ourselves.

There was a good many horses on that show as they moved all the stuff from the train to the showgrounds with horses. They had six beautiful white horses that pulled the band wagon in the street parades. Campbell had good stock and good teamsters. The one good thing I can say about him, he took good care of the stock.

There was a big tent where Campbell fed the teamsters and the roustabout help. He used to hire roustabouts by the month. When he hired them he would tell them that he paid off the first of each month. About the last of the month when he had the carnival all loaded on the cars he would send the roustabouts somewhere down the track where he said there was a car to load. While they was gone the train pulled out, without them. It was known around the carnival as "red lighting." Poor devils, they was left flat broke and couldn't do anything. Next stop Campbell hired another crew.

There was what was called a "Privilege Car." It was a coach with the seats all taken out with a bar on one side where lunches and liquor was served. On the other side of the car there was a crap table and card tables for gambling. Word was passed out on the carnival grounds that there was gambling in the "Privilege Car." The games was all fixed. If somebody did happen to win there was a spotter followed him and held him up.

One day I was talking to a Jew that run a Hoop-a-la game. That is one of those places where prizes are put on blocks of

WITH THE CARNIVAL

wood. If you can throw a ring over the blocks you get the prize. My little girl was with me. He wanted to be nice and gave her a box of chocolate candy. She thanked him and opened the box. The candy was just swarming with little red ants. He took it back and said, "You can't eat that but I see where the folks will win a lot of chocolate candy tonight. I will put them on the easy row and let them throw the big hoops." It just made me sick that night to see the people eat those chocolates.

We had to cross the Mississippi River to get to Baton Rouge, Louisiana. There was no bridge there as the river was better than a mile wide. There was a ferry to haul the trains across the river. Our train was too large to go at one time so they took half of it and then came back for the other half.

While they was stalling around getting the train on the ferry George Williams and I got out to see what was going on. After we had our look-see we went to the Privilege Car to get a lunch. We had just started to eat when a big fight started.

The cook throwed an iron kettle at someone he was quarreling with. It missed the guy it was aimed at and hit a teamster on top of the head. Someone made a pass at the cook who grabbed a big butcher knife, I swear it looked a yard long, and come out cutting at everything he saw.

By that time it was a rough and tumble, go as you please. Williams grabbed a long poker that was hanging by the range and I got a fire shovel. We backed in the corner as we didn't have any finger in the fight. Somebody turned off the lights but that didn't stop the fighting. Williams said, "Don't move, if they get over here do your stuff."

There was fighting going on until someone got the door open. The cook dived out and run off in a cane field with several men chasing him. The train whistled and they all came back but the cook. Someone got the lights on and that car looked like a slaughter house. There was blood all over the car. The teamster was laying on the floor with blood spurting out of a cut on his head. Jimmy Don, one of the carnival barkers, had an arm cut half off. There was a lot of others cut and bruised up.

When we had crossed over and was coupling up with the rest of the train some railroad man had called to the law. There was about thirty police and plain clothes men met the train. Campbell told the police that the cook went crazy and got among them with a knife and done the damage, escaping in the cane field. And that was that.

Williams and I had been busy trying to stop the blood that was spurting out of the teamster's head. We didn't have anything but a sack of Bull Durham. We poured that on the cut in his head. It checked the blood some. We got him to a hospital just as quick as we could but heard later that he died.

Two or three stops later "Bill Huntington's Wild West Show" shook the carnival.

AT CHADRON, NEBRASKA, we had a lot of excitement. At one time, I thought, here goes the show all shot to hell. If it hadn't been for a little quick management and some luck, there would have been some heads busted, maybe some cutting and shooting.

In the Indians that I had signed up to go with my show was two of the best riders on the Crow Reservation. Believe me, they was the best Indian riders I ever saw ride. They was Shobe Daylight and Mortimer Dreamer from Crow Agency. Naturally, I advertised those riders pretty high.

Chadron, Nebraska, is close to the Sioux Reservation. The Sioux Indians and the Crow Indians have always been at logger heads. The Sioux didn't want the Crows to beat them at anything and the Crows didn't want to be outdone by the Sioux.

When the Sioux Indians heard that some Crow Indian riders was coming in their country to ride bucking horses they fetched in a horse from the Sioux Reservation to buck off the Crow

WITH THE CARNIVAL

riders. They never fetched in a sheep, you can bet on that, but a real stem winder that was hard to uncork.

We generally started the carnival shows about two o'clock in the afternoon. My show was a feature show and not a grind show. I opened the first show with the band and the grind shows got my blow off.

The first day at Chadron we had a nice crowd and a lot of outside horses to ride. We got lots of applause and everything went fine.

The second day, every seat was taken and most of the standing room. There must have been two hundred and fifty Sioux Indians in the audience. A good many of them had had too much firewater but everybody was peaceable and seemed to get a big kick out of the bucking horses.

The show was about half over when a breed Sioux Indian with two Sioux Indians and two cowboys came to the back of the arena leading two horses. They tied one up and fetched the other in to be rode by a Crow Indian rider.

He was a pretty good sized horse, raw boned and heavy muscled, as active as a cat. Anybody with horse savvy could see that he was a volcano and ready to explode.

The breed had been drinking. They wanted their horse rode right then. I told them that we had a horse already saddled and we would ride their horse next.

The breed said that their horse was mean and they didn't want to tie him up as they was afraid he would get away. He said they didn't want their horse to get away until he spilt one of them damn Crows. So we left our horse to be rode later.

As the breed lead the Indian horse in the arena, the Indians in the audience all let out a big yell and the white people joined in. They made a terrible racket. When they finally quit yelling so the announcer could say a few words, that Indian horse just stood there quivering and never made a move until the announcer had made his talk.

Shobe Daylight, the Crow Indian rider, grabbed his saddle and started over toward the horse. The horse threw up his head and tail and looked about twice as big as he was. He let out the biggest snort out of him that I ever heard out of a horse. The crowd went crazy.

Shobe Daylight and Mortimer Dreamer, the two Crow Indian riders, always worked together. When one rode a horse the other one always helped him saddle. They blindfolded the Sioux horse and he wasn't too bad to saddle.

Just when they pulled the blind off, Mortimer grabbed the strings on the back of the saddle and jumped on behind Shobe. Of all the pawing and scratching I ever saw, those two Crow Indians done it. They was mad at the breed for calling them "the damn Crows" and was getting even.

I, nor anyone else had any idea they was going to two-time that horse. They gave him a horrible time, one spurring in front and the other behind. All the time giving out some blood curdling yells. Hair was really flying in the air.

The horse was a bucking fool and he done it all, but two buck Indians on his back soon wore him down.

When the snubber had caught the horse and the riders was on the ground, hell sure began to pop.

The Sioux breed had Mortimer Dreamer backed up with a six-shooter aimed at his belly. Mortimer had a knife in his hand. Indians was boiling out of the seats into the arena. It looked bad for my Indian riders.

I knew that I had to do something quick. I hollered for everybody to clear out the arena as there was another bucking horse coming. I told George Williams to fetch the horse that was already saddled and ride him quick.

When the horse began to buck and bawl the crowd rushed to the front to get out of its way. That broke up the near riot. While the crowd's attention was on the bucking horse, I told my Crow Indians to go out the back way and over to the Privilege Car and stay out of sight until things quieted down.

WITH THE CARNIVAL

There wasn't any of the Wild West Show hands very popular around the Sioux Indians after that ride but we had no more trouble.

OMAHA, NEBRASKA, was the first large city that we showed in and one of the toughest places we come in contact with in our two and a half years on the road. It seemed that there was several tough gangs there that went around hunting and making trouble. Any time a show came to town some member of the gang would start an argument with one of the small shows and before the show man would know just what happened, he would be slapped on the head with a black jack, his tent cut down and a lot of stuff ruined. The gang worked fast and before the police or someone of the carnival outfit noticed the commotion the gang would run and scatter in the crowd.

Carnival people as a whole are a hard lot and plenty tough.

I will say, they never went hunting trouble. They had the public beat to start with. They paid for a license to show and for protection from the city. If they quarreled too much and got a tough name for their show or concession it hurt their business.

They had a rule, if any trouble started that the police didn't stop, the show or person in distress would holler, "Hey Rube." The carnival people would come running to the rescue armed with stakes, clubs or anything handy. Generally, several that was in the mix-up got pretty well skinned up.

The police was generally the last ones there. As soon as they was spotted, someone of the carnival would holler, "Jigger the bulls." Everybody got in the clear.

Our Wild West Show was a feature show and had a lot of people connected with it. We hardly ever had any trouble. The cowboys generally had guns on for the show. That might have been why they respected us.

The first night we showed in Omaha there was a gang tore up a China concession and started to tear up the Human

Roulette Wheel that was adjoining our show. They was really making a mess of things until someone hollered, "Hey, Rube!" and run them off. We was so busy we never heard the commotion.

After the show a boy handed me a note. It said, "We will visit you next."

I just turned it over and wrote on the back, "We will be ready to receive you when you come," and gave it back to the kid.

I went to the Chief of Police told him about the note and asked for protection for my show. He was a fine understanding man. He told me he didn't have enough men to protect all the shows but for us to protect ourselves and if we had to kill any of the tough gang in doing so, to drag them over in the alley where the dead wagon could pick them up in the morning.

We gave our show and there was no disturbance. Just off the carnival grounds about a block away there was a place where you could get a lunch and a glass of beer. George Williams and I was tired and hungry after the last show and started over to get something to eat. There was a lot of people leaving the carnival too. There was five or six men standing in a huddle on the sidewalk. When we came to them they stepped on the outside of the walk to let us through, we thought.

There was three on each side of the walk. There never was a word said. The first thing we knowed, someone hit Williams on the jaw and knocked him plumb in the middle of the street. Another one made a pass at me but I dodged and he only connected with my shoulder. It knocked me off the sidewalk into a pile of brick where the city had been repairing a hole in the street.

I came up with some brick bats and I was making good use of them. I got over to where Williams was and he was coming out of it kind of walking on his hands and knees.

Someone hollered, "Police" and the gang disappeared. The police run up to us. They saw Williams was hurt and asked what was the matter. My story and that of several witnesses was accepted. They said we had probably been attacked by the gang that was trying to tear up the carnival. I wasn't hurt much but Williams had his jaw broke and it was really hurting him. We limped back to the carnival grounds.

The next day George couldn't eat. He was quite a tobacco chewer but that was one time he couldn't get a plug in his mouth. George was a peaceable man until he got riled but he was really on the prod that time. He got a claw hammer and stuck it in his belt. He swore he'd get revenge on that "son of a bitch" that hit him on the jaw if he could find them. George had as much red in his eye as an old bull that has just lost a big fight. We was ready to do battle if anyone tried to tear our tent down but nobody showed up.

There was a Free Attraction on the grounds. A man would jump off a platform a hundred fifty feet in the air into a small tank of water. While the crowd was watching the Free Attraction a squabble started near there.

George located his man in the ruckus and made a wild dash for him. He went on a one-man warpath, hammer in hand. He was swinging it right and left. He laid two out before he got to the man that had broke his jaw—probably with brass knuckles.

The guy saw George and his hammer coming and started to run down the midway. George was fanning his coat tails with the hammer. It looked like the "wild man" had got out of his cage and was having a hydrophobia fit.

George run him about a hundred yards before he got close enough to lay him low. George was using the hammer pretty wild and reckless when the police broke it up. The tough guy paid for George's broken jaw with an arm and three ribs broke. The police didn't do anything to George. They was plenty pleased to see that gang of toughs get a beating. That wound up the trouble with the gangs and we gave our shows without any more trouble.

I SHALL NEVER FORGET the town of West Plains. I believe it was in Arkansas. There was a big banner hanging close to the depot that said, "This Town For Christ." After we'd spent a week there I didn't think it was for Christ or for man. All I could see that the people had that they was willing to share was Chills and Fever. It was the most hide bound town I ever run into.

It was there that George Williams got a grudge against the blacks. Since the town seemed to have such a prejudice against shows we was doing our best to change their opinion. The only place we could stretch our canvas was in a grove of trees. There was seven or eight big trees right in the arena. I don't know if it gave the crowd a thrill to see the bucking horses dodge those trees but I know it bothered us cowboys.

One evening there I was riding Duck Creek, the best bucking horse on the show. In fact he was one of the best bucking horses I ever saw. He was a hard horse to mount when not in a chute. When you snubbed him to the snubbing horse he used to fight something awful.

We was trying to break him from fighting and would get on him as quick as possible for as soon as you started on, Duck Creek started raring and plunging. Williams was snubbing him, as I started on I hollered, "Turn him loose." Duck Creek gave a big lunge and jumped plumb over the snubbing horse. That was the first and last time I ever saw it happen. He sure gave me a good ride that night.

In the course of the show we had several acts using extra saddle horses. We had them tied to some trees at the back of the canvas. While we was busy inside bucking out some horses, a black man slipped up and took one of George Williams' own saddle horses and ran off with it.

The show was close to the railroad tracks. The black man was in such a hurry to get away he didn't look where he was going. Consequently, a switch engine hit the horse and broke a hind leg. The man got away, but we had to shoot the horse.

WITH THE CARNIVAL

All the old-timers that knew George Williams will go along with me when I say he was a swearing man. He didn't swear that night, he cussed. His language would have made a bull whacker hang his head in shame. From that time on it wasn't healthy for a black to hang around the back of our canvas.

"The cowboys wore jeans for the show."

Now at that time those blacks and what they called poor white trash just didn't have any spending money, but they liked to see a show. They just about ruined our canvas cutting small holes in it so they could peep in.

From the time he lost his horse George took vengeance on the peepers. He got himself a big hardwood club about like a baseball bat. He whittled the handle nice and smooth. At each show he went around the canvas and when he saw a shadow he stepped back, spit on his hands, took a good hold on his club, waved it at the audience and then swung with all his might at the figure behind the canvas.

Two or three treatments and we didn't have to sew up any more canvas in that town. The audience seemed to think that was part of the show but George wasn't clowning, he was in dead earnest.

I TOOK ALONG seventeen Crow Indians. They was all fine looking young bucks. They was all outstanding riders on the Crow Reservation. They all had war bonnets lined with eagle feathers and beautiful beaded vests, moccasins, belts and cuffs.

They was a fine addition to any parade and all nice fellows. I cannot remember all their names but the three that stayed the longest and was the best riders was Shobe Daylight, Mortimer the Dreamer and Hartford Bear Claw.

They was all good and seemed to like the show business while it was new to them but after about a month they got homesick. Every morning some of them would come to me and say, "Bill, me lonesome, me want to swim in the Big Horn." There was nothing to do but buy him a ticket home. When they left they'd say, "Bott Sots (heap good) me see you at the fair."

It wasn't long after the first three left until I didn't have any Indians. I had a bad time to take care of them as I was paying them pretty good wages and they would get drunk and raise the dickens. They liked the hootchie-kootchie shows just as much as the cowboys did.

I remember one funny incident that happened in Kansas City at the carnival grounds. One big buck went to a Men Only Show and saw a "fairy in the well." You went on a platform and looked down into a kind of well that was lined with looking glass. There was a very pretty woman in her birthday clothes showed in the glass.

I missed the Indian and went to hunt him up as I didn't want him to get in any trouble. He had got hold of some liquor some way or another. I found him alongside of the Fairy Show digging as hard as he could. I went over and asked him what he was doing. He said, "Me digging up Fairy, me ketchum Fairy."

I had a hard time making him understand what it was all about and to get him back to the Indian camp.

WE WAS DOWN in Louisiana on our way to Baton Rouge. I cannot just remember where it was, but we went over some awful bad railroad beds. It seems to me I heard that part of that railroad bed was corduroyed with timber to get it above the swamp. I know it was awful rough. The train went real slow over it. We could see bubbles oozing up in the nasty green slimy water on either side of the tracks.

The train stopped at a siding to take on water. It was just dusk. I got out of the coach to go to see how my stock was doing. I was walking along the edge of the ties. I came upon a black looking object laying half in the water that I took to be a burnt log. I got pretty close and just as I was about to explore it with my foot it opened its mouth, snapped its teeth and swam off. I left that spot in a hurry, having no curiosity left for the welfare of my horses.

That was my first meeting with an alligator but saw a lot of them later, in the daylight, from the train windows.

We had been having a long rainy spell. There had been little profit in the show business. The show people called it a bloomer and was sure stroking their rabbits' feet and lucky charms in the hope of getting some sunshine.

We got into Shreveport, Louisiana. The show was right close to a livery stable where I put up my horses. Two doors from the livery stable was an undertaking parlor. Standing in one corner of the undertaking parlor was an ossified black man. It seems he had been holding that corner down for several years. I had never seen a body standing in a corner for an ornament and was all ears to hear the why for.

They told me, and I guess it was the truth, that the black man died in a lumber camp. The company had sent him to the undertaker but no one had come to claim the body or pay the funeral expense and they'd kept him. I didn't have any lucky piece to stroke so I thought maybe if I touched that black man it might change my luck. The undertaker seeing my interest and hoping maybe I'd be tempted in taking a bad investment off his hands told me to pick him up if I wanted to.

He wasn't very heavy. I put him on my back and carried him to the livery stable where my cowboys was hanging out. They didn't seem to think he was a very happy companion. They all assured me I'd have a Wild West show and no riders if I didn't take him back and put him in his corner, which I did.

He was lucky all right, just as I knew he would be, for that night I got in a poker game with some of the show people and some Cajuns. One of the Cajuns was pretty well liquored up and losing. He accused the players of cheating and they threw him out and locked the door.

I had just quit playing at the time and had my chips in my pockets as I had to cash them in at the bar in the other room. The Cajun got a gun and went to shooting through the window at the poker table. There was a mad scramble, the table turned over, poker chips flew all over the floor as well as the players. One fellow got his hat shot off but no one was hit.

WITH THE CARNIVAL

As soon as the shooting stopped I yelled for them to let me out. The Cajun, with some reinforcements, was in the bar by that time. As I came through the door the Cajun told them to let me through as I was okay, it was the rest of them he was after. I cashed my chips, bought them all a drink and then made some fast tracks away from there.

I know that black man made me lucky for I came away $75.00 winner and everybody else got all skinned up in a big fight that took place after the game. The weather changed for the better right after that and we had good crowds.

IT WAS THE RAINY SEASON and for three weeks we hadn't done any good. All the shows lost money. While we was showing at Baton Rouge, Louisiana, Hort Campbell said that Longview, Texas, our next stop, wasn't a big place but it would be the last show before he shipped to California to layover in winter quarters until spring.

Several of the shows left the carnival at Baton Rouge but we went on to Longview. We decided to make a wagon show there and make our way north that winter.

We got into Longview just before Christmas and was showing there through the holiday week. It rained the first two days and we couldn't show. The third day it cleared up and most of the shows opened up but it was cold and wet and too slippery for the horses to work so we didn't open. The fourth day we showed but didn't get much play but we throwed the best show we could, hoping it would advertise for us for the next two days. It rained the next two days and we never showed.

I was expecting to make some money there. Four weeks of bad weather, paying good wages to the help, had pretty near cleaned out the money sack. I wasn't broke but had to build some wagons and had other expenses to get organized. I had to have more money. I could have sent to Billings and got money but thought I would borrow it there if I could.

I went to the bank and told them my troubles. They didn't give me much encouragement, said I would have to see Mr. Ike Killingsworth. He owned the bank and he okayed all loans. They said he wouldn't be to the bank until after two o'clock as he was at the mule yard selling some mules.

It was about eleven o'clock. I thought I would walk to the yards and talk to Mr. Killingsworth. I would rather talk to him in the open anyway as I always thought a man felt more even standing on the ground than him to be in the bank setting before a lot of money.

I went about a couple of blocks when I saw a man followed by a big black man leading a mule coming down the street. I asked the man if he had come from the mule yards and if so, if he had seen Mr. Killingsworth.

He said, "I'm Killingsworth and what can I do for you?" He was a very intelligent looking man about forty-five years old, was pretty good sized with sharp grey eyes. You would never have taken him to be a banker by the looks of his clothes. He had on a pair of leather boots, baggy pants, a common work shirt but had a good Stetson hat.

I told him why I wanted to see him.

He said that he didn't think that loaning money to a show man was a very good investment.

I thought there wasn't no chance to get a loan but started down the street visiting with him. A paper blowed past the mule and scared it. The mule almost got away. I mentioned what a good looking mule he was. It was a pretty good sized black mule with a mealy nose and acted pretty scarey.

He asked me if I knew much about mules.

I told him, "Not too much. In the north where I come from there ain't many mules but I have rode several of them since I come south with the show."

He asked me, "Do you think you can ride that mule?" Right then I had a hunch. I figured he was a little sporty.

I wanted to make an impression on him as a rider. I told him that I'd like to have fifty cents a head for all of them I could ride in a week and I wouldn't have to borrow any money.

He sure looked me over. I don't think he had saw me until then. He said, "I'll give you fifty cents to ride this mule."

I said, "I didn't say just one mule, I meant a herd of mules." He gave me a nice smile and said, "I think this one would about be all you'd want."

That was just what I wanted. A mule was just duck soup to me after I had learned to ride them. I told him, "Alright, I'll just take you up. I will ride him here in the street if it is all right with you but I won't stand for paying a fine if the authorities kick."

He said, "That part will be all right."

I asked him if his black man could ear down that mule. He replied that he could ear down any mule in the state of Texas.

I told the black man, "Get busy, ear him down. I want the halter rope to tie around his equator." To make it strong, I said, "I can ride any mule in the state of Texas with ten feet of rope."

The black man eared the mule down. I untied the halter rope and tied it around the mule and jumped on. That mule was a hard bucking mule and he sure went to town. He was giving me a hard ride as I didn't have any spurs on. He done his darndest but I rode him. He quit bucking and started back to the corral on a run. When he got to the corral someone opened the gate and let us in and I got off.

I went back to the bank to get my half dollar. Mr. Killingsworth met me with a smile and asked me in his office and said, "I thought you was overestimating yourself."

Mr. Killingsworth was ready to talk loan. He asked me where I had lived in Montana and if I had done banking there.

I gave him the address of the State Bank where I had done a lot of business.

Mr. Killingsworth told me he would check with the State Bank and for me to come back the next day.

When I went back the next day Mr. Killingsworth said that my connections was good and that he would loan me a thousand dollars to start my wagon show. He said, "I'd like to make you a proposition. I'd like to have you give a show in Longview that will be remembered and I will help you out."

"The Elks are having a convention here next week and I want to entertain them. The Elks Lodge will sponsor your show, furnish the Longview band, show grounds and license. I have lots of wild cattle and mules and will fetch them in. Put on a parade and I will ride in it."

I took him up quick on his proposition and asked him, "On what percentage?"

He said that he didn't want any cut, just wanted to help me out and wanted to see a good show.

We got busy and made chutes and some corrals as we had close to a hundred head of outside stuff to ride.

The way I found the south in 1913 and 1914, there was three classes of people. There was the upper tens (10%) that held the money, the middle class and then the poor white trash (as they was called) and the blacks. The classes didn't mix.

Ike Killingsworth must have been a self made man, a kind of Abe Lincoln. As a banker, he mixed with all the classes. He must have been a good square man for everybody had a good word for him. He owned a lot of Longview and a lot of land in the surrounding country. He had a hundred and fifty black families working for him on his land raising cotton, corn, cattle and mules. He was counted one of the richest men in East Texas.

Mr. Killingsworth had a beautiful, silver mounted saddle that had been presented to him by the Elks. The saddle had a pure silver horn with an elk head engraved on it. The elk head had diamond eyes.

The show was on Saturday with the parade set for 9:30 in the morning and the show was to start as soon as the parade was over.

WITH THE CARNIVAL

The Longview band lead the parade, followed by Mr. Killingsworth riding his silver mounted saddle on a beautiful bay horse. Fifteen or twenty Elks followed Mr. Killingsworth. My wife and I was next. My wife was dressed in a blue velvet riding habit trimmed with white pearl buttons. She wore her hair in two long braids under a pearl grey Stetson hat. She carried her rifle over her arm and was riding a very good looking sorrel horse.

George Williams and his wife was next, followed by a western stagecoach. Montana Jack Ray, world's champion trick and fancy roper, and my daughter Daisy, who was also a trick roper, followed the stagecoach. The other cowboys and cowgirls followed them, then some pack mules lead by a packer, the two clowns on trick mules, with a roundup grub wagon at the end of the parade.

We had stretched every foot of canvas we had and had a nice sized arena to work in. We didn't have near enough seats as they was all taken and all the standing room, too. When no more people could get in we took the back canvas down where there was a lot of people standing that wanted to see the show.

After the introduction of the cowboys and cowgirls we opened the show with a bang. We turned six bucking steers out of the chutes at the same time with black riders. We was giving them five dollars if they rode an animal but only a dollar if they bucked off. That was a lot of money to a black man in those days. Those steers made a good showing bucking all their riders off. It was a mad scramble followed by three bucking kicking mules.

We had several western acts but on account of having so much outside stock to ride we cut some of them out and others we cut short and only used them if there was a delay at the chute.

There was something going on every minute of the show. The clowns was working all the time or the trick ropers or my wife entertaining the crowd with her rifle shooting, while out of the chutes came a steady stream of bucking horses, mules and steers. We kept that up until noon. The crowd was well pleased and was cheering us all the time.

The announcer closed the show with a short spiel and told them we would open the next show at two that afternoon.

We had just as big a crowd for the afternoon show and I had to open the canvas. We started off with my wife's shooting act. She shot small targets out of my fingers, the ashes off my cigarette and an empty .22 shell off my head. That last was really a dangerous shot as a .22 shell is pretty small and she never did that stunt if there was any wind or dust, and another thing, we thought a lot of each other.

There is always a lot of things happen where there is so much stuff to ride. Mr. Killingsworth alone furnished us forty head of wild steers and thirty two head of unbroke mules and other people brought in some horses and mules.

Jack Ray was entertaining the crowd with his rope tricks while we was filling up the chutes with mules. One mule got down in the chute. I didn't want the mule to get hurt and hollered for the chute man to open the gate and let him out.

The mule came out on high and ran past me. I was coming from the back end of the arena where I had been helping get the saddles off some bucking horses and had my rope in my hand. I made a long throw at the mule and made a good lucky catch.

There was a bunch of cotton buyers standing by the rope fence and one said, "I'll bet you can't do it again."

I got my rope off the mule and told the chute man to turn another mule out. The mule came out running in just about the same place. I made a throw and caught him, too.

The cotton buyers just went wild and the crowd thought it was part of the roping act. I had on a pretty bright cerise colored shirt, that my wife had made for me to wear in the show. The cotton buyer said, "Cowboy, I'll give you ten dollars for that shirt you got on."

I said, "Okay, we need the money." I took my shirt off and handed it to him. He gave the ten dollars to me and I started back to the chute.

Another buyer hollered, "I'll give you two dollars for your socks." I sat down, pulled my boots off, pulled my socks off and handed them to him. The crowd got a big kick out of the deal.

"Parade."

There was too much that happened in that show to try to tell it all. There was a lot of Mr. Killingsworth's black men tried to ride the mules and steers, but they didn't have any luck. When we turned five or six mules or steers out at once it just seemed to rain black men but none of them got hurt. None of my riders got throwed.

We made more than enough to pay off the loan. Mr. Killingsworth got the kind of entertainment he wanted. We loaded all our equipment in wagons and drove the bucking horses behind. Our next show was at Kilgore, Texas.

WHEN YOU ARE in the show business, the show is given for the entertainment of the audience but sometimes the audience entertains the show people. Such was the case one time when I gave a show in Texas in 1914 to a complete black audience.

I believe it was near Marshall, Texas. There was a grant almost like a reservation for blacks. I don't know how it was arranged but it must have been forty miles long and I don't know how wide, but no white people lived on it.

We was on our way to Marshall with the wagon show crossing this grant when Cow in the Woods, one of our best bucking horses got awfully sick and we had to stop near a store and post office. I got permission from the store man to stay there and rented a pasture for the horses from him.

The blacks seemed curious about our outfit but acted scared of us. Finally the store man—a great big fat black man—told me there had been an axe man in there that had cut up a lot of blacks and they was afraid I was the axe man.

I told him that I was a show man not an axe man and that I was from Montana.

He said, "Mister, I never done heard of that place, what country is that?"

I told him that it was in the northern part of the country and that my grandfather fought to set black folks free. I was his friend right then. He passed the word along and all the blacks got real friendly. They asked about my shows and said there had never been a show in that grant. The store man wanted me to put a show on but he said I'd better see the parson about it. We didn't have anything to do while the horse was getting well so I thought I might as well give them a little entertainment.

The church was about four miles from the store. I rode over to see the parson, who seemed to be the head man in the settlement. I told him that I had a Wild West Show and the folks around the store wanted me to give a show.

He asked me if I had any "bad" women in my show or if I was selling whiskey. When I told him that I had my family with me and that it was a good clean show, he gave me his okay and said he would announce it in church. He said the people didn't have much money but they had produce. I told him to tell them to bring their money, or chickens or eggs or anything, or if they had any mean mule, horse or bull they wanted rode, we'd ride them free of charge and give the owner a pass.

I gave him a bunch of free passes for his friends and told him to come early so he could get a good seat.

The evening of the show, wagons began coming from all directions loaded with black folks. They was dressed in their best calicos that was all colors of the rainbow and they looked mighty nice. As the preacher had said, not many of them had cash money, but I never saw so many chickens, young pigs, eggs, butter and vegetables piled in one pile as there was by the ticket box that night. There was even a possum. We used the butter to grease the wagons for a long time. They also brought a lot of mules and bulls for us to ride.

We had a full house and a more appreciative audience I never showed to. When my wife did her shooting act, I gave a talk telling them what a dangerous act it was and that we'd like them to be perfectly quiet. There was hardly a sound. She shot several objects out of my hand, then I put a potato on my head. The audience, as one person, moaned. When the potato blew apart there was a sigh of relief. Some of them was so afraid she'd miss that they shut their eyes.

We rode the mules all out and then as a final act I had a Jersey bull to ride that some of them had brought in. He was a good bucking bull and was putting his heart into his bucking. He went straight for the ropes that separated the seats from the arena. Just as he bucked into the ropes the cinch on my surcingle broke and I went right over the ropes on my head and landed in a great big black woman's stomach. It knocked the wind out of her and from the noise that she made trying to catch her breath I'd say I jolted her considerable. If I had of hit one of the seats instead of her stomach, I probably would not be telling about it now.

The roads wasn't so good at that time, it was in the spring just after a rainy spell.

I had a wonderful pulling team, but I had them split up as one of the bucking horses had quit bucking so I thought I'd make a work horse out of him.

We came to a small creek, either the bridge was washed out or there had never been one. There was several places where people had crossed but they all looked bad. I followed the main line of travel. One wheel dropped into a deep hole, cramped the wagon and the green horse fell over the wagon tongue and broke it.

I spoke a few expressive Montana words to fit the occasion and set out to cut a pole to make a new tongue. I made one, but working in the water and mud I couldn't get it to fit very good, but tried it anyway. I hooked my good team on it, they gave a good pull and it broke.

Just about that time a long geared Texan came up on a little red mule. He looked the wagon over and said we'd have to unload and carry the stuff across as there wasn't any six mules in Texas that could haul that wagon out of that mud hole.

I was pretty much disgusted with Texas roads, people, mules and mud by that time. I told him there might not be six mules in Texas that could pull it out but I had two Montana horses that could do it if I could get things to hold together.

He looked at me, at the wagon in the mud hole, and at my team, then he got off his mule, sat down in the shade of a tree, reached for his plug of tobacco and said, "I want to see them do it."

While I was cutting another pole for a tongue he sat and chewed tobacco. He didn't say anything more or offer to help like a Montana man would have. He just watched us sweat and cuss.

It must have taken over an hour to get another tongue cut and wired on. I took plenty of time because I didn't want to have to do it over. We was headed north and I guess that team wanted to get out of that country as much as I did. When I tightened up on the lines and let a whistle out of me, mud and water began to fly. The wagon gave a big lurch and out we came.

The Texan who'd been watching the proceedings in comfort, got up, spat out a big cud of tobacco, hoisted his britches and said, "You've got the best God bursted pulling team I ever seed."

Then he got on his little mule, rode around the mud hole and went on his way.

WHEN WE GOT to Marshall, Texas, we layed over to rest up our stock. There was a large livestock market there for horses and mules and I thought I might pick up some good bucking stuff.

It was some time in February and the feed yards was full of horses and mules getting them ready for the spring demand. We put our horses in a large feed and sale yard. They had about five hundred head of stock in small corrals or pens, somewhere between twenty five to thirty in a pen. The principle feed was cotton seed and cotton seed meal. It was a cheap feed and sure put the fat on.

There was quite a lot of activity around the sale yard as there was lying, trading and dealing every day and a big sale once a week on Saturday. George Williams and I picked up quite a lot of cash riding at the Saturday sales. We generally made around $25.00 apiece. It was easy money as the stuff we rode mostly wasn't too tough.

In Texas, at that time, every town had a livery stable and a few head of stuff for sale. We wasn't doing anything only waiting for our stuff to get in condition so we made the close towns and rode for collections. One place, we got fourteen head of mules to halter break, two horses to break to ride and picked up a good bucking horse cheap. We always managed to get back to Marshall for the Saturday sale.

There was all kinds of mules and horses in the yards, some broke gentle stuff and some that was wild that had never been handled. Most every day that we was there we got a chance to ride something. Williams didn't like mules so we made an agreement, I would ride the mules and he would ride the horses.

At the Saturday sale they sold all kinds. If a mule or horse was good and salty we would get them to halter break or ride. Some of those buyers was pretty sporty and would make a five or ten dollar collection most any time if an animal looked like it would make a good show.

There was a big young black man probably around twenty years old called Sam that used to feed the stock in the pens. He had a mule hitched to a wagon that he drove in the pens and shoveled the feed into the feed troughs. The first time we left Marshall, I gave Sam a dollar and told him to take good care of my stock. After that he always tipped his old straw hat whenever he met me and called me "Mr. Bill."

I remember so well one freak mule that Sam showed me. Sam said that the other mules didn't like that mule and they all fought him. When they got too rough, the mule would jump over into another corral.

WITH THE CARNIVAL

It was a horse mule and the tallest mule I ever saw. He had a long body, long legs and was built more like a grey hound than a mule. He had long pointed ears and his body was thin with high withers. As a general rule, mules have low withers. He was an unbroke mule and pretty wild. He had plenty of action. He would jump those fences like nobody's business and those partition fences was anyhow five feet high or higher.

One morning there was a lot of buyers at the sale yard. They noticed this mule jumping from one pen to another. One of them said, "I'd like to see that mule rode."

I told him that I'd ride the mule if they'd make up a purse, which they did.

There was large swinging gates between the pens. We worked the mule easy so he wouldn't jump out. We got him where we could get him between a gate and a fence, then closed the gate tight against him. We tied a rope around him and I got down on him.

When they threw that gate back, oh boy, how that mule did buck. The other mules in the pen got scared and was trying to kick him. Between riding him and dodging the other mules' heels, I was plenty busy. He made about two revolutions around that pen and jumped into another pen.

There was more mules in that pen and it was worse than ever. They was all trying to kick him and they wasn't missing him or me either. I got kicked on the legs several times.

The mule didn't like that pen any more than I did. The next pens was just the same. I wanted off, but couldn't quit him in a bunch of kicking mules.

He jumped in and out of seven pens with me and finally came to the show corral where the people was standing. They sure was scrambling to get out of the way.

The mule finally ran under a wagon shed. There was some cross pieces above the top. I grabbed hold of the cross pieces and the mule ran out and jumped into a pen again. That was the only mule I ever rode that could jump like that.

I HAD NEVER had much experience riding mules until I got in eastern Texas. By the time I got up into Missouri, I'd had a lot of it.

Missouri was always known as a mule raising state. The government used to buy a lot of Missouri mules for the army. The best mules I ever saw was raised in Missouri. You hardly ever saw a horse team there. They used mules to ride too. Many a time I saw a black man riding a mule back with a sack of corn in front of him taking it to a mill to get it ground into corn meal.

We used to advertise for outside stock to ride, with a good reward for anything that the public could lead, drag or drive in our canvas that we couldn't ride.

We got a lot of mules and sometimes some salty, spoiled outlaw stuff. We liked it as the people knew about a mean animal in their neighborhood and would come to see it rode. It saved using our own bucking stock too.

A mule is naturally a low withered animal. We had trouble with getting our saddles bucked off several times. A mule is a kicking animal and with a saddle we had trouble getting them rode quick, so we rode them bareback.

I was the only one in the show that rode bareback so most of the mule riding fell to me. We would put a blind fold over the mule's eyes, get a rope around his equator. Someone would give me a leg up, pull the blind off and there would be a mule in the air.

We was in Dade County, Missouri, I have forgotten the town, a farmer fetched in a mule to ride. He was a freaky looking mule with the longest legs I ever saw on a mule. He had a long slim body, a rather short neck and extra long ears.

The farmer said to watch that mule's hind legs as he could kick the soda out of a biscuit. The farmer never exaggerated a bit. That mule was the kickingest thing I ever saw. If you got within ten feet of that mule, he would try to whirl and kick you.

We threw a rope on his front legs, pulled them back until his knees was on the ground and his hind feet well in front of him where he couldn't use them. We got a rope around his middle and I got on him.

WITH THE CARNIVAL

The first jump he kicked both my legs and just about tore me off. I had to get my legs in the air to keep him from kicking them again.

Oh boy! That was a limber bucking, kicking mule. He had his head down between his front legs. He was bawling and making more noise than a clown brass band.

He seemed to double up when he left the ground and kick ahead with them long legs. They was sure making me squirm.

I kind of got in time with him and would grab him with my spurs about the time he pulled his legs back to light on the ground. He was bucking right in front of the seats. He whirled back to keep from hitting the ropes in front of the seats. I missed when I went to grab him and spurred over the top rope. My crooked shank spur caught in the rope. The mule went on while I hung on the fence to the amusement of the crowd.

The farmer said he didn't think I had a fair deal as I had got tangled up with the rope fence and he would give me another try at the mule if I wasn't satisfied.

I tried the mule in the show the next night to my sorrow. He threw me off and kicked me three times before I hit the ground.

I would have liked to have seen someone ride that mule. I couldn't get it done.

SINCE THE AUTOMOBILE and tractor have come in common use the old time horse trader has faded away. There was more traders in the south and east where it was thickly settled. Their disappearance was no loss to the country for as a whole class they was a scummy lot. I think most of them went into the used car business for they are just about as deceiving in their line of patter.

In Oklahoma I met a typical horse trader, he followed my show for a while. I'll call him John Doe. He was a big, stout, sandy complexioned man with lots of savvy. He had two faces, one he used for the public which was charming, the other one he turned toward his family which was mean and overbearing. Since most folks have never come in contact with a horse trader, I am going to tell you about John Doe, his outfit and how he worked.

John had a little better outfit than most traders. He traveled with his family of five children. He had a covered wagon drawn by a team of good mules, another wagon loaded with a large tent and camp equipment trailing a buggy, followed by fifteen or twenty trading horses, John on horseback bringing up the rear.

Mrs. Doe was a very nice refined woman with a talent for painting. Whenever they stopped and set up the tent it looked just like home. A bed was set up with rugs on the ground, little tables set up with nick nacks on them and always a bowl of wild flowers if they was available.

She would take the buggy and one of the children to drive it and peddle laces, silver polish or some of her paintings. If she couldn't get money for her goods she would trade for chickens, vegetables or anything that was useable. She was the one that kept the family together.

It was a shame such a nice family was wasted on that horse trader. There was a boy about sixteen named Roy. He was John's stepson and was treated by John like one. There was two nice girls probably about fourteen and thirteen, a boy about twelve called Dude the favorite of John and a spoiled brat. The other little boy was Ernest, a bright likeable boy of eight who was right handy at ducking out of sight when John was getting over a hangover.

John knew most all the tricks in horse trading. He could doll an old mule or horse up so he would look like he was seven or eight years old.

Most old horses'—that ain't range horses—teeth get long. John had a fine tooth saw that was made to fit a horse's mouth. He would cut their teeth off nice and even. He had a cupping outfit that he could put cups in their teeth, then he would take caustic and burn the cups black. If anyone looked in the horse's mouth to tell their age and wasn't an expert they sure would be fooled.

Old mules and horses get grey around the head, their eye brows get white and there is a hollow that comes above their eyes. John had a way to fix them up. He used potash to color all the white hairs. He had a bulb syringe with a hollow needle that he used to blow up the cavities over their eyes. He would trim their mane and tail, cut the foretop, clip the long hairs off their legs and give them a shot of dope to pep them up and they was ready for a trade. Someone got a good beating.

He had a good line of talk and never traded horses unless he got some boot money.

If he saw a horse he wanted to trade for and he could get to it, he would take a needle and thread it with hair that was pulled out of the horse's tail, stick the needle through the horse's front leg between the knee and the ankle where the cords in the leg are, and the leg is small. Then he would cut off the ends of the hair so it didn't show.

The horse would go lame in ten minutes and just hold up his foot. If anyone tried to move him he would just hobble off barely putting his hoof on the ground. You could examine the horse to see what made it lame and you couldn't find a thing.

John would just happen around, tell the owner of the horse he thought the horse had slipped a joint in his shoulder. If John couldn't trade for the horse he would tell the man to leave the horse and he thought he could heat some pads and get the joint in place for about ten dollars.

He generally either made a nice trade or pulled out the hair in the horse's leg and the horse was okay. After he got ten dollars for curing the horse he would try to sell the owner a bottle of water with some ashes in it and a few drops of potash in it to color the water, cheap for about $2.50 to use as a rub on the horse's shoulder for a few days.

The boot money John got in a horse trade never did the family any good for John spent it on a jug of moon. He'd hunt a horse trader to share it with and when they got pretty well lit up they'd swap tricks of the trade to each other of how to trim a sucker. When the moon was all gone John would go back to his camp and raise hell with his family.

15: Rodeos

I REMEMBER the first rodeo I ever went to, although it wasn't called a rodeo, that name came along time afterwards. I was just a small boy about six years old. That was at North Platte, Nebraska on the Fourth of July, 1882.

As far as can be determined, it was the start of the rodeo game and the first rodeo given in the world according to a North Platte paper. It was given and managed by Buffalo Bill Cody.

It was a far different deal than the rodeos given today. There was no big parade, fancy clothes, hot dog stands. There wasn't even any rodeo grounds with grand stands, chutes and catch pens.

That first show given by Buffalo Bill was given in a big corral that held the stock. The audience stood around and watched the performance over the fence. I can remember standing between my mother and Aunt Clara clutching tightly to their hands just spell bound.

There wasn't much entertainment at that time and I think everybody and his dog in the country was there. There was wagons, buggies and saddle horses everywhere. Everybody took their lunch and made a day of it.

The rodeo consisted of riding bucking horses and roping big steers. There was several buffaloes rode. It was a salty show in the rough. I was just a very small boy, but I remember it well.

They would rope a horse, drag him out of the bunch, ear him down, blindfold him, saddle him and step on.

Cody would call out the rider's name and tell what cow outfit he represented. The buffalo was a harder proposition. They would have to rope them and throw them down, pull the saddle cinch under their bellies, cinch it up and ride them up. Some of the buffalo riders didn't get very far. As I remember, they rode buffalo cows as the bulls was too mean and dangerous. If a bull got on the fight nothing would hold him and they was afraid he might get in the crowd and kill somebody.

Well I remember one announcement Buffalo Bill made. He said, "These cowboys can ride anything that has hair on it." It was a saying that was used around North Platte for a long time after that.

I don't remember seeing any gaudy shirts, colored decorated hats and loud off colored boots. The riders there was real honest to God working cowboys, the top hands of the various spreads. Their decoration was a cartridge belt around their middle full of cartridges with a scabbard holding a six-shooter on the belt, a pair of high heeled boots, a good hat and a pair of overalls.

Their saddles was low and flat with two cinches and a horn as big as a dinner plate, but they got the job done on them. There wasn't any bareback riding or bull dogging at that time.

I think that I put bareback riding in the rodeos for I never saw anyone ride bareback before I rode bareback on exhibition in Billings over fifty years ago.

I had never seen or heard of anyone else ride that way, but some Indians in Utah as they didn't have saddles. They tied a raw hide rope around the horse's belly. They had a rope with a loop around the horse's mouth and used one rein. When I made my first ride, I did the Indians one better, I left the rope out of the horse's mouth and just held on to the one around the horse's middle.

It wasn't long after I started to ride that way that a lot of other riders took it up, but for a long time they was all exhibition rides. For a long time I never used anything but a rope, then I went to old Bill Tenacks, Tenax, (oh hell, I don't know how to spell his name). But anyway, he was an old timer and one of the first and best saddle makers in Billings. We got our heads together and designed what we called a "bull saddle." They was later called a surcingle. Now the rodeo boys call them a bareback riggin'.

At first the bareback riders used two hands to hold on with like the Indians did, but then we got to using only one hand.

To those young people wanting to learn to ride bareback I'll tell you how to do it easy, "Just keep the horse between your legs. And for gracious sake, don't let go and roll off like a sack of dirt. God put legs on you to use. Use your arm to push you away from the horse. Hit the ground running. You don't need any pick up man to pull you off and drop you or run over you."

SOME OF THE best riders that I knew in the early days of the rodeo game was Earl Stroud, Bob Askins, Jesse Coats, Howard Tegland, Jack Coats, George Williams, C. R. Williams, Leonard Stroud, Paddy Ryan, George Clark, Powder Faced Tom, Earvin Collins, Gene Ross, Buggar Red, Billy Wilkinson, Yakima Kanute, Floyd Stillings, Bob Cole, Thad Sowder, Otto Plaga, Sam Scoville, Hugh Strikland, Pinkey Gist and Ed McCarty.

There are more good riders that I haven't mentioned, but I knew these boys well and rode with them. Some of the best riders of the last few years are Artie Oser, Mert Osness, Clyde Kipp, Slim Schultz, Turk Greenough, Pete Knight, Casey Tibbs and the Linderman brothers.

Some of the riders have gone over the big divide but there are stories about them all.

There is an old saying among riders, "All horses get rode and all riders get throwed," but I don't think the horse ever lived that some of the above riders couldn't have topped him off.

The first shows was just about all bucking horses, steer riding, steer roping, bull dogging and wild horse races. Then they began to add trick riding and roping as added attractions. In the roping they changed from steers to calves.

When the trick roping and riding turned into contests the boys really began doing dangerous stunts to get the top money. Some of the trick riders began going under a horse's belly while it was running full speed and even between their hind legs.

Leonard Stroud used to stand up on his horse while it jumped over an automobile that had its top down. Later he rode "Roman Stand" and jumped the two horses over an automobile.

Montana Jack Ray, one time world's champion trick roper had a lot of fancy catches. One of them was making a big loop in front of his horse and running him through it.

The bucking horse riders pulled some crazy stunts, too. Way back in 1909, Yakima Jim used to come out of the chute on a horse with no saddle or surcingle. He came out one hand full of mane, the other ahold of the horse's tail which he pulled over his shoulder. He used to call it "riding the hard way," but Jim used to get it done. It sure looked wild when he came out of the chute riding a bucking, bawling horse without even a string on it.

The most comical ride I ever saw was put on by Whitey Rains at Hardin, Montana, in 1930. I believe Johnny Wientz furnished the rodeo stock for that show. As everyone knows a show managed by Johnny is always tops for he really has some good bucking horses.

Anyway, Whitey Rains was a rider that followed the rodeos from Montana south into Texas and back into Canada. It seems that Whitey and C. Anderson of Billings got their heads together figuring out a new stunt for the rodeo business. Anderson got a chair, cut off the legs, fastened it above a saddle and Whitey was to ride a bronc sitting in a chair.

There was a lot of speculation among the crowd when the announcer said Whitey Rains was coming out of the chute riding a bucking horse on a chair.

Whitey was plenty busy staying on the chair as he had drew a good bucking horse. The crowd went hog wild. Whitey got the job done though the chair got kind of loose and bucked harder than the horse.

At one time it looked like Whitey was going to lose his seat as he and the chair got sort of tangled up. When Whitey and the chair got unscrambled he was okay except he was minus two front teeth.

The ride made a hit with the crowd and I guess Whitey made rodeo history as the first chair rider. I think he was the only one to try it. Whitey lives on a ranch now near Forsyth, Montana.

IN MY TIME, I have come in contact with a lot of the world's best riders. Of all the riders that I have seen ride in the rodeo game, the two that was the most outstanding was Jesse Coats and Bob Askins. In their day, I believe they won more contests than any other two riders in the world.

Jesse Coats was a nice looking man. He had dark hair and brown eyes, was about five feet eight or nine and weighed about a hundred fifty five. He was a good mixer, had quite a sense of humor and was popular among all the cowboys. He was a good straight shooter. He never cheated a horse to win his money. He was a natural born rider.

Jesse's folks was in the stock business and lived near Mountain Home, Idaho. He won his first bucking horse contest at Mountain Home when he was fifteen years old. Later he rode and broke horses for the United States Government at Fort Keogh. He broke horses to ride in Idaho, Wyoming and Montana before he started to ride in the rodeos.

Jesse rode in most all the large rodeos in the United States and Canada. He went to England when Tex Rickard put on a rodeo in London and won more day rides than any other man there. Jesse was a good all around man but seldom did anything but ride saddle broncs in the rodeos.

I have seen him ride some of the worst horses in the rodeo game and never seen him lose his seat or grab for leather. When he rode a rough horse he made three jabs in the shoulder, then went back. He would hit the cantle board of his saddle with his spurs every jump. He was an artist with those gut wrenches and could put them anywhere the judges wanted them put, forward or back.

I saw Jesse make one of the prettiest rides I have ever seen at the Billings Fair about 1922 or 1923. I was one of the bucking horse judges at the time. It was the last day of the contest. There was some real salty riders in that contest and there was a lot of the boys sitting pretty high in the finals.

They was coming out of the chute scratching for first money. Howard Tegland was setting way in the lead on points and looked like a sure winner. He drew a sorrel mare owned by Nate Cooper. Howard was making a pretty ride when he scratched off.

Jesse came out on a horse by the name of Butterfly owned by the McDowell brothers. I think that everybody around Billings at that time had seen or heard of Butterfly.

He was a very pretty white horse that had dirtied many a rider's back. If a rider wasn't pretty forked he didn't have any business on that cyclone. Butterfly was very well built. He was quick and could handle himself like a small horse though he weighed close to fifteen hundred pounds.

I saw Butterfly do his stuff lots of times and never seen him miss fire, but that day, he turned on an extra dose. Jesse was at the peak of his riding ability. He sure gave Butterfly a scratching cowboy ride. It was first money and a pleasure to see.

I have seen many a ride where the best rider never got a cent. He couldn't show his ability on some old barnacle that was off center. All good rodeo riders like to draw bucking horses. In a contest riding for points, the ride is judged and also the bucking of the horse. If you are a fair judge you have to judge according to the horse that has been rode.

THERE ARE MANY different kinds of bucking horses. The young horse that has never been handled ain't near as hard to ride as an old outlaw that has throwed off a lot of riders. The green horse will do everything he can to slip his pack, but hasn't had the experience of an older horse. The real bucking horse will try every kind of a trick to unload you and believe me, he has lots of tricks. There are a lot of freak bucking horses that will try everything, when he finds a way to unload a man he will stick to that particular trick.

Take the spinning horse, he doesn't buck his rider off, he just spins until the rider is so dizzy he falls off. I once had a real good bucking horse in my rodeo string. He was having a lot of luck just bucking off his riders until one time at Butte, a real salty rider from Canada rode him. The next time he was bucked out was at Anaconda. He gave a couple little short jumps and went to spinning around and around like a top and plenty fast. It made the rider so dizzy that he fell off. That old pony just kept spinning until he was dizzy too and fell down. After that he always spun round and round. A man just couldn't stay on that freak.

There is the horse that runs forty or fifty yards, makes a high dive in the air, loosens up the rider, comes back through himself, swaps ends fast and furious. He is liable to lose any old boy.

There is the falling back horse. Some of them will whirl around a couple of times and fall over backwards lighting right on their back. They are very dangerous horses and have crippled and killed many a rider.

The whirling bucker is not to be mixed up with the spinner. He is generally a very fast horse that does his stunt in a very small space.

The Kangaroo bucker is a hard horse to ride. The first few jumps he lights on his hind legs, never touching his front feet on the ground for several jumps. He stands in the air so high and straight that he scares the rider as he thinks he is coming over and he loosens up as he can't tell what is coming next. The Kangaroo bucker gives his rider a scary ride.

The sunfishing bucking horse is a pretty sight to see with a good buckaroo on top of him. He gets pretty high with all four feet sticking out first on one side and then on the other. It looks like he is going to fall right on his side but always manages to straighten up on his legs before he hits the ground.

There is the back jumper that is hard to sit on. He will jump in the air, instead of going ahead like most horses, he comes back. There ain't too many back jumpers as it ain't natural for a horse to jump backwards. I came in contact with about three of them in twenty five years of riding rough horses. The first one I rode at, I didn't like him so we parted company very fast. I went ahead, he went back.

The running pitching horse is generally a horse that is wild. He wants to throw his rider off. He tries to do it on the run as he is scared and wants to get away. He ain't hard to ride. The straight away high bucker is pretty to look at but not hard to ride.

The most dangerous horse in my opinion is the stampeder. He goes hog wild, just breaks into a crazy fast run and puts all he's got into it. He never looks where he is going or seems to care. He will run into a wire fence, over a cut bank, into a hole or anything. The farther he runs the crazier and scarier he gets until he runs into something or runs himself down. If you try to hold him, he will fight his head and sure fall down with you.

The horse that bawled as he bucked has always amused me. He gets lots of attention and applause. It always seemed to me like he was cussing his rider.

I have heard lots of arguments in regard to flanking a bucking horse, for my part, I don't believe in it. A good bucking horse don't need a flank rope.

The reason a flank rope was first used was on account of a horse being bucked out too much and quit bucking. The rodeo people call it dogging. They flank the dogging horse, naturally a horse don't like something around his flank so he gives two or three jumps, then goes around kicking in the air. It is really harder on him than real hard bucking. Most every rodeo man wants all his horses to come out of the chute doing something. With a flank rope they will always run and kick up, if they don't buck.

I think that the way to spoil a real good bucking horse is to flank him. A good horse will give you all he's got without a flank rope. After he's done his stunt, throwed his man off, or the pick-up man has pulled him off, the horse won't quit as the flank rope hurts him and he runs around kicking in the air. After so much of that flanking he naturally just comes out of the chute kicking over his head instead of doing a right clean job of bucking.

I used a bunch of bucking horses for two years and a few of them quit bucking but most of them never quit. I never flanked any of my bucking horses. If I saw one was slowing up I would try and give him a rest for a week or two and he generally came back. All he wanted was a break. As much as I was bucking those horses, if I had flanked them, I wouldn't have had a bucker left in three weeks' time.

A MEAN MULE is a tricky son of a gun and he can kick the soda out of a biscuit. He can swap ends like lightning. I rode a mule in Stevensville, Montana, that the first jump, he threw his hind feet ahead and tore both of my spurs off.

I rode one in Kilgore, Texas that had the same stunt only more. If he couldn't kick you off he just reached around with his teeth and grabbed you by the leg or arm and believe me, you came off. I got wise to his trick and put a feed bag on him that had a heavy leather bottom in it. He couldn't bite through it but he kept them hind feet going and he was plenty tough.

There is one thing about a mule, he won't buck into a fence, but he may try to jump it. You can't get a mule into a hole. A mule hasn't the jar to them that a horse has. A mule's legs are light and their ankles are long. When they hit the ground there is a give to them, not so much jar.

Another thing I found out riding mules, they can't stand punishment. If you spur a mule hard a few times, he will quit pitching.

For my part I think a horse is a lot harder to ride than a mule. There is, and always has been a few horses that are almost impossible to ride.

I believe the Creator made a horse to carry man for their back is made right to carry weight. A horse is one of the fastest four legged animals on earth.

When it comes to riding bulls, that is a different story. A bull never was meant to ride. He is a different made animal. He has a lot more heavy sharp bones in his back. When a bull that weighs from 1,500 to 2,000 pounds bucks with you, he doesn't buck you off, he just hits the ground so hard that if you ever slip a little he just jars you off.

Take one of them heavy Brahma whirling bulls that hit the ground like two tons of rock and you sitting on a stack of bones under a slippery hide. You ain't got much chance. It ain't a riding contest, it is an endurance contest to see who can stand the most punishment, generally the bull wins.

I have rode a lot of bulls in my time and there was a lot of them I didn't ride. I think, for my part, I would rather take a chance on getting old Dobbin rode.

I HAVE TOLD about the professional riders, ropers and bulldoggers, but I haven't mentioned the cow girls. I take my hat off to them whether they work at home on a ranch or in the rodeos. They are good and do an efficient job.

Of all the women riders that I ever saw on the hurricane deck of a bucking, outlaw horse I think Fanny Sperry had them all cheated. I first got acquainted with her at Deer Lodge in the early 1900s. At that time she lived in Deer Lodge valley and had a reputation of being an expert on a bucking horse.

She rode her bucking horses slick, fair and honest. She never cheated a horse, never hobbled her stirrups nor pulled any leather. In later years she was the undisputed champion woman rider. She rode at the Minneapolis State Fair in the early 1900s when the fair management got the bucking horses from Miles City and their cowboys from Montana and Wyoming. They had the best horses and riders they could get and it was a red hot show. Fanny rode with the cowboys and rode in her turn.

There never was any easy horses picked for her. They filled the chute and Fanny rode whatever horse her number called for. There was several cowboys that got their backs dirtied, but she rode all her horses.

Fanny Sperry was a very well known rider in Montana, a quiet dignified lady, that everybody liked. She didn't care for notoriety, for with her personality, looks and ability she could have went far in the movie world. I never knew of Fanny riding in a contest that she didn't win first money. She was undoubtedly the champion woman bucking horse rider in the United States.

Annie Oakley was another old time favorite. She worked for the Buffalo Bill Show. She was a great shot and bucking horse rider. A horse turned over with her in New York and fractured her skull. She was in the hospital over a year and had a big silver plate in her head. It injured her brain to some extent and her memory was impaired.

In 1914, when I had a Wild West Show in Texas, a man came to our show and wanted to sign up with us. He said that he was a cowboy clown. His name was Joe Shaw. He told me that his wife was with him and her name was Annie Oakley. They had a little baby a few months old. They worked for me about five months. She used to ride sometimes but she had lost some of her marbles, however she was a very nice agreeable person. She didn't do any shooting while traveling with me though she was advertised as the world's best shot by the Buffalo Bill Show for her act of shooting glass balls from the back of a running horse.

Lucille Mulhall a very striking, good looking, blonde woman was a great hand. She used to rope and tie a steer down in astonishing fast time. She made a great showing in 1915 at

Billings in the "Passing of the West" rodeo. She was a champion woman roper without a doubt. She came from Oklahoma.

Kitty Wilks that hailed from Tucumcari, New Mexico, was quite a cow girl. She was a bucking horse rider and a good one. She also used to bulldog steers but on account of not having any competition in the feminine gender she generally had to work on exhibition.

Paris Williams, a Billings girl, at one time was a noted bronc rider. She was a very small blonde woman. She had several first prizes to her credit before she gave up bronc riding for trick riding.

You have all heard of the rough riding Greenough family that live near Red Lodge, Montana. They all take after their old dad, "Packsaddle Ben" a good man and a salty cuss. I worked with him on a horse ranch near Billings in 1899, before either of us was married. Naturally, I have kept tabs on his family, I ain't going to say anything about the boys in these few lines for that is a different story.

I can't say enough about Marge and Alice and their ability but I will say they are a credit to the rodeo game in general. They have no false pride or big heads, but are just good honest cow girls that are natural born riders and get the job done. No horse looks too tough for them.

16: Moonshine

WHEN THE United States went on prohibition everybody wanted moonshine and home brew. It caused more disturbances, arrests, killings and distress than any law that was ever passed in the country. It was a great graft for the lawyers, sheriffs, mayors, policemen and high jackers.

The towns was full of blind pigs where you could walk right in and put down your money and get any kind of poison you wanted. Of course the "Pigs" had to pay a small fee but the town never got much of the payoff. The most of the money paid was hush money.

The law would arrest the bartender, he would plead guilty. The "Pig" would get another bartender and never lose a shift. In the big cities it was the worst. A ring would get together and claim a territory and if any other bootlegging ring moved in their territory there was a lot of trouble. They used armored cars and machine guns to discourage them. As there was a lot of money involved and the law was tangled up with the bootleggers, it was an awful mess.

I remember a serious circumstance that happened at the Billings Fair one year that turned into a joke but for a while it was no joke.

At that time there was a great many Indians attended the fair and several races was made up for the Indians each day. The Indians all got jagged and a couple fell off their horses. The Fair dads was all worked up. They thought that some bootlegger was selling the Indians liquor.

Nate Cooper, one of the officials, came over to the rodeo corrals, where I was one of the judges. He knew that I was well acquainted with a lot of the Indians. He told me to find out where the Indians was getting their booze.

As soon as the rodeo was over I went over to the Indian camp which was in the southeast corner of the Fairgrounds where there was a lot of trees and brush.

I had called the Indian races other years before I got the judge job and was acquainted with the Indian boy riders. I met one I knew, that wasn't too drunk, I warned him that the Fair officials wasn't going to let them run any races the next day if they was drunk.

He told me they would be all right the next day as they had drank about all their liquor. He said they didn't buy the liquor from a bootlegger but that one of the squaws had been getting some wood to cook with and she found a keg of moonshine in a brush pile. She gave all the Indians some.

He said some had it in pots, cans, teakettles or any old vessel. They'd all had a big time all night and day, dancing, drinking and playing the tom toms. He said, "It's just about all gone now. We'll be okay tomorrow."

The next day the Indians was all right, but the cowboys was getting teed up. There was a good looking woman that was furnishing the cowboys their liquor. She had a bottle fastened in her stocking and a rubber hose with a nipple on the end taped up to her breast. She was giving the boys a couple of draws for fifty cents.

Some of the officials got wise to her and arrested her and took her over to the auditorium to search her. She kicked the bottle away, but couldn't get rid of the hose. The clues was there, but the evidence was gone so they ordered her off the grounds and there wasn't any more booze trouble that fair.

I KNEW A COWBOY that used to work for the Antler cow outfit that went to bootlegging. He was getting his liquor over in the mountains of Wyoming about seventy miles from Billings. He was selling his stuff to the Blind Pigs in Billings. I will call him John Doe to protect his name as he is married now and has a nice family.

I was well acquainted with John Doe, also knew his pardner Jim Doe, who was making the moonshine as he worked for me several years later. Jim was to run the still and make the liquor. John was to deliver and sell the stuff. They split the profits 50-50. Jim told me they did real well, but came awfully close to being caught several times.

At first, John hauled his load of wet goods in a car, but it got too hot for him as he almost got caught, so he went to carrying his load on a packhorse. That way he could avoid all the highways and roads that was being watched for bootleggers. He had the trail all figgered out so he could get within seven miles of Billings before he hit a main road.

John had to come through the Crow Reservation, but never sold any liquor to the Indians and always tried to stay clear of them, for he knew the Indian Police patrolled that part of the reservation. It was a common sight in that rough country to see a pack outfit as the sheep and cattlemen used them to haul salt and supplies.

The Indian Policeman's name was Crane. There wasn't much went on around the country that Crane was patrolling that he didn't know about. He was a smart Indian that had caught lots of bootleggers that had sold liquor to the Indians.

Crane was educated. He was a tall, straight Indian with eyes like a hawk. If he ever found a man on the reservation that didn't have a permit to be there, he sure took him into the Agency and turned him over to the agent.

There was a little spring over on East Fork about half way to Billings, where John used to stop and rest his horses. He had two galvanized containers made long and flat to slip in a pannier that hung on each side of the packsaddle. Then there was room for several jugs on top. He wrapped the jugs in burlap to keep them from breaking, then he would throw his bed, which had a heavy tarp around it, on top and tie it all down hard and fast.

John had a good strong packhorse that could carry two hundred pounds easy. He rode early and late so as not to come in contact with anyone. When he was coming through the reservation he always watched for Indians and if he saw any he would keep out of sight and see which way they was going and manage to dodge them.

One morning John overslept on account of riding most of the night. It was about 8 o'clock by the time he'd had breakfast and packed his wet goods. He'd never met any Indians there so he thought he'd take a chance and go on.

He'd just got started when he saw six Indians coming on a long trot. When he took a look at them he recognized Crane as Crane rode a long legged sorrel horse. John had to miss them for he knew as soon as they saw him they would come to have a look at his pack.

He knew there was no use trying to make a run for it leading a heavy loaded packhorse. There was a coulee along the mountainside with a patch of quaking asp trees. He tied his packhorse in the trees and made a run up the coulee, got behind some rocks and watched the Indians.

They must have seen him ride up the coulee for they rode right into the quaking asp grove, lead out the packhorse and began to unpack it.

That was enough for John, while the Indians was busy unpacking the horse, John hit the breeze. The Indians was too busy with their find to look for a man and John made his getaway.

He lost the packhorse along with the liquor but never heard anything about it afterwards. That was John's last trip. He was afraid they'd be watching for him and he thought he had played his string out.

MOONSHINE

THESE TIMES puts me in mind of the times after World War I, when we hit the depression from the effects of the war and had a few years of drought and grasshoppers.

At that time I was running a bunch of cattle over in the Bull Mountains. As soon as a cattleman went in a bank, the banker would begin to gag, hollering, "No! No!" There wasn't any extra work or business on account of no money in circulation. The bankers are getting that same pasty green color at the sight of a cowman today.

About the only ones that seemed to show any signs of prosperity was the ones that handled moonshine. So it seemed as though about everyone that had a copper tea kettle or a wash boiler went to making moonshine. It seemed to me that everyone went to drinking, even the women. You hardly ever saw a woman in a saloon before prohibition. If you did, you can bet your life her reputation was plenty shady. Now there are as many women in the saloons and road houses as there are men.

A lot of the big cattle spreads had gone broke so there wasn't any work for cowboys. A lot of little nesters had already made their fortunes and left the country. Some of the ones that was still clinging to their cactus patches tried to make a living from the only cash crop there was, moonshine. It was hard times all right.

We was having our own troubles holding on to our bunch of cattle and keeping the wolf off our door step. My wife looked after the cattle in the summer and I worked in town. In the winter she worked in town and I took care of the cattle. It took pretty close riding but even so, we lost quite a few fat ones.

My wife was in Billings working and sending our daughter to school. It was in the fall of the year, I had just killed a beef. I loaded my old Tin Lizzie (Model T) with three quarters of the beef to take in to my wife so she could can it for the next summer. I got an early start and got about twelve miles when I burned out a connecting rod. I was in one hell of a fix. I couldn't go on and I was afraid to leave that beef alone in old Lizzie while

I walked after help. I had a team of mules that I used around the ranch and while I was addressing old Liz with some of my best mule language Sheriff Sage came along.

His car was full of Bull Mountain bootleggers and on the running board was tied three stills and some mash and liquor. He stopped to see what was the matter. On hearing my hard luck story he told me to cut a piece of barb wire and tie old Lizzie on behind his car and he would tow me to town.

I guess he sort of had the impression from the load in his car that maybe everyone in that country was "ag'in' the law" for he asked me if I had a hide with my beef.

I had the hide all right but I played it dumb and said, "Hell, my wife don't need any hide, she can't eat it." But before we started off I showed him it was unusual meat, my own.

It was a most disagreeable day, cold, windy and now and then snow squalls. Instead of big snowflakes, it was that hard pellets almost like hail.

Sheriff Sage must have been in a hurry to get to town for he sure poured on the gas and I was bobbing along after him like the tail of a kite. Now my old Lizzie strictly had no class, no top and no brakes. That country is a pretty hilly proposition. Going up the hills was okay but going down was a bugger. He just poured on the gas and had to out run me. I was hanging onto the steering wheel like grim death—too scared to jump. My hat blew off and the sleet was hitting me in the face so I could hardly see. I'd have traded five years of my life to have been out of that car.

He had told me before we started he would have to take his prisoners and evidence to the court house before he could take me home. If the ride through the hills was wild, to make up for it he drove real slow in town, so everyone could see his load. To the people on the streets it looked like I was one of his prizes. Nobody seemed to see him when he towed me home after he put his prisoners in the coop.

I hadn't been home very long when a black man came by who had served a jail sentence and paid a fine for making a little moon. He said, "Mr. Bill, how much did they fine you?"

I tried to explain that I hadn't been arrested, that the sheriff had towed me in because I was broke down. He just laughed and beat his sides.

He said, "I was just towed in too, Mr. Bill, but I didn't get out so quick. I had to serve thirty days in jail and pay a hundred dollars. What I wants to know is how you got out so quick? I done saw those stills on the sheriff's car. Course you wasn't arrested." With that he went off down the street chuckling to himself.

In the face of evidence like that what was the use of explaining.

THERE WASN'T any schools out in Bull Mountains so my wife and daughter had to live in Billings during the school months.

I had to stay at the ranch to take care of the cattle. It was a lonely job batching. I never was much of a cook but I was getting along fairly well for every week or two I would go into town and stay a few days and fill up.

I don't want to brag but my wife was an extra good meat cook and her cakes and pies just sort of melted in your mouth.

It was in the fall. I had raised a pretty fair crop of corn. I had been busy cutting and stacking it for winter feed and had it pretty near all taken care of and was doing some riding. I was out a few head of cattle and wanted to get them all gathered before winter set in.

I went to town and got all the groceries I could haul in the Model T, killed a beef and was set for the winter.

By that time the corn was put up, the cattle gathered and I didn't have much to do. I thought that if I was going to have to eat my own cooking all winter I'd better try my hand at something besides meat and potatoes.

Among the groceries I'd brought out from town there was several boxes of raisins. I always liked raisins so I thought I'd tackle a raisin pie. I never thought about looking in a cook book.

I mixed some water and flour up for the pie crust and rolled it out thin. I put the dough in a pie pan, poured in the raisins that said on the package, "Ready to Use," and put on a top crust, built a big fire and put it in to bake.

It looked pretty good to me and I thought there was nothing to it. I was going to eat good all winter. I set the pie on the table to cool off.

I went out and saddled my horse as I was going out to look at the cattle. The thought of that nice raisin pie setting on the table just made my mouth water. I thought I'd take time out and have a cup of coffee and some pie before I went on my ride.

I poured a cup of coffee and started to cut the pie. That pie crust was really tough. I couldn't hardly cut it but by the time I'd cut it through I knew I could never chew it. I thought at least I'd eat the raisins.

I just took my knife and pried the crust up. I looked at the raisins and there in the middle of them was a big black bug. It looked like it had been as big around as a silver dollar to start with and the juices from the raisins had puffed it up and it looked as big as a toad.

It just about made me sick. I dropped the crust back on the raisins, left my coffee untouched and went out to see the cattle.

I didn't take a very long ride as the cattle was close in.

I was just coming in when I met a very good friend of mine. He lived about twelve miles from me. He was a stockman that I had known a good many years. I asked him to come and have dinner with me.

He said, "No, Bill, I have got quite a lot of riding to do. I have already had dinner on you. I stopped at the house and the coffee was hot and there was a pie so I ate it. It was the best raisin pie I ever ate." He laughed.

I was worried. I thought he had discovered the big black bug and was ribbing me.

When I went in the house I saw where he had had a cup of coffee and the pie was all gone. There was a knife and fork in the empty pie plate so I guess he ate the pie all right. I don't think it made him sick either for he would have told me.

I have never cared to have raisin pie since then.

I TOOK DOWN with a cold or something. My bones all ached, my head ached, I really felt bad. I couldn't eat anything and didn't have any kind of medicine to doctor myself.

The weather was cold and I was afraid to take the chance of going to town. In fact, I just didn't feel up to it. All I wanted to do was just lay in bed.

There wasn't any close neighbors. The day I was feeling about the worst, Jimmy Bryant stopped in. Jimmy was an old cowpoke that was working for John Tolman, who ran a lot of cattle out in that country. Jimmy was wanting me to take him to town in my Ford so he could see Tolman.

He saw I was sick and told me I had the Flu. He said he'd had it and he would tell me how to get rid of it. "This is a sure cure, Bill. Get a quart of whiskey and make a lot of hot whiskies. Soak your feet in hot water, then go to bed. Be sure to cover up good and sweat it out."

It sounded good but I didn't have any whiskey.

I told him to take my Ford as I didn't feel up to driving it and bring me back a quart of whiskey. I would try his "sure cure for flu."

He made the trip okay and got back to the ranch just as it was getting dark. I wanted him to stay all night but he said he had to get back to camp as he had to move a bunch of cattle early next morning. He said for me to go to bed and he would make me a hot one before he left.

He had fetched some lemons from town. He got some sugar and nutmeg and squeezed the juice out of a lemon in a glass of whiskey or moon and hot water. Oh, boy, that first one was sure strong.

He said for me to make another one in about half an hour or even two more, then set the bottle on the stand by the bed and take a drink whenever I thought I could stand another but to keep covered up good.

After taking the glass of medicine Jimmy gave me, I began to feel better. I guess I kind of overdone the medicine taking for there wasn't much left in the bottle next morning.

After taking the second hot toddy I got pretty wobbly but I was sure sweating. It was all I could do to get back in bed and get the covers on. I layed there a while and then reached over and took a big drink out of the bottle. After taking that one I was having difficulties getting the covers on.

In a little while I began to see red streaks all over the house. I shut my eyes as the red streaks hurt them. All at once, the bed started to move off kind of slow. I opened my eyes and saw that the bed and I was going around and around that room.

It began moving faster and faster all the time. Every little while the bed would give a big jump and almost lose me. I thought it was time to pull leather. I grabbed ahold of the bed rail and the head of the bed and thought, "Let her buck!" The last I remember was that old bed was sure doing her stuff. I was thinking, if it got any worse it would sure buck me off. I must have passed out.

When I woke up it was sometime in the night. I was on the floor just about smothered. Somewhere in the deal the bed had got too rough and slipped me for I had a blanket wrapped around and around my neck. I was about froze, on my hands and knees on the floor, in the dark, and couldn't figure how I got there. I began to remember things and went to hunting the bed. I made up my mind to find it if it hadn't jumped out of the window.

I started to get on my feet but no dice. I fell down. I crawled around the room until I finally caught up with the bed. I was cold and oh, what a headache I had.

I took another shot of medicine, covered up head and heels and never woke up 'til about ten o'clock the next morning. I had a headache, otherwise feeling lots better. I was still so wobbly I could hardly walk. I managed to make some coffee. After drinking some coffee I began to get hungry. In three days I was fit as a fiddle.

ABOUT 1901, I was over in the Bull Mountain country about the middle of June helping gather some horses. At that time it was a big open country filled with cattle, horses, sheep, antelope, deer, coyotes and a few wolves. There was also lots of sage hens, prairie chickens, prairie dogs and all kinds of birds. There was a few ranches but they was far apart and had no wire fences.

It had been a wet spring, there was water running in all the creeks and there was lots of grass. It looked to me like a stockman's paradise.

I had seen the country in her best condition. After a few years it started to settle up with dry land farmers. Then most every flat or side hill that could be farmed was taken up, especially those around the water holes. There was a few wet years and they made a living.

It was dry then for several years and they didn't raise any thing. Then two years of grasshoppers fixed it up good, that being a sandy country, after it was plowed up, it about all blowed away.

Most of the dry land farmers had all mortgaged their land, machinery, work horses and anything else they had to raise a little money to live on. When that was gone they all had to leave or starve. For a few years there was empty houses, wire fences falling down, all kinds of machinery laying around rusting. There it was, a good grass country, all shot to hell.

It was about this time I made a deal with Leon Drake for two sections of land about forty miles northeast of Billings in the Bull Mountains. I leased the land for five years to run cattle on.

I bought cows and calves for $86.00. They was good Hereford cattle and I thought I bought them cheap. However, for the next few years cattle went down to practically nothing. If you sold them, you lost money and the more cattle you kept the poorer you got.

Everything got tough. Feed was high, you couldn't borrow money and there was hardly any work. I owed some money on the cattle. The only ones I sold was to pay interest. I was doing all right raising cattle, only the more cattle I raised the more grief I had trying to keep them until they would fetch some money. I wasn't doing so good in the Bull Mountains so I leased some land on Indian Creek in the Crow Reservation.

"For a few years there was empty houses."

We had a real tough trip from the Bull Mountains to Indian Creek. We had moved some of our belongings before we started with the cattle but still had two hay racks full of stuff, including furniture, our chickens, two tom cats and two birds.

I got one of my neighbors, Jay Hodson, to drive one team and my wife drove the other. They each had a saddle horse tied behind their wagons to help me with the cattle when I got in a pinch as we had over a hundred head and I was moving them alone.

It was late in the fall. I gathered all the cattle and had them in a pasture ready to start. The wagons was all loaded to make an early start as I was wanting to make the Lone Tree Schoolhouse by night, which was about a twenty mile drive. There was a fence around the schoolhouse where we could hold the cattle that night.

It started raining about an hour before we got to the schoolhouse and was cold and disagreeable. We got there just as it was getting dark, corralled the cattle in the school yard, then made camp about two hundred yards east of the school yard. After we got supper and was getting ready to bed down, I rode over to see how the cattle was doing. They was tired and seemed to be all right.

It had quit raining by morning. As it began to get daylight, I got up, built a fire and looked at the cattle. I saw that a few head had got out and had headed for their home range. I told Jay to harness the teams while Ella got breakfast and I would get after the cattle before they got too far.

The cattle had drifted about five miles by the time I caught up with them. By the time I got back my wife and Jay had the wagons loaded and the cattle turned out of the school yard to graze. I had a bite to eat and some coffee and we got started. We wanted to corral the cattle that night in the stock yards at Huntley.

The cattle wasn't too wild but they had ranged in the hills away from roads and they hadn't seen many cars. When we got out of the hills and into the Yellowstone valley where there was cars and dogs, those cattle was sure spooked. The first car I met the cattle went through the fence and into a beet field. From there until we got to the bridge north of Huntley we had nothing but grief.

Whenever I got in trouble, my wife and Jay would tie up their teams, jump on their saddle horses and help me until I got started again.

We fought those cattle about an hour getting them across the bridge. It was almost dark as they come off the bridge. Car lights scared the cattle and they stampeded. They separated, one bunch went down the road toward Huntley, the other bunch run on the road that turned east.

We finally got them rounded up and in the stockyard at Huntley about 10 o'clock that night. We just got them in the corral when a freight train came along. They was sure scared but they couldn't get out.

We was all about played out, and about starved as we hadn't had no dinner. We went over to Guy Delman's restaurant in Huntley to get our supper. We was mighty thankful that train hadn't come along fifteen minutes earlier.

The next day we only had about ten miles to go to Indian Creek and made it without too much trouble.

WHEN I FIRST CAME on Indian Creek with my cattle I did quite a lot of range riding. I got quite a lot of inquiries about horses and cattle that had strayed off their home range. Some of the small farmers and ranchers that didn't savvy stock too well used to get me to brand and cut their calves and colts.

George Sturm from Billings told me that he had lost a saddle horse. He said he had heard of the horse and it was running on Broken Leg. Sturm said he would pay me ten dollars if I would get the horse and fetch it in to him. Sturm described the horse as a gentle, broke, bay saddle horse with a ✝S (Cross S) brand on the left thigh.

A few days later I was riding the Broken Leg country and saw the Sturm horse running with a bunch of horses belonging to Tom Snydow that had a ranch on Pryor Creek. I run the horses in to Tom's corral, roped the Sturm horse and took him home and put him with my saddle horses.

I wrote a card to Sturm saying I had his horse and that I was pretty busy, for him to come to the ranch and get the horse. The next time I got my mail I had a letter from Sturm saying he couldn't get anyone to ride out after the horse and for me to bring it in when I found time, and he would take me home in his car.

I had a bunch of cattle in Osness' pasture just north of the Huntley bridge. I thought I'd ride Sturm's horse by that way so I could look at my cattle on my way to deliver the horse.

I'd looked through my cattle and started on to Billings when I met a man by the name of Julius. He was a little Belgian. He looked quite a lot like "Mortimer Snerd" and talked pretty broken. If you listened carefully and guessed a little you could understand what he was talking about.

Julius had a small bunch of cattle on the Billings Bench. In the cattle was a bull calf about nine months old. Julius wanted me to catch the calf in the field, as he didn't have a corral, cut and brand it for him.

He got his branding iron and came with me on foot. There was some cottonwood trees along a ditch. Julius got some dry limbs to make a fire to heat the iron. We went over close to the cattle and built the fire and got the iron hot. I rode over to the cattle to snare the bull calf.

When I took my rope down the horse acted a little nervous. I tied my rope hard and fast as that was a good, big, husky calf. I thought I had better rope him by the head and one front foot, that way I could throw him easy.

When I throwed the calf, the horse seemed to be okay, but when I jumped off to tie the calf down the horse swapped ends and started to dragging the bull calf.

The calf was bawling and kicking. I fell on top of him with my fingers grabbing in his hair. He was hard to stay on. The hair pulled out, the calf kicked me loose and the way that horse made tracks through the field wasn't slow. One good thing, where I had caught the calf was in stubble and not so rough.

Julius was all excited running after the horse, the calf and me. He was hollering, "Jesus, Jesus, I no pay you for to kill my bull. I just want you cut and brand him!"

Julius went past me on high following the horse and calf. That old pony was sure running. The calf was bawling and Julius was cussing me in a mixture of Belgian and English. There was blue smoke in that field.

I wasn't worried too bad as I knew the calf wouldn't choke to death as he had a front foot in the rope and every little while he would get a little air.

The horse drug the bull calf about a hundred yards until he got in some summer plowing where the ground was loose. The calf pulled so hard that the horse played out and stopped for air.

I tied the calf down and cut and branded him, then let him up. The side that he had been dragging on was all bare. There wasn't any hair left on his hide. He staggered around for a while like a drunken Swede.

Julius was so excited he could hardly say, "You think he die?"

I told him that the calf was alright, just a little paralyzed from the dragging.

He said, "I no pay you. I think he die. He look like hell." Julius went toward the house talking Belgian and waving his arms. I was glad I couldn't understand what he said but I knew there was no words of praise.

17: The Last of the Show Stock

MOST EVERYBODY that handles stock and understands the stock business appreciates a good all around cow horse. You can't make a good cow horse out of every horse. A cow horse has to be fast, have a good mouth and a lot of savvy. They are like racehorses for there is one in maybe a thousand that makes the top.

I have rode many a good horse for the different cow outfits in the western states. It was always a pleasure to set on a good well broke cow horse while cutting cattle, roping calves or steers, or doing anything that needed to be done on horseback.

I raised and broke one that I liked better than any horse I ever rode when I lived over in the Blue Creek country. His mother was a very pretty sorrel mare with lots of good breeding. She was kind and gentle with lots of speed. When she had her colt I kept her in a pasture that was close to the road. It seemed like she stayed close just to show off the colt for when anybody went by she would trot off like she and her colt was an exhibition.

He was a light sorrel with white mane and tail. He would stick his tail out, swing his head one way, then another, stepping high and proud. He was a beautiful colt and his build was perfect. He ran on the range until he was three years old. He was never handled, only cut and branded.

I was giving a Wild West show on the Fourth of July, the day of the long distance race. The men's race was from Billings to Lavina and back, a distance of a hundred miles. The women rode from Billings to Hesper, back to Billings, then to Huntley and back to Billings. It was about fifty miles. In the bunch of bucking horses I took for the show I included the sorrel colt.

I thought it would be a good time to have him rode and start breaking him to ride as he had grown into a very nice horse.

There was a lot of riders for the show that day, among them was several Indians from the Crow Reservation that rode in the contest. One of them was an Indian by the name of Jim Carpenter. I don't think he was a full blooded Indian, but anyhow, Jim drew the sorrel horse. We had named him Bald Hornet on account of his having a white face.

Jim rode him about five jumps and sailed away like a kite. The riders was all surprised to see Jim lose his seat. Bald Hornet was declared a good bucking horse.

This he proved to be in the next three months on a trip through the western part of the state. I thought he was too good a horse to be just a bucking horse as the country was full of them and they wasn't worth much as such. I thought Bald Hornet had the makings of a good saddle horse.

When we was in Butte, I decided that it was time to break him from bucking. When I told the cowboys I was going to break Hornet for a saddle horse they all hurrahed me and said I was nuts as Hornet was one of the best bucking horses I had and was getting better all the time.

The next day I told Gail Downing, a top rider, that he would give the last bucking horse ride of the day on Hornet. I'd have the pickup man catch him as soon as he quit bucking, for Downing not to get off but to ride him around for a while snubbed to the pickup horse. I asked Downing to ride without spurs.

Downing refused to ride without his spurs. He said he wouldn't use his spurs no more than to just stay on top.

Instead of using a hackamore, when we was to buck out Hornet I put a bridle on him with a snaffle bit. He did his stuff and they done just as I told them and got him going. That was the last time he ever tried to buck anyone off. Inside of a week we was snubbing broncs to him.

When I got back to the ranch that fall I kept him in the barn and used him for a winter horse. We fed him hay and oats all winter. He got to be a regular pet.

In the spring he got distemper awfully bad. I was afraid for a while he was going to die. My wife and I doctored him until he began to get better and turned him out for a while on green grass.

That summer and fall we used him for a snubbing horse and pick-up horse in the shows. He was one of the best pick-up horses I ever rode. All the cowboys loved him as he had a burst of speed that got him to a bucking horse and he always crowded close as he could to a bucking horse so the rider could get on him.

He turned out to be a wonderful rope horse. He weighed about eleven hundred. If you was roping heavy stuff, you had to be careful or he would break your rope as he sure savvied how to set down when you caught anything. Anything you run him at he would try to catch. If you didn't catch what you run him at, it was your fault for he would take you right up to it. I caught a bobcat off him, also coyotes. I tried to catch many a jack rabbit but never had any luck catching a jack.

ONE SPRING I WAS RIDING HORNET on the head of Blue Creek gathering some of my mares that I wanted to breed to a Percheron stallion I had just bought. I ran into a bunch of Nate Cooper's big brood mares. There was a long yearling stud colt squealing around those nice big mares. I got up close to see what brand was on him. He was a slick.

I didn't want to take that bunch of gentle mares to the corrals to get that slick but knew Cooper didn't want any colts from a small sized horse. He was such a pretty brown I thought he would make a saddle horse in a couple of years. I thought I would rope him and break him to lead on the way to the ranch.

This yearling was wild and snakey. It is pretty hard to catch a yearling on the open range as they can run like the devil and dodge like a fox.

I got my rope down and made a hole in it to be ready if I got a chance to throw at him. I worked around through the mares but that stud colt was plenty leary of me. I finally worked him to the outside where I could take a run for a throw at him.

As soon as I took down my rope Hornet was all ready for business. I ran that stud for about fifty yards when he thought he ought to get back in that bunch of mares and made a quick turn. I made my throw and snared him. If I hadn't had a top horse under me I never would have got that slick.

I had a bunch of horses that ranged over on the Pryor Mountains. It was forty-five miles from my ranch. I'd get started about four thirty in the morning from the ranch, go over to Pryor Mountain, gather the horses and get back with them about sun down. I generally rode Hornet on those long trips and never had him play out with me or act too tired.

When making the ride over on Pryor Mountain I always took a few oats tied on my saddle. When we got there I would pull off my saddle and bridle, turn him loose and give him the oats. He would never leave me. I would lay down under a pine tree and rest for an hour or so. When I was ready to go I'd holler for Hornet. He would always come to me, then we would gather the horses and take them to the ranch. There was a spring on top of the mountain and they was never far from the spring.

MY WIFE LOVED HORNET and used to ride him a great deal. He wasn't a gaited horse but he had a fast running walk, a fast trot and a long easy lope. You could open gates on him and he could run backwards. He could jump over any ordinary wire fence, if one was extra high and you could get a little stretch in the wire and hold it down just a little he would cross it.

LAST OF THE SHOW STOCK

I made up my mind that I never would sell him as he was just like one of the family. I gave him to my wife for her birthday. Any time she walked out where he could see her, he would whinny at her and come to her. She was always petting him and giving him some nick nack. He liked his sugar, in fact, he would eat most anything out of your hand.

It was a pretty sight to see my wife riding Hornet on a fast running walk. She was a good looking woman with pretty blue eyes and two long braids of dark brown hair hanging down her back. She wore a black velvet riding habit decorated with big white pearl buttons, a grey cowboy hat on her head. When she rode in our Wild West Show on that sorrel horse with her gun in her hand to do her shooting stunt, she always made a hit.

WHILE WE WAS SHOWING in the south we was in Texas in the spring of the year. We crossed over the Salinas Bottom for five miles through water from a foot deep to three feet deep. When we got to the Salinas River, it was roaring high. The water was ten to fifteen feet deep but it wasn't over a hundred yards wide. There wasn't a bridge but a ferry boat to cross the river.

We loaded the wagons first on the ferry. We had good luck with the wagons but plenty trouble with the loose horses. They was afraid to go on the ferry boat but we finally got them on it. I stayed on that side of the boat with them. It was a pretty good sized boat.

When we got about in the middle of the river there was a tree that had washed into the river. The horses saw the tree turning end over end. It scared them. They all crowded to the lower side of the boat. The boat dipped and the horses and I went to the bottom of the river.

I had a pair of leather chaps on and a canvas coat as it was raining and cold. I had been holding Hornet by the bridle reins and was standing beside the railing of the ferry boat which was boarded up about four feet. The boat straightened up when the horses left it.

When I came up it was hard swimming to stay on top with all the clothes I had on. The reins had slipped out of my hand as I went overboard. The horses was all around me. Hornet was about fifteen feet to the right of me.

I hollered to him and he swam right at me. I caught the saddle horn and one stirrup and finally got one rein, while the current was carrying us down stream pretty fast. We went down stream about two hundred yards to where the riverbank wasn't too steep and made it out. He saved my life that day for I know I would have drowned if I hadn't got hold of the saddle horn, for I was cold and had my lungs full of water.

ABOUT THREE WEEKS LATER a lady came to me and said she wanted to buy the sorrel horse used in the shooting act. I wouldn't set a price for fear she would take me up. She offered me three hundred and fifty dollars for him. I told her it was a good price and I appreciated her offer but it wasn't enough. She left but came back next day and offered me five hundred dollars. I told her no, that I didn't want to sell him.

I guess she thought I was trying to hold her up but she came back next day and told me to name my price. I had to tell her that there wasn't enough money in the state of Texas to buy him. She went away pretty mad.

I inquired around and found out that her husband was a big cattle man and had plenty jack. However, he didn't have enough to buy Hornet. I've often wondered how much she would have paid for him.

WE GOT BACK TO BILLINGS in 1915. That was the year Charlie Harris put on the show called, "The Passing of the

West." I didn't enter any of the contests except the steer roping. I rode a bull on exhibition and helped my wife in her shooting act.

There was a southern roper there by the name of Buffalo Vernon. He had bad luck, his rope horse was sick. I let him use Hornet to rope on. I cautioned him not to let Hornet run on the rope or he would sure break his rope.

Vernon was a good roper and drew a big steer. Sure enough he wanted to bust that steer hard enough so he would lay still while he tied him down. He let Hornet run on him. He turned the steer head over heels and busted his rope.

I made fast time the first day of the contest. The second day, the wind was blowing awful bad, there was just three steers caught. There wasn't any chance of winning after that so I withdrew from the contest.

I had a job with Sturm and Drake working on commission buying and selling horses, cattle, wagons, harness and saddles. I worked for them nine months. In that time I handled and broke a good many horses.

There was a chute that I would put a green horse in to get the halter on. I would snub the bronc up to Hornet and take the rough out of them. After a little I would pull the bridle off Hornet, turn him loose with the bronc tied to the saddle horn and let Hornet teach them to lead. He seemed to be able to do it faster than I could. I would go back in a couple hours and he would have the bronc halter broke. It saved me a lot of jerking around. It was a pretty sight to see him working with a horse. He knew his stuff.

I LEFT STURM AND DRAKE and went to work for the Northern Pacific Railroad on the survey for a branch road from Hesper to Rapelje. The camp was on Canyon Creek about ten miles from Hesper. I was doing the light freighting with one team from Billings to the engineer camp.

The chief engineer wanted a team to haul the surveyors to and from work. He wanted to know if I could furnish them. I told him I could. He gave me a couple of days to get them.

I had Hornet and another saddle horse named Baully at Billings. Neither one of them had ever had a collar on but they was perfectly gentle. I thought they could get the job done as there wasn't anything heavy, just pull a light wagon with four men in it.

When I hitched them up they thought it was below their dignity to pull a wagon. Neither one of them would tighten a tug. They just turned their heads and shook them. I didn't know just what to do to get them started. I petted them and tried to lead them but they wouldn't move.

I got out on the wagon tongue and got on Hornet's back. He savvied that and started up but Baully didn't want to go. I jumped off Hornet over on Baully and he started but Hornet wouldn't go. I had to get on first one horse and then the other like an acrobat for a while 'til they got the idea of going at the same time.

Then I got them started for camp twenty-five miles away. Every little hill we came to I would have to ride first one and then the other to get them to pull. Finally they both got so they savvied what I wanted them to do so we made camp okay.

I was worried that night for I had to take the men out on the job in the morning. I never told the boss that the horses had never been drove before as I knew they would be alright in a day or two.

In the morning both horses was a little sore and when I looked at Hornet I knew from the gleam in his eye that he wasn't going to start. I jumped on him when the men got in the wagon. After playing leap frog a few times I got them going. After a few trips they was a dandy driving team as they was both good travelers.

It was an easy job for the horses as lots of days there was a lot of figuring for the surveyors to do and they never went out at all. There was lots of grass so I would turn the horses out at night. I'd go out early in the morning and get them as they never was more than a half a mile from camp. I would catch Hornet and ride him in as Baully always followed.

They was getting lots of oats and short drives so they felt awfully good. There was a little flat, then Canyon Creek to cross before we got to the feed tent. They got so they'd have a run when I fetched them in. Baully would be following behind, when they got to the flat, Baully would come up on a run, then they would have a race to camp.

It was fun. I never took a bridle or rope and I didn't mind the race as I knew they would stop for their oats when they got in. So every morning they had their little run.

Along in November the nights was getting cold. There was a little ice on the edge of Canyon Creek. As usual I was riding in on Hornet bareback. He was in the lead that morning and they was sure sailing in. When Hornet came to the creek, he saw the ice and put on the brakes.

I wasn't expecting the sudden stop so I went right on just about knocking all the water out of the creek. Hornet and Baully didn't wait for me to get out but run on to the horse tent bucking and playing, seeming right pleased with the turn of events.

That water was sure cold. My teeth was rattling and I was shaking all over by the time I got to camp.

WHEN THE RAILROAD JOB was finished I went to the Rapelje country to sell horses as it was just settling up. There was several unbroke horses in the bunch I took to Rapelje. One of them was a very nice looking white mare that was plenty wild.

I had the horses at the stockyards. It was a Saturday and there was quite a lot of buyers there. A man looked the white mare over and asked me how old she was and what I wanted for her.

I told him I didn't think she was over five years old and I would take sixty-five dollars for her. I told him I didn't think she was halter broke but I would catch her and look at her teeth if he wanted her.

There had been several people going in and out of the corral. Someone had gone through the gate and not latched it. Just as I picked up my rope to catch the mare the gate blew open and she ran out.

I had Hornet tied on the outside of the corral with just a rope around his neck. I knew if I took time to saddle up that mare would be a long way off and I never could catch her. I jumped on Hornet and took after her.

There was an open section about a half a mile from the stockyards with a lane leading to it. If I got there in time I could head her back to the corrals. There was an old road in about the middle of the section.

I had got around her and started her back for the corrals when she took another notion and didn't want to go back. It had rained the day before and was slippery. I was running to turn her when we hit the old road. Hornet got to slipping and never could gain his feet. He fell and turned over. In the fall, I broke my shoulder and collar bone, cracked some ribs and sprained my ankle.

It doesn't seem reasonable but nevertheless it is true, Hornet jumped up, turned the mare down the lane and came back to me. That's the kind of horse he was.

I was pretty much of a mess and could hardly move but I got him in one of the old ruts in the road. He stood like a statue until I managed to pull myself on him. I rode on to Rapelje to the doctor to get patched up.

There wasn't a hotel in Rapelje. I had a tent at the stock yards where I stayed. When the doctor got through patching me up, a young fellow with a Ford car took me to my tent.

I got a fellow by the name of Matheson to take the horses that was in the stock yards to a pasture. He forgot Hornet as he was standing just where I had left him in front of the doctor's office. I wasn't worried as he just had a short tie rope around his neck and I knew he could take care of himself.

There was a young lady that clerked for Brickley that run the store. She lived on the edge of town. As she went home she saw Hornet grazing close to the path. He was such a nice horse she stopped and petted him. He followed her on home. When she fed the chickens some grain he begged so hard she gave him a handful of wheat.

After that he met her every evening and followed her home. He would beg and paw until she would give him some wheat. That was alright until the gate was left open and he went into the yard and rolled in the flower beds. Someone came to the tent and told me he was getting to be a nuisance around town so I had him taken to the pasture.

When I left Rapelje I bought a bunch of cattle and moved over in the Bull Mountains. Hornet had a pretty soft life over there. I had several saddle horses and never rode him unless we had some branding to do or was working the cattle. He was beginning to show his age and was getting a little stiff in the shoulders.

1921 WAS A GRASSHOPPER YEAR. The grasshoppers had eaten all the grass and the fence posts and started on the wire. I had to get out of there before they ate the cattle up.

I rented some range and bought some hay on Elbow Creek between Fromberg and Joliet. That was one of the toughest winters I ever put in. The snow was about two feet deep and it was all the way from ten to forty below zero. The wind came down that canyon something awful.

I didn't have enough hay to feed all the cattle so I cut out all the steers and dry cows to winter out. I kept two saddle horses up as I had to do a lot of riding. Hornet was a big strong horse and a good snow horse so he was one of them. Before the winter was over I had him down in a lot of snow drifts.

The worst place I got into had me plenty worried. I was riding Hornet, it was about three in the afternoon. I had been getting the dry bunch of cattle up on a long ridge where the wind had blowed the snow off and they could get some grass. I had Hornet down in the drifts several times and he was getting tired. I had to break a trail to get the cattle on the ridge for I couldn't drive them up there unless they had a trail to follow. As soon as I got them up on the ridge I started for camp.

It was about six miles to go back around the ridge, straight across it wasn't over a couple miles, but I would have to cross a deep coulee. In that country, off from the mountains, there was some deep water washes from three to ten feet deep.

There was generally trails through the washes. When I got to the coulee the snow was drifted so deep I couldn't seem to locate the wash as the snow had drifted it full.

I was riding along and didn't think I was near the wash when all at once down we was in a hole. I don't know how deep the snow was below us but we was about five feet down in the loose snow with steep frozen banks on both sides. Hornet was scared but he was a cool headed horse. I petted him to quiet him down and he stood still.

I took off my rope from the saddle and fastened it around his neck. By standing up in the saddle I could claw my way out of the wash. I thought I could help Hornet by pulling on the rope. I spoke to him and pulled on the rope. He tried but couldn't make it.

I caved a lot of snow in the wash, got in and tramped it down but the snow was dry and wouldn't pack very good. I kicked more snow in and tried to stamp it down. We tried again but it was no dice, he couldn't get out.

I kicked more snow in and tramped some more, then I took the saddle off and turned it upside down with the horn in the snow. I pushed more snow on the saddle, then put the saddle blanket down, put more snow on it and then I put my leather chaps on top with more snow packed on them. It was a pretty close place in that wash and the horse didn't have room to tramp the snow.

I got his hind feet on all the stuff so he would have some power with them; I stayed down in the wash that time, to push on him. He wanted out of that hole. I spoke to him, he tried. That time he hung on by his brisket but with me pushing on him, he made it out. I dug my stuff out of the hole and we made it to camp as it was getting dark.

In the spring we trailed the cattle back to the Bull Mountains and stayed there three more years. Then I got a lease on Indian Creek on the Crow Reservation.

BY THAT TIME Hornet was getting old but still a good horse. He had done his work and was a privileged character. My wife's brother had three kids that used to come and visit us a great deal. When they came we would pile them all on Hornet's back and he would take them for a good ride. When he thought they'd rode long enough he would go down to the creek and begin to paw. If they didn't take the hint and get off he would lay down in the water and that was it.

After a few more years we turned him out on the range in the summer. He was an old horse but he didn't look it though his teeth was about all gone.

He got sick several times and crawled through two or three fences to get home. He would come right to the yard fence by the kitchen and nicker for help. When we'd doctored him up and he felt all right, he would head back for the hills and the other horses.

Late in the summer while we was threshing my wife saw Hornet coming for the house. She went to the gate to let him in. He was pretty bad off. Ella gave him some medicine. He took it, then went down by the barn and layed down on the butt of an old straw stack.

Ella came over to the threshing machine and told me Hornet was on his last legs and had come home to die. It was almost supper time and I couldn't get away just then. She cooked supper, put it on the table and went down to take care of Hornet.

Just as soon as I could I went down to see if there was anything more I could do for Hornet. He was laying down in the straw with his head in my wife's lap. She was petting him and crying. She said that when she came to him he whinnied at her. As I came up to them he raised his head just a little, laid it back down on Ella's lap, closed his eyes and passed away. He was twenty-four years old.

I told the threshing crew there would be no threshing until noon the next day as I wanted to bury my horse. The man that owned the machine wasn't any too pleased. I guess he thought I could haul the old horse up some coulee and leave him.

WE DUG HORNET'S GRAVE on a little point of a hill close to some pine trees not too far from the house. We got a stone boat and hauled him up on the hill with a team. We rolled him in the grave on his knees with his hind legs under him. We put his head to the east to face the rising sun.

There wasn't any prayers said but we shed some tears. He wasn't just a horse to us but a member of the family. We had raised him, took him everywhere with us and he had always done his job well. He was the last of my show stuff.

It wasn't like he was just a pet horse that we liked for his looks or what he was worth in money. It was the wonderful good deeds he had done in a lifetime of labor and love.

I have just told a few of the nice things he did. It would take a big book to tell all the smart and intelligent things Hornet done for us.

LAST OF THE SHOW STOCK

"Hornet's grave—spirit horse."

Made in the USA
Lexington, KY
12 November 2019